Feminism's Forgotten Fight

FEMINISM'S FORGOTTEN FIGHT

The Unfinished Struggle for Work and Family

K IRSTEN SWINTH

Harvard University Press

Cambridge, Massachusetts
London, England
2018

Library of Congress Cataloging-in-Publication Data

Names: Swinth, Kirsten, author.

Title: Feminism's forgotten fight : the unfinished struggle for work and family /
Kirsten Swinth.

Description: Cambridge, Massachusetts : Harvard University Press, 2018. |
Includes bibliographical references and index.

Identifiers: LCCN 2018017984 | ISBN 9780674986411 (alk. paper)

Subjects: LCSH: Second-wave feminism—United States.

Classification: LCC HQ1421 .S92 2018 | DDC 305.420973—dc23

LC record available at https://lccn.loc.gov/2018017984

For Alison and Gabriel

CONTENTS

Think for a minute. Who were you before the '70s began? Trying to remember our way back into past realities, past rooms, past beliefs is a first step toward measuring the depth of change in ourselves and the world. It is also a reminder that the progress we may now take for granted is . . . just the beginning of more changes to come.

—Gloria Steinem, "The Way We Were—And Will Be," *Ms.*, December 1979

INTRODUCTION

———

Feminists' Vision Forgotten

> We must ask why it is that our struggle for survival in an
> unjust system is countered not with political change, but
> with upping the ante on female perfection.
>
> —Letty Cottin Pogrebin, *Ms.*, 1978

S OMETIME IN THE 1970S, a new cult for women was born—or so the feminist writer, activist, and *Ms.* editor Letty Cottin Pogrebin warned the
magazine's readers in March 1978. Everywhere one looked, from the latest
"how-to" book to the magazine covers in the supermarket checkout line
and the faddish seminar for success, the same bait was dangled: "how to
be superwoman," or "having it all." The having-it-all cult, Pogrebin observed, supplied women with the dream of a perfect life, updated for the
feminist age: "Everything," defined as "the three-ball juggling act: job,
marriage, children." With just "the right formula" of timetable, efficiency,
career management, togetherness, and babies—"*Voilà*! You've got it *all*."[1]

The problem was that the juggling act was "a gender-specific hype." Men
were never expected to do it. Even more than that, fetishizing having-it-all
was political. "Let's give her what she wants. Let her do it all. Why not?"
the comfortable establishment conceded. "As long as there are no tremors
beneath the status quo; as long as men don't have to give up their political

supremacy, good jobs, hot dinners, casual fatherhood, sexual services, birthright power." Nothing changed with the cult of everything except a woman's standards and expectations of herself. The burden was on *her* to do it all. "Institutions," Pogrebin emphasized, "are undisturbed."[2]

Pogrebin was horrified. It was a dangerous distortion of all that she and other feminists had been fighting for. "In fact, many feminists became feminists precisely *because* we have been trying to have it all. We discovered it is simply impossible," Pogrebin explained. Change had to happen at every level. Equal parenting had to be accompanied by flexible workplaces. Society had a role to play, particularly in providing childcare. Single mothers, poor mothers, the former housewife trapped in an "unglamorous job"—they deserved real options for equality too. What was needed was a movement committed to broad social reorganization. "This is why," Pogrebin vowed, "feminists are not content to treat a social malignancy—like patriarchy and women's oppression—with a local anesthetic, like 'have a baby, get a job, you'll feel better.'"[3]

Feminists are not to blame for today's superwoman dilemma. Americans often assume that feminists promised that "You Can Have It All." In fact, as Pogrebin's exasperation shows, when feminists argued that American women should be able to have it all, they meant something quite different from what the term has come to mean. Pressure on individual women to heroically be everything to everyone is the exact opposite of what second-wave activists sought. As feminists understood, there would be no such thing as *having it all* without larger structural changes.

This book tells the story of the battles feminists fought to make such changes in culture, society, and law. It illuminates the centrality of second-wave commitments to the very issues of work and family that feminists are now wrongly faulted for ignoring. Steadfastly, often with brilliant insight, and always with burning determination, they imagined remaking society from the bottom up and from the inside out.

THE RESURGENCE OF feminist activism in the 1960s built on a long history of feminism in the United States, sometimes described as occurring in waves. Those engaged in the first wave, which peaked in the early twentieth century, ultimately secured passage of the Nineteenth Amendment, which granted women the right to vote. The emergence of second-wave feminism in the

1960s coincided with a crisis in the nation's family and gender arrangements.[4] Feminists addressed the crisis with penetrating analysis, creativity,
and daring. Their movement unfolded in tandem with the dissolution of
the family wage system. This system had mandated a strict configuration
for the typical American household: a man in the workplace earning a wage
sufficient for his family and a woman at home caring for children. The male
breadwinner–female homemaker ideal dominated labor markets, government policy, law, and culture for more than a century and perpetuated
women's second-class status.[5]

This long-standing family wage system was starting to fray in the 1960s.
Clearly, feminists did not initiate the economic and social changes behind
the splintering family-wage norm. Indeed, feminism was in part sparked
by those changes. Yet women's movement activists seized the opportunity
to attack the family wage system's deep-seated gender and racial inequities, passionately promoting alternative visions of family and economic
relations. Feminists' analysis of and activism on the meaning of work and
family was their core response to the simultaneous dominance and dissolution of the nation's male breadwinning–female homemaking norm.[6]

Over fifteen years of activism, from 1963 to 1978, second-wave feminists put forward a breathtaking vision of comprehensive change that they
believed would produce better lives for women, men, and children in a more
egalitarian society. They reconstructed the entire family wage system from
the ground up. Selves—both male and female—would be remade. Worker
and mother would not be mutually exclusive identities for women. For men,
nurturing and fathering would be viewed as laudable, not laughable. Feminists strove to build new partnerships in intimate relationships and the
home, dividing up childrearing and housecleaning among men, women, and
the community differently. Housework and childcare had to be recognized,
valued, and properly compensated, whether performed by homemakers of
either gender, poor mothers on public assistance, or paid workers. Public
policies and laws designed to fit the male-breadwinning ideal would
end, replaced by new ones facilitating equal choices about roles and life
pathways. Government would take up some of the responsibility—and
expense—for supporting families, which had previously fallen on individual households and whose costs women had borne the brunt of. Workplaces would be altered. The assumption would be that all workers—not
just women—had families to care for. Employment benefits and workplace

structures would ensure that workers could make a living and care for vulnerable family members. Second-wave activists fought for a world in which no woman faced the no-win choice to care for her family or remain dependent and relinquish her full economic and social citizenship. Feminists did indeed fight for women to have it all, but they insisted that achieving it required real change in private lives and public policy.

Feminists undertook three principal forms of activism for work and family. First, they worked to reconceptualize gender identities, sex roles, and the family order. Second, they endeavored to reorganize familiar divisions of paid and unpaid labor among men and women. They fought to reshape the sexual division of labor within the home as well as outside of it, without pushing household labor onto low-paid, often minority domestic workers. They looked beyond the private sphere to call for new rules for workplaces and to demand public provision of childcare, maternity benefits, and guaranteed incomes for mothers. Finally, second-wave activists waged legal challenges and legislative crusades to put policies in place that reallocated the costs of family labor among individuals, business, and the state.

Feminist ideas aroused fierce resistance. Their demands upset so many entrenched beliefs that they did not always even win the support of fellow liberals and radicals. The conservative opposition that developed into the "pro-family movement" fought hard to preserve the family wage system and domestic ideal, forging what historian Robert O. Self has called "breadwinner conservatism."[7] These reactionaries pitted women's autonomy against others' needs, especially those of children, the elderly, the sick, and the disabled, for whom women had long been caregivers. Opponents additionally took issue with redrawing the line between public and private. Finally, feminists' insistence that poor mothers had a right to public assistance to care for their children without being forced into low-paid domestic labor provoked a racially charged backlash. Feminist progress in the face of this opposition was uneven, with both significant headway and heartbreaking setbacks.

The measure of the movement, however, lies not in its setbacks. Although the feminist attack on the family wage system called forth a conservative response, it laid critical institutional and intellectual groundwork for a more humane society. As a new postindustrial order made waged work increasingly insecure and a "family wage" for men increasingly rare, feminists provided the first viable alternative to the dominant gender and family arrangement. They offered a countervision premised on gender equity in the home *and* the workplace. In law and policy, feminist achievements extended from valuing a homemaker's contribution to marital property to eradicating barriers to mothers' employment. The movement spurred an astonishing number of men and women to do everything from revamping their relationships to getting out and starting their own childcare centers, even if that meant building the tot-sized furniture themselves. But perhaps the movement's most significant accomplishment is the one hardest to see today. Feminism transformed what we consider fair and normal, so much so that we often can't imagine a time before it. In short, it changed our nation's gender imaginary, altering its deepest expectations for and beliefs about "men" and "women."[8] Furthering this paradigm shift in both belief and practice would be one of the great long-term struggles of the movement, and it would extend into the twenty-first century.

WHEN THE SECOND-WAVE women's movement first emerged in the early 1960s, postwar faith in the expanding abundance of the American economy remained high. With the family wage system at its peak in the 1950s and 1960s, white married women's earnings could legitimately be seen to supplement their husband's income, adding guitar lessons for children, summer vacations and a new dishwasher, a refrigerator, or even a car. In the 1970s, a set of economic shocks changed all that. Disappearing unionized factory jobs, energy crises, persistent high unemployment, and crippling inflation posed severe challenges to the family wage system. Yet waged employment did not disappear in the United States in the 1970s; it transformed. A new postindustrial economy brought with it surging employment in the service sector, which had long been women's occupational domain. Three-fifths of the new jobs created in the United States from 1970 to 1984 went to women.[9]

As the blue-collar manufacturing sector waned, so too did wages. The economic shifts of the 1970s inaugurated a decades-long stretch of little or no real wage growth. By the end of that decade, the entire male-breadwinner system seemed on the rocks. By 1980, half of all married American women had joined the labor force, up from less than a quarter thirty years earlier. The trend was even more pronounced for families in which married couples had to take care of children. In husband-wife families with children under eighteen, 70 percent were supported solely by a working father in 1960; in 1980 the proportion of married-couple families relying on dual incomes surpassed that traditional arrangement. By the end of the 1970s, over two-thirds of African American wives worked for pay—a reversal from 1950, when over six in ten remained out of the labor force. In short, a male-breadwinning system, which had held for a majority of white as well as black married families, was collapsing. As the economy guru Eliot Janeway put it in October 1977, "the single-paycheck household is rapidly going the way of the dinosaur."[10]

Paradoxically, the second wave of feminism emerged during good economic times, in a period of optimism and belief that society could change—yet it addressed challenges to the male-breadwinner ideal that would only become more relevant as economic shifts undercut that standard in the 1970s. Feminists of the 1960s were inspired by the decade's powerful movements for social justice—the black and Chicano freedom struggles, the War on Poverty, and the gay and lesbian liberation movement. A radical New Left that rose up against America's involvement in the Vietnam War and more broadly against the inequalities that beset US society was a training ground for many younger women in the movement. Radical politics fostered a deep skepticism about established institutions and a critical edge that nurtured visionary thinking. Starting in 1963, the first seven or eight years of the movement were thrilling times in which every possible assumption Americans had grown up with about womanhood, manhood, and their place in society seemed up for grabs. Mass demonstrations, acts of political theater, and private discussions in living rooms all drew millions to the movement and inspired women and men to reorganize their personal lives and participate in the groups that blossomed to fight for changed laws and institutions.

These exhilarating days continued into the early- to mid-1970s, as barriers to women's full participation in society fell away. Employment opportunities opened up; universities, professional associations, and men's clubs dropped their male-only policies; an Equal Rights Amendment to the Constitution seemed unstoppable in state ratification drives; domestic workers obtained the minimum wage; childcare centers popped up everywhere; pregnant women began winning the right to keep their jobs; marriages became more egalitarian; and long-term homemakers started to get their due at divorce. Americans learned that sexism (a term coined by feminists) pervaded their society.

Then, in the last four years of the fifteen that this study covers (1975–1978), the ground shifted. The momentum of the civil rights, antipoverty, and New Left movements that had inspired the women's movement faded, as did the economic growth of the postwar era. Conservative opposition to the liberal establishment and to the women's movement in particular grew. It gained political ground, attracting adherents appalled by the changes to women's roles that feminists pursued. Phyllis Schlafly, the antifeminist activist, gained national prominence. The "pro-family" network she forged joined forces with newly politicized evangelical Christians and economic neoconservatives to form the New Right, which would successfully lift Ronald Reagan to the presidency in 1980.[11] So, while feminists kept hammering away at many of the same issues, they met new resistance, compelling them to devise more pragmatic strategies and adopt a less utopian vision. Their gains increasingly came in the courts, legislatures, and local halls of government. Historians have typically seen the late 1970s as a low point for the movement, as it poured its energies into the stalled-out ERA ratification drive, but that is far from the whole story: in the year in which this study ends, 1978, Congress enacted three major pieces of legislation that fulfilled long-standing feminist goals.

THE FEMINIST MOVEMENT was led by three overarching groups. The first was liberal feminists. These were often older women, many of whom had come of age in the 1930s. They were frequently professionals or college-educated women whose ambitions had been curbed to meet the societal expectation that they would care for homes and children. They created formal organizations modeled after civil rights organizations. The National Organization for Women (NOW, 1966), Federally Employed Women (FEW, 1968), the Women's Equity Action League (1968), and the National Women's Political Caucus (1971) were among the most prominent. Activists with roots in postwar labor activism joined their ranks and brought a labor perspective in the Coalition of Labor Union Women (1974). This branch of the movement tended to work through established channels to reform institutions, laws, policies, and union contracts. Many liberal feminist leaders worked in government or were lawyers. Betty Friedan, a journalist who became a founder of the National Organization for Women, has been cast as the archetype, but the pioneering civil rights and feminist lawyer Pauli Murray, the founder of the ACLU Women's Rights Project Ruth Bader

Ginsburg, the New York State Representative to Congress Bella Abzug, the union lawyer Ruth Weyand, and the federal government insider Catherine East are equally worthy emblems of the liberal second wave.

A second, much more *outré* branch of the movement generally scorned the seemingly staid methods of their older counterparts. Radical feminists were younger; they came of age in the civil rights and antipoverty movements of the 1950s and 1960s. They participated in the anti–Vietnam War movement and radical New Left. They formed smaller, local organizations, including Redstockings (1969) in New York City, Bread and Roses (1969) in Boston, Sudsofloppen (1968) in San Francisco, the Women's Majority Union (1968) in Seattle, and the Chicago Women's Liberation Union (1969), to name a few. These groups believed that a transformation in consciousness preceded—and shaped—political action. They questioned mainstream sexual norms. Some were lesbians who built bridges to the gay and lesbian liberation movement. Radical feminists felt that trusted wisdom about women's nature and place in society had to be aired, scrutinized, and challenged. Their unwavering refusal to accept established norms of personal and family life stimulated demands for changes in the private sphere as much as in the public sphere. Childrearing, housecleaning, and marriages had to be made more equal, and government had to shoulder more of the burden for childcare and family support. Significant figures include Alix Kates Shulman, whose template for a marriage contract became renowned; Frances Beal, who questioned black nationalism's patriarchy; Martha Shelley, who scoffed at marriage and urged women to find intimacy with each other; Rosalyn Baxandall, who sparked a cooperative daycare movement; Vivien Leone, who battled for wages for housework; and Naomi Weisstein, who eviscerated the "science" behind experts' characterizations of womanhood. Radicals wrote furiously, publicizing their vision in manifestos, bestselling books, and more than five hundred newsletters and magazines nationwide. They also led some of the movement's most notorious actions, such as a protest against the Miss America Pageant in 1968, in which they characterized one of the nation's hallowed traditions as nothing more than a degrading charade that treated women like cattle being judged at a county fair.

Although women of color joined the cause on both its liberal and radical fronts, their analyses were distinctive enough to constitute a third major arm of the feminist movement. Pauli Murray belonged to a group of liberal black feminists who made the connections between racial civil rights and women's rights. Many of them joined the National Black Feminist Organization (1973). Frances Beal was a leader within the Student Nonviolent Coordinating Committee and brought its black radicalism to her feminism. Black feminists also led movements to secure welfare rights for poor mothers and improved working conditions for household employees. Johnnie Tillmon spearheaded the National Welfare Rights Organization (1966) in a battle for a guaranteed income in the early 1970s, while Edith Barksdale Sloan directed the Household Technicians of America (1971) in a campaign for a minimum wage for domestic workers. Chicana feminists emerged out of the Mexican American civil rights movement in the late 1960s and found their way into groups like Hijas de Cuauhtémoc (1968) and Comisión Femenil Mexicana (1970). Keeping their energies more tightly bound to the Chicano struggle, these activists countered *machismo* in the movement and fought for an equal place in the *familia* that was the primary political symbol of the movement. Activists like Enriqueta Longauex y Vasquez and Ana Nieto Gómez theorized a new kind of selfhood for Chicanas. Women's groups, national conferences, and newspapers advanced black and Latina women's collective demands for the movement to address their concerns for bodily autonomy, roles outside the family, and political leadership.[12]

Chicana and black feminists often viewed white activists with suspicion. They perceived white women as insensitive at best, and hostile at worst, to their needs and situations as women of color. Organizing separately from white women seemed essential in many instances. Activists of the second wave did not always work in lockstep. Their advocacy for work and family brought underlying conflicts to the surface. Which should be prioritized: battles for workplace change or for compensating non-waged mothering? And if workplaces had to be changed, what needed attention most urgently: decent conditions for paid domestic labor or the arbitrary firing of pregnant women? In the fight for childcare, feminists struggled among themselves to reconcile their demand for universal childcare with securing funding for those most in need. Class divides and the separate realities of white women and women of color made for distinct needs and concerns. Liberals and radicals also envisioned diverging means for change. Feminists thus advanced their goals differently at different moments—sometimes in separate organizations, sometimes in coalitions. Recent histories of the feminist movement have begun to explore how and when these alliances formed, as we will see in the childcare, welfare and antipoverty, and domestic worker campaigns.[13]

It is by thematically connecting the three branches of the movement, their alliances and overlapping mobilizations, and the ups and downs of fifteen years of activism that second-wave commitments to work and family issues come to light. This synthetic approach gives us a new angle of vision into the movement, clarifying its aspirations and achievements. Feminists began with deconstructing the social roles that circumscribed women's as well as men's identities (Chapters 1 and 2). They reimagined female and male selfhoods in ways that led to struggles to remake relationships, parenthood, childrearing, marriages, and families (Chapters 3 and 4). They called on society to support parenting with universal childcare and guaranteed incomes for poor mothers (Chapters 5 and 6). And feminists turned their attention to workplaces, securing the rights of mothers and pregnant women as workers and leading some of the earliest campaigns for flexible work schedules (Chapters 7 and 8).

THE REALITY OF THE MOVEMENT'S systematic effort to remake and humanize the nation's decaying family wage system challenges the now-conventional story about feminism. Variants of the having-it-all myth that Pogrebin so cuttingly excoriated have cropped up in women's magazines, newspapers, and the blogosphere about every other year since the mid-1970s. These narratives about having it all normally focus on working moms who are white and professional. Pushed to their limits, these mothers settle for the "mommy track" or simply "opt out" altogether. Occasionally, women opt in. Or they "lean in." But they do so typically in the context of supposedly bitter "mommy wars," between mothers working for wages and housewives working for family alone. Nearly all of these popular "working mommy" plots feature the great feminist betrayal. Feminists, we are repeatedly told, promised women they could have it all, but what we got instead was mothers who were male clones in the workplace. They sleepwalk through stressed-out and exhausted lives, with little meaningful time for their children. Feminism ignored the family, the story goes. Indeed, in many versions of the having-it-all tale, feminists are outright hostile to the needs of family. The blame for women's struggles falls squarely on the shoulders of feminism, full of false promises and promoting nothing more than the selfish advance of individual career women in the workplace.[14]

Many scholars of 1960s and 1970s feminism have bought into the basic premises behind the conventional story, even if they reject its attack on the movement. Histories of the second wave frequently describe mainstream, liberal feminism as principally redressing job discrimination. In particular, this is how the work of the most famous and visible national organization, the National Organization for Women, gets characterized. Younger, radical feminists appear either focused on dismantling the family or generally indifferent to the issue. Much more attention has been paid to how this branch of the movement tackled reproductive rights, domestic violence, and sexual assault. Historians have pointed out feminists' desire to make sustainable work and family lives possible for women, but they have mostly stopped short of exploring their far-ranging analysis of how that goal could be attained and the activism they carried out to reach it. The most in-depth examination of feminist interest in issues related to work and family has been a spate of studies on the welfare rights movement, although these activists have often been set apart from the "mainstream" women's movement. Several legal historians have also illuminated the painstaking work of feminist lawyers who took on the male breadwinning–female homemaking norm in law and the courts. But no comprehensive study has yet tackled the entire issue.[15]

A number of factors explains this lacuna. First, the backlash against feminism has been powerfully effective. It has made it difficult even to see many of the stands feminists of the 1960s and 1970s took on behalf of work and family. That history has been hidden in feminism's defeats. Second, some women active in the movement recall disinterest in either children or work and parenting issues. Even Betty Friedan reported a lack of interest in children among both NOW members and radical feminists.[16] Their recollections have stood in for a more complex historical record. Third, histories of second-wave feminism have often focused on conflict and fragile alignments between liberal and radical feminists, seeking to understand the struggles over strategy and priorities between these two major wings of the movement. Divisions between white women and activists of color have been foregrounded as well in many studies, although recently scholars have considered new areas of collaboration and coalition-building. Finally, feminist campaigns involved diverse sets of activists over long periods of time, often at the local level. Recent histories of these disparate threads have helped forge new ground in understanding the movement, but only once these diverse stories are connected in a comprehensive whole does a new history of feminism come into focus.[17]

By laying out what feminists truly wanted, this book provides a fresh story of second-wave feminism. It's not that feminism failed American women, but that society failed to deliver on the promise of fairness for which feminists fought. Today, it is common for people to talk about "work and family." We have work and family policies, we have calls for paid family leave and flexible workplaces. This book restores US feminism of the 1960s and 1970s to its rightful place in this unfinished struggle. Feminists fought on many fronts for work and family, long before we knew what that term meant.

This is the promise of their vision: once we realize the audacity of their dream, we can see what they accomplished and build upon their struggles to reclaim the true meaning of *having it all*.

1

SELF

The Feminist Reconstruction of Female Selfhood

The great romance between women and the experts was
over. . . . Confronted with something resembling the essence
of real scientific thought—the critical and rationalist spirit
of the new feminism—they could only bluster defensively or
mumble in embarrassment. . . . As the old authorities fell
into disgrace . . . it became possible for women to ask once
again the old questions: What is our nature as women. . . .
How shall we live?

—Barbara Ehrenreich and Deirdre English, *For Her Own Good:*
150 Years of the Experts' Advice to Women, 1978

I N SEPTEMBER 1960, the soon-to-be bestselling feminist writer Betty Friedan
challenged her readers to a thought experiment: what if American women
stopped listening to experts and followed their own internal voices instead?
What lives might they create? Friedan's audience for this article in *Good
Housekeeping* was largely white and middle class, the women most likely
to seek to uphold the postwar ideal of a wife at home and a husband at
work. Friedan's piece, coyly titled "I Say: Women are *People* Too!" was
based on the research that would eventually appear in her book *The Feminine Mystique* in 1963. Psychologists, psychoanalysts, and sociologists had
all failed women, declared Friedan. "In the millions of words written for

"I am woman giving birth to myself," by Marta Thoman. Frontispiece to Sue Cox, *Female Psychology: The Emerging Self*, 1976. The woman rising out of the detritus of traditional womanhood symbolized the new self that feminists imagined creating. This reborn figure opened the pages of an early textbook on the new feminist psychology.

women about women these past 20 years" and in the "thousand expert voices pay[ing] tribute to our femininity . . . our devotion from earliest girlhood to finding the husband and bearing the children who will give us happiness," there was no expert who guided women struggling with feelings of insufficiency and emptiness as they went about their daily lives.

Friedan bid the reader to "shut her ears to all the voices of the experts and listen instead to the voice inside herself which tells her something else."

There was, believed Friedan, extraordinary possibility in that challenge. "Who knows what women can be," she mused, "when they are finally free to become themselves?" Without those droning authorities herding women down ever-narrower paths, a new kind of female self might come into being. Friedan was ebullient at the prospect: "The pattern of women's search for self-fulfillment is so new that experts, blinded by the clear-cut male labels of 'education,' 'career,' 'family,' sometimes don't recognize it all. A woman doesn't have to seek fulfillment by established routes, for why should a woman's pattern be the same as a man's? Or why should it be like that of any other woman's, for that matter?" Her message cheering on a quest for new types of female self-fulfillment struck a chord. Letters poured in, as they would again with the publication of *The Feminine Mystique*. "My deepest thanks," wrote Irene Saylor from New York, "I am so sick of being told I should want to be 'feminine.' . . . I want to be treated as somebody in my own right—because I am."[1]

In this early formulation of the bestseller credited with launching the feminist movement, Friedan made it clear that her intention went far beyond identifying the problem of a stifling suburban domesticity that afflicted women. Rather, she aimed to authorize a whole new female selfhood. In this goal, she was not alone. The reconstruction of the self was one of the most revolutionary achievements of the women's movement.

Before they could take on employment policies that denied mothers jobs or insist that men share childcare and housework, feminists had to engineer a shift in culture and consciousness. They succeeded in making what seemed natural and normal appear contrived and unfair. Second-wavers subjected expert definitions of women's identities, roles, and aspirations to searing scrutiny, and they proposed new conceptions of female selfhood. In pamphlets, manifestos, cartoons, interviews, and more, women of the second wave dissected their own lives and the roles they had been taught to inhabit, then imagined an alternative identity, something they called a whole human self. Feminist intellectuals devastatingly critiqued settled academic truths about women and their nature too, dethroning revered authorities and dismantling foundational paradigms. The charges they leveled against the fields of sociology and psychology reverberated for decades.

That feminists of the 1960s and 1970s questioned dominant beliefs about women and their roles is well recognized. How they specifically reconceptualized the working mother is less well understood, yet that reformulation represented an indispensable foundation for broader activism on behalf of women, work, and family. Three aspects matter. First, feminists disaggregated motherhood from womanhood, making it instead one component of a broader female identity. Movement backers also insisted that a working mother was a positive: better for children, better for women, better for men, and even better for society. Third, second-wavers argued that fixed sex roles ascribing the home to women and the public sphere to men were nonsensical; women could—and should—cross those divides.

Psychological models that regarded female aspiration as deviant came under attack, and biological frameworks that defined maternity as women's sole destiny went by the wayside as well. With impassioned, razor-sharp critiques that thrilled their audiences, feminists exposed every seeming truth about women's nature and place in society as a sham justification for keeping them down. The result was a far more expansive and gender-neutral conception of women's psychology and social roles. The reorientation that followed this process legitimated pursuits for women outside the family and household—particularly for white women—and made it acceptable to earn wages not simply to meet the needs of family but also as a source of self-satisfaction and independence. In breaking the iron grip that wifehood and motherhood held on the publicly sanctioned definition of womanhood, feminists paved the way for the contemporary acceptance of working motherhood.

Full human selfhood for women was a goal shared by feminists, regardless of their race, yet black women and other women of color sought it on distinctive terms. When they insisted on fulfillment of their human potential, it was less to legitimize roles beyond the domestic sphere and more to seek dignity and respect for the roles they already occupied, as well as to undo the ravages of racism. Social scientists and policymakers in the mid-1960s portrayed black mothers in particular as domineering and emasculating; black feminists waged war against those negative stereotypes. Similarly, feminists of color were troubled less by violating sex roles as working mothers and more by the impact that demeaning and dead-end employment had on women's psyches. They pushed middle-class white feminists to recognize that life beyond the home was not necessarily a place of opportunity, fulfillment, and expanded horizons.

In a fertile decade of thinking, writing, and consciousness raising—from the publication of *The Feminine Mystique* in 1963 to the formation of the American Sociological Association's division on sex roles in 1973—feminists forged and sought to live by such new, more expansive selfhoods for women in theory as in practice. Second-wave calls for a renovated female self appealed widely to Americans both inside and outside the movement. Beliefs about women's appropriate roles in work and family began to change in earnest as early as the first years of the 1970s, not long after the movement went into high gear. The feminist rallying cry of a full human self for women became one of the movement's most broadly disseminated calls, and it attracted woman after woman to the cause. But more than that, it shifted the cultural terrain, changing the ground on which the correct shape of women's lives would be understood in the decades ahead. What Americans took to be normal womanhood would never be the same again.

Healthy Womanhood: Experts and Feminine Fulfillment in Postwar America

Social science, particularly psychology, enjoyed unprecedented standing in postwar America. Popular magazines placed Freud alongside Copernicus and Darwin in the ranks of great scientists. A 1957 tome titled *Freud and the Twentieth Century* mused, "Will the Twentieth Century go down in history as the *Freudian Century*?"[2] One of the field's central preoccupations in these years was gender. But womanhood weighed more heavily on the minds of both the practitioners and their popular audience than manhood did. Fear crept throughout society that, after being in charge for four years during World War II, women might resist making way for returning veterans. Other, contradictory anxieties compounded this fear, as experts predicted that overweening mothers, safely ensconced back at home but lacking outlets for their energies, would emasculate their sons.

Fulfillment in marriage, home, and motherhood defined the experts' healthy adult woman in the twenty years after World War II. Psychologists warned mothers that they trod a fine line between being rejecting and being overprotective. A precise course of development was plotted in which young women trimmed their aspirations to home and mature women "adjusted" to their roles as mothers and homemakers. Sociology lent a seal of approval

to such a course: its most influential theorists ratified sex-role differentiation as the most functional arrangement for highly developed modern
societies. Economic dependency and second-class status in both employment
and law followed as a matter of course. With psychology and sociology enjoying extraordinary public credibility in the decades after World War II,
failing to fit these norms tainted women with deviancy.[3]

In the same years, social scientists increasingly described black mothers
only in terms of aberrance. Conflating all black families—and especially
those headed by women—with poor ones, sociologists identified a crisis
in the "Negro family": absent or emasculated men and domineering
women. A "matriarchal" family structure—one which reversed "proper"
sex roles—led to "disorganized" black families. This line of thinking culminated in 1965, when Daniel Patrick Moynihan, the assistant secretary for
labor in the Johnson administration, published *The Negro Family: The
Case for National Action*—widely known as the Moynihan report. The
report blamed poverty in black communities on failed families rather than
lack of jobs or unfair pay, and it pinned responsibility on black mothers
for violating sex roles, which ostensibly led to family dysfunction.[4]

As the 1950s wore on, and even more so in the early years of the 1960s,
cracks appeared in this highly wrought construct. Popular magazines celebrated women's achievements in business, politics, and in the world well
beyond the home. A swelling number of mothers, defying or ignoring pro-
scriptions against maternal wage earning, took jobs. Even government officials acknowledged a "manpower" crisis, and called for "womanpower"
to fill labor shortages—at least in areas suited to feminine talents. A few
social scientists debunked psychologists' claims about working mothers.
Under the auspices of the Committee on Maternal Employment, formed in
the mid-1950s and sponsored by the American Association of University
Women, a group of largely female sociologists pored over data, method-
ology, and conclusions in existing research. The psychologist Lois Meek
Stolz encapsulated the group's findings as she dismissed one colleague's list
of seven "costs to children"—ranging from tired, irritable mothers to no
one at home to do the mending—noting acerbically that his "conclusions
[were] presented without factual documentation."[5]

In 1961, under pressure from women working inside the federal government, President Kennedy created a commission on the status of women.
Discussions among commission members reveal the doubts materializing

about women's appropriate roles. Commissioners debated whether married women and mothers should be encouraged to join the labor force and argued over what might constitute discrimination once they were there, as the historian Alice Kessler-Harris has shown. Yet in the end, on the question of the working mother, they would favor the primacy of home and children. Their final report appeared in 1963, the same year that Friedan published *The Feminine Mystique*, and it bequeathed to feminists the dueling messages that postwar society sent to women: the official façade—a formal commitment to maternity and wifehood—masked simmering disagreements about women's roles and maternal employment. Bringing the full implications of those disagreements to light would be feminists' first order of business.[6]

Feminists Renovate the Female Self and Demand Full Humanity for Women

Envisioning new selves required smashing the old ones first. Authorities who insisted that motherhood and homemaking constituted *the* correct role for a woman had to be taken down. Shaking loose old assumptions and freeing women—and men—from the male breadwinner–female homemaker dyad was necessary in order for social change even to begin. Activists drew freely on concepts from both psychology and sociology—selfhood, identity, human potential, and roles—to make their case against what the culture told them women should be and, somewhat ironically, to envision what might stand in its stead.

Betty Friedan launched some of the first missiles. *The Feminine Mystique* was, in part, a rigorous and relentless deconstruction of conventional social-scientific theories. Friedan described Freudianism and the "pseudo-Freudian theories" that so many self-proclaimed experts spouted as an "all-embracing American ideology, a new religion" that had settled everywhere, "like fine volcanic ash."[7] The book took its name from her attack on the idea that women found fulfillment exclusively in home and mothering. That, she said, was a myth, a "feminine mystique." Instead, women faced constraint. Friedan's own life story was one of the book's primary object lessons in the feminine mystique's ravages: she recounted turning down a graduate fellowship at the request of "a boy" and spending years as a suburban housewife. "I could sense no purpose in my life," she avowed. "I could find no peace." Into the 1970s, collections of feminist writings targeted to liberal audiences raged similarly against "a slowly formed, deeply entrenched, extraordinarily pervasive cultural (and therefore political) decision" to make women into "a class of human beings utterly deprived of self-hood, of autonomy, of confidence."[8]

Once young, radical women's liberationists took the stage at the end of the 1960s, they opened the floodgates. Stories of female suppression poured out into newsletters and manifestos. What had remained unspoken, buried as the slights, indignities, and limits of a normal woman's life, rose to the surface. In a December 1969 profile of the women's movement for *Life* magazine, Sara Davidson described the "rankling resentment" that simmered among women trained to live lives "determined not by ourselves but by the men we married." Diane Narek, a member of the New York City radical feminist group Redstockings, recounted the discouragement and harassment she faced in pursuing a career as a scientist in late 1969. For fifteen cents, readers could order from the Redstockings a copy of "A Woman Scientist Speaks," in which Narek reported that scholarships, for which she was not allowed to apply, went to men with lower grades. Her colleagues assumed that she was not really interested in her work but actually wanted to find a man. "I was constantly asked why I was wasting my time and told to get married. I was told that [my colleagues'] wives preferred homemaking and since I was a woman I wouldn't be happy unless I did the same. My work was considered to be a waste of time, while my co-workers who were doing the same thing were considered to be conducting important research."[9]

Readers of feminist tirades against the restrictions on women's lives were inspired to respond with their own stories of smashing society's expectations. "I failed at every 'female' thing I attempted except having babies," wrote one woman after reading the first issue of *Ms.* magazine in 1972. This working mother, writing to the magazine's editors about her own growing feminist awareness, described the turnabout in her life: as a child, she loved "the neat things my father did in electronics and printing," she remembered, but her father "broke his heart trying to turn my brothers on" to those interests. Like most young women of her generation, she had been directed away from what were seen as her masculine passions and shunted into clerical work at the telephone company. Despite having five children, the women's movement had inspired her to join "an all-male trade," and she loved it. "I'm into presswork and camera stripping," *Ms.*'s correspondent explained. "What a trip! Ten years ago, I knew nothing, nothing of the world but babies, a women's auxiliary, and a car pool. I'm happier now—but then, I'm not trying to be a woman any more. I'm me."[10]

The selves that postwar experts demanded women cultivate were deeply stunted in feminists' eyes. Vivian Gornick, a journalist and prolific writer on feminism, explained to *Village Voice* readers in November 1969 that women had been socialized to believe what they *wanted* was to be wives and mothers. This, said Gornick, was "an act of trickery" that "mutilated [women's] natural selves and . . . deprived them of the right to say 'I' and have it mean something."[11] As those words sank in, Gornick's readers would have shivered in sudden awareness. Their culture told them only about the exalted state of American womanhood.

Motherhood did not escape their scrutiny either. Feminists took on the veneration of motherhood and argued that, as American society defined it, motherhood actually reduced women to mere ciphers living through the accomplishments of their children and husbands. Confinement to such a role shrank a woman to a mere "satellite" of her husband, unable to "develop herself as an individual, having been reduced to only a biological function."[12] To be sure, a strain of hostility toward motherhood permeated some of these writings. For all of its scathing rebuttal of psychology's reigning theories, *The Feminine Mystique* rehabilitated the period's mother-blaming when Friedan relied on studies foretelling the dangers of unfulfilled and overbearing mothers. Such attacks on mothering, however, did not dominate feminist writings, and most stemmed from a desire to critique motherhood as the exclusive basis for women's identity.[13]

Stories of suppressed ambitions and of selves shaped to men's lives and motherhood made the pages of feminist publications bristle with rage. In jettisoning the womanhood ascribed to them, second-wavers transformed what it meant to long for life beyond the home and family. It was not neurosis; nor was it failed "adjustment" to the proper female role. Rather, the culture unjustly suppressed women's legitimate human desires and ambitions. Martha Shelley, active in the Gay Liberation Front, attacked absolute "sex-role differentiation" as "pure artifice." "The makeup is cracking," she warned, "The roles—breadwinner, little wife, screaming fag, bulldyke, James Bond—are the cardboard characters we are always trying to fit into,

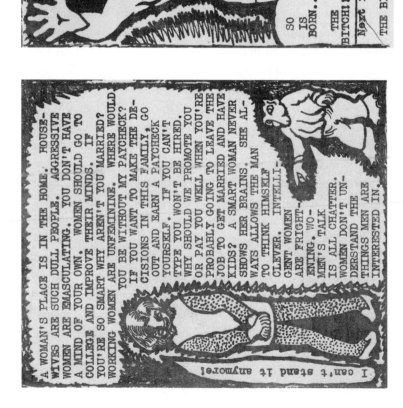
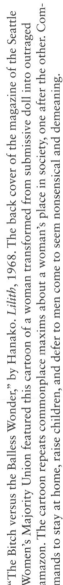

"The Bitch versus the Balless Wonder," by Hanako. *Lilith*, 1968. The back cover of the magazine of the Seattle Women's Majority Union featured this cartoon of a woman transformed from submissive doll into outraged amazon. The cartoon repeats commonplace maxims about a woman's place in society, one after the other. Commands to stay at home, raise children, and defer to men come to seem nonsensical and demeaning.

as if being human and spontaneous were so horrible." Concerned largely with the dominant middle-class male breadwinner–female homemaker norm, feminists argued that everyone from psychologists and policymakers to male comrades in the civil rights and student movements expected women to mold themselves to others and assume a kind of passivity that prevented their full development. In the process, the movement redefined domesticity as discrimination, not privilege. It was a shocking jolt to the system, and it stood every assumption most women held about how they were *supposed* to live their lives on its head. Even black women and other women of color had felt the pressures to conform to the female-homemaker ideal, if only in the negative. Looking back on the world she inherited as a young college graduate in the 1950s, Letty Cottin Pogrebin, a cofounder of *Ms.* magazine, recalled, "It [was] night and day from today."[14]

BY FEBRUARY 1972, the Cambridge, Massachusetts group Female Liberation had run its millionth piece of paper through its mimeograph machine. Weekly newsletters, flyers, pamphlets, and more had spun over the barrel, circulating feminist ideas locally and beyond. The women's movement spawned hundreds of periodicals and newsletters that made it possible for women across the country to encounter the feminist message. Most publications were the work of small grassroots collectives, with many black and Chicana groups producing their own publications. The top priority of the radical lesbian collective The Furies was publishing its ideas. NOW, the Women's Equity Action League, and other national organizations supported local chapter newsletters as well as their own member updates. Regional periodicals, such as Iowa City's *Ain't I a Woman*, invited area groups to send in pages. Minot, North Dakota; Wooster, Ohio; Milwaukee, Wisconsin; Bloomington, Indiana; and Kansas City, Missouri, among other places, took them up on their offer. More formal journals, including *Feminist Studies* and *Quest*, followed. Feminists had a virtual compulsion to write down, publish, and circulate their ideas—in part to make them tangible, in part to connect a highly dispersed movement.[15]

They succeeded in getting their ideas out. Not only did periodicals arrive in mailboxes, but alternative news services like KNOW, Inc. also routinely republished feminist tracts and manifestos. Soon, feminist presses printed them and feminist bookstores sold them. The bookstores, like burgeoning women's centers, became hives of activity where women encountered the movement and its ideas. At A Woman's Place, a bookstore that opened in Portland, Oregon in 1973, patrons attended classes, settled into the reading room, and showed up for films and feminist speakers. Dayton Women's Liberation opened the doors of its Women's Center the same year. The Center sponsored classes, welcomed walk-ins (and provided childcare for them), organized a lending library, and provided meeting space for area groups. The mainstream media gave the movement extensive coverage as well. Not all of it was helpful, however, so feminists inaugurated their own forays into the publishing world. The bestselling book *Sisterhood is Powerful* was an all-woman production, and the group assembling the collection persuaded Random House to publish it. The first issue of *Ms.* magazine, supposed to be on newsstands for eight weeks, sold out in eight days.[16]

In the crucial years of ferment, these books, mimeographed zines, and manifestos brimmed with alternatives to the confining version of womanhood that activists had left in tatters. When feminists envisioned new selves, however, it was not to emulate a male identity tailored to breadwinning and achievement at work. Neither radical nor liberal second-wavers wanted a simple substitution exercise, however highly the culture valued manhood over womanhood. As we shall see in the next chapter, feminists considered any system that denied nurturing traits to men just as distorting as one that foreclosed ambition and striving for women. Movement writings expressed a wish for a reconstructed womanhood with two dimensions: a total or full human selfhood and a balanced role that combined caregiving with work beyond the family.

The founders of the National Organization for Women premised their demands for social change on such an expansion of female identity. Their founding statement of purpose declared in October 1966 that "women, first and foremost, are human beings, who, like all other people in our society, must have the chance to develop their fullest human potential." Liberal feminist activists continued to emphasize the theme of a new female selfhood. The "real sexual revolution," said Friedan in 1970, was "the emergence of women from passivity, from thingness, to full self-determination, to full dignity." Addressing an audience on the theme "Human Rights are Indivisible," Wilma Scott Heide, vice president of NOW, defined autonomous female selfhood as a basic right: "We must think and say: 'Women *are* people.'" "The human right to personhood," Heide concluded, "independent of sex or race is indivisible and must be self-defined and preciously

LIBERATION, NOW!

Theme of Women's Liberation

Words by
BETTY FRIEDAN and
JACQUELYN REINACH

Music by
JACQUELYN REINACH
and J. RENE

"Liberation, Now!" by Betty Friedan and Jacquelyn Reinach, music by Jacquelyn Reinach and J. Rene. 1970. An anthem for the movement, "Liberation, Now!" captured feminists' bravado as it told women, "It's time to spell our own names, we're people, not 'dames.'"

nurtured." As catchy lines from the women's liberation song "Liberation, Now!" summed it up, "We're breaking out of our cage of ruffles and rage / . . . . We're more than mothers and wives with second hand lives." "Femininity, what's femininity? / Masculinity, what's masculinity? It's humanity that we both share."[17]

Among younger activists, calls for a new female selfhood were ubiquitous. Manifestos of numerous women's liberation groups reflected the demand for a transformed female selfhood. Chicago Women's Liberation, asking in February 1969, "What does women's freedom mean?" defined it as "the freedom to be one's own person," living "an integrated life of work, love, play, motherhood." Radicalesbians, a group of New York lesbian feminists, contributed to the discussion of the expansion of female selfhood by suggesting that as long as a woman tried to be what society deemed an ideal woman she would "sense some conflict with that incipient self, that sense of I, that sense of a whole person." For them, the solution was to forge identities in relation to other women, to discover "authentic selves" not deformed by what the culture decreed. As separatists, Radicalesbians envisioned breaking from men but, just as importantly, also from gendered ideals of the feminine in a quest for what they called the "whole person."[18]

The movement's highly influential advice manual *Our Bodies, Ourselves*, first published in 1971, perhaps best sums up the kind of selfhood these largely white feminists envisioned. The book opened with a chapter dedicated to "Our Changing Sense of Self," in which the authors observed that "it became clear that we did not really feel ourselves to be separate, independent people." The writers considered "the confusion and unhappiness that many of us feel at least some of the time when faced with motherhood" as "positive indications to us that our total selves, not just our mother-selves, are struggling to make themselves heard." Repeatedly contrasting "total selves" with "mother selves" and "satellite" identities with full personhood, white feminists demanded a personhood for women that stretched beyond their "mother selves" into expressions of their individual ambitions and desires. As the young sociology professor Marlene Dixon wrote in *Lilith* in the fall of 1968, "Career *and* wife and mother or career *versus* wife and mother, are false dichotomies resulting from a male dominated society. Rather, the issue is *career and wife and mother* as a unit, possible for every woman in this society."[19]

For feminists of color, the question of selfhood was just as urgent, but it was informed by the distinct histories of African American and Chicana women, as well as by the context of the civil rights and Mexican American movements. If Freud was the obvious target for many white activists, black feminists grappled with the Moynihan Report and its damning portrayal of black women. Baldly repudiating popular conceptions of the domineering black matriarch, Frances Beal, a founder of the Black Women's Liberation Committee in the Student Nonviolent Coordinating Committee, published the path-breaking and widely reprinted essay "Double Jeopardy" in 1969, in which she bluntly informed readers that "it is a gross distortion of fact to state that black women have oppressed black men." To anyone who repeated the myth of black women's matriarchal domination, Margaret Wright, an activist from South Los Angeles and a member of the black feminist group Women Against Repression, told the *Los Angeles Times* the next summer, "I tell them they've bought Whitey's bull about the black matriarchy. In a matriarchy the women rule. Hell we get bossed at work and we get bossed at home." Black women's resilient organization of their lives in the face of this "double jeopardy" of race and sex was a sign of strength and functionality, said black activists like Wright, not dysfunction and emasculation. At the same time, black feminists insisted that black women's equality was not antithetical to black liberation. Beal argued that black men in the movement who were "telling black women to step back into a submissive role" were taking "a counter-revolutionary position." Rather, liberation and dignity for black people lay in easing men's feelings of inadequacy without assigning black women a historic white-woman's role.[20]

Indeed, African American feminists noted that *their* concerns about sex roles were not anchored in women's oppression within the home or motherhood. "Black women," Frances Beal declared, have never been allowed the "phony luxuries" granted the stereotypical white women. Decrying women's confinement to the home made little sense from the perspective of black women, as they had always had "to work to help house, feed, and clothe their families." Moreover, Beal pointed out, "the reality of the degrading and dehumanizing jobs that were relegated to us quickly dissipated this image of womanhood." Doris Wright, one of the founders of the National Black Feminist Organization, called attention to the fact that "black women have proven over and over again that they are capable leaders, not only as necessary heads of families but out in the world as well." Beal summed up the position this way: the model of a woman "surrounded by hypocritical homage and estranged from all real work" promulgated in white official culture was antithetical to black women's experience.[21]

In reimagining women's roles, young African American feminists confronted black nationalist pressures to have babies and help reproduce a robust, healthy black nation. They echoed white activists in defining such a vision as too limiting. According to Frances Beal, any woman whose exclusive role was staying at home and caring for children led "an extremely sterile existence." "She cannot develop herself as an individual, having been reduced to only a biological function," Beal argued in a manner parallel to many white activists. There was no reason to embrace as the right direction for black women and men an idealized version of the male-breadwinner and female-homemaker norm. Doris Wright warned black sisters that "The Age of the Pedestal is about to dawn for us" and challenged black men not to embrace sexist ideas about roles that were not only chauvinistic but were also mere copies of white ideals of "making it." Black feminists thus reiterated white feminist condemnations of roles assigning women exclusively to the home, but they blamed that sexual division of labor on whites and called on men in the black liberation movement to resist embracing such sexist roles as emblems of black liberation.[22]

Older liberal black feminists, such as Eleanor Holmes Norton, a lawyer and chair of the New York City Commission on Human Rights in the early 1970s, and Pauli Murray, also a lawyer and a pioneer in linking race and sex discrimination—"Jane Crow" as she named it—shared the concerns of radicals. They feared that black nationalist pronatalism and black women's self-defense against the black matriarch image would perpetuate an idealized male breadwinner–female homemaker norm. Norton observed that, "if we are to avoid this disaster [of emulating the patriarchal white family], the best, perhaps the only, place to begin is in our conception of the black woman. . . . Whether black or white, if American women are to find themselves, they must begin looking outside the home. . . . Inevitably, women are going to acquire new goals and a new status." Toni Morrison pointed out that the selves black women forged in the face of racism's effects on the black community were uncannily the very ones that white women's liberationists called for. The black woman had already "invented herself": "She combined being a responsible person with being a female—and as a person she felt free to confront not only the world at large (the rent man, the doctor and the rest of the marketplace) but her man as well."[23]

Having a full selfhood was less of an issue for black women than it was for their white counterparts, but gaining dignity and respect for that selfhood was a central problem. In addition, fighting for a role outside the home was irrelevant when the majority of working-age black women were already there, facing a race- and sex-segregated labor market. Black feminists argued that what needed changing was the occupational segregation that assigned black women to the lowest paid, most demeaning employment. Faced with a crying need for supports like childcare and adequate income, transformations in identity often fell lower on black women's priority list. Still, the Third World Women's Alliance, which united black feminist activists with Puerto Rican, Chicana, Native American, and Asian American women, called in 1971 for "role integration," so that women could be "human beings" not "sex objects." We are, they asserted, "women in our own right."[24]

A similar push and pull between racial and gender liberation movements shaped Chicana feminists' critique of contemporary American society. Las Hijas de Cuauhtémoc, a group of young Chicana activists who began meeting at California State University, Long Beach in 1968, named themselves after a group of feminist women active in the Mexican Revolution in 1910. Las Hijas struggled to reshape the sexist roles allotted to women while remaining within the Chicano rights movement. Chicano activists wished to resurrect an idealized Chicano national family—la Raza—with women as its backbone. The model Chicana in this nationalistic formulation was strong, enduring, and ensured the survival of Chicano culture. Las Hijas de Cuauhtémoc argued instead that a history of Chicana female activism and self-determination legitimated roles for women that carried them far beyond the home, wifehood, and motherhood to which men's formulations assigned them.[25]

One of the best-known efforts to outline a Chicana feminist perspective was by Enriqueta Longauex y Vasquez. Vasquez, who was active in the Mexican American civil rights movement, began editing the Chicano newspaper *El Grito del Norte* in the summer of 1968. A year later, in an essay lambasting the idea that Chicanas did not want liberation, Vasquez explored the place of "The Women of La Raza." She relied on the metaphors of family that were at the heart of Chicano movement rhetoric, but like Las Hijas, she demanded women's equality: "The family must come up together," she commented, and avowed that "we must strive for the fulfillment of all as equals, with the full capability and right to develop as humans." For middle-class Chicanas, Vasquez saw a fate similar to that of middle-class white housewives: a dependence on a husband that gave a woman no way of "realizing herself as a full human."[26] But, for most Chicanas who were poor, a different struggle for selfhood unfolded.

As Chicano men, much like black men, grappled with lousy jobs and discrimination, poor Chicana women faced their fury. They often ended up alone, as had Vasquez, who was a single mother and sole breadwinner for years after she left an abusive husband. In the strength such Chicana working mothers exhibited, Vasquez saw the resourcefulness of women who "had to live all of the roles of her Raza"—enduring racism in the larger society, struggling as providers, and being mothers. Vasquez used the contemporary history of Chicanas, typically ignored by male activists, to promote an expansive selfhood for women that encompassed mothering and breadwinning. "There [was] little room for having a definition of woman's role as such" when the challenges of race, sex, and class together faced Chicanas. "Roles," she concluded, "are for actors."[27]

The idea of reevaluating women's roles surfaced repeatedly in Chicana feminist texts. A 1975 article on "Roles" for *Chicana Week* at the University of Texas argued that women should not assume there was only one role for them dictated by tradition. Just like men, women had been breadwinners and activists throughout history. "We must stop apologizing for our aspirations to be good career women, good community advocates, and good mothers at the same time if we want to; or at different intervals in our lives as we need to." This, the author notes, is not an alien or Anglo understanding of women's lives. To speak of women's rights did not undermine tradition; rather, it was "improving the conditions under which Chicanas already enact[ed] their reality as mothers at home, mothers at work, single employed women, and as community advocates."[28]

Both black and Chicana feminists struggled with doubts about white liberationists, who often appeared too caught up in their own class- and race-defined worlds to comprehend African American or Chicana experience.[29] Yet all groups shared the demand for women's full humanity. All agreed motherhood should not assume an exclusive or even primary role in women's identities. In working through how such a new selfhood fit into movements for racial equality, black and Chicana feminists were a core part of the second-wave struggle to rewrite female selves.

Consciousness Raising as Method:
New Feminist Selves in Practice

The movement gave life to this new self in the searching, often excruciating self-examination of the consciousness-raising group. Letty Cottin Pogrebin's group of twelve women met every Tuesday night for four years. Each week they had a topic: one week it was patriarchy, another it might be how to ask for a raise. They had a naked session to learn to appreciate the beauty of women's bodies through their own eyes, not men's. Across the country, thousands of such groups brought women together, crowded into tiny city apartments or comfortably sprawled around suburban living rooms. Every session had a question, and women took turns answering it, using their own experience to teach themselves what society refused to say about women's condition. "Telling it like it is may be the most difficult action of our movement," women's liberationists in Gainesville, Florida wrote. "It is an act of great courage and an act of faith in our sisters."[30]

Through consciousness raising, women struggled to translate newfound awareness into different lives and identities. The Women's Radical Action Project (WRAP), a group of about forty women from the area around the University of Chicago, began meeting in 1967. Estelle Carol described the "groping" discussions of the group's early meetings as they began to consider "the conflict between an identity as a woman and as a person" and explore how "society prevents most women from realizing their full potential."[31] In a very different context, and with very different politics, suburban New York housewives participated in the same exercise. In 1970, *Family Circle* profiled a "suburban liberation group" of 150 housewives and mothers along the Hudson River north of New York City. One member, Elaine Disick, sported a women's movement pin with a symbolic clenched red fist on her otherwise conventional suburban attire. When she spoke with the reporter, Disick described the group's discussions over cups of coffee about political action, women's status, and new feminist ideas. They even brought their husbands in for a joint couples session. The group meetings fed Disick's belief that "I have to be more than a wife and mother. Look, I've got 40 years after the kids grow up. It makes me ask myself, 'What am I going to do when I grow up?'"[32]

There is no good count of how many women found their way to a consciousness-raising group. Women's organizations, unions, schools—from high schools to universities—all sponsored such meetings. Popular women's magazines helped spread the word. *McCall's* readers learned in September 1973 about a group of thirty-two suburban women in Long Island, New York who had been treated to a demonstration consciousness-raising session while participating in a five-session course on "Ms: The New Status of Women."[33] The gatherings, which drew in liberals and radicals, white women and women of color, all had a similar form. Some met for short, intense periods, while others went on for years. The Combahee River Collective, a radical black feminist group, identified consciousness raising as its method of expanding political awareness. The historian Kimberly Springer observes that all black feminist organizations had consciousness raising at their origins in common. At California State University, Long Beach, the Chicanas who founded Las Hijas de Cuauhtémoc came together initially in a "rap group" that was instrumental in forging their feminist consciousness.[34]

A 1974 study surveyed nearly 1,700 women from forty-one states about their experiences in consciousness-raising groups. Participants most often cited "to share thoughts and feelings about being a woman" and "to examine problems women have with their traditional roles (mother, wife)" as their reasons for joining a group. The meetings were the grassroots embodiment of the feminist pursuit of new selfhoods. "The group woke me up, made me start asking questions," one woman in New York remembered. "Maybe the questions can cause you a lot of heartache, but if you're a woman in this society and you don't know how to ask the questions, I think you're done for." Another woman, from Maine, recalled that in her group, the women "struggle[d] to give ourselves back to each other." "It wasn't me," she added, "giving me the license to take myself seriously again. It was the group." Consciousness raising pushed women out of their comfort zones, forcing them to face deeply held assumptions and come to terms with how degrading their treatment had frequently been. One fifty-year-old student from the Long Island group reported her sudden insight that "for too many years I had been an expendable person—filling whatever niche I was placed in. In doing so, I had negated myself completely."[35]

The writer Vivian Gornick described at length how the soul searching in a consciousness-raising group circled again and again to the question of forging a new self. Gornick visited a gathering of ten middle-class women—almost certainly all white, but none "committed feminists"—who spread themselves out on couches and cushions in a Greenwich Village apartment one cool autumn evening in the fall of 1970. The women in the room, as Gornick recounted, voiced fear, anxiety, and frustration over "this business of identity." They went back and forth, scrutinizing their lives. Lucie told the group, "For God's sake! We're in here trying to be ourselves. Whatever that turns out to be," while Laura identified one group member, Claire, as a model because "she has the most integrated and most *separate* sense of self of anyone I know." In Claire, Laura saw a woman whose identity reached beyond husband and family, someone who embraced traits normally allotted to men. Jen ended the discussion by remarking, "*Knowing* what you want for yourself . . . that's everything, isn't it?"

For Gornick, these intense collective acts of self-exploration were the heart of the women's movement, where "the soul of a woman is genuinely searched and a new psychology of the self is forged. . . . [Here] I am the full occupant of my feminist skin, engaged in the true business of modern feminism, reaching hard for self-possession." In the intimate, behind-closed-doors talk of the consciousness-raising group, Gornick saw feminist activism as important as any movement demonstration. Breaking down society's prescriptions about what a woman *should* be and conjuring up more satisfying possibilities was essential feminist work, and astonishingly exciting. As a young Toni Morrison observed, when women come together, "talking about human rights . . . the air is shivery with possibilities."[36]

Taking on Social Science: Rewriting Psychology and Sociology's Gendered Paradigms

Feminist intellectuals turned their sights on their own disciplines and, in the process, fleshed out feminist ideas of the female self. Lacerating in their appraisals, feminist psychologists tore down biological accounts of female development, defiantly rejected the stereotype of the mannish career woman, and repudiated the belief that female psychological normalcy lay in maternity. In sociology, their peers critiqued dominant models of male and female sex roles and demonstrated socialization's importance in shaping social roles. By the middle of the 1970s, a generation of feminist scholars had undercut once-hegemonic beliefs about women's psyches and roles.

Feminists exposed the false biological reasoning pervading the social sciences. Perhaps the most influential attack was Naomi Weisstein's 1968 analysis of how "psychology constructs the female." This essay, originally titled "Kinder, Küche, Kirche as Scientific Law: Psychology Constructs the Female," is easily one of the most well-known texts of the second wave. Weisstein famously turned the field's vaunted claims of scientific empiricism on their head. The notion that "anatomy decrees the life of a woman," as the Harvard psychiatrist Joseph Rheingold averred, came under devastating condemnation. "The fundamentalist myth of sex-organ causality" produced no meaningful analysis of human behavior, Weisstein said. A withering dissection of the biased assumptions and unverifiable conclusions of psychological studies followed, whether the research compared humans to primates or studied human personality. For example, after listing multiple instances of clinicians' failing to diagnose psychological problems correctly from their own test batteries, Weisstein reported her own experience as a psychology graduate student, when only a fifth of her Harvard peers had accurately identified the sex of blind respondents to a clinical psychology test—a result worse than chance alone would have produced. The broad field of psychology operated, Weisstein claimed, on "theory without evidence."[37]

Kate Millett's pioneering 1970 book *Sexual Politics* emphasized Weisstein's point. Turning to studies that showed the acquired character of gender (a concept new at the time and which Millett had to define carefully as an acquired social identity rather than a biological character), she concluded "psychosexual personality is therefore postnatal and learned." Millett emphasized the experiences of early childhood and socialization in the formation of identity. Weisstein concurred, arguing that no assessment of human personality made sense without accounting for social context; in this, she was at the forefront of calls by feminist social scientists to assess "the social contexts within which people move . . . the expectations about how they will behave, and . . . the authority that tells them who they are and what they are supposed to do."[38]

In making these arguments, feminists like Weisstein and Millett rebutted the scientific claims that had propped up the domestic ideal's exclusive identification of women with childrearing, mothering, and the home. They showed that what society saw in female nature had nothing biological about it; rather, it was highly social and explicable as the end result of discrimination. Feminist thinkers directed the attention of social scientists to workplace culture, occupational segregation, and the family, and they encouraged researchers to investigate the barriers to women's participation in many of these areas rather than assume women's natural preferences.[39]

Feminist psychologists also repudiated the notion that motherhood represented fulfillment and the sole avenue for women's psychological health, asserting instead that organizing female identity around mothering was psychologically unhealthy. An influential study by Pauline Bart, for example, demonstrated that women who had been "supermothers"—women particularly dedicated to being perfect mothers, as society expected—often suffered from severe depression in middle age as their children left home. "If one's satisfaction, one's sense of worth comes from other people rather than from one's own accomplishments, one is left with an empty shell in place of a self when such people depart," argued Bart. Bart rejected arguments made by the Freudian psychoanalysts Therese Benedek and Helene Deutsch contending that a woman who does not follow the traditional female role is castrating and "pseudo masculine." Quite the opposite, Bart found that a woman with independent achievements had less vulnerability to breakdown when significant others left.[40]

A final area in which feminists questioned psychology's accepted wisdom was the "career-oriented" woman, particularly the married mother who still desired success in the labor force. Feminists located the bias in decades of psychological research that characterized career-oriented women as frustrated, internally dissatisfied, and, for some analysts, victims of childhood trauma. Other second-wave scholars refuted the psychoanalytical tenet that a woman's desire to have meaningful employment represented neurotic masculine strivings. For example, feminists disputed the Freudian-based assessment that choice of occupation and dress reflected an unresolved penis envy and failure to accept the female sex role. Influential work by Matina Horner on Radcliffe College graduates' ambivalence about achievement also showed that a "*motive to avoid success*" dogged women, as they feared becoming less feminine when they succeeded. Horner contended that society actually instilled this motive in women from their very earliest days, as sex-role socialization occurred.[41] Put simply, feminists proved that the root cause of male/female differences in career success lay not in inborn sex-differentiated traits but in gendered socialization.

Feminist sociologists led a parallel assault on their field's orthodoxy. When Alice Rossi was a graduate student in sociology in the 1950s, she paid little attention to the roles of women; it took an experience of blatant and crude sex discrimination to "jar [her] out of a romantic cocoon of political innocence." Out of the "slow burn" ignited by that experience, Rossi wrote one of the movement's earliest commentaries on the field, "Equality between the Sexes: An Immodest Proposal," which appeared in the spring of 1964. Rossi's immodest proposal was "a socially androgynous conception of the roles of men and women." "Traditional conceptions of masculine and feminine," she argued, "are inappropriate to the kind of world we can live in in the second half of the twentieth century." For much of the past, women had labored far more in productive household work than in mothering. Only within the last hundred years had any women converted mothering into total employment: "The woman in 1964 who holds down a full-time job will probably have as much or more time with her children as her grandmother had." In an abundant, technological society, housework consumed only small portions of a woman's time; and with life spans lengthening, a mother expended ever-smaller segments of her life in childrearing.[42] To confine women's social roles to mothering and household made little sense on practical grounds, let alone equalitarian ones. Sociologists had allowed themselves to treat mere stereotypes as legitimate science.

Rossi launched a full-blown critique of her discipline. She argued that the field had simplistically borrowed from social anthropology and psychoanalytic theory to declare sex "a universally necessary basis for role differentiation in the family." Like many feminists, she critiqued Talcott Parsons. A dean of American sociology, Parsons had famously argued that the functional demands of modern society required role differences between men and women. Rossi's feminist awakening involved a break with the field's Parsonian dogma that only one person in a family should have an occupation outside the home. This claim, Rossi came to believe, was "an intellectual put down" justifying male dominance.[43]

To Rossi, sex equality meant redistributing human characteristics across the sexes. She wanted "enlargement of the common ground on which men and women base their lives together by changing the social definitions of approved behavior for both sexes." Feminist sociologists like Rossi tended to argue for transforming *both* women's and men's sex roles. Men should be involved more in parenting; men should express more tender and caring qualities. Critical to this transformation, from Rossi's perspective, was the employment of mothers. With mothers employed, maternal dominance of the family would be attenuated, and fathers could assume roles as "equal partners in family life." Rossi envisioned mothers for whom childbirth and early parenthood were "among many equally important highlights in her life" not "the exclusive basis for a sense of self-fulfillment and purpose."[44]

Literally hundreds of studies on women's sex roles had been undertaken by the time Arlie Russell Hochschild completed a review essay on sex-role research for the *American Journal of Sociology* in 1973, just under a decade later. Between Rossi's immodest proposal and Hochschild's review charting multiple critiques, feminist sociologists elaborated a thorough reevaluation of the field's approach to sex roles. As they had done with psychology, feminists objected to the biological assumptions underlying the assignment of sex roles; they also dissected sex-role socialization and showed how American society produced a narrow and fixed set of sex roles. Lenore Weitzman, for example, identified the "relentless conditioning" that straitjacketed women and men into particular roles through a system of reward and punishment for sex-appropriate behaviors from infancy through college. The feminist-oriented work that appeared in sociology during these years thus disputed not just the field's dominant functionalist presumptions but also the origin and development of sex roles. This burgeoning scholarship emphasized the impact of socialization and social pressures for adjustment rather than natural sex-role differentiation, paving the way for the development of the concept of gender a few years later.[45]

Jessie Bernard, one of the most prominent feminists in sociology, published *The Future of Motherhood* in 1974, culminating this early round of work. Writing for a popular audience, Bernard announced her position simply by titling her first chapter, "Mother is a Role, Women are Human Beings." The book was an intellectual *tour de force* and a ringing defense of changing women's roles. She countered the belief that motherhood was a woman's primary purpose and source of self-fulfillment with a barrage of evidence, citing women's history, cross-cultural comparisons, and studies of alternative lifestyles, along with psychological and sociological research and facts about the changing modern workforce. Roles were not intrinsic, but acquired. They were malleable and expandable, with space for women and men to acquire a full range of human traits. Role scripts for motherhood, argued Bernard, were already undergoing revolutionary change: women's mother-role and worker-role were converging, and transformation was inevitable.[46]

Bernard's watchword was integration. Combining motherhood and wage earning was happening; it made no sense to "write about the future of motherhood by writing separately about the role of mother and that of worker." American women, whether professionals or working class, had already learned how to fulfill both roles, and without the "role strain" that social scientists assumed they would incur. Mothers had lived and breathed the false dichotomy between roles. "Roles, not women, were stereotyped," said Bernard. "Structures, not women, were rigid. Women themselves were multi-dimensional. They could be competent *and* nurturant both at home and at the office."[47]

Blue-collar and working-class mothers also experienced little psychological conflict between their two roles, as they typically considered their worker role "an extension of the mother role," with their wage earning providing support for their families. (Exhaustion was another matter, and Bernard acknowledged the lack of concessions to a working woman's double day.) Bernard dismissed as mere sexist bias the conventional assumption that women's two roles were in conflict. In fact, Bernard insisted on women's *right* to work, not merely out of the comforting convenience of economic need but as "urgent emotional necessity." Work was as much of an emotional need—a human psychological imperative—for women as it was for men. Bernard buttressed her claims by turning, like other feminists, to growth psychologists' models of human development. These humanistic psychologists jettisoned the model of adjustment to rigidly fixed sex roles as the imperative of psychological health, favoring instead a model of human development based on finding and developing an authentic self. With this model as ammunition, Bernard maintained that work was a fundamental means for human self-actualization, for women as well as men.[48]

Bernard also turned the tables on the very question of dual roles. Men were both workers and fathers; why hadn't their two roles come under scrutiny? One positive trend, according to Bernard, was that many younger men and women were involving men in childrearing in ever deeper ways. Bernard saw role sharing, as it came to be called, as a surprisingly far-reaching innovation. "On the surface, role sharing appears to be a relatively mild kind of change. It does not challenge the isolated household nor call for any tampering with conventional family relationships. All it does, seemingly, is call on the father to participate more extensively and intensively in a basic family function. Actually, of course, it would entail a revolution in the whole concept of work for both men and women." The potential for male involvement in the family struck many feminists as one of the most critical insights of the movement: role transformation extended across both sexes. Bernard called it a "new balance."[49]

Dethroning the Experts: Feminists Reshape the Field

Feminist psychologists and sociologists did not stop at intellectual critique; they also fought entrenched bias against women in their fields. Feminists founded the Association for Women in Psychology in 1969, and in the same year, a women's caucus held its first discussions at the American Sociological Association annual meeting. Sociologists for Women in Society emerged shortly thereafter. Both organizations demanded changes in the profession to end hiring discrimination, open their respective fields to female graduate students on equal terms, address topics relevant to women in their scholarly journals, and include women in leadership roles in their professional associations. Outraged feminist sociologists, for example, presented a dramatic set of resolutions to the American Sociological Association directly following their 1969 organizing session. They critiqued men in the field for complacently accepting what is as what ought to be, citing "a great and pressing need for critical reassessment of many psychological and sociological assumptions in the area of sex role and family structure." Special journal issues in the early 1970s explored the impact of feminism on their respective fields. In 1973, the American Sociological Association established a section on sex roles; in 1975, the journal *Sex Roles* printed its first issue. Four decades later, both the Association for Women in Psychology and Sociologists for Women in Society continue to advocate within their fields.[50]

In addition to eroding male dominance within the fields' institutions, feminists revised the principal theoretical and methodological frameworks of each. They changed the kinds of questions asked, the designs of studies, and the assumptions embedded in each field's theories. This paradigm shift had a series of important consequences. First, feminist scholars dethroned the psychological establishment, delegitimizing their claims to define women's identities and roles. Second, in emphasizing social context and socialization, feminist intellectuals explained women's status as a consequence of changeable social forces, not women's nature. The horizon of female selfhood and women's sex roles expanded accordingly.

The work of these feminist psychologists and sociologists transformed expert opinion and changed how young women—and men—were educated. Because experts defined and policed women's roles, and because Americans looked to them for guidance about how to be women, men, mothers, and fathers, change required successful feminist dismantling of these authorities' tenets about identity and sex roles. Key feminist texts in both fields were reprinted again and again, in women's liberation literature and elsewhere. Popular books such as *Woman in Sexist Society* and *Voices of the New Feminism* reprinted essays by Kate Millett, Pauline Bart, Jessie Bernard, Alice Rossi, and the psychologists Phyllis Chesler and Nancy Chodorow, among others. Naomi Weisstein's "Psychology Constructs the Female" could be found in the bestselling classic *Sisterhood is Powerful*, along with *Woman in Sexist Society, Radical Feminism*, and *Liberation Now!*, to name just a few. A couple of them, like Jessie Bernard's 1972 *The Future of Marriage,* became bestsellers. Their themes and arguments surfaced routinely in media coverage of the fields.[51] Feminist social science thus undergirded the feminist-led reorientation of cultural norms around female roles and identity.

FEMINIST IDEAS ABOUT the self percolated through American culture in the 1960s and 1970s. Feminists broadcast their own scholarship and writings, while consciousness raising drew even those far from the movement's core to the issue of identity. And significantly, virtually every story on the movement in this crucial decade made the new selfhood a basic theme. *Newsweek*'s dramatic March 1970 special report, "Women in Revolt," for example, described the "New Feminist" as one of "thousands of women with lovers, husbands and children . . . talking about changes . . . that will allow every female to function as a separate and equal person." Just a few months later, *Redbook* quoted an earnest, "gentle and pretty computer analyst" in her twenties attending a NOW meeting in Chicago saying, "Look, we have these stereotypes. . . . It doesn't matter to me if I'm feminine, because I'm *human*." "Again and again," commented the article's writer, "they returned to the theme of humanity. In fact, a slogan for a button being considered by NOW is 'Women Are People Too.'"[52] A full human self for women was among the most frequently cited longings when journalists asked women what they expected from the movement.

The media's focus on a new selfhood had downsides for the second wave. By seizing on the question of self-realization, journalists helped cement the belief that what defined the movement was individual women's transformation, a key building block of the having-it-all myth. Still, feminists' demand for a whole human self for women became the framework against which future visions of American womanhood would be tested and constructed. By the mid-1970s, increasingly higher numbers of women agreed that maternal wage earning hurt neither school-age nor preschool children. They supported men sharing in housework as well as employment rights for pregnant women.[53] Second-wave feminists came on the scene as long-term trends in women's employment and a changing outlook on female roles were moving in the direction feminists wished for. It was feminism, however, that framed those beliefs in ways that, over the long term, Americans came to accept as the norm.

If the culture had been dominated for over a century by an ideology of domesticity which located female identity in nurturing, caretaking, and the "softer" traits while defining men as aggressive, competitive, and "harder," feminists proposed distributing all human traits across both men and women. The remade feminist self normalized working motherhood, and it set the foundation upon which a broad edifice of changes in personal lives, workplaces, and society could be built.

2

FATHERHOOD

Male Feminists and the Nurturing Father

As long as women have to fulfill the demands of two roles
(family and employment) while men are responsible only
for employment, inequities will remain, and women's
advancement will be constrained. Apparently, then, further
improvement in the status of women seems to depend on
the increased involvement of men in their family roles.

—Michael E. Lamb and Abraham Sagi, *Fatherhood
and Family Policy*, 1983

THE PROTESTORS GATHERED in front of Brentano's bookstore on Fifth
Avenue in New York City on a hot August 26, 1973. It seemed like an
odd place for a demonstration, but the men in NOW's Task Force on the
Masculine Mystique had chosen it deliberately. As Warren Farrell, the task
force's national leader, explained, "in children's books men are always
shown as doers and women as always housekeepers. This leads men to develop contempt for women." The fifty or so men who lined the street in
front of the bookstore, along with wives and children, brandished banners
announcing the new men's liberation movement. "Men's Liberation. Men
Are More Than Success Objects," trumpeted one. "Let's Share Child Care,"
read another, more hopefully. "I want to be seen as a warm man sharing in
child raising, not as that cold cigar-smoking man after power, money and
prestige," observed Farrell.[1]

Bettye Lane, "Let's Share Child Care," (June 20, 1976). Fathers with child rally to end the masculine mystique and support women by taking a greater role in children's lives. This sign appeared at multiple men's protests.

The Task Force on the Masculine Mystique that Farrell headed had its roots in arguments Betty Friedan began making in the years after publication of *The Feminine Mystique* in 1963. She contended that the sex roles enshrined in the domestic ideal constrained men as they did women. Men, Friedan underscored in the early 1970s, were "fellow victims suffering from an outmoded masculine mystique that made them feel unnecessarily inadequate when there were no bears to kill."[2] Begun in September 1971, the Task Force on the Masculine Mystique was NOW's answer to that insight. The task force addressed "those problems of masculinity which simultaneously hurt both women and men." Such problems could be part of the ordinary give and take of daily life, such as men's tendency to dominate conversations and fail to listen to women—today's "mansplaining"—or systemic, such as men's investment in breadwinning, which ensured female economic dependence and limited men's involvement in family life.[3]

Warren Farrell ended up leading the masculine mystique task force after he became involved in the women's liberation movement as a doctoral student in political science at New York University. As he worked on his PhD, he felt increasing pressure to succeed as a breadwinner, even if it meant working in a field that he now cared little about. With his wife taking a prestigious position in Washington, DC, he began seriously questioning men's and women's roles in the family.[4] He served on the New York NOW branch's board of directors, and then took on leading the Task Force on the Masculine Mystique. He taught courses on sex roles at colleges in New York and Washington, and he started writing a book originally titled *Beyond Masculinity*, eventually published in 1974 as *The Liberated Man*.[5]

Farrell's book popularized the work he was doing with NOW's task force. He defined the masculine mystique, argued that alterations in men's roles must accompany women's liberation, explored men's position in the family and as fathers, and shared strategies for change—strategies he was pursuing as leader of the task force. The task force organized men's consciousness-raising groups, supported other NOW committees, and promoted actions for the organization that engaged the male side of liberation. For example, in an open letter to NOW members in 1972, Farrell urged feminists to take cases for paternity leave to the courts and to "demonstrate or draw up legislation for a quota of men to participate in child care centers."[6]

For his role in men's side of the feminist movement, *The Chicago Tribune* dubbed Farrell "the Gloria Steinem of Men's Liberation." A media darling like Steinem, he appeared on the *Today Show*, the *Michael Douglas Show*, and the *Phil Donahue Show*, among others. Admiring profiles in *Cosmopolitan*, the *Washington Post*, and *People Magazine* showcased his take on the negative effects of the masculine mystique.[7] Farrell became the public face of a new men's liberation movement in the early 1970s. His effort to remake masculinity exemplified the claims and aspirations of a small cadre of male profeminist activists.

This antisexist men's movement took two major forms across the 1970s. The first sought to transform normative ideals of masculinity. Men's liberationists organized consciousness-raising groups modeled on those created by women and buttressed by the work of sympathetic male academics, particularly in psychology. In work paralleling that done by feminist intellectuals, these academics upended expert dogma to conceive of a new male psyche. One critical aspect of this new selfhood included caring and nurturing fatherhood. Building on this foundation, a second strand of the men's liberation movement focused solely on fatherhood, combining intellectual work to reinvent fatherhood with the promotion of men's involvement in childcare both inside and outside the home, as in childcare centers and elementary schools. The fatherhood projects they started in the 1970s led the way to a new popular ideal of male parenting. Throughout these years, profeminist men's activism was antithetical to the so-called "men's rights" movement, which also gained momentum in the same period and maintained, in contrast to men's liberationists, that women were subjugating men.

Always few in comparison with women in the movement, male liberationists nonetheless represented an important component of second-wave feminist activism, one focused on altering men's roles in order to build an egalitarian balance between work and family. They made men part of the solution rather than part of the problem.

Breaking with Postwar Manhood

When Farrell and his fellow men's liberationists denounced postwar masculinity, they were reacting against mores they considered as restrictive and stultifying as those regulating women. *The Liberated Man* claimed those norms funneled men exclusively into breadwinning and did not allow them to be emotionally expressive. American culture had made men into "success objects," Farrell contended. "Men become scared of acting warm or gentle, or sacrificing their career in any way for their children."[8]

That manhood was the normative masculinity of midcentury America, and it mirrored the femininity prescribed for women. Psychologists, turning to the same Freudian theories they had used to trace female development, identified adult male maturity with assuming the role of provider. Signs of "effeminacy," such as nurturing children, signaled a failure to develop proper manhood and could manifest themselves as homosexuality or bachelorhood. "A single man over thirty," observed one psychoanalyst in 1966, "is now regarded as a pervert, a person with severe emotional problems, or a poor creature fettered to mother." Breadwinning so dominated theories of men's identity in the 1950s and 1960s that psychologists filtered all manhood through its presumptions. According to dominant psychological beliefs, for example, black men faced systematic emasculation because society short-circuited their role as providers. This hypothesis became a widely circulated companion to the Moynihan Report's attack on black matriarchy, and it reinforced dominant social prescriptions for black families.[9]

Sociological principles fell into line behind the breadwinner notion of masculinity. Men fulfilled their "instrumental" function—in contrast to women's "expressive" purpose—by providing for their families. Those presumptions colored expectations for men's role as fathers. Providing was good; too much "mothering" was bad. As the renowned psychologist Dr. Bruno Bettelheim explained the accepted wisdom to the readers of *Parents' Magazine* in 1956, "the relationship between father and child never was and cannot now be built principally around child-caring experiences. It is built around a man's function in society: moral, economic, political." Nearly two decades later, not much had changed. One popular parenting manual still warned that if a father fed or bathed his infant too much, "the baby may end up with two mothers, rather than with a mother and a father."[10]

In the eyes of the new men's liberationists, this conventional masculinity bound men into a straitjacket of professional success and achievement. Loosening those restraints would become their major project, one linked to the liberation of women as well.

Antisexist Men Organize

In June 1971, Rick Bingham of Florence, Massachusetts wrote in gratitude
to the *Female Liberation Newsletter* of Boston. The newsletter came to his
home addressed to his wife Ilene, but he often spirited it away and read it
before she did. He eagerly anticipated "more jewels" about women's liberation in upcoming issues, and he added a personal request to his letter:
"I would like to hear from men trying to free themselves from sexism." As
Bingham's hopeful query reveals, men's liberation developed directly in response to the women's movement. The earliest manifestation came in the
form of "gentlemen's auxiliaries": men's groups organized to provide childcare for women involved in the movement. In Portland, Oregon, the collective Men Doing Child Care for Feminist Functions coordinated with the
local women's center to find men willing to care for children while their
mothers attended feminist events. Denys Howard, the Portland organizer
of the collective, recalled discovering he could relate to small children and
even liked it. His childcare work "gave [him] a vision of how non-masculine
men and non-feminine women can provide models for children that just
might enable them to be real people when they grow up." Howard went
on to work full time in a daycare center as an openly gay man.[11]

The men's auxiliary model evolved into more independent organizing.
The men who found their way to the men's liberation movement frequently
had ties to the women's movement through their partners and typically had
roots in the antiwar, New Left, or civil rights movements as well. They were
often middle class, white, and college educated. A significant portion was
gay, bisexual, or queer, and a fair amount of energy in the movement went
to thinking about the relationship between heterosexual and homosexual
members. Gay activists provided an important voice questioning what
normal masculinity was supposed to be. Byron, an early leader in the movement interviewed by the sociologist Judith Newton in 1999, was typical
of men drawn to men's lib: involvement in the civil rights and antiwar movements preceded his interest in feminism, and his partner was also active in
the movement. Through her, he worked on feminist politics—a childcare
center he organized with another man, a collection of feminist writings he
produced with his wife. In 1970, Byron started a cooperatively run men's
center, where men could meet, attend consciousness-raising groups, and
learn about the movement. He was among those organizing the national

"Men and Masculinity" conferences which began in 1975 in Nashville, Tennessee.[12]

Black men were rarely drawn into the men's liberation activism led by white men, nor did they organize an explicitly feminist black men's movement, for a variety of reasons. The Black Power and black cultural nationalist movements of the 1960s and 1970s called for a revolutionary black manhood. Often tangled up in efforts to disprove the notion that matriarchs controlled black families and displaced black men from their rightful roles, this militant manhood stressed a visible masculinity, including men's leadership of their families. At the same time, these movements advanced a more nurturing, expressive vision of manhood that took form in Black Panther Party community programs for children and families. The Panthers leader Huey Newton balanced his revolutionary machismo with an emphasis on what Judith Newton described as "loving ties to family, friends, and community, along with vulnerability, sensitivity, and thoughtfulness as part of a masculine ideal."[13]

Overtly feminist men's liberation adherents took their cues from their female counterparts and typically made consciousness raising their first order of business. They formed men's liberation groups in which they questioned the masculine ideals they had grown up with and explored men's perpetuation of sexism in a patriarchal society. Workshops offered at early women's movement meetings on "the male liberation movement" provided opportunities to connect with other sympathetic men. Men's centers cropped up in smaller towns and cities, many of them home to universities—Fresno, California; Lawrence, Kansas; and Lansing, Michigan, for example—and in metropolitan centers, including the San Francisco Bay Area, Chicago, Boston, and New York. Men's centers sponsored consciousness-raising groups and organized childcare for women in the movement. They also participated in demonstrations, notably antirape and antiviolence marches, and served as clearinghouses and places to publicize events, often through a series of regional and ultimately national magazines.[14]

At the national level, the NOW Task Force on the Masculine Mystique was the most formal male feminist organization in the early 1970s, but by mid-decade, activists coordinated annual men and masculinity conferences that drew several hundred participants. Groundwork laid as early as 1977 nurtured the formation in 1982 of the National Organization for Changing Men, still active today as the National Organization for Men Against Sexism.

Even so, the numbers of men involved remained small. By one estimate, the movement consisted of just several hundred consciousness-raising groups with five to fifteen members each and an additional thirty to forty men's centers at the end of the decade.[15]

The influence of the movement reached well beyond the tiny numbers of men involved, as its ideas gained a broad audience through a series of texts put out by large and small publishing houses. As was true for women in the second wave, print literature—books, newsletters, pamphlets—was a crucial medium for profeminist men. In addition to Warren Farrell's *The Liberated Man*, books by Jack Nichols, such as *Men's Liberation: A New Definition of Masculinity* (1975) and Marc Feigen Fasteau, such as *The Male Machine* (1974), presented men's liberation for popular consumption. Like Farrell's *Liberated Man*, both books railed against masculinity's constricting focus on competitive toughness and breadwinning. These mainstream handbooks had counterparts in smaller but widely circulating collections by men more tied to the radical side of the movement. *Unbecoming Men* was an early example. The work of a New York men's consciousness-raising group started in 1969, it was a small pamphlet with the revealing subtitle, *A Men's Consciousness-Raising Group Writes on Oppression and Themselves*. Jon Snodgrass, an anti–Vietnam War activist and sociologist, was a founding member in 1974 of the Los Angeles Men's Collective. His edited collection, *For Men against Sexism* (1977), along with another volume put together by the profeminist psychologists Joseph Pleck and Jack Sawyer, *Men and Masculinity* (1974), provided early equivalents of the feminist classic *Sisterhood is Powerful*.[16]

Men's liberation groups routinely took these texts as starting points for their discussions. Their sessions not only examined the suffocating traits of masculinity in detail but also unpacked society's requirement that "true men" fulfill the role of successful provider and its companion, the distant father. Writing in the collection *For Men against Sexism*, Paul Carlo Hornacek advised men organizing "anti-sexist men's consciousness raising groups" to include among their ten essential topics five that addressed men and family, including "work and housework," "fathers and sons," "the nuclear family as a bastion of sexism," "maleness and masculinity," and "childhood training for sex-roles." "We, as men, want to take back our full humanity," announced the Berkeley Men's Center collective, which began meeting in 1970 and issued their manifesto in 1973. "We no longer want

Warren Farrell with his consciousness-raising group, as featured in *People* magazine January 20, 1975. The article was subtitled, "Getting Men to Hold Hands—On the Road to Liberation."

to strain and compete to live up to an impossible oppressive masculine image—strong, silent, cool, handsome, unemotional, successful, master of women, leader of men, wealthy, brilliant, athletic, and 'heavy.'" Instead, "we want to love, nurture, and support ourselves and other men, as well as women. We want to affirm our strengths as men and at the same time encourage the creation of new space for men in areas such as childcare, cooking, sewing, and other 'feminine' aspects of life."[17]

SEX-ROLE STEREOTYPES WERE a focus of men's liberation writings. Douglas Robbins, a psychologist in Brooklyn, New York, remarked that they owed their awareness that men were trapped in a sex role to women's blazing attacks on gender norms. "As soon as they blew the whistle on the stereotypes they were stuck with," he observed, "it raised questions for me about the phony parts of masculinity that I had bought—and that had always existed." Just as women's liberationists had done, men embraced socialization theories which viewed sex roles as learned, not intrinsic, and culturally specific, not universal; they even pointed out that in some societies, normative masculinity looked suspiciously like American femininity. "Male liberation," Jack Sawyer wrote in one of the very early movement manifestos, "calls for men to free themselves of the sex-role stereotypes that limit their ability to be human." Indeed, men's liberationists were often as scathing about the male sex role as women activists were about the female sex role. "Impoverished," "unhealthy," and "lethal" were just a few ways male activists described men's roles and identities. This restrictive manhood was virtually always implicitly white, and the question of race rarely surfaced in these men's analyses. More commonly, men's liberationists addressed the social consequences of the male provider role: to carry out the exploitation required of a dehumanizing capitalist system.[18]

"The Male Sex Role: Our Culture's Blueprint of Manhood and What It's Done for Us Lately," written in 1976 by the psychologist Robert Brannon, listed four unbreakable rules of manhood: "No Sissy Stuff," "Be a Big Wheel," "Be a Sturdy Oak," and "Give 'em Hell." It became a virtual bible for men's consciousness-raising groups and for courses on gender and sex roles. In the hands of male liberationists, those basic tenets encapsulated everything society deprived white men of: no softness, no openness, no vulnerability, no crying, and no dependency. In consciousness-raising groups, men voiced dismay at the strictures those attitudes imposed on their selfhoods and how they made it difficult to have close relationships with women and children, as well as with other men. After meetings with his Chicago men's group, Mark, "a 40-year-old burglar-alarm specialist," marveled that he saw his wife "more as an equal partner, a whole person, a friend. Before I saw her primarily as a mother and housekeeper, and I was always playing the big protector, the man around the house. That's really a pretty crummy role, and besides, you can't have a really open relationship with a servant. It's been a lot nicer lately."[19]

Men's liberation groups frequently practiced an alternative masculinity during their meetings. Participants described touching and hugging other members in their groups, crying with each other, and opening up about their feelings. Activists hoped to translate this different kind of maleness into more caring and open relationships with women and children as well as with each other. The psychologist and activist Robert Fein complained that "economic pressures and the press toward a successful career often force a man to choose between his work life and his family life, an anguishing choice that some men now are refusing to make."[20] For male liberationists, transforming the male sex role was a precondition to parity between the sexes, and they always understood comprehensive changes in men's identities as indispensable to a fully equal society.

No such society could exist without transforming fatherhood. As they questioned conventional male sex roles, men's liberationists also reevaluated inherited traditions of fathering. Men, they argued, were capable of nurturing, intimacy, and close relationships with children—but these required men to relinquish much that they were invested in. Marc Feigen Fasteau, a New York lawyer and husband of the prominent feminist Brenda Feigen Fasteau, who co-directed the ACLU Women's Rights Project with Ruth Bader Ginsburg in its early years, dedicated a chapter of his book *The Male Machine* to rethinking fatherhood. "Being a father, in the sense of having sired and having children, is part of the masculine image," Fasteau informed his readers, "but fathering, the actual care of children, is not." Men had to let go of the idea that care for children was "a diversion from men's 'real' work, the building of a successful career." To counter that influential belief, activists routinely claimed that close relationships with children benefitted men, enabling them to get in touch with more open, expressive, and "childlike" sides of themselves that would free them of the rigid constraints of masculinity. "Men are finding," Robert Fein claimed, "that contact with children leads them back to themselves, allowing them to integrate their childlike selves with their grownup selves."[21]

The desire for a less aggressive and competitive manhood pervaded feminist men's thinking. In addition to promoting a gentler fatherhood, they took up the question of male violence. Writing in the shadow of the Vietnam War, men's liberationists were convinced that the conventional male sex role fostered male violence. They followed many women's liberationists into antirape and anti-domestic-violence work, particularly in the late 1970s and 1980s. Among the most enduring outcomes of men's liberation as a social movement are the programs begun in this period to work with men on ending their violence.[22]

In the end, though, good will more than action typified organized men's liberation. The Task Force on the Masculine Mystique was effectively a one-man show, more the work of Warren Farrell than any groundswell of grassroots involvement. Farrell claimed sixty men's liberation chapters made up the task force in 1975, but these were more likely the many consciousness-raising groups that Farrell made it a priority to organize. Consciousness raising and participation in a men's group did not spur men into the streets as they did women. Sporadic demonstrations encouraged alternative images of men and manhood, while some in the movement labored to involve men in the care of young children in daycare centers and elementary schools. The quarterly journal *The Nurturant Male* and a National Men's Child Care Caucus formed the visible spine of this work, and the Nurtury, a male-run childcare center, opened in southern California in 1975. A few voices lent support to alternative and part-time work schedules for men as well as women. But as Rick Bingham's letter and the widespread circulation of men's liberation books and manifestos illustrate, profeminist men left a broader and deeper footprint on the culture than their numbers alone suggest.[23]

Dismantling the Myth of Masculinity

The texts that circulated in men's consciousness-raising circles were not simply those by popular authors like Warren Farrell, Marc Feigen Fasteau, and Jack Nichols. Just as commonly read were studies by a small cadre of psychologists whose work was published in men's liberation collections, such as *For Men against Sexism* or the widely disseminated primer *Men and Masculinity*. Involved in the movement themselves, such academics often devised studies to respond to issues raised by the movement; frequently, they went on to be long-term leaders of the profeminist men's movement. Psychologists provided the intellectual underpinnings for men's liberation work, and their ideas and research are among its greatest legacies. In similar fashion to what women's movement activists did to rethink female selfhood and women's sex roles, studies by men's activists dethroned the voices of authority—psychologists, government officials, educators, and the media—to put forward new models. Their impact was twofold: they forged new paradigms of healthy relations between men and women, envisioning fatherhood anew—particularly for white men—and they simultaneously built the intellectual infrastructure to support such revisions, producing scholarly work that carried weight not just in popular belief but also in framing policy and drafting legislation.

For the most part, this research applied primarily to white men. Black sociologists did not embark upon the same quest to reframe fatherhood. Saddled with their own field's depiction of the black family as pathological for its supposedly emasculated men and domineering women, these social scientists' studies of black manhood and the family were largely devoted to refuting the Moynihan Report during much of the second half of the 1960s and early 1970s. In 1970 and 1971, the sociologist Robert Staples published a pair of influential essays—"The Myth of the Black Matriarchy" and "The Myth of the Impotent Black Male"—that countered beliefs in the "feminization of the black male" and inadequate black fathering. "That many black fathers never realize their aspirations for their children," Staples observed pointedly, "can be attributed to America's racist social structure."[24] Staples and other leading scholars led a defense of black families that reframed the roles within them as a positive, adaptive response to the circumstances they faced. Robert B. Hill's 1973 *The Strength of Black Families*, for example, highlighted the "role flexibility" that facilitated black families' survival and nurtured an "equalitarian" family structure. In November 1978, a special issue on the topic in the *Journal of Marriage and Family* drew attention to the distinctive strengths and traits of "ambicultural" black families, whose members could simultaneously navigate white culture and thrive in the black community. As the decade came to a close, a few studies began to argue that black middle-class fathers in particular had taken on greater involvement in childrearing and a more nurturing style.[25]

The most important of the white social scientists tackling the question of manhood and fatherhood was Joseph H. Pleck. Born just after World War II, Pleck had ties to the student movements of the 1960s and had begun writing about men and psychology in the early 1970s for radical magazines linked to the antiwar and New Left movements, such as *Rough Times*, a small magazine produced originally as *The Radical Therapist*, and *WIN Magazine*, a journal sponsored by the New York–based Workshop in Nonviolence. His 1974 piece in *WIN Magazine*, "My Male Sex Role—and Ours," would become one of the most influential men's liberation essays.[26]

Pleck found his way to the study of manhood through the women's movement, and he co-authored work with his feminist wife, the women's historian Elizabeth H. Pleck. "The women's movement," he proclaimed in 1975
at a workshop in Aspen, Colorado, "has really been one of the most important events that I have experienced in my life, in an intellectual way, in a
political way, and also in a very personal way." With a PhD in clinical psychology awarded by Harvard in 1973, Pleck led the decade's research into
the male sex role.[27]

For Pleck, the dilemma was change. How could changes in men's and
women's roles occur, and what were the psychological forces at work? What
would happen when sex roles altered, and how could healthy male sex roles
supplant existing limiting ones? Pleck understood psychology historically, as
both an evolving field and one with social power. "People's behavior," he
surmised, "often follows psychologists' theories about it." His early publications dissected standard sex-role theories and argued for a paradigm
shift—"a new psychology of sex roles"—that emphasized socially acquired
gender roles.[28] No normative presumption should be made that white
middle-class manhood was the bar by which men's fulfillment of their role
should be measured, whether for working-class white men or black men.

Straddling both the activist and academic worlds, Pleck wrote of his own
socialization into a male sex role, describing his uneasy and conflicted relationship to such traditional male domains as sports and intellectual
achievement. "My Male Sex Role—and Ours" connected his personal feelings of failure as a white man to the stifling pressures of conventional manhood. He came to think of patriarchy as a "*dual* system . . . in which men
oppress women, and in which men oppress themselves and other men."
Addressing male-male oppression was, for him, one of the fundamental purposes of men's liberation. Hopefully, he declared, "Men's liberation means
undoing the effects of patriarchal competition among men and finding out
what we can be with each other."[29]

In outlining how to make change happen, Pleck combined psychological
and social perspectives. For example, he argued that defining breadwinning
as a necessary masculine trait reinforced male dominance over women as
psychological compensation for enduring unsatisfying work. "For the
large majority of men who accept dehumanizing jobs only because having
a job validates their role as family breadwinner, their wives' taking paid
work takes away from them the major and often only way they have of

experiencing themselves as having worth." For Pleck, this psychological dimension meant that no matter how much women gained equality in employment, sexism would maintain its grip on social relations unless men also conducted rigorous self-examination and transformed their male identities. At the same time, he observed that men would not do any meaningful family work without reorganizing their paid jobs and work expectations. "What ultimately limits men's ability to change," he warned, "is not innate male need for dominance or for 'security' in their sex role identities—though men *are* socialized to have these concerns—but the current institutionalized structure of the male work role, which is incompatible with role change."[30]

The Myth of Masculinity summed up this decade of work. Published in 1981, the book was, according to one historian, "the culmination of men's liberation theory as academic social psychology." In it, Pleck forcefully discarded the field's long-standing explanation of sex-role formation, arguing instead for a paradigm of sex-role strain. His model foregrounded the ways that contemporary society created pressures in men seeking to uphold a nearly impossible ideal of manhood. Indeed, for Pleck, it was no accident that the intellectual and cultural authority of the breadwinning, competitive man was greatest at the peak of the feminine mystique in the 1950s. He thought the forces of history were already swinging toward social change in men's and women's roles, particularly in the workplace, creating strain. To look at men's roles from the perspective of sex-role strain held promise for the future. "I can assign to the social sciences only a modest part in furthering the liberation of the sexes," Pleck confessed, yet "the part they can play for men is clear: understanding the roots of the strains men experience, analyzing men's aggression and their inability to find and express intimacy, and examining the burdens and conflicts arising from assigning men the role of family provider."[31]

Pleck completed *The Myth of Masculinity* as his research began to take up new themes. Shifting away from examining strains in male psychology and efforts to transform men's relationships to each other, Pleck turned to projects analyzing sex, family, and work roles as interdependent, requiring change in both homes and workplaces. He conceptualized a newly named structure, "the work-family role system" that showed how the structures of *both* workplaces and families blocked egalitarian distribution of household and wage-earning roles between men and women. In 1976, he began a research program jointly funded by the National Institute of Mental Health and the US Department of Labor on "Men's Two Roles: Family and Work." In it, he promulgated the "changing roles perspective" on men's involvement in the family. This perspective acknowledged that men did relatively little around the house, but argued that they could and would "if appropriate educational and social policies are implemented."[32] Pleck's participation in an emerging "family field" was a product of his collaboration with one of the other leading thinkers and activists of the 1970s, James Levine. Levine's starting point: the problem of children.

Who Will Raise the Children?

James Levine's interest in children began with securing a draft deferment. In 1968, while working on a doctorate in English, he took a job at the Circle Preschool in Oakland, California. While teaching there, he became aware that no one asked his female colleagues the question that he was always asked: "What do you *really* do?" That question raised his consciousness; he became curious about other men adopting traditional female roles and caring for children at work or home. After directing a nursery school at Wellesley College in Massachusetts, he became a consultant with the Child Development Foundation and wrote a do-it-yourself guide, *Hustling Resources for Day Care*. He took equal responsibility for parenting his two children with his wife, a children's book writer. And with a grant from the Ford Foundation in 1974, he spent eighteen months traveling around the country, interviewing 120 men caring for children. "The women's movement has drawn attention to women in male occupations and I wanted to redress the balance by showing men in female roles," he spelled out for a *New York Times* reporter.[33] The result, *Who Will Raise the Children? New Options for Fathers (and Mothers)*, appeared in 1976.

In it, Levine told the stories of involved, capable fathers—men who were divorced parents with custody or working part time in order to spend more time with their children. He even located a few "househusbands" who had breadwinning wives. In focusing on fathers, Levine aimed to make them visible in public discussion. Fathers and the changes they needed to make in their childrearing roles were completely absent from the decade's heated debates about the family. Government counted the rising numbers of working mothers, but it kept no statistics on working fathers; reams of research worried over the effects of maternal wage earning on children, but none looked at the effects of working fathers, "even if these working fathers are so busy that they rarely see their children." Levine found it dismaying that daycare proposals, part-time work, Congressional scrutiny of the future of the family—all included only women and children as actors. Typical was a summer day in Congress with hearings in both the House and Senate, where "there was not one word spoken about the 'average' American father. . . . There was no mention of the role of men in child care. It was as if the changing American family consisted only of women and their children."[34]

Ignoring fathers left a trail of incomplete change that made equality impossible to achieve. "If everybody thought nurturing was a rewarding and healthy thing to do," Levine commented in 1974, "it would slowly transform society." Breaking down sex-role stereotypes about nurturing fostered greater options for both men and women—"a broadened sense of manhood" and fewer "pressures on women to pin their identities on motherhood." It created the possibility for both men and women to have "lives that offer us equal opportunity, that allow us to be productive and to be loving and caring for our children." Levine proposed a host of social and policy changes to achieve this end. "The changes most likely to promote male involvement in child rearing are economic ones," he contended, "ones that would allow men and women to meet their child-care needs flexibly, without compromising on family income: restructuring of working time, parental leaves with guaranteed employment on return, payments for work done in the home, guaranteed income policies."[35] Anything that advanced women's economic opportunities, Levine also emphasized, would support change.

Levine shared with other second-wave feminists a vision of thoroughgoing reconstruction both of homes and of workplaces. Solutions that today seem radical—payments for homemakers and guaranteed income—were, for him, viable mainstream liberal policies to consider. Levine traced at some length the part-time, job-sharing, and flex-time options the fathers he profiled were pursuing, and he showcased the organizations, businesses, and cities experimenting with such policies. Karl Lenz, a fifty-three-year-old administrator working for Lufthansa's US offices, loved the time over breakfast that flexible scheduling gave him with his children, because it

"Father and Child at Demonstration," by Bettye Lane. June 20, 1976. The role of fathers in their children's lives was a common theme in men's liberation actions.

put him on the same "wavelength" as them.[36] Where legislation was under consideration, as in the bills for flex-time for federal employees covered in Chapter 8, Levine drew attention to its benefits for women *and* men.

To demonstrate that these ideas were feasible, he described for his American readers the father-supportive policies that were working in Scandinavia. Sweden surfaced as an ideal, as it would so often in 1970s feminist thinking. The Swedish program of Parents' Insurance not only provided 90 percent of pay to the parent at home with a newborn for seven months, but also encouraged splitting it between both parents. And if the father took any leave, the family gained a month of parental insurance. The Swedish viewed the problem as one of interdependent men's and women's roles, with awareness that sex-role stereotypes affected men as much as they did women. Quoting "The Emancipation of Man," the frequently invoked speech that Swedish Prime Minister Olof Palme made in 1970, Levine found a society whose leaders proclaimed that "the men should already from the beginning have just as much contact with their children as the women. And we should have both men and women as child nurses, kindergarten teachers and infant-school teachers."[37]

Levine insisted that children and men needed new types of socialization in schools and the broader culture. He encouraged children's books that showed men in nurturing roles, parenting handbooks without bias against men as fathers, career counseling that didn't funnel girls and boys into sex-typed work, and fathering classes, groups, and programs that encouraged men to believe in their nurturing and caretaking abilities. Levine himself became a spokesperson for involved fathering. The *New York Times* profiled him as a model "Homemaker-Father"; *Ladies' Home Journal* turned to him for expert opinion when it asked in 1979, "Do Fathers Make Good Mothers?"; and *Newsweek* anointed him an advocate for working fathers in 1981 with their exploration of "A New Kind of Life With Father."[38] *Who Will Raise the Children?* launched Levine himself into a career of research and advocacy on fatherhood and families, making him part of a set of male feminist activists and social scientists who focused on fatherhood beginning in the mid-1970s.

Like Levine, other fatherhood advocates made the case that fulfilling the objectives of the women's movement required changing men's roles as fathers. They conducted the social-science research that demonstrated fathers' importance to child development, refuted biologically based ideas of fathers' limited roles in children's maturation, and revealed that father-infant bonding was as possible and successful as mother-infant connections. Many came out of the men's liberation movement. Robert A. Fein, for example, wrote an early piece on "Men and Young Children" for Joseph Pleck and Jack Sawyer's *Men and Masculinity*. In 1978, he reviewed recent fatherhood research in *The Journal of Social Issues* and explored what he called the emergent perspective on fathering, a view which he described as androgynous for its presumption that "the only parenting behaviors from which men are necessarily excluded by virtue of gender are gestation and lactation." By 1981, Ross D. Parke, a psychologist at the University of Illinois, could publish *Fathers*, a short book fully refuting psychologists' and sociologists' conventional theories and summarizing the new fatherhood research for a popular audience.[39]

Backing this new scholarship was an expanding network of fatherhood programs. James Levine began working with Joseph Pleck at the Wellesley

College Center for Research on Women in 1978, and with Michael E. Lamb at the University of Utah, he led the Fatherhood Project, funded by the Ford, Levi Strauss, Ittleson, and Rockefeller Foundations starting in 1981. The Fatherhood Project cross pollinated scholarly research, public programs, and policy reports. In the early 1980s, for example, Joseph Pleck and Michael Lamb invented the "Lamb-Pleck conceptualization" of paternal involvement, a measure of the impact of fathers' engagement with children. At the same time, they organized playgroups and classes for fathers and produced handbooks on starting father-child classes and daycare centers. The US Commission on Civil Rights commissioned Levine and Pleck to write a report on *Child Care and Equal Opportunity for Women*.[40] All would go on to be advocates for legislation supporting paternity leave.

The Fatherhood Project anchored a profeminist fatherhood movement. The project itself acted as a national clearinghouse, fielding over ten thousand requests for information by 1984. The Fatherhood Project's 1984 manual, *Fatherhood USA*, demonstrated that a host of small-scale fatherhood centers and projects existed across the country, listing more than five hundred such programs and organizations nationally. Its bibliography ran to nearly three hundred entries and identified forty-four newsletters on men and fatherhood. Sections included resources for single fathers, gay fathers, working fathers, and stepfathers, as well as an extensive compilation of "Books for Children Featuring Fathers and Men in Nurturing Roles." *Fatherhood USA* provided a sense of the range of activities that could fall under the umbrella of the new fatherhood. Courses in boys' schools in New York on infant care coexisted with postpartum support groups for fathers in Boston. Los Medinas Community College offered early childhood parenting classes for Mexican American men, while Cleveland Planned Parenthood sponsored programs on teenaged fathers' involvement. There was little manifest attention to the needs of black fathers or other minority men, but there was some acknowledgment of the needs of gay parents. Single fathers were a focus.[41]

Two issues that exemplified antisexist fatherhood concerns were child custody in divorce and paternity leave. With divorce rates tripling between 1960 and 1982, household breakup became a major social concern. The feminist movement tackled it through women's efforts to value housework in divorce settlements, as Chapter 4 explores, along with male feminists' push to erode the preference for maternal custody. Levine and his colleagues promoted the use of new divorce and custody mediation services during the divorce process. Mediation, they claimed, was "more effective and humane" than traditional divorce proceedings, and it led to longer-lasting agreements, less postdivorce conflict, and, most importantly, higher levels of involvement by fathers over the long term. They identified sixteen centers across the country as examples and referred men to The Divorce Mediation Research Project in Denver, Colorado.[42]

The antisexist men in the Fatherhood Project additionally called for custody decisions that reflected children's experiences within the marriage prior to divorce. "Custody," they argued, "should usually be awarded to the parent who has played a primary role in the care and nurturance of the child." They noted that in today's world, that would most likely be the mother, but that in principle, it had to do with the parents' "responsibilities and roles" in children's lives, not their sex. Joint custody, in their eyes, should not be ruled out, but depended on how parents had shared caretaking prior to splitting up. This argument eased the concern that formal principles of equality between mothers and fathers at the moment of divorce set aside the underlying reality of different (and potentially unequal) roles during the marriage.[43]

Providing paternity leave was the second policy priority of the Fatherhood Project. James Levine and his colleagues made much of the "work-family conflicts," as they were just coming to be called, that affected men as well as women. Indeed, working fathers had as much stress as working mothers, just for different reasons. The provider ideal of the "good" father created internal conflict for many men, while employer resistance made it difficult for fathers to take advantage of any policies in place. "Pervasive sex discrimination," Michael Lamb and his colleagues also emphasized, allowed men to earn more than women, preserving "the status and importance of men as primary breadwinners." The Fatherhood Project offered its own host institution, the Bank Street College of Education, as an exemplar of the kinds of policies needed for fathers of newborns and recently adopted children. Bank Street offered a "Family Leave Policy" that included three months paid leave for either parent of children under three years old, with a possible extension of up to one year of unpaid leave.[44]

Men's Rights and the New Father

Kramer vs. Kramer won nearly every film award possible—five Oscars, four Golden Globes, plus more than two dozen others. In many ways, it was a cultural barometer, signaling the shifting winds of feminism, the men's liberation movement, and the new fatherhood. The 1979 film told the story of Ted and Joanna Kramer's divorce; at stake was custody of their five-year-old son, Billy. Early in the film, Joanna, played by Meryl Streep, leaves Ted and Billy out of frustration, suffocation, and a desire to find herself. Ted, portrayed by Dustin Hoffman, starts out the film as an utterly inept father, overwhelmed by a world he was never involved in. By the end, Ted has withstood getting fired from his job for conflicts over his parenting obligations, managed to cook a meal without burning it, and learned to be a devoted father. When Joanna returns, seeking custody of Billy, the audience knows that the judge wrongly favors her distant mothering over Ted's new involved fathering. Joanna knows too. In a painful scene at the end of the film, she relinquishes custody, leaving parenting Billy to Ted.[45]

The film enraged many feminists. It blamed feminism for Joanna's seemingly selfish and callous abandonment of her son. At the same time, it depicted a working father heroically doing exactly what brought criticism raining down on working mothers. Film critic Molly Haskell captured some of the wrath as she observed that finally, a film "took on the crisis central to the modern woman's life, that is, the three-ring circus of having to hold down a job, bring up a child and manage a house simultaneously, and who gets the role? Dustin Hoffman."[46] While critiques like Haskell's expressed feminist frustration at the depiction of motherhood, *Kramer vs. Kramer* also spoke to powerful crosscurrents within the men's movement.

The film seemed to give credence to a burgeoning "fathers' rights" movement. Growing demands to protect fathers' rights were part of a larger divide within the men's movement between men's liberationists and "men's rights" supporters. Men's rights proponents, antifeminists who accuse women of oppressing men, see men as the victims of discrimination, particularly in divorce settlements. Fathers, they alleged, were also losing rights as feminists made gains for women. The men's rights movement picked up surprising support from one of men's liberation's early leaders, Warren Farrell. Since his earliest writings, Farrell had hinted that he prioritized freeing men from the burdens of high-powered careers over ending men's oppression of women. By 1988, Farrell would aver that "men are just as powerless as women in relationships." His book *The Myth of Male Power* (1993), a summation of his move into the men's rights camp, proffered a lengthy list of men's needs for protection from overreaching women, who were now in the position to discriminate against them. Among those items was recognition that men were good fathers and had a right to their kids.[47]

Farrell's men's rights perspective helped advance the fathers' rights position as well. In *The Myth of Male Power*, he demanded that women stop forcing men to work at jobs they despised to support children. Women had to do their "financial share" so fathers could enjoy their right to "sharing child care." Fathers' rights activists resisted the idea that divorcing fathers were merely "cash registers" for child support and alimony. They faulted divorcing women for denying men greater closeness to children. At times, fathers' rights and feminist goals overlapped, as fathers' rights activists helped advance the joint custody revolution of the late 1970s and early 1980s. However, fathers' rights advocates were often disgruntled, recently divorced men who believed the system was rife with antimale bias. The Fatherhood Project's guide to fathers' rights groups rather wryly prefaced its listing with the warning that the men in these organizations "often take a position that is emphatically hostile towards women."[48]

Although *Kramer vs. Kramer* gave a burst of energy to these fathers' rights activists, the film also ironically stimulated support for profeminist fatherhood activism. After *Kramer vs. Kramer*, foundations rushed to fund the Fatherhood Project, while inquiries about programs for fathers poured in from the public. The "new fatherhood" was in vogue, and *Kramer vs. Kramer* marked the tipping point. Other films early in the next decade, such as *Mr. Mom* (1983) and *Tootsie* (1982), portrayed men in nurturing roles. A raft of popular books dished out advice to the "new father." Bill Cosby's 1986 book *Fatherhood*, published long before he became known for sexually assaulting women, was a bestselling paean to the caring father, while *The Father's Almanac* (1980) provided advice on everything from diapering babies to business travel for working dads.[49] Popular magazines and news stories depicting nurturing fathers outpaced those depicting good-provider dads by a ratio of nearly three to one.[50]

The shift had been afoot since the mid-1970s, as feminist pressures on both motherhood and fatherhood began changing attitudes. As early as

1974, 44 percent of American men in a Roper survey said that the most satisfying and interesting way of life was a marriage with shared wage-earning, household, and childcare responsibilities. Dr. Benjamin Spock even changed his tune on fathers and infants. Spock's *Common Sense Book of Baby and Child Care*, first published in 1946, served as America's postwar childrearing bible. In its 27 years, 201 printings, and 3 editions between 1946 and 1973, it had sold 23,445,781 copies—virtually one for every first-born child.[51] Liberal in his politics and a committed antiwar activist, Dr. Spock would hardly seem likely to have invited feminist wrath. But he did. In March 1969, an inflammatory answer to the country's feminist stirrings appeared in Spock's monthly *Redbook* column. "Biologically and temperamentally," he proclaimed, "women were made to be concerned first and foremost with child care, husband care and home care." Education of women had had the unfortunate effect of making them dissatisfied with their lot. "Imagine how much more fun it was way back in the simple days," he said, with chatty condescension, "when to produce a baby was the greatest miracle any woman could perform—like discovering radium or writing a best seller today." In response, Gloria Steinem publicly chastised Spock, comparing him to Sigmund Freud and pronouncing him a force for women's oppression. A mea culpa was not long in coming. "Male Chauvinist Spock Recants—Well, Almost" was published in September 1971 in the *New York Times Sunday Magazine*.[52]

Spock admitted embarrassment at his earlier opinions about women and their roles. For example, he repudiated his assertion "that women will always play the major role in child care, that the mother is more obliged than the father to give up whatever career time is necessary for the care of small children, [and] that fathers' outside jobs will be the main ones." He still had reservations about paid substitute caregivers, but a mother, father, or grandparent could do the trick. "I recognize that, in justice, a wife has as much right to an uninterrupted career as her husband. How they want to reconcile their various aspirations is for them to decide, democratically." He later cleansed *Baby and Child Care* of more than 10,000 gendered pronouns that referred to the baby in question as "he, him, his" and issued a new, post-feminist-conversion baby manual. There is perhaps no greater index of feminist inroads into popular culture than Dr. Spock's change of heart. A wage-earning mother supported by an involved father became his model family. By 1982, *Ms.* magazine hailed Spock as a *"Ms.* Hero"—

among the "men who have taken a chance and made a difference" to women's causes.[53]

Paralleling Dr. Spock's new faith in fathers and Hollywood's vogue for caring dads were the fatherhood programs sprouting up across the country. Some of these programs targeted black fathers. Still not overtly feminist like the efforts led by white men, these undertakings concentrated on a loving, involved, "in-charge husband and father." Rites-of-passage programs focused on adult black men mentoring boys. Jawanza Kunjufu, a leading proponent, used the image of "bringing your son to your chest" as a central symbol of fathering for men within the programs. In 1984, the National Urban League began a "male responsibility campaign" to involve unwed teen fathers in the lives of their children. The Brooklyn-based Sisterhood of Black Single Mothers organized groups of fathers who discussed how they could connect with their children. Middle-class black consumers of magazines like *Ebony* read regularly about black Mr. Moms. Often not egalitarian in their import—the ideal of a "benevolent patriarch" hovered over many of these programs, and girls more or less disappeared as needing good fathering—they connected engaged black fatherhood to strengthening communities, while countering the charges leveled against many black men of being "deadbeat dads."[54]

Profeminist white men channeled their efforts into programs like those the Fatherhood Project promoted. Stories on Levine and Pleck's work appeared on television and radio, as well as in newspaper and women's magazine articles. The Project sponsored a Fatherhood Forum in New York on Father's Day weekend in 1983, followed a year later by similar forums in Boston, Chicago, Houston, Los Angeles, Minneapolis, and San Francisco. The New York event included nearly fifty workshops and attracted four hundred participants, about half of them professionals and the other half interested parents. Michael Lamb warned attendees not to get sucked into "the fathering hype," reminding them that fathers belonged within a larger "caretaking network." And James Levine added, "It's not easy for men, or for women either, who have the responsibility for childcare and also for breadwinning outside the home." One motivation for the Fatherhood Project was the belief that men's limited participation in childcare reduced women's equal opportunity. Increasingly, Levine and his colleagues highlighted the need for changes in public policy, law, and workplaces along with changes in attitudes. Without systemic change, they insisted, "the major stumbling block[s] to equal opportunity and egalitarianism" remained in place. Joseph Pleck would testify on the need for parental leave at the first hearings in 1986 for the law that was finally signed as the Family and Medical Leave Act in 1993.[55]

Pleck and Levine took these positions in an increasingly politicized context. By the end of the 1970s, profeminist fatherhood advocacy came up against more than antifeminist fathers' rights adherents. The coalescing "pro-family" movement rejected the involved father ideal that men's liberationists pushed. The pro-family defense of male breadwinning was part of the broader backlash against feminism. Conservative leader Phyllis Schlafly called feminists "antifamily and antimen" and berated them for their supposed "hatred for husbands as family providers." Seeking to restore what they perceived as men's proper role as breadwinners, pro-family activists argued that shared parenting and wage earning in families deprived men of their most basic identity; without it, said Schlafly, the husband and father "tends to drop out of the family and revert to the primitive masculine role of hunter and fighter."[56] This logic backed up conservatives' dual focus on restoring traditional homemaking and motherhood and on attacking single-parent households with "missing" fathers. Whatever gains feminists would make in the long run, whether in the broader movement or by fatherhood activists, would have to overcome this conservative response.

Other stumbling blocks slowed real change in fathers' involvement in children's lives. With Ronald Reagan's election in 1980, cuts in social programs pushed Levine and others to focus on corporate family-friendly programs. Despite the popularity of the new fatherhood in the 1980s, business culture provided no incentive and little support for men altering their roles. Speaking to the House Select Committee on Children, Youth, and Families for hearings held on "Babies and Briefcases: Creating a Family-Friendly Workplace for Fathers" in 1991, James Levine decried the gap between official policy and the reality that men who took time from work for family responsibilities were "branded . . . as uncommitted."[57] The wage gap that continued to make men's earnings significantly higher than women's also complicated involved fatherhood, as economic changes in the late 1970s and 1980s produced mounting pressure on household earnings.

PROFEMINIST MEN'S LIBERATIONISTS carried on. Consciousness-raising groups, men's centers, and national conferences remained in existence, some even up to the present. Yet over the 1970s, the movement translated more often than not into occasions for men to get in touch with themselves and experience masculinity differently. It was often quite touchy-feely—literally. Men learning to touch other men lasted as a goal. Cultivating opportunities for men to express and experience alternative masculinities continued to be an important outcome of men's liberation. Byron, the men's liberationist active in the early 1970s, reported that at the National Organization for Men Against Sexism conferences, workshops on sexual harassment and on advancing the ERA were on the schedule, but the rooms that filled to overflowing were for sessions on male bodies and health—sessions that ignored men's role in discriminating against women. The NOW Task Force on the Masculine Mystique petered out within a few years as a force to advance policy changes, but small groups of men remained active in M.A.N. for ERA—Men Allied Nationally for the Equal Rights Amendment—the pro-ERA men's liberation group for which Alan Alda was the most visible face. Since the late 1970s, the antisexist men's movement has focused much of its organizing work against domestic and sexual violence.[58]

In asking how men's roles needed to change and insisting that true equality required new male selves as well as female ones, men's liberationists added a crucial piece to the feminist movement that has often not been recognized. The feminist movement and feminist analysis of society, sex roles, and the family inspired Pleck, Levine, and other activists and scholars in the field to broaden the movement by making change in the character of manhood and fatherhood part of the feminist agenda. Their commitments to gender equity came out of feminism, and they believed firmly that reshaping masculinity was an essential complement to transforming women's lives. Psychologically and socially normative ideas about men deformed selves and society just as much as those about women did, and for these activists, opening the door to a different manhood was essential to any vision of equality. This was equally true of fatherhood. In asking who will raise the children and suggesting that men could do it as well as women, fatherhood activists like James Levine and his profeminist male colleagues embarked on a feminist project that held onto the insight that it was insufficient to move women into paid work lives. Men's identities had to change also, and workplaces had to change so that men and women could raise children together. Feminist men joined the movement's broader fight to remake American society from the inside out, and they were crucial forerunners of still sorely needed changes in men and in men's lives.

3

PARTNERS

Dismantling the Male-Breadwinner Ideal

> I realized that the only way we could possibly survive as a
> family . . . was to throw out the old sex roles . . . and start
> again. Wishing to be once more equal and independent . . .
> we decided to make an agreement in which we could define
> our roles our own way.
>
> —Alix Kates Shulman, "A Marriage Agreement," 1970

JOAN DIDION READ IT and despaired at women's liberationists mired in "sullen public colloquies about the inequities of dishwashing." Norman Mailer parsed it and raved that he could love a woman but would watch her "sprain her back before a hundred sinks of dishes in a month" rather than "help her if his work should suffer." More than two thousand letters inundated *Redbook* after the magazine published it in August 1971, and *Ms.* magazine inserted it in its inaugural issue a few months later. "A Marriage Agreement" was a sensation, a *cause célèbre* of the early second wave.[1]

"A Marriage Agreement," the invention of the writer Alix Kates Shulman, made its first appearance in August 1970 in the feminist journal *Up from Under*. Sparked by the frustrations of her marriage and fueled by a roguish mixture of feminist outrage and bravado, the agreement detailed with military precision Shulman's egalitarian division of household and childrearing

"The Shulmans at Home," by Arthur Schatz. *Life*, April 28, 1972. *Life* magazine featured Alix Kates Shulman and Martin Shulman jointly making their bed. Text from their agreement was superimposed on the bed's white sheets. "The Shulmans Have a 50–50 Marriage Agreement That's Down in Writing" is how the magazine announced the story.

labor with her husband. "The idea was simply this," explained Shulman, "that a woman and man should share equally the responsibility for their household and children in every way, from the insidiously unacknowledged tasks of daily life to the pleasures of guiding a young human to maturity." This idea, and the agreement that expressed it, symbolized feminist remakings of long-standing family structures.[2]

Shulman encountered the women's liberation movement at its very beginnings in New York, but she was already older than most of the feminist activists around her. Born in 1932, Shulman had been married twice and had children ages five and seven when she heard an announcement on the radio for a women's group meeting. Feminism was instantly comprehensible to her. "The minute I heard feminism articulated," she explained, "I recognized it as an explanation of all my puzzles. Until then, I only felt the anguish of it, and felt that it was demeaning to complain. This was my fate: I was a woman, I was a mother, and to complain about it would be beneath me. So I couldn't complain about it. But I had my secret thoughts."

She joined the radical feminist groups Redstockings and WITCH—Women's International Terrorist Conspiracy from Hell. Shulman was among those who planned the first high-publicity action of the new liberation groups, a protest at the Miss America pageant in Atlantic City in September 1968, financed in part by money she secretly withdrew from her joint checking account because she feared her husband would oppose it.[3]

The movement imparted courage. Inspired by her feminist companions, who bravely questioned the rules and roles they had inherited, Shulman assuaged her anger at her husband, who was routinely absent for business in Pennsylvania and having an affair, by having an affair of her own. In the same period, she stopped writing in secret and under a pseudonym, and she began publishing on the anarchist and women's rights activist Emma Goldman. She penned what she described as "the sex article for my Redstockings group," titled "Organs and Orgasms." The essay, Shulman recalled, "brazenly ended . . . with the admonition, 'Think clitoris!'" She wrote the marriage agreement early in 1969 as her rage and newfound fearlessness crystallized.[4]

"Like most women of my class and generation born in the United States before World War II," Shulman recalled, she accepted, "if sometimes grudgingly, traditional gender arrangements whereby the home belongs to women, the world to men." Once her children were born, she slipped into the role of homemaker and mother, until the women's movement provided its jolt to her consciousness. Yet Shulman resisted divorce. She did not want her children raised without their father in their lives, and she feared losing his financial support: joint custody was not a legal option in New York in 1969. And, although some radical feminist groups did vow to smash marriage altogether, Shulman's urged differently. Redstockings, she thought, "was concerned less with overthrowing the institution than with overhauling it to better serve women's interests by somehow forcing men to be responsible mates and reliable fathers."[5]

Her marriage agreement sought that end by divvying up household and childrearing labor—down to tucking the children into bed—equally between partners. For Shulman, however, this roster of duties was the least important part of the agreement, even though it was the one most often discussed—and most often mocked. The "soul of the agreement," she insisted, was its "principles," in which Shulman and her husband accepted the idea that earning more money did not make one's work more valuable, nor did it allow "the larger earner to buy out of his/her duties and put the burden on the one who earns less, or on someone hired from outside."[6] Trading male breadwinning for female homemaking could no longer be presumed or even accepted. By remaking men's roles within the home and family, feminists like Shulman hoped to free women to remake their roles outside of it.

Shulman's agreement is an emblem of how feminists disassembled a family order that had been in place for over a century and a half.[7] Second-wave feminists passionately critiqued the patriarchal assumptions embedded in marriage practice and law, then experimented intrepidly with new models of intimacy and family relations. Some radical and lesbian feminists abjured marriage and monogamy altogether. Feminists put forward alternative models of marriage whose changes stretched from bedrooms to legislative chambers. While neither radical nor liberal white feminists fully agreed on the root problem and solution, all placed remaking marriage and family at the center of feminist work. For black feminists, who also took up the problem of intimate relationships, the starting point was the pervasive stereotype of black families as disordered and matriarchal. Regardless of background or ideology, feminists of all stripes sought egalitarian relationships, invented new family forms, fought for shared breadwinning and household labor, and valorized single-parent households. The second wave's challenge to marriage was game-changing. It percolated into homes and altered the relationships of even those lightly touched by the movement, helping to remake fundamental cultural beliefs about intimacy and equity in relationships. The model of marriage as a partnership that came to the fore paved the way for changes in law and policy that substituted new sex-neutral "functions" for the older duties and obligations of wives and husbands, and the word *spouse* supplanted married men's and women's gendered identities in court opinions, legislation, and divorce decrees.

Putting the Male-Breadwinner Ideal under the Microscope

Before they could articulate new models of marriage and family, feminists had to topple the old one. Step by step, they dismantled the male-breadwinner ideal of the household economy. To do so represented a turning point in women's-rights thought. As the historian Dorothy Sue Cobble has shown, mid-century feminists largely acceded to a gendered order of female household and childrearing duties, even as they advanced women's causes. Based in the labor movement, these activists sought working conditions that would make it easier to manage women's "double day" of work at home and on the job, but without disputing that managing that double day was their responsibility.[8] But second-wave feminists would call into question all such suppositions.

The male-breadwinner norm assumed that husbands were wage earners by right of manhood and by necessity of labor, both physical and intellectual. Economically dependent, wives in this model remained responsible for household labor and childrearing. In culture and in politics, the dominant assumption was that this division of labor embodied a kind of parity between men and women, each given their due in their own sphere. Families adhering to the male breadwinner–female homemaker norm, moreover, supposedly anchored a stable social and political order.

Labor victories that had been won first at the turn of the century, then in the years of the New Deal, and finally after World War II meant that in the postwar years male breadwinning was far more than just an aspirational ideal. Less than one quarter of all American married women were in the labor force in 1950. This arrangement was even more pronounced for families where married couples had to take care of children. In husband-wife families with children under eighteen, 70 percent of households had a working father and stay-at-home mother in 1960; not until 1980 would dual incomes predominate. Although working-age African American wives worked at rates more than 50 percent higher than white wives did, the male-breadwinner norm held for married black families in postwar America as well. In black husband-wife households, over six in ten women remained out of the labor force in 1950. Still, lower rates of marriage among black women contributed to a lower proportion of black households fitting the ideal. Employment and housing bias also meant that black families and other families of color faced further difficulty in emulating the suburban version of the domestic norm. While there's no doubt that the ideal never described all households, when postwar Americans looked around them, they saw households that fit what the culture prescribed. Just as importantly, the model held sway in popular culture, expert opinion, policy, and law.[9]

As they had in reconstructing female selfhood, feminist activists tore apart biased biological, historical, and economic assumptions propping up this model. They showed that inherited stereotypes rather than biology determined these roles. Instead of finding equity in divvying up spheres, they shed light on its discriminatory effects. Black feminists proved that rather than being matriarchs, black women stood at the bottom of the heap in terms of both responsibilities and income. Sweeping critiques of the family wage ideal emanated from both liberal and radical feminists, with some distinct emphases, but all shared disdain for the old model. To rethink the relationship between work and family, the feminists' first step was an intellectual and cultural critique of the male-breadwinning family that deconstructed beliefs so deep that they seemed natural. Relentless, resentful, but sometimes hilarious and hopeful, it sparked a shift in mentality.

The first target was the sexual division of labor within the household, which feminists found capricious and unfair to women. For liberal feminists, the gendered assignment of breadwinning and homemaking handcuffed both sexes. Betty Friedan argued that the homemaking role did not occupy all of women's capabilities—nor their time—and that restricting them solely to this position led to unhappiness within marriages and unfair limits on women's opportunities. And as we saw in Chapter 2, she believed that men, too, faced unhealthy confinement: the lifelong pressure to be providers weighed them down. "Obsolete sex roles" had made marriage strained and unhappy. Indeed, speaking at the NOW Marriage and Divorce Conference in January 1974, Friedan claimed that "our movement to liberate women and men from those polarized, unequal sex roles might save marriage." Liberal activists involved in Women's Lobby, Inc., the Washington, DC women's interest group, described for readers of their quarterly newsletter the revealing impact of reversing roles in marriage. When Pat Caplan, a real-estate investigator for the state of Massachusetts, supported her family, and her husband Denny Andrews remained at home after the failure of his hammock store, both discovered the stigma of household labor and the pressures of breadwinning. Their happy marriage provided a kind of object lesson in the negative consequences of arbitrarily designating roles within marriage by sex.[10]

Even more scathing attacks on restrictive women's roles within the family peppered the writings of radical women's liberationists. Explaining the rush of discontent among women in the radical student movement, Heather Booth, Evi Goldfield, and Sue Munaker, young members of the Chicago Women's Liberation Union, argued in a 1968 pamphlet that the "age of promise" so touted in postwar American popular culture had not extended to women. "The housewife role, offered up as the most fulfilling for women, was expanded, elaborated, filled up with trivia." But this role was "not serious, not involving." It "merely whittled away the long endless hours." Like their liberal counterparts, these young radicals emphasized confinement, constraint, and the essentially limited nature of wifehood and homemaking. Women's prescribed roles, radicals contended, made them servants of men. As Kate Millett summed up in her influential 1970 treatise *Sexual Politics*, conventional sex roles allotted "domestic service and attendance upon infants to the female, the rest of human achievement, interest, and ambition to the male." The radical feminist analysis likened women's status within marriage to enslavement by contrasting the legal obligations of wives with the rights of husbands. In a letter to the early radical feminist publication *Voice of Women's Liberation*, Flora Ellen Hardy declared that in marriage and motherhood, "I will not choose slavery. I will not choose denial. Those roles must change."[11]

Merely adding the opportunity for women to take jobs and be active in the public sphere in addition to their homemaking roles would be insufficient to correct the fundamental inequalities in marriage. Activists pointed out that working women typically bore the double burden of full-time wage-earning and home responsibilities. The Marxist feminist Evelyn Reed argued that working-class women's waged work compounded their servitude, as "shouldering two responsibilities instead of one," they became the "doubly oppressed." At times, the two jobs borne by women described the nature of female abjection: wage work was the extension of the domestic servitude that, in some feminist analyses, dominated women's lives. Shulamith Firestone, the author of the movement classic *The Dialectic of Sex: The Case for Feminist Revolution*, criticized those who used evidence of women's rising employment to claim women had already been liberated. That one-third of all women were in the workforce was not progress, as many claimed; rather, said Firestone bluntly, women "have merely taken over the shit jobs," with the burden of housework, cooking, and childcare still theirs. Kate Millett described wage work as a double burden imposed atop unremitting housework and childcare, "unrelieved either by day care or other social agencies, or by the co-operation of husbands."[12]

Black women had no doubt that wage work had not been a force for their liberation in marriage. Married black women had long labored for pay at significantly higher rates than white women and in jobs that were frequently backbreaking and poorly compensated. Black feminists fought the remedy for black families proposed by the Moynihan Report and by most social scientists: a restored patriarchal family combined with programs to promote male breadwinning. Should black women take up "white woman's familial cocoon?" Eleanor Holmes Norton, a lawyer and founder of the National Black Feminist Organization, thought there was "no reason to repeat bad history." Radical black feminists similarly criticized black male nationalists who were attracted to the idea that black liberation required installing men as the heads of households. Instead, black feminists turned the attack on black families on its head by asserting that the history of the black family actually gave African Americans a head start on equality. Norton told the *New York Times* in 1970 that "the black woman already has a rough equality which came into existence out of necessity and is now ingrained in the black life style."[13]

The rigid roles and unequal burdens of the idealized nuclear family certainly angered feminists. But just as frequently, they noted that the domestic ideal was also illogical, inefficient, and out of step with historical change. Whatever justification there might have been historically for a sexual division of labor, today "the incessant childbearing role [was] a lame excuse for confining women to domestic chores." Technological change made work in and out of the home cleaner and less physically demanding. Labor-saving devices limited the time housework would take. NOW pointed out that with a life span of nearly seventy-five years, women simply couldn't spend their entire lives in child-bearing and -rearing.[14]

Many radical feminists went further than liberal activists by calling for the eradication of marriage and the patriarchal family altogether. Sheila Cronan, a member of New York Radical Women, Redstockings, and The Feminists, concluded in an often-reprinted critique of marriage that "freedom for women cannot be won without the abolition of marriage." Many lesbian feminists similarly rejected marriage. Martha Shelley, president of the New York City chapter of the early lesbian-rights group Daughters of Bilitis, saw unhappy, heterosexual marriages all around her. She had no desire to enter an institution which bound her to one sexual partner and gave that person "jurisdiction over my friendships and finances." In her eyes, gay marriage was "a form of Uncle-Tomism." Lesbian separatists argued that marriage was just another patriarchal, heterosexual tool of domination. When the short-lived Washington, DC collective the Furies announced they would live apart from men, they declared, "We have broken our last dependence on male privilege which kept us from being revolutionary."[15]

Radical feminists insistently shifted attention from the public sphere to the private, arguing that without change at home, equality was impossible. Indeed, the family and marriage were patriarchal institutions that must be ended. Naomi Weisstein, a Chicago activist and the author of "Psychology Constructs the Female," stated that quite simply, "the family oppresses, and it must be fought." Radical second-wavers drew attention to how much the legal structures of marriage constrained wives. They couldn't move at will. They couldn't demand meaningful support from husbands. They couldn't refuse sex with their partners. It was a myth that marriage protected and benefitted women. The opposite was the case. "The word 'protection,'" instructed Sheila Cronan, "in this case is simply a euphemism for oppression."[16]

At the same time, the family was the primary means of socializing men and women into false roles. In an extended analysis of the family in 1969, Linda Gordon, a member of Boston's socialist-feminist group Bread and Roses—and now a renowned US women's historian—dissected the family's role in perpetuating gender roles: "We are trained from the day of our birth to accept these roles and to behave toward men as menial, supportive inferiors." Within a capitalist system, marriage and the family further oppressed women by devaluing their productive work as wives and mothers.[17] While divisions emerged among radical liberationists about how to attack marriage and the family, they agreed that women's equality depended on their thorough reconstruction. That penetrating appraisal of these institutions fostered openness both to alternative forms of marriage and family and to wide experimentation in sex roles within marriage.

In rejecting the male-breadwinner ideal, feminists also took on the long-standing presumption of female dependence, particularly economic dependence. The National Organization for Women, in its earliest formal statements, declared the question of limiting women's roles to wives and mothers one of its central concerns. The fledgling organization's 1966 Statement of Purpose declared, "We do not accept the traditional assumption that a woman has to choose between marriage and motherhood, on the one hand, and serious participation in industry or the professions on the other." Eradicating the male-breadwinner model of the family was their explicit goal: "We reject the current assumptions that a man must carry the sole burden of supporting himself, his wife, and family, and that a woman is automatically entitled to lifelong support by a man upon her marriage, or that marriage, home and family are primarily woman's world and responsibility—hers to dominate—his to support. We believe that a true partnership between the sexes demands a different concept of marriage[,] an equitable sharing of the responsibilities of home and children and of the economic burdens of their support."[18] It is hard to recapture now exactly how revolutionary such a declaration was. NOW proposed roles for men and women that flatly rejected the idea of separate, gendered spheres. Breaking with the assignment of noneconomic and economic roles by sex, they insisted instead that women and men shared responsibility for earning money and taking care of the home.

Despite their more far-reaching critique of the family, radical liberationists came to similar conclusions. Linda Gordon explained that a revolutionary social and economic order would "[permit] people's needs for love and security to be met in ways that do not impose divisions of labor, or any external roles, at all." Drawing on a socialist-feminist perspective, the economist Heidi Hartmann would translate this point into an influential, comprehensive analysis of the division of labor between men and women both at home and in the workplace, concluding pointedly that "not only must the hierarchical nature of the division of labor between the sexes be eliminated, but the very division of labor between the sexes must itself be eliminated if women are to attain equal social status with men."[19]

Single mothers most radically challenged expectations for female dependence on a male wage, as Chapter 5 explores. Writing for the Los Angeles-based *Momma: The Newspaper/Magazine for Single Mothers* in the winter of 1972, Karol Hope criticized "the shrinks and the social workers and the politicians" trying to picture the ideal family. "They will be years at it, even if they do know what they're talking about." Instead, she says, single mothers have a unique status—"solely responsible for the care and well-being of ourselves and our children." The Sisterhood of Black Single Mothers, founded by Brooklynite Daphne Busby in the early 1970s, rejected the notion that single black women's families were incomplete. As the feminist and African American women's historian Barbara Omolade recalls, "the Sisterhood challenged patriarchal, middle-class, and even cultural nationalist assumptions of women's roles and the family." In the early 1980s, the Sisterhood went on to sponsor the fatherhood groups discussed in Chapter 2, in keeping with their commitment to families composed outside the bounds of conventional marriage.[20]

Gloria Steinem summed up the feminist vision of reconstructed family roles for *US News and World Report* in 1975. She dismissed the "old imperative of the patriarchal nuclear family." Rather, "Responsibility for children won't be exclusively the woman's anymore, but shared equally by men—and shared by the community, too. That means that work patterns will change for both women and men, and women can enter all fields just as men can."[21] From critiquing marriage built out of an inequitable, outdated sexual division of labor and an unfair legal regime, feminists turned to imagining alternatives to the male-breadwinner household.

Experimenting with the "New Marriage"

In March 1971, in a fifty-page screed in *Harper's Magazine*, the writer Norman Mailer issued one of the most infamous broadsides against the new feminist movement. Alix Kates Shulman's "Marriage Agreement" featured prominently. "I remember the mounting excitement with which I read Mailer's notorious attack on feminism," she recalled, "I exulted over having hit the mark." "Oh, exquisite triumph! The first principle of my Agreement, that a woman's work was by definition as valuable as a man's—indeed, that the comparison was henceforth impermissible, not least because absent the opportunity that must follow domestic equality no one could know what women might do—this Mailer could not swallow."[22] Shulman's glee at Mailer's discomfiture reflected how much the Agreement was a provocation—an inside joke for feminists and a sly stab at male pretensions.

At the same time, the Agreement was serious. As Shulman observed, it opened the door to questioning why labor in the home was not valued and was women's alone. It revealed how women's countless hours of household labor suppressed opportunity. The Agreement, along with the thousands of other marriage contracts it spawned, envisioned a new model of male-female standing in marriage to replace coverture, the long-standing legal framework under which a wife's legal, social, and political identity was "covered" by her husband's. Nearly a century of challenges had substantially eroded coverture by the 1960s, but feminists pointed out the continued legal enshrinement of male control in marriage and family law. By substituting a marriage contract for coverture, feminists advanced an ideal of marriage forged by equal partners in a negotiated agreement.[23]

Marriage contracts—both formal and informal—proliferated in the 1970s. Feminists deployed them creatively. From Shulman's regularly reprinted agreement to samples of "Utopian Marriage Contracts," feminist activists made women's legal disability in marriage visible, giving value to women's labor in the home and demanding that men share in it. But the contracts were often merely a starting point. Many commentators also drew attention to how engaging with partners over a contract stimulated heightened consciousness in the marriage and forced negotiations over how to share family and household labor equally. In other words, contract-talk helped a new kind of marriage to emerge and flourish.

Marriage contracts could be found easily. The very first issue of *Ms.* magazine, which was printed as an insert in *New York* magazine in December 1971, included Susan Edmiston's instructions on "How to Write Your Own Marriage Contract." Not only did she reprint Shulman's agreement, but she also added a ten-point "Utopian Marriage Contract" that covered "the wife's right to use the name she chooses, the children's names, division of housework and child care, finances, birth control, whether or not to have children and how many, the upbringing of the children, living arrangements, sexual rights and freedoms, and anything else of importance to the individual couple." A proposal for a "Model Marriage Equality Bill" that would require legal recognition of marriage contracts appeared in many feminist publications, and in 1974, Lenore J. Weitzman, a sociologist at the University of California at Davis, laid out the legal case for "Individual Contracts and Contracts in Lieu of Marriage" in the *California Law Review*. Ten pages of sample contracts covered the bases from "Traditional Marriage—Partnership of Doctor and Housewife" to "Middle-Aged Working-Class Couple" and "Alternate Lifestyle, Homosexual Couple." *Time* magazine reported in 1972 on the contract of the Terrys of Detroit. Stimulated by a struggle over a new car, the Terrys' contract stipulated responsibilities for household labor, family care, and how Bob would treat his wife. An early reader of *Ms.* described her thrill at the effect of her new agreement. "We split all the household chores into two lists. Each list has a week's work to be done. Then we switch lists," she explained, "This is the first time in 12 years that I have ever had a week off from doing laundry."[24] By 1975, the sociologist Marvin Sussman had compiled over 1,500 contracts.[25]

Many couples went further. The Terrys dropped their contract after their first child was born in 1970, not because they abandoned its premises, but because, as Bob Terry underlined, "we found we couldn't just switch roles. We've had to redefine our relationship completely." Similarly, in May 1973, Madelon Bedell maintained for her readers in *Ms.* that eventually she and her husband "came to an agreement. It isn't exactly a contract. It has no ironclad clauses. It is subject to continual revision; it occasionally breaks down completely and must be painfully reassembled." Two of its core understandings: "Your work is important and so is mine. Care of the children and home is also important—to both of us."[26] As Susan Edmiston concluded, the mere fact of drawing up a contract forced partners to examine their assumptions and differences, negotiate over them, and consciously choose their roles. The ultimate intent was to free men and women from established gender roles and to facilitate broader male participation in the private sphere as well as female involvement in the public realm.

Beyond contracts, widespread experimentation with family form characterized feminist efforts to reconstruct intimate relationships. Such experimentation took inspiration from the 1960s and 1970s movement to set up communes. Intentionally breaking with the norm of the isolated nuclear family, members of communes tried to share everything from living spaces to money, children, and partners. Cheri Register, who was active in a cooperative women's bookstore in Minneapolis, remembered that "it was the way people were living. There were more communes. . . . [My husband and I] bought a house and people moved in and out of it. . . . This sense of privacy was a lot different."[27] From Los Angeles to Boston, women and men explored new configurations of adults and children, from communes to cooperative playgroups, often requiring equal participation by all adults in household and childcare tasks. Many women moved into women-only households, some of which were exclusively lesbian. Some of these communal households were childless, while others included children, but all put questioning the nuclear family and the conventional arrangement of men's and women's roles at the heart of their missions.

Often vexed by internal conflicts and members' ambivalence, these ventures required tremendous effort by participants, who, with a high degree of self-consciousness, tried to change their own expectations about how to create a family. Radicals endorsed household transformation as part of their view that nuclear families perpetuated patriarchy. For the radical feminist and University of Chicago sociology professor Marlene Dixon, alternative lifestyles, communal living, and collective childrearing constituted means to liberate women from "the constriction and spiritual strangulation inherent in the role of wife." Activists like Dixon foresaw the dissolution of the nuclear family as the solution to the double burden, and they predicted that new arrangements would emerge for the industrial production of housework and communal childcare.[28]

Communes struck many as highly promising avenues for liberation. Kate Millett highlighted the possibilities for a journalist from *Look* magazine: "We should try to keep the positive values of the family—like the affectional side, which doesn't have to be based on blood," she urged, "and get rid of the negative (like economic dependency)." Lesbian separatists, some of whom decamped for "womyn's lands"—communes set up in remote rural locations—argued that all-women communities freed women to find true closeness away from the struggle of relationships with men.[29]

Shared living arrangements spread out household labor and costs, freeing up time and resources for both men and women. At the Earthworks Community in Vermont, all members performed all tasks, from nail pounding to floor mopping. Barbara Balogun Jackson set out a series of principles for communes in her 1970 think piece "Marriage as an Oppressive Institution/Collectives as Solutions." Among them was the tenet that all members, male and female, "will be freed to work if they are able and find this desirable." "This distinction," she underlined, "will not be determined by sex, but rather by the needs of the various individuals and the collective." Twin Oaks, a Virginia community founded in 1967 on principles of race, gender, and class equality invented the pronoun "co" to replace he and she as part of the members' ambition to eradicate distinctions between men's and women's roles.[30] Not all communes practiced such egalitarianism, however: hippie communes notoriously exalted an earth-mother role for women. When women's liberation filtered into these counterculture farms and rural compounds, many women left in disgust, some to found their own woman-only communes. Others challenged men to change, and if they refused—as at the Diggers' Black Bear Ranch in 1974—women ousted the "cowboys."[31]

Second-wave activists also proposed publicly sharing previously privatized family labor. For example, a feminist group took over the offices of the popular magazine *Ladies' Home Journal* in March 1970 and, a few months later, published an insert with articles calling for free childcare centers, collective food preparation, and food co-ops to reduce hours of shopping. Joan Jordan, a feminist from California, contended that housework should be reorganized "by application of mass production methods." The collective publishing the magazine *Up from Under* advocated emulating the Black Panthers and the Young Lords in setting up children's breakfast programs, a model they thought could be "extended to other meals so that more people can share the cooking and cleaning." Following in the footsteps of early twentieth-century feminists, *Up from Under* writers called for altered housing and communal kitchens.[32] While few communal kitchens appeared and few communes outlasted the economic shocks of the early 1970s, feminist advocacy for them signaled their commitment to securing transformed relationships and roles within the private sphere.

Imaginatively rethinking how to raise children was at the heart of many of these alternative arrangements. Alix Kates Shulman's marriage agreement was as much about involving her husband in raising their children as it was about dividing up housework. Just four months after implementing their agreement, Shulman's five-year old daughter told her husband, "You know, Daddy, I used to love Mommy more than you, but now I love you both the same." Shulman considered this sweet observation a sign of their arrangement's success. Robin Morgan, the editor of *Sisterhood is Powerful*, divided care of her infant son with her husband as well, each taking part-time jobs and spending half the day with the baby. "We're both mothers," Morgan told Sara Davidson, a reporter with *Life* magazine. "He bottle feeds, I breast feed." Feminist activists theorized that men's involvement with children was better for both. Writing about "Child-Rearing and Women's Liberation" in 1970, Sheli Wortis, a psychologist and childcare activist in Cambridge, Massachusetts, decried children's losses if they were deprived "of the opportunity of interacting equally with men as with women."[33] Radicals more broadly viewed nuclear families as oppressive and restrictive to children as well as to adults, and they argued that, by reordering marriage and gender relations, they would also liberate children from both conventional gender norms and the soulless, achievement-oriented selfhoods required by capitalist societies.

Lesbian feminist activists suggested that lesbian couples exemplified reconstructed intimate relationships. Sidney Abbott and Barbara Love, who

fought together for recognition of lesbian rights in the early 1970s, sum-
marized it succinctly: "Lesbians are the women whose relationships attempt
a true break with the old sexual-emotional divisions." In fact, in lesbian relationships, women embodied the ideal of shared responsibilities, rooted
in individual desire, skill, and temperament. "Both partners have maximum
opportunities. . . . In the absence of roles there is no prescribed way of
thinking or acting. Everything is open for new consideration, from who will
wash the dishes, to who will aggress in love, to who will relocate for
whom. . . . Like all freedoms, freedom from role playing requires work.
Each couple has to find its own way and there is no 'how to do it' book available." Framing lesbian intimacy in these terms aligned it with the feminist
movement's broader goals to eradicate sex roles and the sexual division of
labor in marriage. It also helped nudge women to see that they could rely on
themselves and each other rather than assuming they had to depend on
men for both emotional and economic support. "I can only hope," Martha
Shelley wrote in 1970, "that, as the Movement grows, more and more
women will come to depend on other women for emotional support, for
love and comradeship."[34]

In April 1972, *Life* magazine published a feature section called "The
Marriage Experiments" with a blazing red cover. Among the five arrangements profiled was Alix Kates Shulman's marriage agreement. Additional
stories of an unmarried couple with a child, a collective household of seven
adults and four children in Berkeley, California, a "frontier partnership"
in Idaho, and a marriage in severe stress allowed *Life* to ask about "new
forms in a cherished institution." Women's liberation did not directly affect
all of the breaks with tradition outlined in the story, but *Life* framed each
household's beliefs developing alongside the sexual revolution, left and
counterculture politics, and a growing desire for self-fulfillment.[35] *Life*'s feature led the way in a broad, popular fascination with new marriage and
family forms in the 1970s. *Glamour* reprinted the Shulmans' marriage
agreement in 1978. *Time* and other magazines told repeated stories of feminists reconstructing marriage. Questioning, inverting, or altering presumptions of male breadwinning and female homemaking predominated,
and both making space for women's work and cultivating men's nurturing
were constant themes.[36] At a NOW conference on marriage and divorce
in January 1974, all but two of the 175 people attending the workshop
"Marriage or What?" said they no longer wanted a traditional marriage.

Alternate lifestyles—from communes, single parenting, lesbian parenting, or open marriage—were their preferred option. A cottage industry of advice books on how to update your marriage appeared as well, among them *Becoming Partners: Marriage and Its Alternatives* and *The Love Contract: Handbook for a Liberated Marriage.*[37] A kind of feedback loop emerged as feminist critique encountered on-the-ground experimentation just as a weakening economy put combustible pressure on the male-breadwinning norm. Feminists' creative alternatives in turn opened the door to new possibilities for intimate relationships and marriage.

The widespread power of the feminist-inspired rethinking of marriage took many Americans further than they ever imagined they might go. Wealthy suburban Connecticut housewives who had begun meeting in a consciousness-raising group in the spring of 1971 provide a telling example. Ten to fifteen women gathered at the group's weekly sessions to discuss everything and anything—marriage contracts, role playing, abortion, volunteerism, the "destructive aspects of marriage." One intense gathering took the theme, "You Belong to Me." The topic emerged after one woman reported that her husband ended every argument by saying, "You belong to me, and you do what I say." One of the group's members left, stunned by the conversation, and asked her husband, "'Do you think you own me?' He said 'I absolutely do. I pay the bills.'" Shocked, the woman pressed further, and the conversation ended with a changed attitude by her husband. Another member commented optimistically that "when your husband goes along with it and admires you and lets you be equal, you start loving him more than ever. For a while it's rough going, but when you get together on this new basis, my God, it's better than anything."[38]

The Liberal Model of Marriage as a Partnership

That radical feminists experimented broadly with family structures is not so unexpected. After all, their politics led most to assess the family negatively as an instrument of capitalism, patriarchy, or both. Liberal feminists, however, similarly emphasized transforming intimate relationships as a necessary precondition to women's meaningful equality in the public sphere. The liberal outlook was rooted in the report that the groundbreaking President's Commission on the Status of Women issued in 1963, which called for recognizing "marriage as a partnership in which each spouse makes a different but equally important contribution."

A certain ambivalence about the implications of this demand filtered into the report. Produced on the cusp of the resurgent women's movement, commission members insisted that "the husband should continue to have primary responsibility for support of his wife and minor children," but suggested that "in line with the partnership view of marriage," a wife should have the legal obligation to support herself and their children "to the extent she has means to do so." This uncertainty about the degree to which a married woman should be responsible for earning some of the family income reflected abiding commitments to a male-breadwinner ideal mixed with recognition of women's economic vulnerability in the labor market. Liberal feminists would seek to flesh out and give substance to the commission's vision of marriage as a partnership of equals.[39]

African American feminists were among the first to make the case. They had responded to the Moynihan Report with calls to strengthen black families by advancing black women's economic opportunities rather than by propping up a male-breadwinner system. Eleanor Holmes Norton argued that it was "too late for any group to consciously revert to old familial patterns of male dominance and female servility." New "functions" for women outside the home had to emerge, giving the nation "a chance to pioneer in forging new relationships between men and women." The eminent black feminist and civil rights lawyer Pauli Murray thought black women had the opportunity to blaze the trail for egalitarian marriages that could be a model for young people, whatever their race or sex. The outlook of such middle-class professional black women was not far from that of welfare rights advocates who argued that benefits should not be contingent on mothers remaining unmarried, and that they should be allowed to maintain fulfilling, equal relationships with men outside of marriage. As the historian Serena Mayeri has noted, black feminist lawyers' collaboration with white feminists led to pathbreaking Supreme Court rulings that found government policies which favored male-breadwinning households over other forms violated the constitution.[40]

With Pauli Murray as one of its founders and Aileen Hernandez, the daughter of Jamaican immigrants and a member of the Equal Employment Opportunity Commission (EEOC), as one of its earliest leaders, it is not surprising that the National Organization for Women's outlook was shaped by the egalitarian perspective on marriage. The fledgling organization's Task Force on the Family informed NOW's members in 1967 that since the group's "basic ideological goal" was "a society in which men and women have an equitable balance in the time and interest with which they participate in work, family and community," NOW intended to seek changes in policy and personal life. The goal was to keep men from "disproportionate involvement . . . in work at the expense of meaningful participation in family and community," while ending women's "disproportionate involvement . . . in family at the expense of participation in work and community." In March 1970, NOW took the next logical step at their national conference in Chicago: NOW members resolved "that marriage should be an equal partnership with shared economic and household responsibility." A second resolution of the conference recognized the greater earning power men generally enjoyed and called for sharing economic responsibility proportionate to earning. Still, NOW members expected women to be economic contributors to their families, just as they pressed men to be active participants in the household and childrearing. Their 1970 conference resolutions included demands for paternity as well as maternity leave.[41]

Advocates of the liberal partnership model focused almost as extensively on men as they did on women. As with profeminist fatherhood advocates, Sweden was frequently their exemplar. The Swedish prime minister's speech on "The Emancipation of Man" as well as a special report on the status of women in Sweden for the United Nations in 1968 were frequently

"NOW=Partnership in Marriage." New York State Conference on Marriage and Divorce, January 1974. The New York state chapter of NOW organized this conference, featuring speakers Bella Abzug and Betty Friedan. This banner hung prominently on the podium.

reprinted—in the edited collection *Voices of the New Feminism* in 1970, in the *Journal of Social Issues* in 1972, and in the pioneering sex-discrimination casebook co-edited by Ruth Bader Ginsburg in 1974. American feminists were enamored with the ways Swedish programs for tax reform, social benefits, preschool, shorter work hours, and women's employment all aimed to eliminate differentiation of roles by sex while supporting families by encouraging *parental* involvement.[42]

The partnership model effectively "degendered" marriage—that is, it took gender out of the assignment of roles and responsibilities within marriage and turned them into a matter of a couple's preferences. The model envisioned spouses performing functions that were not sex specific. Shared responsibilities, inside and outside the home, would be negotiated. Separate spheres assumptions collapsed. As the future Supreme Court Justice Ruth Bader Ginsburg would argue in 1975, marriage and family law must substitute a "functional description" for "a gender pigeonhole" in setting the roles and obligations of wives and husbands. Elizabeth Duncan Koontz, head of the Women's Bureau, similarly preferred function to gender when she proposed "child rearing leave," which, she noted, was "a very new concept." To her mind, either "a working mother or father with a firm attachment to the labor force" might seek leave: a mother might wish to nurse an infant; a parent might need to provide care until daycare could be organized; some couples might "alternate periods at home for child rearing." Koontz insisted society had an obligation to support such leaves for both men and women because "assumption by men of a full share in the rearing of children would contribute to the welfare of the whole family."[43]

Many couples tried the "50/50 Marriage" model. It featured in abundant news and magazine stories covering the experiments. In 1971, for example, *Look* magazine profiled Ted and Sally Oldham, a couple "living out a current feminist theory that men and women can and ought to share equally the joys and tasks of home and parenthood as well as the thrill of professional achievement." The Oldhams struggled to shift the balance of power and roles in their relationship, particularly ensuring that Ted took a shared role in parenting their infant daughter. Federally Employed Women (FEW), the organization fighting for the rights of women working in the federal government (as we see in Chapter 8) featured the marriage of two psychologists and professors at Stanford University, Drs. Sandra and Daryl Bem, in their newsletter. The Bems formed a perfect model—shared research on androgyny in sex roles and equal division of homemaking and child-care. The feminist partnership model thus not only spread as media outlets described new 50/50 marriages but also as the women's movement influenced women and men to rework the terms of their relationships. By 1977, a CBS News poll found that 48 percent of Americans believed that a marriage in which "the husband and wife both have jobs, both do housework and both take care of the children" offered a "more satisfying way of life" than traditional marriage.[44]

To make partnership marriage a reality, liberal feminists sought not just the alteration of individual relationships but legal and legislative change as well. Feminist lawyers led the effort to reshape family law and social welfare programs so that, as Ruth Bader Ginsburg described, "precise functional description" could be substituted for "gross gender classification." Cases brought by feminists in the first half of the 1970s converted an understanding of the privileged protection of women in marriage into awareness of sex discrimination. Hundreds of laws that reinforced stereotyped roles for men and women in the family received feminist scrutiny. Ruth Bader Ginsburg pioneered this legal strategy at the Women's Rights Project (WRP) of the American Civil Liberties Union. Founded in 1972, the WRP represented a series of female and male plaintiffs who had faced discrimination because they occupied roles traditionally belonging to the opposite sex. As the legal historians Neil and Reva Siegel note, Ginsburg's arguments in these cases "[contested] legally enforced sex-role differentiation" and maintained that "the prevailing system of sex-role differentiation . . . [perpetuates] the subordinate status of women."[45]

Ginsburg believed constitutional limits prevented state action to force men and women to fulfill sex-role stereotypes. "The breadwinning male/homemaking female division of functions deserves neither special favor nor condemnation by the law," she emphasized. Rather, "it is a pattern individuals should be free to adopt or reject, without government coercion." She then called on the court "to confront the particular gender discrimination cases presented to it as part of a pervasive design of government-steered sex-role allocation" that must be overturned. As the legal historian Cary Franklin has shown, Ginsburg "promote[d] a new theory of equal protection founded on an anti-stereotyping principle . . . [that] dictated that the state could not act in ways that reflected or reinforced traditional conceptions of men's and women's roles."[46]

"First Women's March down Fifth Avenue," by Bettye Lane. August 26, 1970. Women listen to speeches at the Women's Strike for Equality in New York City. The signs reveal the movement's concern, even in its early days, with women's vulnerable status inside marriage.

In developing this approach, Ginsburg drew on two contemporary sources. The first came from Sweden. While working for the Columbia Law School's Project on International Procedure in 1961, Ginsburg researched Swedish law, learning Swedish, living in the country off and on, and producing more than a dozen books and articles on Swedish law from 1963 to 1970. Ginsburg credited her exposure to Swedish thinking about equality with shaping her outlook. Olof Palme's "Emancipation of Man" speech appeared not only in her 1974 sex-discrimination casebook but also in lectures, articles, and briefs, and she frequently quoted the speech alongside the 1968 report to the United Nations on the Status of Women in Sweden. Challenges to the arbitrary sex-role system, of course, also defined US–based feminist activism. For example, Ginsburg's anti-stereotyping logic built on feminist sociologists' breakthrough challenge to sex-role theory. And it echoed the demands made by NOW and other liberal feminist groups to distribute household labor, childrearing, and wage earning evenly between men and women.[47]

Ginsburg and the Women's Rights Project consistently argued cases that revolved around either male caregivers or pregnant workers in order to break down the stereotyped breadwinner and homemaker roles.[48] Ginsburg has always insisted that the "most spectacular" gender-discrimination decision by the court was *Weinberger v. Wiesenfeld*. Stephen Wiesenfeld protested the Social Security Administration's denial of "mother's benefits" to him and his infant son. His wife, Paula, who had been the family's primary breadwinner, died in childbirth. He sought benefits traditionally awarded to widows to enable them to care for children at home after the death of a breadwinning spouse. Ginsburg argued that this denial unfairly excluded women from benefits they had earned by paying into the system, while enforcing stereotyped sex roles in requiring a widower to enter the wage labor market. In 1975, the Supreme Court upheld the WRP's reasoning. It was a crucial victory, and Ginsburg celebrated. With this case, she crowed, the Court began "to strike classifications based on the notion that social roles are preordained by sex, that woman's first job is wife and mother, man's, doctor, lawyer or Indian chief."[49]

Feminists also struggled to eradicate family law and state benefits that enshrined a male-breadwinner model of marriage and family relations. Led at the national level by feminist legislators like Bella Abzug, Shirley Chisholm, Patsy Mink, and Martha Griffiths, they persistently attacked unfair treatment of wives in inheritance, property, tax, and social security laws. Martha Griffiths, for example, described the American social safety net as "designed for a land of male and female stereotypes, a land where all men were breadwinners and all women were wives or widows . . . in other words, where all of the men supported all of the women." Drily observing that this imagined land never came close to matching reality, she helped spearhead feminist legislative campaigns to revise social security.[50] Other feminists noted that the requirement that a wife take a husband's name, the husband's right to choose where the family would live, and limited tax relief for childcare expenses (not to say lack of public provision of child-care) took for granted a secondary status for wives. Even the right to a hus-band's support devalued wives' labor in the home, making it a service rather than work with monetary value. By the end of the decade, virtually all of these laws had been altered. Recognition of the homemaker spouse's contribution to the couple's property, for example, became routine, as Chapter 4 explores. Encouraging states to pass the Uniform Marriage and Divorce Act was also a component of feminist activism. Describing obliga-tions within marriage in functional rather than gendered terms, the Uni-form Marriage and Divorce Act was meant as a model for states revising discriminatory marital and family law. By the late 1970s, most states had adopted revisions along these lines.[51]

In seeking change in marriage and family law, second-wave feminists saw the possibility to generate substantive equality for homemaking spouses— and recognized that women stood to gain the most from such changes. "Functional description," predicted Ruth Bader Ginsburg, "should preserve, and indeed might enlarge, rights and benefits accorded women who work full-time within and for the family unit." The basic thrust of the changes in law proposed by feminists were aimed at this very outcome: to value women's contribution in the home, acknowledge the second-class status in which marriage had historically placed women, and widen their oppor-tunities. A novel proposal by the Missouri-based feminist lawyers Joan M. Krauskopf and Rhonda C. Thomas in 1974 for a "partnership family model" exemplifies the creative alternatives feminists advanced in this fer-tile period. To rectify unequal and ineffective support laws, Krauskopf and Thomas called for equal service obligations for husband and wife; shared property between husbands and wives, including that acquired during the marriage; and the freedom to alter the terms of a marriage by contract between the partners. Just over a decade after the President's Commission on the Status of Women called for expanding the partnership ideal, this pro-posal fleshed out its full feminist implications.[52]

Marriage change became a prominent feature of feminist Equal Rights Amendment advocacy as well. Ratification of the Equal Rights Amend-ment was a priority for feminists, and they pushed hard to persuade state legislatures to pass it. By 1974, thirty-eight states had endorsed it, and more than a dozen states added ERAs to their constitution in the decade.

By the middle of the decade, debate over the addition of a sex equality amendment to the constitution focused increasingly on the status of the housewife. ERA supporters insisted that the amendment would enshrine the partnership ideal of marriage, and the National Commission on Observance of International Women's Year (IWY) made that case in a fact sheet on the "Legal Rights of the Homemaker and the Impact of ERA" in 1975.[53]

The fact sheet discussed how common-law traditions merged a wife's legal identity with her husband's and denied her independent rights. Only "slowly and spottily" had the law evolved "to give independent identity to the wife and to treat marriage as an economic partnership." The ERA would hasten reform. Uniform marriage and divorce laws had already required states with those alterations to their constitutions to define roles in a marriage "neutrally in terms of functions and needs rather than in terms of sex." Speaking to the National Press Club in April 1976, Catherine East, the coordinator of the IWY Commission, predicted a new domestic legal order. State ERAs had generated new domestic relations codes; courts had begun to interpret marital dissolution in new ways. Molded by functionalism and gender neutrality, marital roles and obligations would be defined by activity and contribution, not by sex. Support acquired new meanings, expanding from a narrowly economic concept to include a wide array of contributions to family wellbeing. These contributions could be made by either spouse and given value by policy and the courts.[54]

Under East's auspices, the IWY Commission issued pamphlets for every state in the union to analyze its family and divorce laws. These fifty pamphlets are an astonishing piece of feminist labor. Each detailed the specific state laws that put wives at a disadvantage in marriage, and as a whole, they sought to remake the legal superstructure of unequal marriage and family law state by state. Such rewriting of domestic law was urgently needed work. Collectively, the pamphlets painted a picture of a dire state of affairs and recommended "reform based on the concept that marriage is a partnership, in which each partner's contribution deserves equal value and dignity."[55]

Liberal feminists placed change in marriage—personal, institutional, legal—at the core of their activism. They advanced a new vision for intimate relationships which involved a functional division of responsibility for homemaking and earning between both partners. These second-wave activists wanted to introduce a fundamental reorientation of value into

American society—to grant the homemaker role both dignity and economic recognition, while inspiring men to commit to home and family as
much as they did to work. As Ruth Bader Ginsburg would write in 1975,
"Solutions to the home-work problem are as easily stated as they are hard
to realize: man must join woman at the center of family life, and government must step in to assist both of them during the years when they have
small children."[56]

SECOND-WAVE FEMINISTS left marriage a changed institution. Legally, it had
new parameters. Culturally, it drew on new egalitarian models of shared
roles and contributions. Critics of feminism, who accused women's activists of obsessing narrowly over sex when they took up problems of the private sphere or of ignoring the family altogether in favor of securing equal
employment, have it wrong. Second-wave thinkers, legislators, and lawyers
all scrutinized, deconstructed, and then rebuilt marriage along new lines.
Many thousands more took courage from the movement, confronted partners, and forged new kinds of intimacy. The success of this work is perhaps most concretely embodied in the new legal architecture of marriage
and family law in place by the end of the 1970s, but two other results demonstrate it as well. The first is the utopian vision of alternative ways to
manage work and family that required changes in business and government
as well as in private lives—the early glimmers of "child rearing" leave, family
medical leave, and alternative work structures, some of which shaped long-
term campaigns for maternity, family, and sick leave. The other is the dis-
crediting of the male-breadwinner household as a national norm. Feminist
challenges to sex-role stereotyping within marriage and a concomitant
insistence on negotiated responsibilities between spouses made dramatic
inroads in disestablishing that deeply entrenched ideal.

In addition to removing hundreds of head-of-household and other traditional laws of coverture, second-wave feminists proposed a host of policy
changes to move men to the center of family life, as we saw in Chapter 2.
Feminists demanded "child rearing" leave specifically in order to make it
available to fathers as well as mothers.[57] Early on, the NOW task force on
the family also resurrected a long-standing feminist demand to extend protective labor laws to men. Protective labor laws typically regulated women's
working hours, but not men's. NOW's family task force emphasized that

shorter hours were necessary to give both working fathers and mothers the opportunity to "participate equally in the pleasures and responsibilities of home care and child rearing." "Men's jobs," one NOW member informed the sociologist Maren Carden, "have to change so they don't have to work so hard and so long at them." By July 11, 1973, when Aileen Hernandez, the former EEOC commissioner and the former president of NOW, testified to the Joint Economic Committee of Congress about women's economic status, her ten-point policy proposal to redress inequity included not only "a system of high quality child development centers for all parents who wish to use them," but also a "Humane Labor Standards Act." The act would extend to *all* workers, male and female, and include "adequate wages, flexible hours of work, shorter work days and weeks, [and] child care facilities," along with basic insurance and pension protections.[58]

Change in marriage cannot be attributed to feminism alone, of course. Long-term changes in the economy, in education, in marriage norms, and in reproductive control all undergirded the change.[59] But feminists offered concrete alternatives. At a time when traditional practices seemed at best suspect and at worst untenable, they provided provocative new understandings of family relations that appealed to women's surging demands for equality. Conservatives understood the deep shake-up this vision represented. It is no accident they mobilized in a "pro-family" movement aimed at maintaining male breadwinner–female homemaker households and took on everything from lesbian and gay men's desires for recognition of their relationships to feminists' withering critiques of men's preeminence in the family. Phyllis Schlafly scornfully dismissed Alix Kates Shulman's marriage agreement as full of "petty provisions," a model of lovelessness, discontent, and disorder rather than a struggle for equality.[60] The outrage of conservatives over Shulman's feminist dream and the political victories they won as Ronald Reagan ascended to power have overshadowed Shulman's and other feminists' intentions—which were nothing short of upending American culture's entrenched practices and replacing them with new, egalitarian relationships.

4

HOUSEWORK

"Don't Iron While the Strike Is Hot"

Everybody's in favor of equal pay, but nobody's in favor of
doing the dishes.

—Mary Jo Bane, Wellesley Women's Research Center, 1977

TEACUPS SHATTERED rather than washed. Shirts left "wrinkling in laundry
baskets." Housework boycotted for a day. Women were on strike for
equality. On August 26, 1970, American women gathered in the largest
women's rights march since the suffrage demonstrations of the early twentieth century. Protests across the country featured women carrying signs:
"Oppressed Women: Don't Cook Dinner Tonight! Starve a Rat Today!!"
and "Housewives are Unpaid Slave Laborers! Tell Him What to Do with
the Broom!!" In Los Angeles, marchers responded to heckling men by
chanting, "Go do the dishes, go do the dishes." Cooking, cleaning, and
laundry were everywhere in a day of protest whose slogan was "Don't Iron
While the Strike is Hot!"

The Women's Strike for Equality was the brainchild of Betty Friedan.
Held on the fiftieth anniversary of women gaining the right to vote, the
strike dramatized the strength of the new movement and its demands for
change. The day's events brought together a wide-ranging coalition of

"Women's Liberation, New York," by Ken Regan. August 1970. Protesters at the Women's Strike for Equality demand that housework—and housewives—be valued.

women's groups, and as many as fifty thousand marchers to Fifth Avenue
in New York. NOW was at the forefront, but so were radical groups like
The Feminists and traditional women's organizations like the Young
Women's Christian Association. The Third World Women's Alliance, Women
Strike for Peace, Older Women's Liberation, and even teens, under the
banner "H.S. Women Unite!," joined as well. The strike had three demands:
free twenty-four-hour community-controlled childcare centers, free abortion on demand, and equal opportunity in jobs and education.[1]

The strike was conceived as a revolt from women's daily second-class
status—in dead-end, low-paying jobs, in lack of childcare, and in housework
that was solely women's domain. As Betty Friedan told the assembled
crowd, "All of us are housewives, but from now on it shouldn't be
housewives—'housespouses' is a better word. Both of us will share the
world inside the home and walk equally in the world outside the home."
Calling the lack of economic value granted to women's work in the home
the "unfinished business" of the women's revolution, Friedan asked, "What
will happen to architecture, to city planning, when women are no longer
the unpaid free servants of the home?"[2]

There was no mistaking the revolutionary implications of the call to
replace housewives with "housespouses." Most commentators actually
agreed on the reasonableness of the strike's official demands, particularly
childcare and equal job and educational opportunities. But challenging men
to "go do the dishes" seemed, as ABC news anchorman Howard K. Smith
editorialized, "abhorrent," and a bizarre demand for "sameness." "*Vive la
différence!*" he proclaimed as he closed his commentary the night before
the strike. (This was a cry that would reappear on many signs, and in the
jeers of male onlookers to the day's protests.) Coverage of the strike, particularly in network television news reports, returned repeatedly to the prospect of an unsettling and unappealing gender reversal. Cartoons showed
browbeaten husbands caring for bawling babies while their wives, sporting
women's lib paraphernalia, headed out the door. News stories reported men
throwing pennies at the marchers and carrying signs reading "Back to the
Kitchen."[3]

That household labor and gender roles were at stake became even more
evident in the movement's opponents, who were featured in most stories.
The Strike for Equality Day coverage followed a familiar pattern. News
stories about the women's movement rarely asked men for their opinion.

Reporters relied instead on women—typically women who in unthreatening ways affirmed their enjoyment of housekeeping and childrearing, and their commitment to familiar gender roles. On strike day, interviews of women entering or exiting local stores captured predictable soundbites of happy mothers and housewives, none of whom could imagine embracing feminist demands.[4] Partnered with the male hostility that seeped through much of the commentary and in the footage of cameras panning over the onlookers, such formulaic wife-as-happy-housewife imagery revealed just how provocative feminist demands to share housework were. Recasting responsibilities within the home brought charges of inequality and injustice into the most intimate spheres. Yet the movement's exponents contended that sharing the work at home was as constitutive of equality as equal opportunity at work.

Second-wave activists critiqued male prerogative in making housework women's work. Advertisers and moral authorities were scorned for romanticizing cooking and cleaning as natural female labors of love. Feminists demanded proper economic valuation of household labor and recognition of housewives' contribution to family wellbeing. A "wages for housework" campaign proved the economic significance of labor in the home. Other activists participated in a movement to upgrade the status of household workers like domestics, nannies, and housecleaners, pursuing labor protections and professional respect and dignity. In telling men to "go wash the dishes," in other words, second-wave feminists sought to recognize the work of social reproduction and to share it equally between the sexes. Social reproduction—the process by which new generations of citizens and workers get clothed, fed, and raised—happens in the home, but it is also more than a private matter. Women's rights proponents fought for society's responsibility for social reproduction by advocating for laws and policies that provided social benefits, such as social security, to "housespouses" and labor rights to paid domestic workers.

HISTORIANS HAVE JUST begun to trace second-wave feminists' sweeping activism on the question of housework.[5] The timeline I propose here differs significantly from these scholars' timelines in showing earlier, broader, and more sustained activism. It includes important efforts predating second-wave reactions to conservatives' charge that feminists hated housewives.

My interpretation also challenges the narrative that denigration of housework dominated feminist activism. Second-wave interest was extensive. It began with questioning gendered notions of housecleaning as women's work and their female destiny and ended with battles for homemakers' and domestic workers' rights. In all cases, we find feminists struggling to achieve two objectives: to get the social value of housework recognized and to overturn the assumption that it was uncompensated work that should be assigned to women alone. Three broad strands of feminist organizing overlapped to take on the problem of housework. In the first phase, loosely from 1963 to 1970, feminists tore apart bland assumptions of women's happy destiny in cleaning house and challenged men to share housework equally. This phase began with Betty Friedan's scathing attack on housework in *The Feminine Mystique*. This is when the myth that feminists disparaged housework and belittled housewives was born, yet these years also witnessed some of the first efforts to name housework as labor and to creatively reimagine men's participation in it as a foundation for gender equity.

In the second stage, which unfolded roughly from 1968 to 1975, feminists in a variety of venues calculated the value of housework and the contributions of homemakers. This second phase had roots in the 1963 report of the President's Commission on the Status of Women, which issued recommendations on domestic workers, housewives' benefits, and social security reform. Black domestic workers fought to define household employment as skilled professional work and, between 1971 and 1974, led a broad coalition in a fight for the minimum wage for household employees. Radical wages-for-housework activists called for salaries for homemakers; economists and policy wonks toted up the dollar value of housework and demanded changing national economic measures to include household labor. Their calculations provided ammunition in battles to reform social security and alter divorce settlements, exemplified by the NOW Task Force on Marriage and Divorce's forceful 1975 recommendation to make recognition of homemaker contribution in the division of marital property a standard in divorce.

Finally, between 1973 and 1978, "homemakers' rights" moved to the forefront. In these years, often in the form of pro-Equal Rights Amendment advocacy, feminists insisted on "rights" for homemakers. Housewives for ERA formed in 1973. Later in the decade, liberal activists laid out claims on behalf of homemakers in a NOW Homemakers Bill of Rights and in a homemakers' plank endorsed at the gigantic National Women's Conference in Houston. In this last phase, feminists responded angrily to a growing conservative movement and the pronouncements of leaders like Phyllis Schlafly, the antifeminist founder of STOP ERA, to be "pro-family." Furious that the work they had been doing for years on behalf of home-makers was increasingly obscured in the press, second-wave feminists stepped up their assertion that household labor must be valued in a truly equal society.

Taking the Shine off Housework

That "who should wash the dishes?" was a hot political question frequently made feminists a target of derision. Yet for many feminists, the joke was all on the other side. Alix Kates Shulman insisted that her marriage agreement's portioning out of dishwashing and bed-making was done with "a sardonic lift of eyebrow . . . a curl of the lip . . . [and] a wicked chortle as I mocked man's self-importance as a mere ruse for getting out of the dishes." Sensitizing Shulman to the issue was a widely circulated piece written by Pat Mainardi, a member of the radical feminist group Redstockings in New York City. "The Politics of Housework" made its first appearance at a conference of New Left women in June 1969. It immediately touched a nerve, and in 1970, it was included in the pioneering collection *Sisterhood is Powerful*. Its brilliant wit made it a touchstone for feminist consciousness raising about housework.[6]

"The Politics of Housework" took the form of a dialogue between a man and a woman about cleaning house; in it, Mainardi slyly dissected men's excuses for not contributing. He says, for example, "Housework is too trivial even to talk about." She explains: "*Meaning:* It's even more trivial to do. Housework is beneath my status. My purpose in life is to deal with matters of significance. Yours is to deal with matters of insignificance. You should do the housework." Mainardi not only exposed her partner's cavalier attitude of superiority, she also rejected his presumption that his time had greater value than hers. "One hour a day is a low estimate of the amount of time one has to spend 'keeping' oneself," Mainardi tartly pointed out, "By foisting this off on others, man gains seven hours a week—one working day more to play with his mind and not his human needs."[7]

What feminists discovered was that household labor was invisible in two fundamental ways: as an expression of male privilege and as work. The second wave's steadfast rejection of sex-role stereotypes extended to housework as they showed that nothing in women's "nature" made housework a feminine trait. Women were no more suited for or inclined to cleaning house than men were. In fact, in "The Politics of Housework" Mainardi offered up a few choice facts and comebacks to use as men trotted out such arguments to justify avoiding housework. When men introduced wolves and gorillas to suggest that by nature some were just top dogs, Mainardi prompted women to bring up bees and spiders, species in which females dominated hapless males. When men implied that they were "best at" more meaningful jobs and that work should be divided by talent, Mainardi interpreted it sarcastically for readers as "*Also Meaning:* Historically the lower classes (black men and us) have had hundreds of years experience doing menial jobs. It would be a waste of manpower to train someone else to do them now."[8]

In the context of rising numbers of women participating, like their husbands, in the paid labor force, the injustice of men's continuing avoidance of housework became painfully evident. Another frequently reprinted feminist skewering of men's taken-for-granted privilege was "Why I Want a Wife," by Judy Syfers, a member of San Francisco's radical women's liberation group Sudsofloppen. Formed in 1968, Sudsofloppen gave itself this nonsensical name to signal the members' desire to define their own agenda, free of New Left dogma and expectations. Syfers, a married housewife and mother, taught about women's oppression at Breakaway, a Bay Area community liberation school. "All three of those factors serve to keep my anger alive," she reported. Imagining having a wife for herself, Syfers tallied up the raw inequity of that wife's double day. So that Syfers could go back to school to get a better job, her wife would keep the children clean, fed, and nurtured, make sure the house was tidy and running smoothly, manage Syfers' needs for clothes and doctors' appointments, type her school papers as necessary, and entertain guests warmly. The wife would, of course, do this around her own full-time job, out of which the wife paid for childcare and negotiated all her children's illnesses and school and doctor's appointments (without losing her job). As Syfer's chronicle of labor and service sardonically concluded, "My God, who *wouldn't* want a wife?"[9]

In more mainstream venues liberal feminists echoed radical liberationists, although in less withering terms. One NOW member told the sociologist

Maren Carden that, although she herself was not particularly interested in alternative family arrangements, she did believe in redefining men's and women's roles: "Family responsibility should be viewed as a fifty-fifty thing; so should careers," she contended. Letty Cottin Pogrebin made the same point in her April 1972 monthly column "The Working Woman" for the *Ladies' Home Journal.* "When it comes to division of labor at home," Pogrebin advised a reader, "two job-holding partners must split the chores 50–50. No other way makes equitable sense. They aren't *your* chores or *your* dishes or *your* laundry; they're a joint responsibility. Husbands must not be allowed to feel that they're doing our work for us. They aren't doing us a favor; they're just holding up their end of an equal bargain. Don't ask him to 'help'—expect him to 'share.'"[10]

Consciousness-raising groups made the household division of labor a standard topic. Women recalled marching home to issue ultimatums of male participation in housework. Some men embraced it. "Every week when I clean the house, I feel like I'm striking a blow for women's liberation," declared one young man. Frequently, though, male partners agreed to divide up the labor, but then dragged their feet and shirked their new commitments. Housework became a zone of friction for many. Feminists proposed a variety of schemes for splitting up the chores. *Ms.* featured a clever tale of a woman sending a letter of resignation to her family:

> This is to inform you that I am no longer running this household. The cupboards, the Lysol, the linoleum, the washer, the dryer, the marketing—they're all yours. I HEREBY RESIGN AS KEEPER OF THIS HOUSE, AS YOUR LIVE-IN MAID/COOK/MENTOR/NURSEMAID.
> You can fend for yourselves. Best of luck.
> Mom

The family in this story winds up guided by "THE CHART," a detailed list for sharing housework among family members. Picking up on this theme, feminist writers printed sample charts, along with helpful hints for filling them out, in advice books and elsewhere.[11]

Unsparingly, women's liberationists stripped the glow from housework and even childcare. For every glossied-up advertisement of dish soap, laundry detergent, or shirt-collar cleaner, for every smiling kitchen-mopper in the movies, feminists had one answer: there was nothing glamorous, fun, or rewarding about housework. Readers of the tracts of early second-wave women's liberationists could not have missed this litany of charges against housework: "monotonous repetitive work," "uncreative," "endless repetitious drudgery," "dirty and boring," "routine work," without "lasting let alone important achievement." A standard placard carried in the Women's Strike for Equality March read, "End Human Sacrifice! Don't Get Married!! Washing Diapers is Not Fulfilling." Pat Mainardi bluntly declared that the basic truth about housework is that "it stinks." Housework consisted of a series of "dirty chores" which had to be done, and done again, and had been routinely assigned to women of all races—but especially to African American women. In 1968, in *Notes from the First Year*, two members of New York Radical Women, Carol Hanisch and Elizabeth Sutherland, objected to the idea that women's identity inclined them to fulfillment through housework. Instead they argued that such work "provides a pathetic sense of being needed, of identity, to many women. But anyone who thinks she feels good as she surveys her kitchen after washing the 146,789th batch of sparkling dishes isn't being 'natural'; she's literally lost her mind."[12]

Second-wave feminists subjected glorification of domestic labor to relentless debunking. "The housewife's work is treated by society simply as though it did not exist as work!" observed Meredith Tax, an incensed member of the Boston socialist-feminist group Bread and Roses, in 1970. "It is as if the 60 to 80 hour week she puts in . . . were imaginary and all she really did as far as others were concerned, was to sit on the sofa, munch chocolates, and read *True Romances*, as she does in cartoons." Women's housework was not a labor of love as society told women over and over, but service work with cold hard cash value. Vivien Leone, a writer and a member of Older Women's Liberation (OWL), had a rude awakening to the hidden productive value of her labor after a car accident put her in a hospital bed with forty-seven stitches in her face and an arm in traction. That's when she learned she was a "lawful domestic servant." Her husband, uninjured, could still file suit, a lawyer advised them, for loss of Leone's services in the home. Leone's lawyer commented that, "A housewife is a very valuable piece of property." The number of people needed to replace her was "staggering," he told Leone, and, he added, the cost "astronomical." Yet, she marveled, "it remains unpaid, undignified and unrewarding." The housewife had a job, with onerous working conditions, according to Leone, which included no sick leave, no vacation time, no disability insurance, no social security. Her unpaid labor then reinforced poor treatment of domestic workers, whose work remained similarly devalued. "As long as housewives are the scabs who do this job for free, domestic work must remain degrading.[13]

The Economics of Housework

There was no more effective way to show the terrible working conditions of housewives than by calculating the monetary value of household labor, and feminists delighted in pointing out that, according to the Department of Labor, it would cost $8,000–$9,000 a year—more than the annual income of nearly 40 percent of American households—to purchase all the services a housewife provided. One of Gloria Steinem's stock punchlines in her speeches on feminism introduced this staggering fact, although she coyly tweaked audiences by adding that the figures excluded "on and off prostitution."[14] Feminists devoted considerable effort to campaigns to recognize the worth of household labor despite the image of feminist hostility to housework. Betty Friedan's controversial pronouncement in *The Feminine Mystique* that the suburban housewife occupied a "concentration camp" provided ample fodder for such a view.[15] And certainly, the drive to unmask the labor behind household work fed that notion, particularly as radical women's liberationists foregrounded the drudgery and mind-numbing repetition in housecleaning. Yet feminist efforts to shed light on the work that went into sparkling homes developed into campaigns to assign economic value to housework and secure its recognition as productive labor.

In doing so, second-wave feminists had several aims. The first was to give household labor the value historically accorded to paid work. Second, they wanted to end the inequality of women's disproportionate burden of family work by compensating and supporting housewives who had devoted themselves to home and family. Such support, they believed, should also be available to spouses—whether male or female—in the future. Third, movement supporters argued that social benefits such as social security and tax deductions should be distributed by role and contribution rather than by marital status. And finally, feminists fought for recognition that years of homemaking diminished opportunities for women in the larger society. They strove to facilitate movement between home and work in a variety of

Help Wanted

REQUIREMENTS: Intelligence, good health, energy, patience, sociability, skills: at least 12 different occupations. HOURS: 99.6 per week. SALARY: None. HOLIDAYS: None (will be required to remain on stand-by 24 hours a day, seven days a week). OPPORTUNITIES FOR ADVANCEMENT: None (limited transferability of skills acquired on the job). JOB SECURITY: None (trend is toward more layoffs, particularly as employee approaches middle age. Severance pay will depend on the discretion of the employer). FRINGE BENEFITS: Food, clothing, and shelter generally provided, but any additional bonuses will depend on financial standing and good nature of the employer. No health, medical, or accident insurance; no Social Security or pension plan.

"Help Wanted." *Ms.*, July 1972. The first regular issue of *Ms.* magazine included this tongue-in-cheek job description for a housewife in an article by Ann Crittenden Scott, "The Value of Housework." It noted a homemaker's nearly hundred-hour work week and lack of job security and fringe benefits.

ways—from social security credits for time out of the paid labor force to job-training programs for divorced or widowed women with a long tenure in the home. In all of these cases, feminist activism swirled around identifying a way to value housework so that it could be placed on a level playing field with waged work.

The arguments feminists put forward and the tactics they pursued to value housework went in two major directions: either showing the dollar value of household labor or showing homemaking as a job without benefits that left homemakers dangerously dependent and vulnerable. Quantifying how much housework and childcare added to the nation's economy was one way to draw attention to its dollar value. The readers of *Ladies' Home Journal*, confronted with the pages young women's liberationists had persuaded the magazine's editors to insert in the August 1970 issue, learned an estimated $270 billion would be added to the country's wealth if women's childcare and housework were measured.[16] A vigorous debate unfolded among radical feminists about how to view household labor within a Marxist analysis of capitalism. As early as 1969, Marxist feminists Margaret Benston, then a young chemistry professor, and Marlene Dixon, the University of Chicago sociologist whose firing had become a *cause célèbre* in the movement, wrote influential analyses of how women's responsibility for unpaid housework rendered them invisible to the monetary economy. Despite considerable disagreement about the specific way that housework was productive labor, socialist feminists pointed out that capitalism depended on women's labor in the home for the reproduction of workers and for the availability of a cheap reserve labor force. Their general conclusion was that "women in the home are doing work which is of economic value for capital and not merely serving an economic function inside the individual family."[17]

Liberal women's organizations also advanced arguments to include housework in national accounts. In testimony to the Joint Economic Committee of Congress, the American Home Economics Association urged as early as 1973 that homemaker production be included in national economic statistics. "Inclusion of Homemakers in National Measures of Production and Income," a fact sheet written by longtime women's and labor activist Katherine Ellickson in February 1975, included this little ditty: "Through women in labour/Life keeps on its course;/But mothers don't count/In the Labour Force!" Ellickson claimed that better collection of national data on homemaking would increase awareness of the dollar value of homemaking, thereby fostering needed policies on social security for homemakers and deductions of homemaking expenses. Feminist economists also used their perch in universities to develop methods for calculating the value of housework for use in economic data. The pressure of feminist activism was strong enough that, in the late 1970s, the Bureau of Economic Analysis of the US Department of Commerce undertook an official effort to calculate household work's monetary equivalent. The goal was to provide a number to use in combination with more conventional calculations of the gross national product. In 1976, they concluded, housework totaled $752.4 billion, which was 44 percent of the GNP, a value nearly equal to half of all goods and services produced that year and a proportion even higher than earlier estimates.[18]

Just as frequently, feminist champions asserted the value of an individual housewife's labor. In June 1970, a Chase Manhattan study repeatedly cited by second-wavers estimated a housewife clocking 99.6 hours a week; it put the cost of replacing her labor at well above $10,000 a year. According to Housewives for ERA, when you added up all of homemakers' jobs—food buyer, nurse, waitress, seamstress, maintenance worker, cleaning woman, bookkeeper, interior decorator, and chauffeur, to name just a few—"The Worth of Wives" was $549.60 per week, nearly $30,000 per year, which would have put them among the highest paid workers in America when these figures were put together in 1974 by the *Washington Post*. In 1975, the federal government's Social Security Administration Office of Research and Statistics performed its own calculations, a more modest $4,705 per year on average for a housewife's labor. Kathryn Walker, an economist at Cornell University, led a series of widely cited studies based on time use, which arrived at amounts varying by number and age of children—from just under $10,000 per year for a family with one child to over $13,000 if there were 3 children and the youngest was under one.[19]

Everyone from radical liberationists to the most mainstream feminists enlisted in such efforts to calculate the dollar value of housework. In the process, they fortified the feminist undertaking to see household work as productive labor. Official census and government labor statistics had long placed "Occupation: Housewife" outside the category of productive occupations. The idea of the "unproductive housewife" developed in the early nineteenth century, as official government census takers categorized housewives first as "unoccupied" and then wholly as dependents. Such categorization made their labor so invisible that dictionaries in the early 1970s described a housewife as one "who does not work for a living," while the Labor Department's *Dictionary of Occupational Titles* placed housewife at 878 on a skill-rating scale of 1 to 887 (with 887 the lowest).[20] Making homemaking disappear as an occupation meant that "I'm not working. I'm just a housewife" had been a ready reply for women until second-wave feminists changed the discussion.

While efforts to add housework to the GNP ultimately produced more discussion than action, the question of the dollar value of individual women's housework spawned several other movements. One of them was the campaign to secure "wages for housework," the demand for which had its roots in a critique of women's unrecognized contribution to capitalism.

Socialist and radical feminists envisioned paying housewives as a provocative tactic toward the larger goal of revolution. Wages for housework would not end capitalist exploitation, but its advocates believed paid homemaking provided a tool to raise consciousness about productive work long invisible even in Marxist analyses. Although the idea percolated among American feminists starting in the late 1960s, the movement was international in origins and had outgrowths in Europe as well as the United States in the early 1970s.[21] Vivien Leone first heard about the idea of wages for housework in 1969 at meetings of her OWL group in New York. She laughed at the concept then, but her hospital-bed epiphany changed her mind, and she began to support government-paid wages for housewives and mothers. Linda Gordon had also argued in 1969, for Bread and Roses, the Boston socialist women's group, that the work of housewives deserved "a salary just as much as that of their husband in the office or factory."[22]

The New York Wages for Housework Committee was founded in 1973 and opened a storefront office in Brooklyn not long afterward. Similar groups emerged in places as diverse as Los Angeles, Philadelphia, San Francisco, and Tulsa, Oklahoma. Sometimes they organized jointly as Black Women for Wages for Housework (New York and Los Angeles) and Wages Due Lesbians (Philadelphia and San Francisco). Members of the wages-for-housework committees participated in women's movement demonstrations, provided speakers, led discussion groups, and distributed videotapes, cassettes, and pamphlets.[23]

The Marxist-feminist Silvia Federici summed up the campaign's argument in her 1975 treatise "Wages against Housework": "They say it is love. We say it is unwaged work." Indeed, Wages for Housework activists argued that paying for housework supported the feminist goal of disassociating housework from women's nature. "To say that we want money for housework is the first step toward refusing to do it," Federici pointed out, "because the demand for a wage makes our work visible, which is the most indispensable condition to begin to struggle against it."[24] They demanded, instead, that government or business provide salaries for housewives.

Highlighting the connections between women's unpaid labor in the home and their status in the workforce, the movement reasoned that as long as women had no meaningful choice but to be housewives, they remained second-class citizens. New York Wages for Housework called unpaid housework a "crime against women internationally," arguing that "this

NO ONE WORKS AS HARD AS WOMEN DO FOR NOTHING

WE WANT TO BE PAID FOR THE WORK WE DO

WE NEED MONEY OF OUR OWN TO MAKE CHOICES IN OUR LIVES

NO WOMAN SHOULD HAVE TO DEPEND ON A MAN

WE DEMAND

WAGES FOR HOUSEWORK

FROM THE GOVERNMENT

FOR ALL WOMEN

COME TO DISCUSS WITH US AND FIND OUT WHAT TO DO FOR THE
CAMPAIGN FOR WAGES FOR HOUSEWORK

in Manhattan:

WEDNESDAY   FEB. 11   7 – 10 p.m.

COMMUNITY CENTER   119 9th Ave

HUDSON GUILD FULTON CENTER (at 18th St.)
Child Care Provided

New York Wages for Housework Committee 288 B Eighth St. Brooklyn, N.Y.
Wednesdays and Saturdays 11 a.m. to 4 p.m. 965 4112   11215

"All Work and No Pay." New York Wages for Housework Committee, 1975.
With a witty pictograph of stacked dishes, wailing children, and piled-up laundry,
the Wages for Housework Committee invited people to a February 1975 meeting
to learn about the movement and their demands for government-provided wages
for housework.

crime of work and wagelessness brands us for life as the weaker sex and delivers us powerless to employers, government planners and legislators . . . as well as [to] individual men for a lifetime of servitude and inprisonment [sic]." Adding paid employment to women's lives made no difference in the absence of waged homemaking. The right to "refuse the double shift of a second job" complemented these activists' call to provide a wage for homemaking.[25]

The movement also made connections between salaries for housework and other women's causes. Wages Due Lesbians noted that because households of two women faced a discriminatory labor market, a government wage for housework made it possible to afford real sexual choices. Black Women for Wages for Housework had ties to the welfare rights organizations discussed in Chapter 5 and connected pay for housework to mothers' need for income to care for their children. Margaret Prescod, for example, had organized breakfast kitchens for the Black Panthers and fought for welfare rights in Brooklyn, New York, when she discovered the wages for housework movement through Wilmette Brown, a black feminist who was friends with Selma James, one of the movement's founders. "I was active in civil rights. I was black. I was seeking to organize as a black person and also as a woman. I thought there has to be a way to put these together," Prescod recalled. "Wages for Housework had money in its name. In organizing in the black community, you always organize for resources." New York Wages for Housework also linked salaries for housewives to the campaign to end forced sterilization of women, which was sometimes justified as a way to prevent poor women from having children they could not afford. With wages for housework, women had "the power to decide whether or not we want to have children, when, how many, and under what conditions."[26]

While the long-term overthrow of capitalism was the goal of the radicals leading the Wages for Housework movement, they contended that providing a wage for housework was a crucial first step. "When we struggle for wages," Federici explained, "*we struggle unambiguously and directly against our social role.*" The wage was more symbol than salary: it forced awareness of how the capitalist system thrived on women's supposedly natural yet unrecognized labor in the home. Conflict raged among radical feminists about the wages for housework campaign. Critics feared waged housework would legitimate keeping women in the home while reinforcing the low status of female-dominated occupations. They also worried that wages-for-housework advocates gave short shrift to patriarchy, especially male investment in dominance over women in the home. Wages-for-housework supporters refuted this criticism, insisting that a wage for household labor put broader questions on the table. Adding housework into the calculus exposed the real length of the working day for both men and women. It forced discussion of the limited benefit of a "second job" for women if housework remained their unpaid labor. It also revealed that their dependency and lack of options took a psychological toll. "It seems to us," Federici explained with her collaborator Nicole Cox, "that if instead of simply relying on love and care, our mothers had had a financial reward, they would have been less bitter, less dependent, less blackmailed, and less blackmailing to their children who were constantly reminded of their mothers' sacrifices."[27]

Radicals were not alone in promoting wages for housework. Writing for *Ms.* in the summer of 1972, Ann Crittenden Scott noted that paying a housewife for her work was an idea in the air. "This salary," she observed, "would reflect the value of her individual services, what she could be earning in the labor market, or the official minimum wage. She could receive a percentage of her husband's salary to be paid by him or paid directly by his employer in the same way as the military sends allotment checks to the wives of servicemen who are stationed overseas." Male feminists like Warren Farrell and James Levine, as Chapter 2 noted, supported homemaker payments as well. Various schemes to "trade-a-maid" pointed out the ironies of the current system. Homemakers could hire each other, clean each other's home, and pay each other a daily wage from their husbands' earnings. In the process, they would make social security payments and, as workers, would qualify for disability and other employment benefits. As Jessie Hartline, a Rutgers University economist who proposed such a scheme, pointed out, "This isn't a gimmick at all. If I put an ad in the paper to hire a housecleaner, and it turns out that the lady across the street answers the ad, that's fine, right?"[28]

For NOW's tenth national conference, an elaborate program celebrated the movement's achievements. Inside its pages, a sly *Doonesbury* cartoon captured feminists' caustic humor about household labor. Nichole, the "alternate life stylist" for WBBY radio, reported the latest hot tip for women at home—"Trade-A-Maid." Housewives A and B, best friends, spend their days cleaning each other's home and get paid by their friend's husband.

Doonesbury, by Garry B. Trudeau. February 20, 1977. Feminists delighted in Trudeau's clever mockery of paying women for housework, reprinting the 1977 "Trade-A-Maid" strip multiple times, including in NOW's 10th national conference program.

The husbands learned the value of household work and the wives felt they were contributing to family income. Besides, the wives each built up their own social security benefits and earned tax deductions for the costs of their cleaning equipment. "Why . . . why . . . that's the most amazing system I've ever heard of, Nichole," comments D. J. Mark, "It's illegal, though, right?" "Not yet," quips Nichole.[29]

The idea had surprisingly broad appeal. One quarter of Americans surveyed in 1976 agreed with the radicals in Wages for Housework that homemakers should earn pay for their work. A Connecticut homemaker told Crittenden Scott in *Ms.* that "it's not just the money. It's what it would mean psychologically. It would put a value on your work and make it clear that you've earned part of the family salary—that he's not just *giving* it to you." Other homemakers emphasized the humiliation factor: their husbands constantly questioned their use of money, and they repeatedly had to *ask* him for more. As feminist debate spread nationally, the topic of wages for housework became a focus for discussion. A 1974 Wisconsin conference on the homemaker generated a vigorous back-and-forth about paying a housewife, who would do it, and its potential risks and rewards. State assemblywoman Mary Lou Munts, a leader of the discussion, suggested that a guaranteed income might better solve the problem. At a minimum, she concluded, a new model of social insurance based on need, not workforce participation, seemed necessary. "The more we can do that—making old age and medical insurance, for example, the right of everyone—the more we can solve some of the problems of the homemaker."[30] Much liberal feminist energy would go into these very efforts to structure employment, retirement, and divorce law to provide for homemakers independent of their status as wives.

The Rights of Housewives

If wages were not about to come the way of homemakers, feminists insisted other rights should. During the Strike for Equality's highly scripted events, activists arrived at 26 Federal Plaza, New York's Federal Building, at 2:35 p.m. Locked doors did not prevent Betty Berry of NOW's Marriage and Family Committee from reporting to the assembled protestors on her earlier meeting with Joseph Kelly, the regional Social Security

Administration commissioner. Berry had delivered NOW's call to extend social security benefits to divorcées and housewives, which Mr. Kelly had dutifully promised to forward to Washington.[31] As this action illustrates, by the 1970 Strike for Equality, second-wave activists had begun to articulate a set of legislative and policy proposals to reform social security, government pensions, and tax and divorce law.

One of the great ironies of the second-wave era is that the blame for the ways that America disparaged housewives landed on the shoulders of feminists. It was feminists, not their opponents, who most vociferously challenged the inequities and putdowns that housewives faced, and it was the defenders of the status quo who made feminism the source of housewives' difficulties. Conservative activists, particularly Phyllis Schlafly's STOP ERA campaign, systematically described feminists as hostile to homemakers. In a familiar move, media reports also routinely set up the issue of homemaking as a conflict between women, leaving men, law, and policy out of the story. As Pat, a divorced homemaker, succinctly pointed out, "I'm in favor of the movement, but women like me, we can also see how the movement has been used against us. I don't mean by the feminists, but by our ex-husbands who say go out and get liberated and get a job so we don't have to support you."[32]

To complicate matters, systemic class and race tensions ran through the housework debates. For many professionals, escaping housework did seem ideal because they had employment opportunities they found more rewarding. But for pink- and blue-collar women, labor in the home often looked better than a dead-end job. While many appreciated feminist efforts to expose housewives' vulnerability and to create real choices between homemaking and paid employment, some resented a feminist presumption that economic independence was indispensable to women's equality. Even if they had small children or wished to be caretakers, many white women now felt pressure to be in the paid labor force. As one housewife explained, "I got the feeling, you know, that women shouldn't want to be dependent. That we're fools if we do. . . . But the fact is many of us, maybe most of us, like leaning on our husbands—he leans on us, too, you know."[33] For black women, who until the early 1970s were disproportionately confined to domestic labor in white women's homes, often at exploitation wages, bitter ironies abounded. As we will see, some shared the goal of making housework real work, but others resented middle-class liberationists' scathing comments about the work they paid black women to do.

Feminists addressed these charges of insensitivity and misplaced priorities with revelations about homemakers' true status and with wideranging efforts to redress the inequalities of both paid and unpaid work in the home. "A blissful state of false security" was how Betty Berry, head of NOW New York's Marriage and Divorce committee, described the typical homemaker's comprehension of her status in 1970. Berry went on to enumerate "her lack of rights and precarious financial position." NOW's Fourth National Conference in March 1970 passed a series of resolutions to rectify the homemaker's vulnerability that ranged from calling for shared economic and household responsibilities between spouses to demanding a whole battery of health insurance, social security, and pension protections for divorced wives. And in the very month of the Strike for Equality, a "Housewives' Bill of Rights" demanding paid maternity leave, health insurance, social security, paid vacation, a six-day work week, and free twenty-four-hour childcare centers was printed in the *Ladies' Home Journal* as part of the insert feminists produced for the magazine.[34]

Efforts to explore women's economic status in the early 1970s revealed what Jane Roberts Chapman, the co-director of the Center for Women's Policy Studies, called "the fearful side of the homemaker-breadwinner bargain." Congressional hearings led by Representative Martha Griffiths in the summer of 1973 showed in exhaustive detail how national law and policy built on a family wage model disadvantaged women. Members of the Joint Economic Committee heard testimony on the unfair bargain in social security, tax law, divorce, and pensions.[35] The groundwork for policy changes laid by the NOW demands and the Griffiths' hearings gathered steam after the middle of the decade. Eleanor Smeal, a homemaker newly elected as president of NOW in April 1977, proudly declared, "I am a housewife and I am a mother and I am interested in homemakers' issues because they are things that have happened in my life. Now people will have to realize that . . . feminists are people like me." Smeal made homemakers a priority and announced the establishment of a new National Homemakers Committee by the organization. Congratulating Smeal on her election, Representative Patricia Schroeder of Colorado observed that "it is important that the homemakers of our country be brought into the mainstream of the women's movement."[36]

Testifying to the House of Representatives Subcommittee on Retirement Income and Employment in May 1979, Smeal challenged Congress to address "the crisis of women in midlife." It was myth, pure and simple, she argued, that housewives were protected by their husbands and society; in

widowhood and divorce, Smeal insisted, American women found themselves with "no rewards, no recognition, and no financial security." Women
far outstripped most men in their service to the country, giving ten, twenty,
and thirty years of unpaid service in the home, yet while society rewarded
veterans with multiple benefits, it gave to women "a lifelong handicap—a
blank resume." Just as the GI Bill enacted after World War II had paid for
veterans to get an education, so should homemakers be rewarded for their
years of service with support for education and workforce re-entry. Smeal
told the assembled representatives that fulfilling the goals of NOW's ambitious Homemakers Bill of Rights would rectify this injustice.[37]

The Homemakers Bill of Rights that Smeal touted to Congress had been
endorsed by NOW at its October 1978 national conference. It was the work
of Susan Brown of Pennsylvania, who had organized Housewives NOW as
a "work-site organization of Housewives." Brown argued that homemaking
must not be thought of as an instinctive talent of women, but a "real job"
that would garner government support in the form of social security benefits, the right to credit in their own name, childcare, and a calculation of
housework in the gross national product.[38] She thought that in marriage,
and at its termination, homemakers should benefit from the kinds of employment supports and labor protections granted other workers. NOW
took up the theme.

"We must think of the homemaker as a worker who has a right to certain fringe benefits," Eleanor Smeal chided lawmakers at the 1979 hearings.
She called upon them to "design either national programs that [the home-
maker] can participate in or change the concept of her spouse having the
sole rights to the wages and benefits of his work." To think of homemakers
as workers was, for activists of the 1970s, a stepping stone to a larger reorganization of everything from family roles and social policy to workplace
relations. On distinct policy fronts—displaced homemakers, credit reform,
flexible and part-time work, and social security reform, for example—NOW
fought hard to advance changes relevant to homemakers. Among their and
other proponents' most radical proposals was income sharing, which would
have housewives legally earning half of the breadwinner's wages. NOW ad-
vertised the "Bonnie Plan," proposed by Bonnie Cowan, a lawyer from
Tennessee, which would have required joint income tax filers to sign an af-
fidavit affirming that all property and income was jointly owned. But income sharing remained more aspiration than reality.[39]

More successful feminist efforts led to social security reform, new models of equitable marital property division at divorce, and displaced homemaker legislation. Social security reform had been a focus of feminist activism from the earliest days of the second wave. The 1963 President's Commission on the Status of Women had recognized the need to provide homemakers with benefits beyond those they received as dependents of their husbands. Because social security payments were tied to employment-based contributions, housewives who had largely been out of the paid labor force had little entitlement of their own, and even when they worked, their pay was so low that they often received a better benefit as a spousal dependent. As one feminist analyst explained in 1977, "the social security system promotes dependency by defining women as family members rather than as individuals, by ignoring the prevalent phenomenon of the working wife and by failing to recognize the value of housework."[40]

In 1965, Congress made an early change in the law and provided a divorced woman the social security benefits she would have received as a wife as long as she had been married twenty years and had not remarried prior to eligibility. The limits of this legislation were patently clear: a woman married nineteen years and eleven months received no benefits; those eligible had to wait until a former husband drew benefits, and then he received 100 percent of his benefit and she received 50, rather than splitting the total allowance of 150 percent between them. In response, feminists systematically put forward proposals to lower the number of years of marriage necessary for eligibility. NOW resolved in 1968 to support reducing the number of years of marriage for eligibility to ten, and by 1970 had argued that there should be no requirement on years of marriage at all for divorced women to receive social security benefits. Their demands were reflected in legislation that Representative Bella Abzug of New York introduced in Congress as early as 1971.[41] In 1977, the law finally set the bar at ten years of marriage for a divorced wife to be eligible for an ex-spouse's benefits.

Feminists also attacked other inequities ingrained in a social security system designed with male breadwinners in mind. They prioritized providing benefits to homemakers as individuals to reward the value of the work they had done in the home. During Congresswoman Martha Griffiths' hearings on American women's status in the summer of 1973, Carolyn Shaw Bell, an economist at Wellesley College, pointed to precedents in awarding noncontributory credits to servicemen and servicewomen and in extending benefits to unpaid members of religious orders, as well as to other countries, such as Belgium and West Germany, where such systems were in place. Proposed plans ranged widely. NOW argued that employers should make additional payments based on husbands' earnings to build up a homemaker's benefits. Others proposed giving credits for years spent outside the labor force to give birth or care for children. Bella Abzug introduced legislation to pay for homemaker benefits from the general tax fund, a back-door channel to award homemakers recognition for their labor while also acknowledging their work's import for the national economy. In 1974, Congresswomen Martha Griffiths and Barbara Jordan proposed a bill to provide eligibility for homemakers as the equivalent of self-employed workers. Feminist lawmakers, with the support of activists, repeatedly introduced such legislation in a flurry of creative proposals that focused attention on the issue through the 1970s.[42]

They ran into considerable opposition. Some were angered by the prospect of what was effectively an increase to a husband's social security taxes. Others pointed out new contradictions in the program that the proposals would create, such as a working, married woman's additional social-security tax payments to cover homemakers, especially when their own husbands could not receive dependent benefits, since married men were not eligible. Efforts to ensure that the proposals would not unfairly burden single earners, particularly lower-paid women, with social security taxes that would then be distributed to homemakers addressed some concerns about the plans benefitting wealthier households. Although feminists pointed out that welfare recipients *were* homemakers deserving of similar benefits, the proposals were oriented to married housewives with wage-earning partners. They did little to grapple with the long-term disadvantages the system created for poor, single mothers on public assistance.[43]

Modest changes emerged, however. In 1977, in addition to the reforms in divorced women's eligibility, Congress granted remarried women the right to retain benefits from a previous spouse and made it possible for homemakers to establish Individual Retirement Accounts, which allowed them to build up independent retirement savings. More substantive proposals toward disentangling government-provided benefits from marital status and, alternatively, toward awarding them based on shared contribution to the couple's well being—whether paid or unpaid labor—did not succeed. A system of earnings sharing in benefits has remained a feminist aspiration, with ongoing efforts to advance it over subsequent decades.[44]

Reform of the division of marital property at divorce emerged from similar desires by feminists to redress homemaker vulnerability. A NOW spokeswoman was already explaining to a reporter in 1970 that "many housewives who don't work outside the home are shocked to discover that they are not automatically entitled to half the property." As divorce rates spiked in that decade, feminist groups from NOW to OWL shed light on the lack of protections for divorcing women and the economic difficulties they faced. NOW even went as far as endorsing "end of marriage" insurance to provide a measure of financial security for divorcing women. Other ideas under discussion included establishing defined shares of property and creating a divorce pension plan that would take annual payments during marriage for benefits payable if a marriage dissolved.[45]

NOW's Task Force on Marriage, Divorce and Family Relations made the division of property at divorce a specific concern by 1972, and in 1975 it made equal distribution of marital property at divorce a component of its recommendations for reformed divorce laws and displaced homemaker support. The task force took resolutions to NOW's 1974 national convention that would "subject the states, their agencies and/or their employees to legal actions and passive civil resistance" if they did not provide legal protections to divorcing women.[46] Feminists devised several strategies to count homemaker contributions for the purpose of property distribution in divorce settlements. In the growing number of states where state-level Equal Rights Amendments had passed, courts increasingly required that a homemaker's contribution be calculated. The Pennsylvania Supreme Court, for example, ruled in 1975 that property belonged to divorcing spouses equally, regardless of who was the family provider, observing, "We can not accept an approach that would base ownership of household items on proof of funding alone, since to do so . . . would fail to acknowledge the equally important and often substantial non-monetary contributions made by either spouse." Feminist lawyers often framed such arguments for courts, contributing to a series of influential law review articles and shaping the model Uniform Marriage and Divorce Act.[47]

In states without state-level ERA's, feminists found ways to advance recognition for homemakers' labor in reformed divorce law. In Illinois, 1977 legislation included a provision for homemaker entitlements at divorce.

Feminist legislators, including Republican representative Susan Catania, a NOW member, advanced the bill. Support from women's activists and legislators helped a 1979 law with similar provisions to pass in Virginia. By the beginning of the 1980s, over half of the cases involving marital property distribution nationwide recognized the contribution of homemakers. By 1983, forty-two states had laws to consider homemakers' labor at divorce—up from none in 1968. The trend was unmistakably in this direction. As the legal historian Mary Ziegler has observed, all of the demands put forward by the NOW Task Force on Marriage and Divorce in 1975 "had either been adopted at the federal level or had passed in more than twenty states" within a decade.[48]

Housework's value drew feminist energies in one additional area: addressing the needs of older women who had expected to spend their lives as housewives. Many middle-aged women found themselves "displaced" when their husbands died or their marriages ended. The realities of widowhood, compounded by a surge in separation and divorce, left more than four million women in limbo by 1977, with many millions more facing such a prospect. Bereft of the support they presumed they would receive from husbands, they faced discrimination and limited opportunities when they tried to get a job. One California divorcée emphasized her narrow options: after thirty-eight years of marriage without a job, the work she could get was babysitting for seventy-five cents an hour. A job counselor told her she "hated to have to say it but . . . they just don't want older women on the job market."[49]

In 1974, the feminist activist Tish Sommers coined the term *displaced homemakers*; in her eyes, these women were similar to persons displaced by war or disaster. She saw a generation whose plans to live out their lives as housewives had been dashed by forces beyond their control, women who had been "displaced from a role, an occupation, dependency status, and a livelihood." Tish Sommers came to the displaced-homemaker movement out of a lifelong involvement in left-wing causes, including years working for civil rights through the Communist Party. In 1971, in her mid-fifties and post-divorce, she moved to Berkeley, California, where she joined the local NOW chapter, became a member of the organization's national board, and soon led the NOW Task Force on Older Women. In 1975, she met Laurie Shields, then fifty-five years old and recently widowed, who had worked in advertising before she became a homemaker. Shields joined Sommers in leading the newly formed Displaced Homemakers Alliance, traveling around the country in her "tennies," which she chose not just for comfort but also, as she drily commented, "as a not so subtle protest against the notion that little old ladies in tennis shoes are flaky."[50]

Sparking a strikingly effective grassroots campaign, the two women received funding and assistance not only from NOW but from such organizations as the Young Women's Christian Association and Church Women United. Historian Susan Hartmann has noted the critical backing that the women's movement received from what she calls "the liberal establishment." The displaced homemaker movement is a good example of the broad support feminist issues enjoyed beyond familiar national feminist organizations like NOW.[51]

Displaced homemaker programs got their start in 1975, with legislation passed in California. In 1978, with the backing of Representative Yvonne Burke, a civil- and women's-rights supporter and the first African American woman elected to the House from California, the movement secured national funding through the Comprehensive Education and Training Act. At that point, twenty-eight states had considered similar legislation in the previous year.[52]

At the heart of the displaced homemaker movement was what Shields called the "special needs" of middle-aged and older women. Their goal was "to bring older former homemakers out of the shadows of a youth-oriented society. To force recognition of the contribution homemakers make and have made to society." By the last years of the decade, this single-minded focus ran up against other currents of the feminist movement. Rising attention to single mothers and the growing feminization of poverty raised questions about making older homemakers a sole priority. As public opposition to welfare grew, moreover, displaced homemaker activists played up the differences between themselves and poor women on public assistance. This approach angered antipoverty and welfare rights activists. In 1979, Beulah Sanders, who as we will see in Chapter 6 was a longtime welfare rights leader, attacked the movement for failing to deal with "poor Third World women, as usual." "They are creating a constituency of middle-class White women with whom they can relate most comfortably," she went on, "but how many minority women will reap any benefits?"[53] Tish Sommers maintained, however, that such older, largely white women did deserve attention. In her eyes, the needs of minority and poor women were being addressed elsewhere in the women's and civil rights movements; the displaced homemakers she advocated for, she feared, would otherwise fall through the cracks.

Over time, programs funded for displaced homemakers expanded the constituency they served and included younger "women in transition." As fewer and fewer women were long-term homemakers, responding to their fears and frustrations faded from program goals and the centers focused more narrowly on job placement. Still, the displaced homemaker movement of the mid-1970s reflected the breadth of the feminist conceptualization of the dilemmas of housework. It revealed a much more capacious vision of homemakers' needs than is frequently understood. At the same time, it identified a solution distinctive to liberal feminism: eradicating dependency. While the displaced homemaker movement had broad aims of emotional support and social recognition for homemakers, its core programs were oriented toward individual economic self-sufficiency and employment.

Homemakers and the ERA

As the battle to push the equal rights amendment through its final few state legislatures heated up in the second half of the 1970s, ERA advocates stepped up their arguments about its benefits for housewives. As we saw in Chapter 3, the amendment's supporters linked the ERA's ratification to the protection of homemakers. They maintained that the amendment would guarantee married women rights, such as shared decision-making over property, and secure recognition of their contributions as homemakers. Opponents disagreed, and the homemaker's fate under the ERA became a contentious focal point for debate. Led by the conservative activist Phyllis Schlafly and the STOP ERA movement she headed, ERA critics dramatically predicted the end of homemakers' traditional "right" to male support.

Feminist and other pro-ERA groups increasingly made disproving such claims about the homemaker a centerpiece of their campaign. The Equal Rights Amendment would actually help homemakers more than other groups of women, NOW stated in 1981, because it would "secure legal and economic rights of homemakers." Outrage over STOP ERA's statements that the amendment would end housewives' privileged status catalyzed the foundation of Housewives for ERA in Illinois in 1973. In 1978, Housewives for ERA went national, and in 1979 it became the Homemakers' Equal Rights Association, with chapters in more than a dozen states.[54]

The most visible moment of the feminist campaign for homemaker rights came in conjunction with the massive national women's conference held in November 1977, as part of the country's observance of International Women's Year (IWY). Thousands poured into Houston, Texas for the meeting, their numbers nearly matched by the conservatives gathered across town. At both meetings, homemakers were on the agenda. Phyllis Schlafly recited the dangers that awaited homemakers if feminists had their way. IWY conference attendees heard a different story: the IWY's homemakers' committee, which had issued the recommendations on marriage and divorce and fifty state pamphlets discussed in Chapter 3, presented delegates with hard facts about the homemaker's disadvantaged legal status. Its final report summed up the decade's feminist analysis that "homemakers are an unrecognized and unpaid part of the national work force." The convention endorsed the committee's recommendations, and then voted overwhelmingly in favor of another plank on "Women, Welfare, and Poverty." This plank offered an implicit rebuke to the ongoing blind spot about single mothers in discussions of the homemaker. Brought to the floor by welfare rights advocates bearing signs demanding "Wages for Housework," the plank declared that, just like other workers, "homemakers receiving income transfer payments should be afforded the dignity of having that payment called a wage, not welfare."[55]

As she rallied the assembled delegates, Bella Abzug reminded them that the women's movement consisted of many parts. Central among them was "the homemaker deciding that raising children, cleaning, cooking and all the other things she does for her family is work that should be accorded respect and value."[56]

"A Revolution in the Kitchen"

Another group of women understood the devaluation of housework all too well. Domestic workers did their jobs in a kind of netherworld of employment. In mid-century America, their labor remained invisible by its location in the private home and its association with housewives' work. But it was also invisible in law. While other workers had acquired protections and benefits over the course of the twentieth century, domestics remained largely outside labor law. Minimum wages, unemployment benefits, workers' compensation, limits on hours worked and overtime regulations—none applied to domestics. A workforce of mostly African American women by the 1960s, domestics faced the added stigma of work associated with racial minorities.[57]

In the mid-1960s, a surge in domestic worker organizing began to challenge such injustice. "We won't go in the back door any more," vowed Jessie Williams, a member of the Auburn, Alabama affiliate of Household Technicians of America (HTA), the organization fighting for household workers' rights. "We won't be told to eat scraps in the kitchen and stay out of the living room except when we are sweeping," Williams declared. "We feel domestic work is just as professional as any other job. If people go on making it degrading, there won't be any workers doing it much longer." Williams' militant warning had roots in the revival of the National Committee on Household Employment (NCHE) by the Women's Bureau of the US Department of Labor. A long-standing network of feminists within the government, along with Dorothy Height, the president of the National Council of Negro Women, backed this renewed attention to household employees. The NCHE sought to upgrade the status of domestic work, to provide training to domestic workers, to educate employers about the skill involved in household work, and to advocate for decent employment conditions. The Committee issued a voluntary code of standards for employers that included a minimum wage, social security contributions, overtime, sick days, and vacation benefits.[58]

The NCHE supported domestic worker organizations that sprang up across the country in the late 1960s. In Atlanta, for example, Dorothy Bolden mobilized domestic workers into the National Domestic Workers Union of America beginning in 1968. Elsewhere, Mary McClendon led Detroit domestics in the Household Workers Organization starting in 1969, and Geraldine Miller brought household workers together in the Bronx Household Technicians and the New York State Household Technicians in 1971.[59] Recognizing the momentum behind these budding groups, the NCHE shifted direction at the end of the 1960s. Under its new leader, Edith Barksdale Sloan, the NCHE spun off the Household Technicians of America in 1971 to unite and represent the burgeoning movement. An activist in her thirties, Sloan had graduated from Hunter College, served in the Peace Corps, and had worked for the US Commission on Civil Rights. Sloan redirected the NHCE's energies towards more militant objectives. No longer would the group focus on providing "better" maids for employers and training mothers on public assistance to be domestics; instead they would rally household workers for decent wages and benefits, and they would educate employers about domestic workers' rights and fair employment conditions. Without change in domestics' working days, warned Sloan, to the raucous cheers of the women gathered at the HTA organizing conference, "'Madame' is going to have to clean her own house, and cook and serve her own meals, because *everyone* is going to quit."[60]

Before a crowd of more than a thousand equally enthusiastic delegates, Shirley Chisholm, the black feminist Congresswoman from Brooklyn, New York, declared at HTA's 1972 national conference a year later, "We want equal pay for equal work, decent working conditions and respect for the long, hard hours we work." The mostly female and black attendees understood the message loud and clear. HTA, Chisholm explained, "is symbolic of what the Women's Movement is about." "We want our piece of the American Dream," she had insisted the year before, neatly linking women's claims for equality with the workers' and civil rights consciousness of the organization. With thirty-seven affiliates and twenty-five thousand members in more than a dozen states at its high point, in 1974, HTA was a thriving black feminist organization.[61]

Momentum for this domestic workers' movement came from a number of sources, civil-rights struggles and the rising militancy of service workers among them, but the women's movement gave its arguments renewed urgency and impact. In its organizing, the movement helped shape feminist arguments about the value of household labor and the necessity of making the home a decent workplace for those working in it—whether they were paid or unpaid. Josephine Hulett, a domestic worker activist from Ohio, made the point clearly that their movement was a feminist one. "After all," she told an interviewer for *Ms.* magazine, "there's a sense in which *all* women are household workers. And unless we stop being turned against each other, unless we organize together, we're never going to make this country see household work for what is really is—human work, not just 'woman's work.'"[62]

Domestic worker leaders forged a strategic alliance with the broader feminist movement. The ties between HTA and mainstream liberal feminism were varied and deep. The National Organization for Women, the National Women's Political Caucus, the National Federation of Business and Professional Women's Clubs, and even New York Radical Feminists supported the domestic workers' cause, testifying in Congressional hearings, organizing fundraisers and speak outs, and serving on the board of the NCHE. Gloria Steinem in particular was a vocal and strong supporter of HTA. The black feminist leaders Shirley Chisholm and Eleanor Holmes Norton also both identified the household workers' cause as a priority and a women's issue.[63]

Activists in HTA participated in major feminist events and rallies. Geraldine Miller of the Bronx Household Technicians joined the Women's Strike for Equality. At the mass International Women's Day Rally in New York in 1975, Carolyn Reed, leader of the Progressive Household Technicians of America, read out the workers' demands one by one. New York Radical Feminists co-organized a speak out in October 1973 with the Professional Household Workers Union. Later in the decade, Reed joined representatives from Black Women for Wages for Housework, members of Wages Due Lesbians, Ms. magazine writers, and professors from the women's studies program at Sarah Lawrence College outside New York at a conference on "The Future of Housework, the Role of the Housewife, and Sharing Arrangements for Child Care."[64]

Leaders of the domestic workers' movement had their own ties to other feminist organizations. Carolyn Reed, for example, had leadership positions in the Women's Action Alliance and the National Women's Political Caucus, and she was also a founder of the National Black Feminist Organization. Geraldine Miller led both the Bronx chapter of NOW and the NOW Women of Color Task Force in these years. She, too, became involved in the National Women's Political Caucus as a way to advance the household workers' agenda.[65] Reed and Millers' activism reveals how domestic worker rights became a significant strand within black feminism. Shirley Chisholm spearheaded the campaign for the Fair Labor Standards Act (FLSA) amendments within Congress, while Eleanor Holmes Norton used the platform of the New York City Human Rights Commission to speak out regularly on domestic workers' issues.

In 1971, Holmes Norton organized a conference, "Toward a Strategy for Solving the Problems of Household Employment in New York City," which brought NCHE and NOW leaders together with union representatives, city officials, and legislators. In her speech to conference attendees, Holmes Norton acknowledged the challenge in forging a coalition of women who employed domestic workers and the workers themselves, but insisted on the necessity of the alliance: "That is why I have sought to highlight the plight of household workers as a question for the women's rights movement. . . . Only the movement for women's rights embraces the entire affected group— those who work as household workers and those who need it most. . . . When the movement for women's rights can claim that it has done something concrete to change these conditions, such as winning legislative protection, it will have established itself as a serious movement that can deliver for all women and will lay to rest the foolishness about black women not having a stake in the fight for women's rights." In her speech and elsewhere, Holmes Norton stressed that domestic workers shared common interests with other women. Household labor attracted the same low wages and lack of respect that other jobs dominated by women commanded. Moreover, as Carolyn Reed pointed out to the *New York Times,* men's presumption that they could get housework done for free by wives and girlfriends kept domestics from getting their "rights as a paid person in the labor force." To Reed, it was obvious: "This is a gut woman's issue."[66]

To resist such treatment, HTA adopted the strategy of emphasizing the value and skill of domestic workers' labor. "If you still want an underclass to do your bidding," Sloan proclaimed to employers of domestics in 1971, "you had better start building robots, because we refuse to play the part any longer. We refuse to be your mammies, nannies, aunties, uncles, girls and handmaidens any longer. What we will be are skilled, professional household technicians." The title "technician" was intentional. The Bronx HTA leader Geraldine Miller despised the word *domestic.* "We felt as though technicians were people that did something and were supposed to be great at it," she explained. "We household workers were great people as technicians." Skilled at many tasks, HTA members demanded "the Three P's: pay, protection, and professionalism." Their fundamental goal was to be treated like real workers.[67]

Ensuring that domestic workers would receive the minimum wage through the requirements of the FLSA became the vehicle through which HTA sought recognition of household laborers' skill and professionalism, and they waged an extended battle from 1971–1974 to extend FLSA protections to domestic workers. Passed initially in 1938 as a raft of legal protections for workers in the New Deal, the Fair Labor Standards Act had excluded domestics, in part because of the work's location in the home and in part because of maneuvering by some in the Roosevelt administration who were nervous about placating legislators from the South, where large numbers of African American domestics labored.[68]

In a series of Congressional hearings on the FLSA amendments between 1971 and 1973, supporters reiterated the movement's feminist demands to uncouple housework from women's work and to understand it as demanding labor rather than selfless love. Domestic workers and their allies insisted that housework was skilled employment and that the home was a workplace. Sloan told legislators that domestic work was "a demanding occupation requiring a variety of skills." "We household workers," she informed them, deserve the wages "offered to the other workers of the land." Kee Hall, a young NOW speaker, commented that women understood that housework was "dirty, tedious work." Women, she continued were "willing to pay to have it done because they, more than anyone else, know what it is worth." While both Sloan and her NOW ally understood the labor involved in domestic work, their differing descriptions of housework—"dirty, tedious work" rather than "demanding occupation"—reveal the challenges of maintaining coalitions among feminists very differently situated by race and class. Nevertheless, Hall echoed Sloan's bottom line: having experienced workplace exploitation outside the home, she knew that without fair pay, domestic workers faced similar abuse. The esteemed labor organizer and NOW founder Dorothy Haener reiterated the organization's absolute support for the legislation. Its passage, she told legislators, was NOW's number one legislative priority.[69]

During their testimony, domestic worker leaders also challenged dismissive Congressmen who brushed off the need for a minimum wage for domestic work as upsetting to their wives and disruptive to the comfortable, familial nature of domestic employment. Congressmen condescendingly claimed, for example, that housewives could not manage complex paperwork or deal with federal bureaucracy in their homes. Supporters angrily called them out, pointing out that the idea that women couldn't add or subtract or organize the necessary forms was insulting. The deeper challenge to male prerogative became clear in a back-and-forth between Secretary of Labor Peter Brennan and Senator Pete Dominick as they fretted over the implications of higher valued—and higher cost—household labor in

June 1973 hearings. "Your wife will want to get paid," worried Brennan. "That means that you or I or we have to pay her. So we have to be very careful unless we are ready to do the dishes."[70]

Finally, advocates for domestic workers called for respect and dignity for their work—and decent pay and benefits to match. For them, a legally mandated minimum wage was a first step toward such recognition. Senator Harrison Williams of New Jersey captured the arguments made by domestic workers and feminist allies when he commented that "many domestics are treated just as they were 150 years ago—as slaves. . . . They are called 'girl' and by their first names while they, themselves, must still address their employers and employers' children as 'ma'am' or 'sir' or 'Miss Jane.'" Their average wages were less than one quarter of the minimum wage. "This hardly seems reasonable," he concluded with understated outrage. When Richard Nixon finally signed the amendments into law on April 8, 1974, the National Committee on Household Employment crowed in victory: "Minimum wage coverage for household workers gives to these one and a half million employees a legal mandate, a recognition of the value of their services and basic equality with other workers. . . . For the domestic worker, whether she is Black, White, Red or Brown, or lives in the North, East, South or West, it means a new respect—for her service and her person—and the ability to support herself and family."[71]

The domestic workers' movement brought another dimension to the second-wave struggle to value housework. In important ways, it shaped the broader feminist view of housework as *work*—work that should be valued with social respect, legal rights, and decent treatment. Yet the alliance of domestic workers and mainstream feminist organizations was also fragile, partial, and complex. The portion of feminist rhetoric that painted housework as tedious, nasty work alienated many domestic workers, and the guilt many feminists felt employing domestics bemused domestic workers, who resented the implicit unwillingness of their feminist allies to make domestic work a good job with decent pay and treatment. When some women complained that they could not afford to pay a fair wage to a household employee, domestic workers argued that their employers had a responsibility to turn around and fight for better pay from their own bosses or greater contributions from their male partners.[72] HTA activists were clear-eyed about the larger problem: systematic devaluation and underpayment of women workers both inside and outside the home.

The class and race differences among these feminist allies made sustaining common ground and shared goals over the long haul difficult. After the FLSA amendments passed, the struggle turned to enforcement, and a new invisibility shrouded domestic work, as responsibility for adhering to the law returned to individual employers. The nature and site of domestic work shifted in the following decades as well. As the historians Eileen Boris and Jennifer Klein have shown, an expanding sector of care work produced more domestics working for multiple households and more working for contracting companies like maid services and home health-aide companies. By reshaping the employer-employee relationship, this restructuring shifted the ground for recognizing and valuing domestic labor.[73] Yet the enduring accomplishment of these insurgent years was to raise the status of the profession as a whole and to enshrine in law, for the first time, the labor rights of domestic workers. It gave tangible form to the feminist claim that housework was work.

THE SECOND-WAVE STRUGGLE to divide housework equitably and value it fairly addressed the problem of work and family in three major ways. First, feminists successfully made labor in the home visible. Radical feminists who dissected the politics of housework, domestic workers who called out the racist legacies in their treatment, feminist economists who recalculated the GNP, and wages-for-housework activists who schemed to Trade-a-Maid all contributed to a feminist-led transformation of Americans' accepted beliefs about female labors of love in the home. In disaggregating sex, nature, and housework, the second wave also successfully redefined both a homemaker and a paid domestic as a worker, in the home and outside it. Second-wavers showed how the idealization of housework as an expression of a woman's devotion to her family had generated a low-status and racialized workforce, both paid and unpaid, that blocked women's equality. Finally, feminists demonstrated that dependency was structured into the homemaker role in law and policy, making the decision to be a homemaker a risky venture indeed. Acknowledging these three contributions reverses the commonplace vision of feminism as a movement hostile to housewives or domestic workers. It also makes clear that feminists did not simply open the door to the house, walk out, and never look back as they entered workplaces long closed to them.

Their battles resulted in new rights for domestic workers, significant social security reform, changed divorce law, and supports for displaced homemakers. Unpaid housework itself became part of an ongoing struggle between partners. In the long term, feminists had the greatest success when their proposals shifted the burden of women's dependency as homemakers out of the home and onto the wage labor market, as in displaced homemaker programs, or continued to link revised social benefits to marital status, as in broadening divorced women's eligibility for social security. Efforts to provide homemakers with benefits as individuals in order to produce security regardless of marital or employment status stalled out, as did radical proposals for homemaker wages. The impact of domestic worker activism was more complex. It, too, challenged individual female economic dependency, yet in demanding that household employment be a *good* job, these organizers collectively fought for workplace rights for a diversifying labor force of nannies, household employees, home health aides, and eldercare workers.

Economic pressures that pushed more and more women into paid jobs compounded the limits of feminist successes in securing benefits for homemaking. Moreover, feminists never really managed to overcome the media characterization of them as hostile to homemakers, particularly as Phyllis Schlafly received more press coverage and pinned her critique of the movement to the claim that it endangered housewives. As feminist work on behalf of homemakers became invisible, it got easier and easier to repeat the "having it all" caricature of feminism.

5

CARE WORK

"Women's Work Is *Real* Work"

The ladies of N.W.R.O. are the front-line troops of women's freedom. Both because we have so few illusions and because our issues are so important to all women—the right to a living wage for women's work, the right to life itself.

—Johnnie Tillmon, *Ms.*, 1972

JUST MONTHS AFTER the momentous Women's Strike for Equality, in October 1970, Beulah Sanders occupied the stage with Betty Friedan at a "Women's Teach-In" at Wayne State University in Detroit, Michigan. Sanders was a New York City activist and a leader in the dynamic welfare rights movement. By then, the two women's paths had been crossing in New York for a number of years. Sanders joined Friedan in a dizzying array of causes: protesting the 1970 nomination of the antifeminist Harrold Carswell to the Supreme Court; marching in the Strike for Equality; testifying at week-long public hearings on women's rights convened by Eleanor Holmes Norton, New York City's human rights commissioner; and establishing the National Women's Political Caucus (NWPC) in 1971. In turn, Friedan joined welfare rights marches and envisioned the welfare rights movement as part of the big tent of feminism she wanted to construct. Asked to provide a list of the ten most powerful "men" in New York City for *New*

York Magazine's annual rundown in January 1971, Friedan named ten women. Sanders was among them.[1]

Sanders led the City-Wide Coordinating Committee of Welfare Groups in New York City, and she was first vice president of the umbrella group the National Welfare Rights Organization (NWRO), formed in 1966. A welfare recipient from New Bern, North Carolina who had come to New York with her twin sons in 1955, Sanders had begun organizing welfare recipients in 1964, recruiting block by block, house by house. Along with other recipient leaders, Sanders had built "Citywide" into an organization of several thousand mothers on public assistance, supported by a robust group of middle-class allies, by the end of the decade.[2]

Welfare rights and women's antipoverty activists made a distinctive contribution to the second-wave struggle for government support for poor mothers, which spanned from the middle of the 1960s to the late 1970s.[3] In another variant of feminists' persistent demand that household labor be properly valued, they expressed a right to public assistance for mothers to stay home and care for their children. The poor, predominantly African American women of the movement insisted on their prerogative to choose between care of their children and dignified employment. They asserted a mother's right to determine by herself where support would come from: her own labor, her partner, or the state.

These feminists rejected the solution favored by both male liberal and conservative reformers: shoring up male-breadwinner households. Through the welfare rights and women's antipoverty movement, second-wave feminists fought for state support to raise children as a right of all women as individuals—not as dependents of men, nor only if middle class, affluent, or white. They extended that right to encompass both income for full-time caregiving and good jobs that allowed mothers to bring up their children. In making these arguments, the welfare rights and women's antipoverty movement reconfigured the maternalism of early-twentieth-century social feminists. They revised and expanded arguments for state support of maternal care of children to envision a universal right for all mothers to adequate income, with the autonomy to determine how to organize waged work and unwaged childrearing in their lives.[4]

Insightful studies by recent scholars of welfare activism have shown how this movement represented a critical strand of feminist advocacy. This chapter situates welfare rights and antipoverty campaigns as part of the

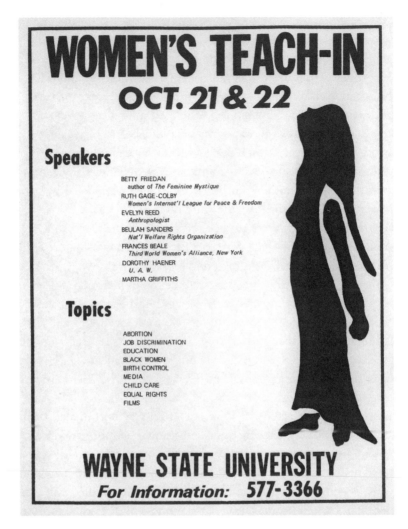

"Women's Teach-In at Wayne State University." October 21–22, 1970.
Joining Betty Friedan and Beulah Sanders at this teach-in organized by
the university's Association of Faculty Women was a virtual "Who's
Who" of the movement, including the radical black feminist Frances
Beal, United Auto Workers leader and NOW founder Dorothy Haener,
and Michigan Congresswoman Martha Griffiths.

broad second-wave drive to redistribute caretaking labor—with men by re-envisioning fatherhood, within marriage by formulating the partner model, within the home by recognizing the value of household labor, and as Chapter 6 shows, with the state by demanding universal childcare. Activists for poor mothers, however, were the vanguard in demanding universal state support for maternal care. Pressing fathers to be equally involved, for example, was largely a private solution, focused on men's roles within the home. By contrast, welfare rights champions reconceptualized the historic family wage supposedly furnished to male breadwinners, imagining a radical new balance of public and private support for families. Welfare rights and antipoverty efforts also shared the broad second-wave call for jobs that supplied more than dead-end opportunities. Like other feminists, activists for poor mothers saw simply opening the door to women's employment as inadequate. Their distinctive angle was that not only must jobs pay adequately, be flexible enough, and provide high quality, affordable childcare, they must never force poor mothers to opt for demeaning low-wage work instead of caring for their children.

Welfare rights activists and antipoverty feminists brought to the second wave a searing analysis of race, gender, and poverty as intertwined systems. Popular discussions of the black family demonized black women's mothering while simultaneously reinforcing long-standing expectations that they should get jobs. In fighting for a universal guaranteed annual income, African American activists thus fought to value the mothering of black women on equal terms with that of white women. Similarly, antipoverty activists were attuned to how race made women more vulnerable to poverty. In the 1970s, it became increasingly clear that social welfare benefits and the 1960s War on Poverty had combined to reduce male poverty, but at the expense of women, whose proportion of the poor population had soared. Feminist antipoverty activists made the connection among growing numbers of single parents, poor job opportunities, and this "feminization of poverty."[5] As a result, they led second-wave efforts to secure a mix of solutions for public assistance and jobs independent of male breadwinners.

Looking at the 1960s and 1970s through the lens of welfare rights and women's antipoverty activism reshapes our understanding of second-wave feminism itself. These proponents pioneered an integrated feminist analysis of women's autonomy, parenting, and employment, and in the process, they took the problem of caretaking in a deeper, more radical direction than other strands of feminism. They put forward the most forceful and direct claims to state funding for women's childrearing. They also made a strong case for discarding the male-breadwinner standard as the guiding principle of policy and social norms. Instead, they envisioned a multipronged system of state, employer, and private supports.

The welfare rights and women's antipoverty movement toggled between the two sides of their rallying cry, "Jobs or Income, Now." These core demands guided the two major campaigns of the movement: the struggle to secure a guaranteed national income from 1969 to 1972, and the effort to get "decent jobs for decent pay" for poor Americans from 1977 to 1979.[6] Grassroots organizing in housing complexes and urban neighborhoods had given life to the welfare rights movement in the years leading up to the founding of the National Welfare Rights Organization (NWRO) in 1966. The NWRO peaked in the high-energy struggle for a guaranteed income that followed President Nixon's proposed Family Assistance Plan (FAP) in 1969. After the NWRO folded in 1975, a second, broader-based feminist antipoverty coalition led efforts to shape the Program for Better Jobs and Income (PBJI), the welfare reform legislation proposed by President Carter in 1977, to better meet the needs of women on public assistance. Neither FAP nor PBJI came to be. Yet feminist campaigns to bring each to life reveal the second-wave ambition to remake work and family as well as the fierce opposition that vision would bring to the fore.

Mothers' Work: A Guaranteed Income for All

The welfare rights movement had its origins in civil rights and antipoverty drives of the early 1960s. Mothers for Adequate Welfare (MAW) in Boston, for example, arose from women with experience protesting housing conditions and school segregation. Before organizing officially, its members came together informally to visit area welfare offices to challenge the arbitrary cutoff of benefits. Organizers with Students for a Democratic Society helped the women form MAW after the mothers had learned, during their participation in the 1963 March on Washington, about benefits gained by other welfare recipients. Westside Mothers in Detroit emerged in December 1965 to meet some practical needs—locks on mailboxes in their housing complex, so welfare checks wouldn't get stolen; support from the local welfare office for babysitters, so mothers could participate in work experience programs; and deposit-free utility hookups, so low-income families wouldn't deplete their monthly budgets just to start up electricity or gas service.

The shabby, degrading treatment Johnnie Tillmon had received from caseworkers inspired her, a daughter of Arkansas sharecroppers and a divorced mother of six, to gather other mothers on welfare. She knocked on the doors of over five hundred Aid to Dependent Children (ADC) recipients in her Los Angeles housing project, and turned out a crowd of three hundred at her first meeting, then went on to form Aid to Needy Children Mothers Anonymous in 1963. As was the case in these three cities, poor women on AFDC (the renamed ADC), overwhelmingly African American, initiated the movement. Mobilization arose out of their experiences as mothers seeking to support their children on meager benefits. In a society whose buzzword was then a War on Poverty, poor women's needs were addressed only glancingly in mostly male-centered community and antipoverty programs.

In the spring of 1966, at a conference on guaranteed income proposals at the University of Chicago, the fledgling movement began to coalesce. Johnnie Tillmon was there, as were Beulah Sanders and George Wiley, a former chemistry professor from Syracuse, New York who had just started a new antipoverty group in Washington, DC. With other activists from places ranging from Chicago, Ann Arbor, and Detroit to Newark, New York City, and Cleveland joining the discussions, the group agreed to a planning session for a national organization later that summer. Surrounded by fellow recipient activists sharing their stories of common frustrations and obstacles, Tillmon said that this August 1966 assembly "was just a buzz, buzz, buzz." NWRO was formed a year later. Its members agreed that four goals would guide the new organization: adequate income, dignity, justice, and democracy.[7]

George Wiley took the position of executive director, with responsibility for fundraising, connecting welfare rights groups around the country, and directing the organization's campaigns. A National Coordinating Committee guided policy; its first chair was Johnnie Tillmon. Wiley and the largely male staff he hired led NWRO, but female welfare recipients dominated its membership. African American women with children represented about 85 percent of members, but the organization was self-consciously interracial in an era of separatist black nationalism, and whites, Puerto Ricans, Chicanas, and Native Americans belonged as well. In Los Angeles, for example, Alicia Escalante founded the East Los Angeles Welfare Rights

Organization in 1967, after attending a Los Angeles NWRO meeting led by Johnnie Tillmon. Escalante and her fellow Chicana activists allied themselves with the larger movement, while focusing on services to Spanish-speaking communities. At its peak in 1969, an estimated twenty-five thousand members had joined, with many more involved in the organization's campaigns. In 1971, 540 local affiliated Welfare Rights Organizations (WROs) spanned the country, with the greatest strength in urban areas. Dissatisfaction with the sexist and racist attitudes of many male leaders (large numbers of whom were white) developed in tandem with NWRO's growth, and a more explicitly feminist outlook grew among leading members. Johnnie Tillmon famously instructed the readers of *Ms.* magazine's very first issue that "Welfare Is a Women's Issue." Middle-class women might find women's liberation "a matter of concern," she contended, but "for women on welfare, it's a matter of survival." In 1972, Wiley resigned, and Tillmon assumed NWRO's executive directorship.[8]

From the movement's first years, welfare rights groups sought alliances with other women's organizations. The Washington, DC Welfare Alliance, for example, invited all area women's groups to a meeting in 1968 to review President Lyndon Johnson's welfare proposals, while Coretta Scott King, the civil rights leader and widow of Martin Luther King, Jr., put out a call for a similar meeting in New York City. Many traditional women's organizations, such as the League of Women Voters, had vigorous antipoverty programs with strong ties to welfare rights organizers. At the local level, welfare rights organizations and chapters of NOW worked together in some cases. Detroit NOW joined the local welfare reform coalition. In Las Vegas, Nevada, Ruby Duncan steered women in her welfare rights group into NOW; in Albuquerque, New Mexico, the leader of NOW's national Women and Poverty Task Force, Merrillee Dolan, built a strong connection between her NOW chapter and the area's WRO. National leaders such as Betty Friedan and Gloria Steinem, as well as organizations they helped lead, such as NOW and the National Women's Political Caucus, all endorsed NWRO goals.[9] Those relationships both guided political actions and shaped the broader feminist consciousness of poverty and welfare as women's issues.

THE MOVEMENT HAD some important early victories. Recipients secured access to special grants for necessities like school clothes, winter coats, and furniture, and they publicized this availability to other AFDC mothers. A standard complaint of welfare recipients was highhanded and intrusive treatment by caseworkers. WROs won the right to appeal welfare officials' decisions, and they successfully challenged invasive scrutiny of recipients' lives. They lobbied public officials for better benefits, while instructing many poor women in their right to assistance. The movement's gains went hand in hand with mounting national attention to welfare.[10]

Aid to Dependent Children, the poorer cousin of the two-tier social welfare system that emerged out of the New Deal, had provided grants for children in poor households since the passage of the Social Security Act in 1935. Full-time wage earners, mostly men, received the benefits of social insurance—unemployment insurance, and social security—while poor and disabled citizens landed in a separate category, with lower benefits subject to greater restrictions. Throughout its history, ADC (renamed Aid to Families with Dependent Children in 1962) was deeply discriminatory, with state and local control guaranteeing that many African American women would not receive benefits, as "suitable mother" requirements made it easy for caseworkers to exclude families arbitrarily. Nevertheless, enrollment numbers in AFDC rose, fed by both the sweeping migration of Southern workers to urban areas, particularly in the North, and inadequate job opportunities in cities, as companies relocated to other, lower-cost labor zones. At the same time, antipoverty militancy arising from the War on Poverty encouraged more poor women to claim their right to benefits. In 1960, 3.1 million were enrolled; by mid-decade it had risen to 4.3 million, and by 1970, welfare lists approached almost 8.5 million. Cries of a "welfare crisis" pervaded media reports, policymakers' speeches, and conservative and liberal accounts of the most urgent problems facing the country. Heightened hysteria about exploding welfare rolls and swirling anxiety about entrenched urban poverty in the aftermath of the riots and civil rights protests of the 1960s sparked demands for action as the decade came to a close.[11]

Amendments to the Social Security Act passed in 1967 mandated, for the first time, work or job training for AFDC recipients with school-age children. Welfare recipients faced growing charges of laziness, immorality, and abusing the system. "Increasingly," historian Premilla Nadasen has observed, "the politics of welfare converged on the stereotypical image of a black unmarried welfare mother with a child born out of wedlock. This image, more than any other, fed the fires of the welfare controversy."[12] The debates over work requirements in 1967, with their racially charged stigmatization of poor women, signaled the direction of the disagreements to come, as conflict over state support for full-time maternal caregiving escalated.

ON AUGUST 9, 1969, President Richard Nixon announced that he would be proposing a radically restructured public assistance program, the Family Assistance Plan. To meet the needs of poor Americans, the AFDC program would be eliminated, and all Americans would be entitled to a guaranteed annual minimum income of $1,600 for a family of four, an amount well below a typical family income of over $9,000. Allies introduced legislation for FAP in October. The legislation solved the problem of welfare by furnishing all households with a baseline annual income. Those payments could be augmented with earnings, and the plan included a work requirement for adults that retained those already in place for single mothers with school-age children. Some job training was included in the bill, but men were its targets in order to meet the FAP's quite explicit goal: to end the poverty of mothers and children by ensuring that men could adequately support their families and would thus stay with them.[13]

Although the idea of a guaranteed income has virtually disappeared from public awareness today, it enjoyed nearly universal support across the political spectrum in these years. There was a consensus among both conservatives and liberals that Americans deserved income security—a guaranteed basic income for all citizens, whether unemployed, disabled, or caring for children. They did not always agree, however, about the best delivery mechanism. Milton Friedman, the conservative economist who was an advisor to Barry Goldwater's 1964 run for the presidency, proposed a negative income tax in 1962; John Kenneth Galbraith, the prominent liberal economist and longtime advisor to Democratic presidents, endorsed a guaranteed income in his influential book *The Affluent Society* (1958). In 1968, twelve hundred economists lobbied Congress to enact income guarantee legislation. The idea received official imprimatur when Lyndon Johnson's Presidential Commission on Income Maintenance endorsed a guaranteed income just as Nixon took office.[14]

The NWRO had made providing an "adequate income" for recipients of public assistance a goal since its founding. The Ohio Steering Committee for Adequate Welfare (OSCAW) was one among many local WROs pressuring local and state officials to raise benefits to meet the basic cost of living for a family. In 1966, OSCAW organized a symbolic "Legislative Assembly for Adequate Welfare," calling on the Ohio governor and legislators to hear their demand to increase welfare grants to match what it took to live in their state. Many local groups sued states for failing to award benefits that met a basic standard of living, and in 1969, NWRO along with the Center on Social Welfare Policy filed suits in a number of states, taking some of them to the Supreme Court. Welfare rights activists sought to enshrine a constitutional right to a basic income—a "right to life," as activists called it—but failed to win the cases before the court.[15]

In the wake of the failure of these efforts to establish a constitutional "right to life," NWRO made guaranteed income a political objective, and with the introduction of FAP in 1969, income security became a signature goal of the welfare rights movement. Signaling the activists' reorientation, OSCAW distributed a flyer in 1969 on "Ohio's Continuing Welfare Disgrace." "Each person in this country has a right to life. Our society must *subsidize life*," they began, before segueing into the new demand: "We call upon this nation to eliminate the inadequate, humiliating hodge podge of programs like food stamps, welfare and the others that perpetuate poverty. This country must get down to business with a Guaranteed Adequate Income for all." Other feminist allies voiced their support as well. Established women's organizations like the League of Women Voters and the YWCA chimed in, as did NOW and the National Women's Political Caucus.[16]

Welfare rights advocates took a more radical stand than most mainstream supporters did. They considered a guaranteed income a means to lift all poor people out of poverty, regardless of employment history or status. During the civil rights movement of the 1960s, antipoverty activists commonly viewed a guaranteed income as a means to redress racial inequality. Most supported it, however, in the belief that it would foster traditional male-breadwinning households. A standard critique of AFDC blamed it for encouraging the break-up of families by handing an independent income over to mothers. In the mid-1960s, it was still inconceivable, even to most liberals, that a social policy should do anything but promote this family structure. The official recommendations of a 1969 presidential advisory committee on income maintenance reiterated the position that any guaranteed income program should be designed to strengthen male-breadwinning families. Male leaders of the NWRO adopted a similar position.[17]

Female welfare rights activists often came from a different perspective. For most, a guaranteed income recognized the contribution women made to society through mothering, "work that is not now paid for by society," as Cassie Downer, the chair of the Milwaukee County Welfare Rights Organization, underscored in 1972. "The greatest thing that a woman can do is to raise her own children, and our society should recognize it as a job. A person should be paid an adequate income to do that." Johnnie Tillmon called attention to the double standard that idealized the full-time mothering of the "society lady from Scarsdale" (as she sat doing her nails) while impugning the care of welfare mothers. Writing in *Ms.* magazine, she also pointed out that, however much the then-governor of California Ronald Reagan might wish the mothers he slandered as "lazy parasites" and "pigs at the trough" would get jobs, "the truth is a job doesn't necessarily mean an adequate income."[18]

Despite its support for the principle of a guaranteed income, NWRO opposed Nixon's plan as supplying inadequate benefits. "ZAP FAP" became the mantra of a coast-to-coast effort to defeat the administration's bill. Launching a full-scale lobbying campaign, NWRO leaders and members testified at hearings and visited representatives and senators in their offices. Local WROs sent letters and spoke out in their communities, while the national organization staged high-profile actions and attention-grabbing demonstrations. "The power structure understands us better," observed Johnnie Tillmon, "when we boycott, jump up and down, pound the desk, break windows and things like that." On May 13, 1970, the NWRO occupied the Department of Health, Education, and Welfare (HEW). One hundred and fifty welfare recipients, mostly African American women from Maryland, Pennsylvania, Rhode Island, and Virginia, chanted outside the HEW building while Beulah Sanders and other leaders ensconced themselves in the office of Robert Finch, the secretary of HEW. They called for an end to America's involvement in Vietnam, criticized the president's plan as paltry and enabling only a subpoverty existence, and demanded an annual minimum income that would *actually* support a family.[19]

The "Adequate Income Act," introduced on April 30, 1970 by Senator Eugene McCarthy and twenty-one House cosponsors, emerged out of a campaign NWRO had launched in June 1969. With a floor of $5,500 for a family of four (a number derived from a Department of Labor estimate for a low budget for an urban household), it contained substantially more generous benefits than Nixon's plan and countered FAP's objectionable work requirements with work incentives. Supplemental support services were integral to the NWRO's plan—childcare, free medical care, special emergency grants, legal services, and fair hearings.[20]

At their 1970 national convention in July, NWRO activists continued to express strong opposition to FAP, particularly against its built-in work requirements. In many ways, the employment stipulations lay at the heart of the matter for the welfare rights advocates seeking to advance a feminist vision. The income side of the NWRO's "income and jobs" motto reflected these activists' insistence that mothers' caregiving merited social support in its own right. Work requirements necessarily undercut that connection. At the same time, women in the movement did not rule out jobs. Beulah Sanders insisted to the House Ways and Means Committee that the "NWRO is for adequate jobs," but with a caveat: only "for all mothers who freely decide that it is in their own and their children's best interest for them to work in addition to their primary job as mother and homemaker." They wanted neither to be denied jobs (in favor of men, in particular), nor to be forced by economic exigency (because they lacked income) or government mandates (that required recipients to work) into traditional black women's jobs as domestics and kitchen workers with exploitative, sub-minimum-wage earnings. This was a real concern. First, policy designers focused narrowly on male breadwinners, providing virtually no childcare assistance to enable mothers to earn wages. Second, the bill's opponents made it clear that they feared that FAP might make a pliable black female workforce disappear. Georgia Representative Phillip Landrum voted against FAP, afraid that with it, "There's not going to be anybody left to roll these wheelbarrows and press these shirts."[21]

In November 1970, the Senate Finance Committee voted down Nixon's FAP. A revised version, H.R. 1, was introduced in Congress in early 1971 and drew even fiercer NWRO opposition. It would have resulted in lower benefits for 90 percent of current AFDC recipients with a work requirement that extended to mothers of preschoolers. The more stringent H.R. 1 reflected the shifting political winds on guaranteed income proposals and the ascendance of conservatives within the Nixon administration. Now dubbing it the "Family Annihilation Plan," NWRO organized nationwide protests. Despite making it through the House of Representatives in June 1971, the revised plan stalled in the Senate, and by the fall of 1972, the legislation was dead.[22]

Not everyone agrees on the impact of welfare rights activists on the guaranteed income debate. Certainly, with unmatched standing to speak for poor people in these years, they shaped the positions taken by many liberal antipoverty groups. Their adequate income defined the parameters of the debate by becoming the standard counterpoint to the official administration proposal. Yet many mainstream liberals at the time, and political historians subsequently, blamed the NWRO for demanding more than was politically feasible and pulling the liberal coalition away from more modest yet more pragmatic legislation. Others counter that such modest proposals left the vast majority of AFDC recipients with worse benefits. Additionally, the disappointing outcome likely stemmed from other factors, notably growing hostility to programs for racial equity, particularly those seen to benefit the "undeserving"—such as poor, unmarried mothers. Conservatives, whose influence was rising within the Nixon administration, also contributed to the legislation's demise. Most significantly from a feminist perspective, NWRO women failed to persuade either male politicians or male allies within their own coalition that supporting mothers independent of men was a legitimate national goal. Blinkered by their focus on fostering men's breadwinning, few male activists and legislators understood the feminist insight that the family wage ideal was disappearing in the face of both changing women's roles and a changing economy. Ahead of their time in insisting on the necessity for social redistribution to support caregiving, the poor black women of NWRO conceived of a very different world than their peers could imagine.[23]

Mothers at Work: Decent Jobs for Decent Pay

If, in the guaranteed income campaign, the scales leaned toward demands for income, in the later 1970s they would tip towards jobs. After FAP's failure, national welfare reform faded from Nixon's political agenda. And in the haze of Watergate, Vietnam, and growing resistance to antipoverty programs, guaranteed income disappeared into political obscurity. As the movement regrouped in the second half of the decade, members of organizations like New York's Downtown Welfare Advocacy Center (DWAC), formed in 1975 just as the NWRO shut down, would pick up the mantle. Dressed in Robin Hood costumes, protesters from DWAC picketed the New

York City welfare office and demanded "Decent Jobs for Decent Pay," a refrain that signified the movement's new orientation as it carried the campaign for welfare rights through the second half of the decade.[24]

In the mid-1970s, feminist antipoverty activism evolved and broadened. Local welfare rights groups took over from the NWRO. Leaders on the national stage shifted. And nearly a decade of work on poverty and welfare slowly produced greater understanding and awareness in other feminist organizations. Growing acknowledgment of the feminization of poverty thrust the issue ever more clearly into the women's movement camp. What the historian Marisa Chappell has termed the feminist antipoverty network took shape in the second half of the 1970s. This network included many welfare rights activists from local groups as well as national feminist organizations, traditional women's groups, and new coalition organizations advancing women's interests in Washington. NOW and Women's Lobby, Inc. both had full-time lobbyists dedicated to welfare reform, for example. All of the major national feminist and women's groups—NOW, NWPC, the Women's Equity Action League, the League of Women Voters, and women's religious groups—weighed in on Carter administration proposals. Welfare rights activists struggled at times to get their antipoverty priorities taken up by these other feminist groups. Even with the strengthened feminist antipoverty network, different emphases on income supports, employment, childcare, and parental leave made it challenging to work together. Those conflicts, however, prevented neither a working coalition nor general agreement that welfare was a women's issue in need of feminist-framed solutions.[25]

In 1976, signaling the network's mounting strength, welfare rights advocates joined forces with antipoverty feminists in mainstream feminist organizations to form the National Council on Women, Work, and Welfare. The group connected remaining local welfare activists nationwide and collected information on women and poverty. It opened an office in Washington, DC, where coalition members reported they brought administration officials and Congressional staffers together with low-income women to develop new ways of addressing women's poverty.[26]

The outlook forged in this new alliance represented feminist analysis of the interrelationship between welfare and the feminization of poverty. Colorado Congresswoman Pat Schroeder acquainted her fellow representatives with these new realities in 1977. Welfare "really is a woman's issue more and more," she informed them. "The fastest growing poverty group in America," she continued, "is not black, and it's not brown, it happens to be female." Nationally, female-headed households were rising as a proportion of the poor, with about one half of all households in poverty in 1978. In an influential 1978 article, "The Feminization of Poverty: Women, Work, and Welfare," the sociologist Diana Pearce elaborated the feminist argument: occupational segregation and labor-market inequality, in combination with pauper-level welfare benefits, left poor women trapped. Inadequate assistance forced them into wage work; "poverty-level" wages pushed them back on welfare.[27]

While the feminist antipoverty network never withdrew from the basic argument for a viable "*guaranteed livable income* for all poor people," employment moved to the fore for a variety of reasons.[28] Changing economic realities meant that virtually all women anticipated spending the majority of their adult lives in the labor force. Prioritizing income *over* jobs made less sense in that context. Feminism itself encouraged different aspirations and visions for women's lives, which public assistance recipients also embraced. At the same time, changes in the political climate made a major new income transfer program virtually inconceivable. Employment was more politically palatable.

However, in the late 1970s, welfare rights activists promoted not just *jobs*, but *decent* jobs, with *decent* pay. Ruby Duncan, a longtime Las Vegas welfare rights leader, informed the platform committee of the Democratic Party in 1976 that the jobs typically employing women—clerical, maid, and kitchen work—simply did not pay enough to lift a family out of poverty. Instead, she contended, "The Democratic Party must develop a national policy for full employment that includes us." As the battleground shifted, feminist antipoverty activists like Duncan insisted that employment had to be without coercion, in "meaningful, productive jobs," as one said during the November 1977 hearings on welfare reform. Existing poverty programs had failed by keeping their sightlines narrowly on male breadwinners, Maya Miller of Women's Lobby, Inc. informed the Democratic National Committee in 1976. Success lay in reconceptualizing jobs programs to meet the needs of recipient mothers.[29]

"In the new feminist vision of welfare reform, then," as the historian Marisa Chappell usefully summarizes, "calls for education, training, jobs, and child care had displaced the cry for 'welfare rights' as the central demand." Increasingly, activists drew attention to the structural barriers re-

cipients faced to holding jobs that would yield livable incomes for single
mothers. Eve Dembaugh, from Chicago's Women, Work & Welfare, told
the President's Commission for a National Agenda for the Eighties that her
status as a low-wage worker with limited skills and education meant
that work was never reliable or consistent. She explained that she inevitably had to move on and off public support if she was going to be able
to take a job at all, let alone support her children. What she needed was
"the security to go to work." As Ruby Duncan boiled it down for legislators, "The barriers [to moving out of welfare] have to be replaced with
bridges."[30]

In August 1977, President Jimmy Carter proposed the Program for Better
Jobs and Income to tackle the problem. In designing the plan, administration officials attempted to respond to both ongoing debate over full employment legislation—in an economy recovering from an unemployment
spike unprecedented in the postwar period—and mounting angst over a

"Pro Day Care and Welfare Demonstrator Confronts a KKK Member in Front
of Convention Center," by Bettye Lane. November 1977. The massive national
women's conference in Houston, Texas, brought women's advocates face to face
with conservative opponents in the rising pro-family movement. Welfare rights
proponents' signs show the demand for jobs that moved to the forefront of their
activism later in the 1970s.

so-called "family crisis," which skyrocketing divorce rates and growing numbers of female-headed houses portended. On the campaign trail, Jimmy Carter had vowed to reform welfare. His solution, however, remained rooted in assumptions about absent male breadwinners. Railing against AFDC as "a divisive force that the Government artificially imposes on the family system," one that "quite often benefit[s] handsomely the divided family," he promised Congress after he was elected to ensure "the dignity of useful work to family heads." Early names floated for PBJI included the telling "Jobs Security and Family Stability Plan." PBJI replaced AFDC with a two-tiered structure. The first—to be administered by the Department of Labor and targeted to households with married adults or school-age children—received a small annual income and job guarantees in the public sector if recipients could not secure a job in the labor market. The second "Income Support Tier," to be run by the Department of Health, Education, and Welfare, offered poor mothers of young children $4,200 for a family of four, an amount that the decade's high inflation still rendered well below the adequate income floor NWRO activists had set during the FAP campaign. Despite all of its guarantees, PBJI added only two million people to the thirty million already receiving some form of public assistance through welfare and other federal programs. Mostly, it redistributed payments away from AFDC recipients. The big winners were two-parent families now cast as the "working poor."[31]

Feminist antipoverty activists were horrified. AFDC recipients were sacrificial lambs to propping up male-breadwinning households, said one Pennsylvania welfare rights activist, denouncing the program. Nevertheless, they initially supported PBJI, hoping to improve its offensive features. Once finally formulated in legislation, however, they opposed it. The National Council on Women, Work, and Welfare concluded the system proposed was "more than deficient and inadequate, it [was] destructive."[32]

The meager supports for single mothers, along with highly constrained employment opportunities, worsened the situation for most current AFDC recipients. Women's Action Alliance warned its members in March 1978 that the Income Support Tier, where single mothers of small children would be assigned, promised a "subpoverty existence" with recipients in three-fourths of the states set to lose benefits. With their new jobs orientation, the feminist antipoverty network was also sharply critical of PBJI's limited work opportunities. According to the National Women's Agenda, single-mother beneficiaries of the program "would be served last, if at all, by the jobs program." Overwhelmingly, the new public service jobs created by the program would go to "principal earners" placed in the employable category, workers who were nearly all male. For those single mothers with older children who did gain employment, virtually no provision had been made for childcare. Carter administration officials, said Carol Payne of the League of Women Voters in 1977, had "decided that it is cheaper to keep women at home than to provide job opportunities."[33]

The feminist antipoverty network also criticized PBJI's "principal earner" provisions for discriminating against women. Prioritizing men had been a standard feature of federal job-training and employment programs. PBJI did the same, making jobs available only to a single primary earner in a household. Feminists called attention to the fact that because wives typically received lower wages than their husbands, just one in ten earned more than their partners.[34] The government effectively denied choice about employment within households because they had already decided which worker was eligible. The requirement also assumed that one low-wage income was enough for a household, an assumption increasingly questionable as economic changes weakened the earning power of men. Moreover, the absence of childcare virtually guaranteed that women would be kept out of the labor force. Feminists thus found PBJI objectionable on multiple counts. After nearly fifteen years of concerted second-wave feminist effort, the program went beyond merely privileging male earners: it put the government behind female economic dependence.

PBJI's sponsors were quite aware that the program maintained second-class status for women. The employment structure it set up presumed a female labor force permanently composed of secondary earners. In that, they misread the tea leaves of historical change. Ruth Clusen, the president of the League of Women Voters, could only conclude that Carter administration officials relied on an "outmoded conception of who the family breadwinner should be." The feminist Jo Freeman commented that policymakers simply failed to understand "that the principal economic unit is no longer, if it ever was, a two-adult family with only one primary wage earner." She warned them that they must stop assuming "economic dependency on men as the ultimate fallback position" and accept "the fact that all adults have a responsibility for the support of themselves and their children, regardless of their individual living situation." Even the president's own

Advisory Committee for Women identified the individual rather than the family as the appropriate unit for setting benefit levels.[35]

The women's welfare rights and antipoverty network countered with a feminist alternative. At the end of the 1970s, women's advocates narrowed their focus even more sharply toward the jobs that now seemed the best way to tackle poverty. A study completed in 1976 for the women's think tank the Center for Women Policy Studies laid out the policy options. It discarded those at the top of feminists' lists earlier in the decade—guaranteed incomes and expanded welfare to support poor women's full-time homemaking—before settling on "Strategy 4—full economic independence for women." The government needed to get out of the business of promoting male breadwinning and design policies supporting individuals. What kept women poor was sex discrimination in the labor market, occupational discrimination channeling them to low-paid sectors, and a dearth of education and training programs. "Moving to help women acquire these [economic] resources for themselves is the most direct solution to the problems which they face and which society faces with them." Welfare policy, the study determined, should not be family policy.[36] It was a double-edged conclusion. On the one hand, it showed the distance feminists and welfare rights champions had traveled from demanding mothers' rights to care for their children full time. The economy had changed; so had women's aspirations. Jobs now outweighed income. On the other hand, it reaffirmed feminists' decade-long fight to demand support for poor women apart from men.

Although a simple guaranteed income for mothering now seemed impossible to demand without greater emphasis on good jobs, women's antipoverty activists still insisted upon a robust system of supports for work and family life to complement employment. As debate over PBJI unfolded, feminists called for access to nontraditional jobs, rigorous sex-discrimination protections, full participation of single mothers in job provision and training programs, subsidized childcare, parental leave, and part-time and flex-time opportunities. All were "innovative things," Pat Schroeder insisted to her Congressional colleagues, which "just have not been looked at, because we still have the concept that every worker in America is a male supporting a family of four."[37]

PBJI never made it to a vote on the floor—in either the House or the Senate. By 1979, inflationary pressures made reining in the budget a Carter administration priority. Such a large social program could not muster support in this climate. Then, debate over welfare and poverty amelioration took a sharp new direction with Ronald Reagan's election a year later. Conservatives beholden to a new militant pro-family movement rejected the feminist vision of social policy based on women's individual autonomy rather than on the traditional male-breadwinner mold. Yet the arguments of the feminist antipoverty network about the feminization of poverty and the needs of women on welfare took hold. Women's activists would continue to push them from their now-established position within the liberal coalition.

WELFARE FACED EVEN stronger attacks in the 1980s and 1990s. In 1996, welfare, in the form of AFDC, came to an end. No able-bodied adult could receive long-term assistance any longer if he or she were poor. Yet the welfare rights and antipoverty feminists of the 1960s and 1970s bequeathed an important set of legacies.

As scholars have widely recognized, these activists showed that welfare is a women's issue and that antipoverty programs must address women's distinctive status. They also exposed the racism embedded in the system. Racism was built into social structures that impoverished black families and pushed high proportions of black and other mothers of color into the labor force. Moreover, as poor *women*, often with limited education and skills, they faced a sex-segregated and discriminatory job market. Many were funneled into domestic labor no matter what their qualifications. The very act of asserting the dignity and value of their mothering repudiated this racist system. In the face of the demeaning stereotypes of AFDC recipients, feminists emphasized that welfare mothers were neither lazy nor shiftless, but hard workers caring for their families, who deserved to be compensated for their labor. Poor women, particularly poor women of color, had a right to choose their lives. Welfare rights and antipoverty activists decried the racial and class bias that celebrated "motherhood" but denied poor minority women that role.

Building on this analysis of welfare's biases, antipoverty feminists demanded public assistance programs that supported women's economic independence. They made the second wave's most forceful case for jobs good enough that mothers could provide for their children on their own. Ruby

Duncan, the powerful Las Vegas activist, chastised Senators at hearings on full employment legislation in 1976: "Don't create jobs that I don't qualify for. Remember that traditional qualifications of white and male exclude me. A job that forces me to abandon my children to the streets is not acceptable. A job must provide a decent wage so that health care and child care are possible." Welfare reform, Beulah Sanders had bitingly warned legislators at the beginning of the decade, "must not be a vehicle for subsidizing slave wage employers at the expense of poor people."[38]

This feminist struggle stands alongside the second wave's other efforts to transform workplaces to make them work for families, such as maternity protections and flexible schedules. By the late 1970s, feminist antipoverty proponents offered a comprehensive vision of what was required for true access to jobs that would lift women out of poverty: income supports, education, training, eradication of employment discrimination, and support services, especially for children. In the process, second-wave activists imagined a new system of shared private and public action to meet the basic needs of American families.

Those actions did not depend on men. Feminists rejected the establishment's assumption that the solution to poverty lay in changing men's circumstances to make them *the* household breadwinner. In part, women's antipoverty campaigners were fighting against the stigmatization of black-female-headed families. But undercutting the male-breadwinner norm was also part of the broader feminist goal to erase society's expectation of female dependency.

Welfare rights activists claimed the right to a basic living that would enable all women to care for their children should they choose. As Johnnie Tillmon proclaimed, "women's work is *real* work." Pay "women a living wage for doing the work we are already doing—child-raising and housekeeping."[39] Second-wave feminists also demanded childcare, maternity leave, and flexible work schedules to support mothers, but from the perspective of combining parenting with paid jobs. Welfare rights and antipoverty feminists started from a different point on the spectrum of feminist claims to remake family and work. They radically reconceived who bore responsibility for caring for children by pushing male breadwinners and female dependents out of the center of policy thinking. Instead, they envisioned a world where, regardless of wealth or race, individual women had the opportunity to support themselves and their children with any mix of state assistance, paid work, or a partner's contribution they preferred.

Without remembering this vision, we fail to appreciate the radical deconstruction and reorganization of social life proposed by second-wave activists, as well as the encompassing vision for which they fought.

6

CHILDCARE

Feminists Pursue Childcare as a Universal Right

Universal day care, after-school care NOW! WORKING
MOTHERS UNITE! FOR YOURSELVES! FOR YOUR CHILDREN!
—*The Working Mother*, 1971

HEAVY INCENSE BURNED REGULARLY at Liberation Nursery, which occupied a rundown storefront on New York's Lower East Side. The nursery's organizers had scraped together enough money to rent and clean up the building on East 6th Street, then carted away the trash piled in the back, plastered and painted the walls, and installed shelves they stocked with toys. Heating was unreliable in the winter. Toilets overflowed, and the incense burned in a vain effort to cover up the smell of a rat rotting in the wall. It was hardly an auspicious beginning. Yet Liberation Nursery thrived on the passion of its parent organizers, who were determined to meet the needs of mothers and children in new ways. Liberation Nursery was one of dozens of underground, illegal daycare centers started by feminists and community activists in New York City and, indeed, across the country in a burst of grassroots activism. Nurseries, explained one Liberation Nursery founder, Rosalyn Baxandall, had cropped up in "apartments, storefronts, churches, community centers, basements—everywhere and anywhere there was space."[1]

Rosalyn Baxandall's work with Liberation Nursery attracted the attention of Betty Friedan, who summoned her to her apartment in the elegant Dakota building overlooking Central Park. Friedan peppered Baxandall with questions about her efforts at the nursery. She hoped Baxandall would do something for NOW on childcare, but Baxandall wasn't interested. NOW, she thought, should do its own thing. Baxandall's audience with Friedan was something of a bellwether. A couple of years later, Bella Abzug got in touch with a request to organize a daycare center in her campaign headquarters. This time Baxandall agreed. It was just the beginning. "We started one in Washington Square Church. We started lots of them all over New York," she boasted.[2]

In radical women's liberation groups, as well as in NOW chapters and women's groups across the country, second-wave feminists tackled the question of daycare. They knew that without it, the movement itself was doomed, as were larger transformations in women's lives and true equality. An outlook that redefined the core meaning of childcare blossomed out of that sense of urgent need. Like public schools, like libraries, like parks, feminists contended, daycare should exist as a basic public service available to all, whether poor or wealthy, on public assistance or self-supporting, employed or simply needing time to oneself. For over a decade, from the late 1960s through the 1970s, feminists sought to breathe life into that right through sustained—at times national, at other times highly localized—activism for childcare. Their efforts spanned do-it-yourself community efforts and a campaign for national legislation, a campaign that led to one of the most heartbreaking losses of the movement.

"Now Is the Hour for Universal Child Care": Making Childcare a Right

In July 1970 Florence Falk-Dickler, Coordinator of the NOW Task Force on Child Care, rallied the organization's chapters to join the fight for childcare. Now is the time to act, she wrote, as she invoked feminists' bold demand for a new right: universal childcare.[3] The feminist cry for twenty-four-hour, community-controlled childcare developed in a political landscape that had been shifting over the previous decade. At the end of the 1960s, community activists, early childhood specialists, and child welfare advocates also ramped up their demands for broadened public support of childcare. While they did not embrace a vision of women's rights as expansive as feminists', they nonetheless joined them in reframing the rationale for public support. Childcare, all these activists now agreed, delivered not merely a service for the most needy or dysfunctional households. Rather, it was a right, and one that should give mothers choices about whether to work or not.

The child welfare coalition had revived its campaign to expand government-funded daycare for working mothers in the early 1960s, before second-wave activism took off. Federal support had been nonexistent since the end of World War II, when nurseries set up during the war closed their doors. Local and state funding was hit or miss and limited in scope.[4] In 1960, the newly formed National Committee for the Day Care of Children put the issue on the agenda at two national conferences—one on youth and another specifically dedicated to daycare. Speakers at the two meetings pointed out that the number of working mothers had doubled in the previous decade and that advocates needed to begin selling rather than apologizing for daycare.[5]

Widespread awareness of exploding maternal employment met deep-seated ambivalence about its moral rightness and effects. In fact, opponents of daycare funding feared it would "recruit" mothers into the paid labor force. The conferences produced Janus-faced recommendations. They acknowledged that the nation needed more daycare for both needy children *and* working mothers, on the one hand; on the other, they issued a call for counseling "to help parents decide wisely whether [the mother's] employment will contribute more to family welfare than her presence in the home."[6] Similar anxiety pervaded debate in the committees of the President's Commission on the Status of Women in 1962 and 1963. Daniel Patrick Moynihan, speaking as assistant secretary in the Department of Labor, vowed that any alteration of tax deductions for childcare must not "indicate any desire to arrange the tax laws so that wives are encouraged to get jobs." In 1962, the first federal funds allocated to childcare since World War II came attached to the Public Welfare Amendments. They were restricted to services for women on public assistance. So, while all early-1960s advocates justified calls for government funding of daycare by citing astronomical growth in the numbers of mothers employed, few viewed this rationale as unequivocally good. They rarely advanced expanding childcare slots as necessary for mothers' rights. Yet the argument was beginning to be promulgated.[7]

"Day Care Demonstration at City Hall," by Bettye Lane. April 17, 1975. Protesting in New York City, these women and children reiterate feminists' resonant call "to make day care a right."

In the same years, early childhood education specialists more forcefully made the case that preschool years were pivotal for child development, insisting to federal officials that children needed far more than custodial care. Early childhood education, they asserted, could counter the negative effects of poverty and family instability. Congress was persuaded. In 1965 it allocated funds to Head Start, a preschool program for poor children, as part of the expanding War on Poverty. Modeled on nursery schools rather than daycare centers, the program focused on children's needs, not those of employed parents. Head Start enjoyed widespread grassroots support, as many parents and community activists saw it as an integral part of the War on Poverty. By convincing many middle-class families of the benefits of early childhood education, Head Start also broadened the base of support for publicly funded childcare.[8]

Thus as the women's movement launched, groundwork had been laid, however tentative, for thinking about childcare on new terms. "True equality of opportunity and freedom of choice for women requires such practical, and possible innovations as a nationwide network of child-care centers." This was the gauntlet the National Organization for Women threw down in its statement of purpose on October 29, 1966. Pointedly sidestepping the educational and caretaking needs of children and the economic pressures pushing mothers into the workplace—issues that preoccupied others—NOW stressed what was necessary for equality. Women could have "true equality of opportunity and responsibility in society, without conflict with their responsibilities as mothers and homemakers," *only* if American society innovated new institutions to meet their needs—just as European countries had been doing for decades.[9]

This claim had even deeper implications. "If women are to participate on an equitable basis with men in the world of work and of community service," NOW's Task Force on the Family reported a year later, then childcare centers had to be like all community facilities, freely available "to be used or not used at the discretion of individual parents."[10] The Bill of Rights adopted by the organization at its November 1967 convention put universal childcare as a public entitlement at the center of its formal vision for equality. "We Demand," NOW members declared, "that child care facilities be established by law on the same basis as parks, libraries and public schools adequate to the needs of children, from the pre-school years through adolescence, as a community resource to be used by all citizens from all income levels."[11] Childcare had been substantially reframed.

Universal, community-controlled, free, round-the-clock childcare, available to all members of society, emerged as a unifying political demand of second-wave feminists. It was axiomatic for radical feminists. The Third World Women's Alliance pointed out that twenty-four-hour childcare mattered for women who worked at night, and at the First National Chicana Conference, the six hundred women attending endorsed free childcare available day and night.[12] In November 1969, five hundred women from Massachusetts to Maryland gathered in New York for the first ever Congress to Unite Women. Organizers convened similar meetings in Los Angeles, San Francisco, and Chicago. In New York, NOW, women's liberation groups, feminist lawyers, and members of the Socialist Workers Party were among the more than two dozen groups represented. The Congress unanimously called for "nationwide free twenty-four-hour-a-day child care centers for all children from infancy to early adolescence regardless of their parents' income or marital status." This demand connected to feminists' aspirations to reshape family life as much as it did to their desire to open employment opportunities for women. Equal staffing by men and women was essential, the Congress maintained, "to encourage the breakdown of sex role stereotypes." For those working in the centers, "their wages should be equal to those of public school teachers." At the top of their list for "priority in political attention": childcare.[13]

Welfare rights activists supported universal childcare as well, although they emphasized both poor women's greater economic need for daycare and the importance of community control for minority areas. The NWRO circulated a pamphlet to local welfare rights organizations on "How to Organize a Comprehensive Community Controlled Child Care Program." Some local welfare rights activists in California dedicated themselves to childcare activism alongside agitating for welfare reform. Espanola Jackson, president of California Welfare Rights, for example, sought to set up community-controlled daycare centers in her San Francisco neighborhood, which she believed could give jobs to welfare recipients from the children's own community. Although Jackson and others saw such employment as an opportunity for poor women, Johnnie Tillmon warned fellow feminists not to assume that mothers on welfare would become a cheap labor pool to staff such centers.[14]

Universal childcare topped the list of feminist demands in the August 1970 Strike for Equality. Strike fact sheets highlighted the appalling inadequacies of existing childcare. Slots failed to come close to meeting the need; nearly half of the states had no publicly funded childcare; two million children were consigned to "poor" or "inadequate" facilities; and the cost of private care ate up one-third to more than one-half of the average full-time working woman's salary. To prove the point, strike actions included setting up impromptu, ad hoc daycare centers across the country. City Hall in New York received a batch of preschoolers, while women deposited their toddlers on the desk of Mayor Lee Alexander in Syracuse, New York. The strike nurtured both sides of feminist claims to childcare as a right. Some drew attention to childcare's critical importance for working parents; others rejected the limited horizons and lack of choices that the absence of childcare meant for *all* women. Karen DeCrow, later president of NOW, remembered that the strikers demanded universal, twenty-four-hour childcare, for "no woman can be at home in the world when her total world is the home."[15]

The Fight for the Comprehensive Child Development Act

At the end of 1970, child welfare advocates, together with feminists, civil rights activists, and antipoverty activists, catapulted the issue of childcare into the national limelight at the White House Conference on Children, giving a boost to comprehensive childcare legislation that was beginning to make its way through Congress. Presidents had sponsored these meetings every ten years since the early twentieth century to showcase the developmental, educational, and health needs of children and youth. Four thousand attendees gathered in Washington, DC, bringing delegations from every state together with a lively array of young people, community organizers, minority groups, and liberal activists. Participants at the conference voted to endorse federal funding for a comprehensive childcare assistance program as its top issue of "overriding concern."[16] In the months leading up to the conference, NOW activists had worked feverishly behind the scenes to put childcare front and center during the meeting and to shape a recommendation that reflected the feminist perspective on childcare as a universal right.

NOW had formed its Task Force on Child Care after its second national conference in 1967, when Florence Falk-Dickler, a young woman from New Jersey, approached Betty Friedan arguing that the organization must address childcare if it wanted to secure equality for women.[17] The task force envisioned a range of activities, from forming chapter daycare committees to lobbying elected officials at the local and state levels. Falk-Dickler encouraged NOW members to work with area childcare advocacy groups and labor unions to ensure that programs in their areas were high quality, served a wide range of social and economic groups, and took advantage of all public funding possible. In May 1970, Falk-Dickler stepped up the committee's activities. She called on local NOW chapter presidents to demand that regional Women's Bureau offices follow up on promised childcare consultations, and she urgently advised NOW members to petition governors in each state to appoint a NOW representative to the upcoming White House Conference.[18]

By the middle of that summer, NOW's national offices were deep into the issue, and Falk-Dickler began preparations for her work on "Forum #17"—the group working on the question of daycare for the White House Conference. NOW's Board doubled the task force's budget and engaged in a lengthy back-and-forth about what official position to take to the conference.[19] The Board's internal debate echoed conflict with the larger childcare coalition over whether to insist on universally available daycare or to pragmatically accept more limited programs for the neediest. Board members also struggled with how to counter hostile reports that demands for twenty-four-hour childcare meant that feminists advocated abdicating mothers' involvement in their children's lives.

How to frame a claim for women's autonomy, choices, and full participation in society without conveying disregard for children was a thorny dilemma. A compromise position emerged that repeated the demand for universally available childcare but agreed to sliding-scale fees for those above a certain income level. NOW also reiterated that high-quality developmental childcare benefitted children, alongside stating its urgent need for women's full citizenship. The compromise hammered out internally was essential for the alliance that NOW sought to build with black child-welfare organizations and with daycare groups like the National Black Child Development Institute and the Day Care and Child Development Council of America.[20] Falk-Dickler and the president of NOW, Wilma Scott Heide, met in advance of the conference to caucus with these groups, which they joined in advancing the final resolution endorsed by the conference. At the White House Conference, Heide and NOW also led an independent

Women's Caucus, which issued a forceful statement "rejecting the idea that mothers have the primary responsibility for child-rearing and a special child care role not to be shared by fathers," while calling for "a national system of quality, comprehensive child care and developmental services . . . developed [not] in order to lessen public assistance rolls but rather as a basic right."[21]

"Though we were few in number," Florence Falk-Dickler reported exultantly to the Board after the conference, "feminists did make things happen there." "The Women's Caucus," she marveled, "made it abundantly clear that the absence of high quality child care is *institutionalized sexism*." "It may be said," she announced with some bravado, that "we touched as many bases as we could in a game that continued far beyond the usual nine innings." Looking forward, Falk-Dickler called on the Board to offer "our continual and vociferous support" for universal childcare legislation planned for the next Congress. The Board responded by making childcare its number one legislative priority for 1971, replacing the Equal Rights Amendment, which had been the group's top goal in 1970.[22]

As liberal feminists geared up for the fight, radical feminists directed their energies elsewhere. Radical second-wavers generally eschewed national-level, legislative childcare activism in favor of battling local and state bureaucrats. Dorothy Pitman Hughes organized the citywide Committee for Community-Controlled Day Care in New York. Formed in early 1969 to network and to protest actions by the city, the group brought together over 150 community groups planning to open daycare centers. Pitman Hughes had founded her own center on West 80th Street in 1966 and went on to be active in feminist organizations, traveling with Gloria Steinem in the early 1970s and joining the National Black Feminist Organization. She objected to esoteric licensing procedures as well as the patronizing treatment city officials dished out in requiring licensed centers to investigate children's families' personal and financial histories. Still, with their shoestring budgets, the black and Latina women operating centers such as Pitman Hughes's generally welcomed state funding, as long as the community retained control of the centers. Keeping centers in the hands of the neighborhood ensured quality and guarded against racism and ethnic bias.[23]

"We blocked traffic and held a nursery in the streets to make our demand for day care publically known," Rosalyn Baxandall remembered. The Committee for Community-Controlled Day Care organized sit-ins, populated by small children as well as mothers, in the offices of New York City officials. By the end of 1970, the city had agreed to fund the community centers.[24] Los Angeles organizers also took on state and local officials to allow parents to open a cooperative daycare program in one of the city's working-class neighborhoods. Heather Booth and Day Piercy of the Chicago Women's Liberation Union led a similarly successful interracial feminist campaign, the Action Committee for Decent Childcare, which targeted the city's byzantine rules and paltry funding for daycare. They won a review of city licensing codes and kept several neighborhood centers open. The committee also supported welfare rights advocates (discussed in Chapter 5) and prepared to resist the "forced childcare for women on welfare" that they anticipated being handed down from the national level if new work requirements for welfare recipients were instituted.[25]

As this local activism burgeoned, federal legislation also claimed feminists' attention. Congress had begun to consider a childcare bill in 1969, but the Comprehensive Child Development Act (CCDA) gained traction only in 1971. By then it looked like everything was in place to smooth its passage. Polls in 1969 and 1970 had shown hefty majorities of American men and women supporting more federally funded childcare centers. The coalition lobbying for the bill had strong leadership from Marian Wright Edelman of the Children's Defense Fund, but it also counted child welfare, social welfare, civil rights, and traditional women's groups among its members, as well as labor unions and welfare rights organizations. NOW belonged too.[26]

Most histories of the campaign for the Comprehensive Child Development Act argue that feminists were secondary partners, at best, in the coalition. It is true that radical feminists kept their focus at the local level. And while others, particularly child welfare and antipoverty activists, were at the forefront of the CCDA coalition, NOW records indicate strong action behind the scenes, especially in keeping the feminist perspective on childcare in the conversation. Edelman told interviewers in 1974 that the women's movement in general, and NOW in particular, was a major force for better childcare. Initially, NOW preferred a bill introduced by Bella Abzug and Shirley Chisholm, but in the end it put all its resources into the CCDA. The organization's leadership lobbied hard for the bill and mobilized the group's membership on its behalf.

The reports and memories of feminist marginalization likely stem from the significant disagreement within the coalition about the feminist focus on universal childcare. Seasoned children's advocates leading the coalition thought feminists had an unrealistic goal. Moreover, the child welfare position emerged from commitments to civil rights and antipoverty work that prioritized meeting the needs of the most vulnerable. Marian Wright Edelman recalled scathing criticism from welfare rights activists angered by "middle-class liberationists who . . . wanted time to go to an art gallery." From this perspective, the universal childcare claims of women's groups seemed to place affluent and middle-class women's needs ahead of poor children's. Moreover, child welfare and mainstream antipoverty activists were not as interested in changing the family or in challenging the male-breadwinner norm as feminists. Their position echoed the liberal policy consensus during the same years over the Family Assistance Plan (as we saw in Chapter 5), in which feminist focus on female autonomy and self-support remained an outlier position.[27]

NOW leaders were well aware of this conflict with others within the coalition. They strove to advance their claims to universalism, explain its validity as a vision of transformative equity for women *and* children (not simply as selfish classism), and manage internal conflicts within NOW over whether or not to stick to their guns on their ultimate goal of universalism or compromise for practical necessity. NOW and the daycare leadership continued to seek common ground and work together even after the CCDA lobbying blitz. The Day Care and Child Development Council of America was printing the NOW position paper on childcare in its national publications at least into early 1973.[28]

NOW made sure the feminist perspective was heard in debate over the bill. President Wilma Scott Heide stated NOW's support to the House Committee on Education and Labor; Vicki Lathom, from the Board of Directors, delivered a NOW statement to several Senate subcommittee hearings and circulated the feminist position paper rolled out at the White House Conference, "Why Feminists Want Child Care," to legislators. "Developmental child care services are a right of children, parents, and the community at large," this policy statement announced, before drawing attention to universal childcare's benefits for all members of society. Women's fight for equality foundered without it, but children, too, would be hindered: "In a circular fashion, the development of children has been intimately influenced by the development of women." NOW thus staked a position for social supports for daycare that started from the mother's perspective. With childcare, women gained the possibility for equality *and* children gained mothers better able to parent them to fuller lives.[29]

On Mother's Day, 1971, NOW staged a rally in front of the White House that drew 150 mothers and children. Denver chapter members joined the march, pushing "baby buggies, strollers, [and] wagons." Children and mothers chanted together, "Power to the mothers! Power to the children!"[30] As debate drew to a close in the fall, NOW Washington staff sent out regular updates to members, asking chapter leaders in target states to lobby their legislators vigorously. By late fall, the legislation made its way through Congress, but as the coalition awaited President Nixon's signature, it seemed increasingly likely that he might veto it despite the administration having declared support for it earlier in the year. Once again, NOW circulated an urgent letter asking members to call on the president to sign the bill.[31]

Opposition to the bill had two dimensions. In Congress, supporters and opponents split sharply on the size of the units to receive federal funds— smaller, local, units, where community-controlled centers would predominate, or larger, city- or state-level units, where urban and state officials would retain control. Conservative opponents feared the smaller units would introduce another mandate for racially integrated state-sponsored centers and preschools. Veiled resistance to civil rights advances helped mobilize Congressional and administration dissenters. A second reason for seeking to scuttle the CCDA came from the gathering forces of the New Right, who rejected a new liberal entitlement and its feminist thrust. This conservative opposition could rely on a strong backer in the administration—the White House advisor and speechwriter Pat Buchanan—as well as vocal support from the conservative press and newly mobilized parents groups. The energy that coalesced against the CCDA provided the early impetus for the "pro-family" movement that would come together later in the decade. Paul Weyrich, the wily New Right strategist, claimed the effort to persuade Nixon to veto the bill opened his eyes—and those of many others as well—to the power of anti-feminism and defense of the family to mobilize grassroots conservatives.[32]

By the time the bill reached Nixon's desk, the White House had been deluged with letters denouncing it as an "invasion of the family." Nixon ultimately agreed. On December 9, 1971, he vetoed the legislation. In his official announcement, Nixon ignored the race-driven, anti-community-control reasons for opposing the CCDA. Instead, he delivered a sermon about the family. To sign this bill, he preached, would "commit the vast moral authority of the National Government to the side of communal approaches to child-rearing over against the family centered approach." In crafting such a rejection of the bill, rising conservatives within the Nixon administration made evident how universal childcare embodied a feminist challenge to the male-breadwinning ideal. Against the feminist vision in NOW's policy statement "that the care and welfare of children is incumbent on society and parents," Nixon insisted that the government must "cement the family in its rightful position as the keystone of our civilization."[33]

The tenor of President Nixon's veto made reviving the CCDA out of the question, and another round of national action on childcare became politically untenable. CCDA sponsor Representative John Brademas declared that the attack on nationally funded daycare "poisoned the well for early childhood programs" for many years to come. Efforts to reintroduce legislation in 1975 and 1979 went nowhere. Yet within one day of vetoing the CCDA, President Nixon signed the Revenue Act. It expanded tax relief for dependent care costs for those itemizing deductions on their taxes, committing the government to a two-stream path for supporting childcare. Middle-class families would receive tax benefits to underwrite the costs of private daycare, while poor women would get direct federal subsidies, increasingly linked to measures pressuring them to enter the labor force. Indeed, Congressional supporters of the new tax deductions touted their job-creating potential for those on public assistance. Deliberation over the Revenue Act recapitulated elements of the CCDA debate and supporters consistently tied the tax benefit to enabling *mothers* to get paid jobs to supplement inadequate earnings by their husbands. Opponents feared that result. They fought to block any proposal that might encourage women to seek employment. As with the debate in the same year for the Family Assistance Plan discussed in Chapter 5, policies that shook the foundations of the male-breadwinner ideal fired up opposition.[34] Conservative success in overturning the CCDA became one of the women's movement's biggest defeats—as well as a boost to the movement's strongest opponents.

"Day Care Centers on Every Corner":
Childcare from the Bottom Up

The political defeat of the CCDA, however, was neither the beginning nor the end of on-the-ground feminist childcare advocacy. Away from the high politics of Washington, women's activists built center after center in their communities. The cooperative daycare centers Rosalyn Baxandall and others fought for in New York were only the tip of the iceberg in the nationwide, grassroots creation of a new childcare infrastructure. A do-it-yourself ethos sprung up in storefront cooperative centers, in church basements, in YWCAs—anywhere organizers could cajole sponsors to give them space. Women's groups across the country founded centers wherever they worked, studied, and lived. Local and statewide political activism continued, with feminists often working in coordination with other community organizations to take advantage of any and all available funding. Second-wavers fought to hold on to the vision of universal childcare as a social right, while striving to meet the growing need for childcare as maternal employment skyrocketed.

Liberation Nursery exemplified the cooperative tradition that radical feminists dominated.[35] The center was organized by neighbors on the Lower East Side, many of them hippies, all of them white (although several were married to black men), but joining together "split people" like Rosalyn Baxandall, who had a career, with those who "felt that children came first." Initially, only Baxandall was heavily involved in women's liberation. Yet, she said, "women, including myself, were willing to exert great effort and energy starting nurseries for our own infants and kids because there were no nurseries available and many women like myself were desperate for some relief. We were slowly going crazy taking care of our children alone in our apartments." Liberation Nursery, like most of the cooperative centers shooting up in the period, existed because of parent involvement. The fees were low, as parents ran the centers—volunteering weekly, fixing up the place on weekends, and attending monthly or even weekly meetings to hash out everything from finances to philosophy. Liberation Nursery, Baxandall emphasized, was designed to solve childcare problems not by hiring nannies but through shared community service.[36]

The cooperative centers varied in their approach to children, with some organizing structured curricula and others far more free-form and flexible.

Philosophy could change from day to day, as at the West Village Cooperative Day Care Center, where depending on the mothers present, a day at the center could be organized by "educational traditionalists" or by "radicals further left than Summerhill."[37] For women's liberationists involved in cooperative centers, creating nonsexist environments and instruction was also very important. At Liberation Nursery, girls and boys played with dolls *and* trucks, while parent volunteers avoided traditional sex-typing. They were, however, less successful in getting sustained involvement by men in the nursery, which was one of women's liberationists' goals for childcare. Lesbians sometimes objected to the heterosexual bias of childcare centers. In Washington, DC, members of the Furies collective called for a "continual gay presence so children can see women loving women and men loving men." Separatist lesbian groups frequently arranged for boys and girls to have separate childcare at many of their events, a practice designed to fulfill their commitment to woman-only spaces where sex roles could be broken down, but one which remained controversial among lesbian communities.[38]

While the involvement of radical women like Baxandall in daycare had everything to do with freeing mothers, it had little to do with enabling mothers to work nine-to-five jobs. There was an exhilarating sense of possibility behind the centers. "Mothers get a lot of advantages from day care," Baxandall marveled in 1971. "They get to meet other women in their neighborhood and have some free time. Everyone should have this. (Rich women always have been hiring other women to watch their kids). Mothers can work, go back to school, talk to friends, shop, or work in the women's movement. Whatever it is she has always wanted to do." Of course, wage earning was acceptable, even beneficial to the extent that it opened up horizons and provided mothers with stimulation, but radical women's liberationists imagined idealistically that new forms of family, community, and employment would develop as horizons expanded. A certain cluelessness about poor and working-class women's motivations in seeking daycare colored Baxandall's vision. But she shared with most radicals the conviction that all women, including those on welfare, deserved time for themselves, away from children. "We did think," she recollected, "that there must be a better way than to imitate careerist men—not that we knew what that was." But nine-to-five jobs, no, "we certainly didn't want that." The radical Deborah Babcox even went so far as to identify full-time childcare for full-time working mothers who came home to the double burden of housework as a kind of feminist dystopia.[39]

Opponents accused radical feminists of being anti-child, and some in the movement remember painful discussions about welcoming children and supporting mothers in the movement. Baxandall recalled that much of her daycare activism did take place separately from the actions of her women's groups. "I enjoyed my separate universes," she reminisced, "and didn't want them linked." Most of the women in Baxandall's feminist circle were still unmarried and not yet thinking about parenting; some struggled with ambivalence about their own mothers' fettered lives and their desire for more choice in their own lives. Age and life stage were typically the factors that drew young women's liberationists into childcare activism. "Most radical feminists were not anti-child," emphasized Baxandall, "they simply ignored children."[40]

Despite the lukewarm enthusiasm of some radical feminists, a daycare network blossomed among radical women's liberationists starting in 1968. One short-lived group connected activists from New Haven, Boston, and New York to work on daycare. It held conferences and issued pamphlets, with one of its members, Phyllis MacEwan, going on to co-author one of the most widely reprinted pieces on daycare in the movement, "On Day Care," which first appeared in *Women: A Journal of Liberation* in 1970.[41] Rosalyn Baxandall helped circulate radical positions on daycare by publishing several pieces in leading women's liberation newsletters.[42] Radical groups also started up dozens of daycare centers across the country. New York Radical Women splintered early in 1969, when several women formed The New Woman to organize around daycare and job discrimination. In Chapel Hill, North Carolina, the Community School for People Under 6 was up and running, organized by Chapel Hill Female Liberation. An activist from Milwaukee, Wisconsin wrote the North Carolina women requesting advice. She wanted to start a "Radical Day Care Center" in her own low-income neighborhood. Dayton, Ohio Women's Liberation members set up their own childcare cooperative. In *New York Magazine* in 1971, Susan Edmiston described the movement's goal as daycare "centers on every corner and the proliferation of various kinds of day care: 24-hour day care, weekend day care, vacation programs, after-school programs, and infant day care."[43]

When Rosalyn Baxandall's son entered public school, she gratefully withdrew from vigorous daycare activism. She had no involvement in lobbying for the CCDA. Yet when she began a new job at the State University of New York, she rallied to organize a childcare center there, joining the ranks of mainstream, liberal feminists setting up centers anywhere and everywhere they could. Liberation Nursery received permanent city funding in 1972.[44]

FEMINISTS AND WOMEN'S GROUPS of virtually every stripe poured their energies into childcare centers. NOW chapters started them, as did unions. Welfare rights organizations, lesbian communities, and feminists inside schools, colleges, and workplaces demanded them. Detroit NOW spearheaded a Conference to Sensitize and Educate Legislators on the Need for Child Care in October 1972. Michigan's governor proclaimed a "Statewide Child Care Day" the next spring. The NOW efforts in Detroit persuaded city and county officials to create a community childcare council that would be eligible for matching state and federal funds. Detroit's chapter was not alone in trying to leverage funds from local and state political systems. In California, Illinois, New York, Michigan, Florida, and New Jersey, and Washington, DC, among other states, women's activists forged ongoing childcare coalitions to organize actions and press for legislation. NOW started or sponsored centers in Brookline, Massachusetts; Princeton, New Jersey; Danbury, Connecticut; Queens, New York; Cleveland, Ohio; and Wichita, Kansas, to name just a few.[45]

Community-oriented and poor-women's groups continued to open centers as well. The Johnnie Tillmon Child Development Center in Los Angeles, named after the welfare rights leader, opened after a decade of effort in 1974. Dorothy Pitman Hughes claimed her center had provided some four hundred mothers on welfare with the childcare they wanted and needed by early 1972.[46] Community colleges and universities had some of the most active campaigns. At Contra Costa College in San Pablo, California; Peralta Junior College in Berkeley, California; the University of New Mexico; Ohio State University; Florida State University; Portland State University in Oregon; and the University of Massachusetts at Boston, among many others, student, faculty, and community parent groups went to work on university officials. A group of student mothers at Wayne State University in Detroit changed diapers on the university president's desk to protest the lack of campus housing for them. They went on to form a feminist cooperative center.[47]

"The Lollipop People. A Case for Child Care NOW!" Circa 1972. NOW created "Lollipop People" in the early 1970s as an "educational and fundraising tool" and used it throughout the decade. With 125 color slides and a full "Child Care Action Kit," this how-to resource included scripts on "why child care programs benefit children, their parents, and the community" and publicity materials for presentations to schools and colleges, hospitals, businesses, and the public.

The Coalition of Labor Union Women pushed for employer-sponsored childcare in collective bargaining agreements, and in 1979 helped to organize a labor conference on childcare in honor of the International Year of the Child. Women's liberationists' childcare actions at Indiana University inspired workers at Westinghouse and General Electric to seek release time to work in cooperative childcare centers. Best known were the daycare centers won by the Amalgamated Clothing Workers in the area around Baltimore, Maryland.[48] A few activists raised concerns about the rise of corporate, for-profit daycare rather than community-controlled centers, including fear that the growth of these centers would pull federal funds away from nonprofit community centers, but they ultimately failed to rally a major movement to stop their expansion.[49]

SEATTLE PROVIDES A good example of how feminists' grassroots childcare activism evolved over the decade. From their earliest days, radical women's liberation groups in Seattle joined forces with liberal feminists and mainstream women's organizations like the YWCA to make childcare widely available. Women's Liberation Seattle took as one of its first issues the fight for free childcare for faculty, staff, and students at the University of Washington. It seemed a logical choice: many of the group's members were connected to the university, which was the second largest employer in the city. One participant, Wanda Adams, director of the North Seattle YWCA and a member of Seattle Radical Feminists, was a white mother of three in her early thirties who had been drawn into women's liberation when she returned to school to study social work. When the university president told to the group to "take their demands to society at large," Wanda Adams reminded him that "the University is part of society and as such must accept its responsibility for the resolution of such problems."[50]

Off campus, the city's NOW chapter, formed in 1970, forged a coalition with the King County Child Care Coordinating Committee, which worked to manage local, state, and federal childcare resources. The two groups sponsored a day-long "Child Care Workshop" in December 1971 under the slogan "Quality Child Care: The Right of Every Family." They undoubtedly drew on the nearly forty-page "Child Care Syllabus" the chapter had produced. The workshop walked participants through issues different from those at Liberation Nursery; rather than focusing on community control, unfair licensing rules, and street protests, the Seattle activists' main concerns were types of childcare services, working with public officials, the logistics of setting up a center, and "feasibility and cost."[51]

As chapter president of NOW in 1972, Elaine Day LaTourelle steered the chapter's involvement with childcare in the post-Nixon veto era. "NOW," she would say, "is dedicated to working within the system and when that doesn't work, to raising hell." Over the course of the 1970s, NOW members became deeply embedded in city advocacy positions and participated in an overlapping group of women's leaders.[52] One such chapter member was Jackie Griswold, a white public-school teacher in inner-city Philadelphia and Seattle. In many ways a classic liberal feminist working from within the system on childcare, Griswold brought a deep commitment to children—particularly in low-income and minority communities—to her activism. Her first foray into organizing was with the League of Women Voters in 1971, when she was forty; a year later, she joined NOW, where she took on leadership for coordinating the chapter's ERA advocacy. Friends described her as "analytical, precise, and a tenacious feminist," "a person concerned with questions of justice and equity."[53]

In 1973, she applied to serve on the Seattle Women's Commission, where she chaired the Joint Committee on Child Care from 1975–1976 and was the commission's president the following year. One of her major achievements was discovering a cache of underutilized state funds that the city could use to finance services. They were badly needed as licensed centers in the city grew from 70 in 1970 to 186 in 1975. Griswold also guided the commission through a yearlong review of childcare in the city beginning in 1976. A key question was the need for childcare by the city government's clerical workers, and in a recommendation that seems prescient, the commission called for allowing city workers to use sick leave to care for their children when they were ill. They also proposed legislation placing all children's services under a single agency.[54]

The commission's efforts resulted in less progress than Griswold and other feminists had hoped. "Reception hasn't been all that exciting," one member observed, and the city council never advanced the proposed legislation out of committee. Unexpectedly, a growing constituency in the daycare world—women running small home-based daycare centers—objected to commission efforts to affiliate them with larger daycare centers. One committee member delivered a mixed postmortem on the year's hard work: "We'll keep addressing [childcare], monitor its progress, and . . . support it . . . through letters to political people. . . . However, we are all tired." Childcare would not be at the top of the commission's agenda the following year. Instead, this commission member said, with more enthusiasm, "what may become a priority is stereotyping in educational programs, in schools."[55]

Enmeshed in officialdom, focused on eking out as many resources as possible from arcane regulations and opaque bureaucracies, and faced with stonewalling by largely male city officials, Seattle feminists' demands for universally available daycare faded away as a clear-eyed politics of the possible shaped their activism. The CCDA's defeat and the sustained resistance to expansive visions of childcare it triggered altered feminists' strategies. More and more, the crying need for childcare to allow women to work drowned out the fight for daycare as a right for all women and as a public resource. Feminists of the late 1970s still understood childcare was a critical issue for women, but a narrower struggle over availability, quality, and cost dominated the practical goals in front of them.

In their organizing, Seattle's feminists could turn to the mushrooming do-it-yourself guides and manuals that feminist organizations produced to help local activists. *Ms.* magazine featured an article by Dorothy Pitman Hughes, "Child Care Centers: Who, How, and Where" in its very first preview issue. Vicki Breitbart pulled together articles and stories from radical women's liberationists' magazines, child welfare publications, and women's magazines to publish *The Day Care Book: The Why, What, and How of Community Day Care* in 1974. James Levine told readers about *Hustling Resources for Day Care.* Similar books and how-to resources appeared throughout the decade.[56] Yet over the second half of the decade, these too shifted course. The earnest and enthusiastic grassroots organizing that animated feminist-inspired manuals slipped more commonly into advice for parents on how to chase down reliable childcare.

Collective campaigns, like those of Jackie Griswold and others from NOW in Seattle, were increasingly eclipsed by placing responsibility squarely in the hands of individual households to find their own solution. The advice *Ms.* offered its readers in March 1975 was typical. "How to Choose the Right Child-Care Program" delivered tips on the kind of caregiver to ask for, good staff-child ratios, and appropriate physical space. Parents were charged to ask nearly fifty different questions about a center and to conduct a basic safety check (no bad electrical outlets or too many things plugged into extension cords; no dangerous street access; medicines and cleaning supplies safely out of reach). "Finding good child-care takes time and effort and can cost you money in missed work," the article's authors advised, but "it will be time, effort, and money well spent."[57] This was a long way from what feminists were worrying about half a decade earlier.

That dream faded for many reasons. Opponents of federally supported universal childcare, who had rallied to doom the Comprehensive Child Development Act in 1971, gained strength in the decade. The National Coalition for Children, founded in 1973, joined forces with the American Conservative Union in resisting new legislation. Added support came from Phyllis Schlafly's Eagle Forum, established in 1975 to expand her anti-ERA activism into a broad assault on feminism, and from the American Family Forum, which organized anti-childcare lobbying under the umbrella of the growing pro-family movement.[58] Still, according to one national study, the number of daycare centers increased 30 percent between 1970 and 1976, with 60 percent of them nonprofit. Grassroots efforts had produced sharp growth in daycare centers, an important achievement of the women's movement in its own right. Growth in the number of formal centers is only an indirect measure of feminist efforts, however. Many of the cooperative storefront centers that radical feminists founded closed when parents' energies went elsewhere; others never overcame licensing hurdles. Direct federal support for childcare narrowed to programs for poor women, and feminists, particularly those in the antipoverty network, continued during the Carter years both to struggle to ensure that adequate support for childcare was built into any programs assisting poor women and to demand that all earmarked funds were actually used by state administrators.[59]

Generally, long-lasting childcare centers, even those founded by feminists, shifted their energies to maintaining funding and enrollments, shaping curricula, and developing professional staff. James Levine, the feminist activist for fathers and childcare, noted that the Carter administration led a subtle shift toward "what might be called 'tuning up' the existing system."[60] In that climate, feminists themselves altered course. Some grew away from childcare organizing. Seattleite Wanda Adams moved to California, where she stayed active in Women in the Trades and worked with domestic violence victims. Jackie Griswold decamped for Florida for a number of years in the 1980s, left political activism behind, and worked in real estate and for Seattle City Light. Eleanor Smeal traded work in the South Hills NOW Day Nursery School, which she had founded outside Pittsburgh, Pennsylvania, for the presidency of the National Organization for Women in 1977.[61]

Others put their energies into existing centers. The Women's Action Alliance, founded by Gloria Steinem, began its Non-Sexist Child Development Project in 1972. Over its nearly two-decade long existence, the program created curriculum guides, toys, and films and sponsored conferences, professional-development programs, and, in 1979, began *Equal Play*, a journal for those interested in sex equity in education. *Free to Be You and Me*, a project of the feminist actress Marlo Thomas and *Ms.* co-founder Letty Cottin Pogrebin, among others, appeared in 1974, creating a far-reaching popular effort to advance nonsexist education for children.[62]

Finally, by the end of the decade, it was increasingly evident that for middle-class and working-class women, childcare involved choosing among a range of options, from daycare centers to small home-based providers. Guiding individual families to the right options through information and referral services seemed more and more important. San Francisco's Child-care Switchboard had its roots in the early 1970s, for example, and provided a variety of related services—connecting parents to providers, offering technical assistance for centers, and gathering data for advocacy work. In Seattle, the state-funded King County Day Care Referral Service, established in 1972 through the combined efforts of women's groups and daycare activists, received a significantly rising volume of calls over its first three years of operation.[63]

Increasingly, feminists who came of age in the late 1970s would look toward the private sector and a new "business case" for childcare. *Ms.* featured debates about employer-sponsored centers, while providing information on the tax incentives, business benefits, and community advantages they held.[64] So while feminists remained involved in childcare activism across the 1970s, their energies went in new directions as political and economic circumstances changed. Writing in the feminist magazine *Sojourner* in 1981, Molly Lovelock lamented the loss: "'Free 24-hour day care!' Day care was part of every feminist and radical platform ten years ago. Now we hear about it mostly when there are cutbacks in state funding, or as another 'dilemma' of middle-class parenthood, like choosing a pediatrician. Where really is day care now in our organizing strategies?"[65] The decade's growing conservatism, feminism's defeats and shifting energies, along with the changing shape and form of feminist childcare work meant that the utopian vision of childcare as a right all but disappeared.

THIS VISION HAD ITS limits. It was economy-specific, as it minimized the necessity of full-time wage earning for many and assumed an economy of abundance, in which part-time employment was sufficient. Yet as an expression of feminism, it embodied two critical components. First, it combatted stretched lives of work and parenting. Feminists *did not* imagine long workdays and women solely responsible for children whom they had little time to parent. In fact, it was quite the opposite. They hoped to create a far more balanced world of work and family, shared with men and supported by society, and available to all regardless of economic status. Second, feminists' fight for universal daycare teaches us something about the defeats they faced—defeats brought both by political opposition and economic change. The CCDA failed because of effective, organized conservative opposition. It also failed because, in a decade when the male-breadwinner ideal still held the imagination of policymakers and many others in society, the feminist vision of universal childcare upset that ordering of the family. At the same time, a sea change in the American economy that squeezed wages for many sent mothers flocking to the labor market. It made the hope for a world of sane working hours that could be combined with parenting seem a dream impossible to finance.

Understanding feminist aspirations for working mothers has too often been shaped by the diminished outcome of second-wave childcare activism. What feminists sought, in coalition with civil-rights, child-welfare, and anti-poverty activists, was far more revolutionary, with feminists pushing the most forcefully to overturn society's norms. In its feminist incarnation, universal childcare represented a basic foundation for women's equality and an expansive social right. Choice and freedom, rather than full-time employment, was the driving vision.

7

MATERNITY

Securing the Legal Right to a Job for Mothers

It is unfathomable why an employer should not let a woman
take her three weeks paid vacation to give birth instead of
sunning herself on a Bermudan beach, but some apparently
have found a reason.

—ACLU Women's Rights Project, "Punishing Pregnancy," 1973

IDA PHILLIPS WAS A MOTHER of seven children, ages three to fourteen, and
the wife of a truck mechanic when she sought a trainee position on an
electronics assembly line at Martin Marietta's plant in Orlando, Florida.
Three-quarters of those working the line were women. "I've always had to
work for a living," Phillips explained. "I was earning six dollars a day, including tips, waiting on tables in Orlando. So I thought I would try to get
a factory job. The hours would be more regular and there would be those
company benefits." Waitressing work demanded difficult and unpredictable
hours, and the pay was lower in the slow season. When she applied at several local factories, though, management pointed to the door as soon as
they heard she had seven children. One day in 1966, Phillips saw Martin
Marietta's ad in the paper for one hundred assembly trainees. She was
among the first in line at the plant; on her application she listed her seven
children, including the youngest, a three-year-old girl, who was in a day

nursery. "It never occurred to me not to be honest," said Phillips, but Martin Marietta refused her a job, citing their policy not to hire women with preschool-aged children. That night, Phillips wrote an outraged letter to President Johnson complaining of discrimination. "One thing I put in there," she later commented, "If a defense plant with government contracts could deny me a job because I had a pre-school age child, I saw no reason why my sons, when they became of age, should have to go to war."[1]

Phillips sought out an attorney, who said he wouldn't "fool with" such a case, but the National Association for the Advancement of Colored People (NAACP) took it.[2] They filed suit, alleging violation of Title VII of the Civil Rights Act of 1964, which outlawed job discrimination on the basis of sex. Although Phillips was white, civil rights activists feared rulings on sex discrimination could endanger civil rights cases. The Fifth Circuit Court of Appeals ruled against Phillips in 1969, a decision that triggered a dramatic showdown with Betty Friedan and the National Organization for Women. When one of the justices denying the appeal, Harrold Carswell, was nominated for the Supreme Court in January 1970, the underground feminist network in Washington leaped into action.

Catherine East, then serving as executive secretary of the government-sponsored Citizens' Advisory Council on the Status of Women (CACSW), called Friedan, passing on the tip that Carswell's nomination was going through. Friedan then testified before the Senate Judiciary Committee to oppose Carswell's appointment, making Carswell the first prospective justice to face opposition for sexism. Friedan condemned Carswell as a "sexually backward judge" and cited his circuit court ruling against Ida Phillips as a dangerous precedent. "Unusually blind in the matter of sex prejudice," Carswell did not deserve to serve on a court that would decide the cases of discrimination against women then inundating the court. Phillips agreed, telling the *New York Post*, "No, I didn't think Carswell was suited for the Supreme Court. I didn't think he'd be for the equality of men and women, of black and white. He didn't understand the changing of things."[3]

Laughter punctuated the questioning just over ten months later, on December 9, 1970, when Ida Phillips's case came before the Supreme Court for oral arguments. Justices—led not infrequently by Chief Justice Warren Burger—and lawyers for Martin Marietta Corporation indulged themselves in snide remarks, mocking questions, and frequent titters, all at the expense of a woman with preschool-aged children who had dared seek employment. *Phillips v. Martin Marietta Corporation* tested whether the constitution permitted employers to refuse to hire mothers with children still too young to enter school.

Justice Burger worried that he himself might be compelled to hire a "lady law clerk," who would, after all, have to leave work at six p.m. every day to cook dinner for her husband. His fears were put to rest. The case before him would not affect federal judges, as the law involved did not apply to public employees. Others joked about "porteresses" on railways and female ditch diggers and "stewards" on airlines (a step certain to put airlines out of business, quipped one, when men didn't have pretty stewardesses to entice them on board). They even avowed women's superior talent for secretarial work over men.[4]

Meanwhile, Ida Phillips kept waitressing. "It's not just for myself that I'm doing this," Phillips commented about sticking with her case all the way to the highest court, "it's for all mothers." In 1966, when Phillips sought her job, and still in 1970, when the case landed on the Supreme Court docket, there were no laws protecting pregnant workers and mothers from employment discrimination. It was legal to fire a woman for being a mother, or even for being pregnant. It was legal to deny a mother a job altogether. Employers refused to hire women if they even sniffed a hint of potential maternity. This too was legal. School boards routinely mandated teacher leave during pregnancy, deeming it "awkward" for the children, even worrying out loud that some children might think women had swallowed watermelons. It was equally legal to exclude the costs of pregnancy and delivery from employer health policies. Childbirth leave was typically of mandatory length, but virtually always unpaid. Even when mothers wanted—and needed—to return to work, employers frequently disallowed it. And, in rules that seemed just as logical at the time, it was legal to strip new mothers returning to work of job seniority and accrued benefits. Bosses and corporations made pregnancy and maternity, in other words, an excuse for treating women differently at work. By 1978, feminists would successfully persuade the courts, Congress, and the country at large that such treatment was deeply discriminatory.[5]

Phillips's case represented the leading edge of a groundswell of feminist activism to redress mothers' workplace rights. Working women like Phillips filed complaints and grievances; union activists and feminist organizations took them forward, pushing the cases into the courts, and an increasingly sophisticated network of feminist lawyers built the arguments that would persuade judges. *Phillips v. Martin Marietta* was the first in a series of landmark cases led by feminists to secure mothers and pregnant women the right to a job. In the process, second-wave activists battled to reverse the presumption that motherhood meant economic dependence, male support, and lack of commitment to work. Instead, they demanded treatment of mothers and pregnant women as workers like other workers, without stigma as either bad mothers or bad workers.

Women's activists named this "the right to bear children"—a broad right that encompassed both ending discrimination against pregnant and maternal workers and putting supports in place for working mothers. The right to bear children complemented and enhanced related second-wave demands for universal childcare and government assistance for poor mothers. Pointing out the no-win situation that women faced between not having children or losing their jobs and being dependent on a breadwinner, these feminist advocates claimed that women needed society to guarantee a right to bear children alongside the right to reproductive freedom.[6] As Ruth Bader Ginsburg insisted to an audience at the University of Cincinnati College of Law in November 1974, "if we are genuinely committed to the eradication of gender-based discrimination, the problem of job and income security for childbearing women workers must be confronted and resolved head-on."[7] For feminists like Ginsburg, the solutions to this problem included preventing pregnant women from getting fired; providing paid maternity leave; using medical insurance, vacation, and sick-day benefits during pregnancy and childbirth; and preserving mothers' seniority, accrued pension benefits, and job rights when they gave birth.

This chapter tells a story of transformation: from seeing workplace discrimination against pregnant women and mothers as right and natural to making such treatment wrong and illegal. It traces a series of steps from 1964, when Title VII, prohibiting sex discrimination in employment, became law as part of the Civil Rights Act, to 1978, when the Pregnancy Discrimination Act, outlawing biased treatment of pregnant workers, made it through Congress. *Phillips v. Martin Marietta Corporation* symbolized the first step in the process: establishing the legal right for a mother to have a job. A second Supreme Court case, *Cleveland Board of Education v. LaFleur*, brought by a pregnant teacher with deep roots in the civil rights movement,

"International Women's Year March," by Bettye Lane. March 12, 1977. With a campaign for legislation to protect pregnant workers gearing up in the spring of 1977, these women demand "Full Rights and Compensation for Pregnant Workers" at a New York City protest.

set out the legal right to keep a job when pregnant. A final step—the right to have benefits like any other worker when pregnant—was more of an uphill battle. A defeat in 1976, in the Supreme Court's ruling in *General Electric Company v. Gilbert*, sparked a strikingly successful legislative campaign that led to passage of the Pregnancy Discrimination Act in less than two years.

The Right to Be a Mother and Have a Job

Until the 1960s, thinking about maternal employment began with two fundamental assumptions. First, mothers were not wage earners—and indeed, most actually were not. Not until 1970 did more mothers of school-age children join the labor force than not, nearly a 10 percent jump in a decade, and almost a 20 percent climb from 1950. The percentage of employed mothers of preschoolers climbed precipitously as well, from

14 percent in 1950 to 32 percent in 1970.[8] The second principle governing mothers' wage earning was that mothers needed their duties as parents to be safeguarded. An important Supreme Court decision in 1908, *Muller v. Oregon*, enshrined this belief in legal doctrine. In *Muller*, the Court ruled that the state of Oregon could constitutionally limit women to a maximum of ten hours work a day. After the ruling, state after state passed hours restrictions and night-work prohibitions for women: thirty-nine of forty-eight states regulated hours by 1920, and sixteen states banned nighttime labor.[9]

Protecting maternal and infant health preoccupied many reformers and legislators in the early twentieth century, but this created a curious disinterest in looking out for mothers in the workplace. As the historian Alice Kessler-Harris has astutely observed, this tendency produced "the paradoxical situation in which the idea of motherhood became the object of protection in the workplace, while women who became mothers acquired no job protection at all." Women warranted a particular kind of citizenship. The state intervened to protect a woman's role as mother and in the family, but it would not protect a mother's right to her job.[10]

After World War II, feminists in the labor movement inaugurated efforts to recognize mothers' employment rights. Working through unions, they pressed to have maternity benefits negotiated in collective bargaining. These postwar activists sought transfers to lighter work for pregnant women and permission for special clothing on the job. Provisions for maternity leaves with guarantees of retaining seniority and accumulated benefits postleave were priorities, as were medical coverage for pregnancy and childbirth. By the mid-1950s, most major industrial unions included some maternity coverage in their standard labor contracts, although there was a great deal of unevenness in how willing local union chapters were to support women's requests to use their benefits.[11] As late as 1970, Labor Department researchers reviewed 252 collective bargaining agreements each covering five thousand workers or more and discovered that only 29 percent stipulated leaves-of-absence for maternity. Union women also turned to lobbying states to extend unemployment and state disability benefits to pregnant women. Labor feminists demanded these benefits in specific terms, however, in the postwar years: they did not question men's and women's traditional roles inside the home, or men's primacy as breadwinners. Instead, they demanded recognition of the distinctive dilemmas working mothers faced, and they urged policies to make it easier for them to accommodate their dual roles.[12]

Despite the gains made for some working mothers, the vast majority had few rights or benefits. Women's status as mothers or potential mothers largely confined them to a second-class position in the labor force and reinforced their economic dependence on men. The emerging feminist movement drew attention to this fact with mounting frustration and vehemence. Relying on the analyses pouring forth from the movement, they began to call sex roles and the male-breadwinner ideal "phony moral rationalization for paying lower wages and providing worse working conditions for women than men." This 1968 condemnation by Joan Jordan, a radical feminist from California, was echoed by the feminist lawyers Kathleen Peratis and Elizabeth Rindskopf seven years later. "Women are tracked into becoming wives and mothers," their review of pregnancy discrimination concluded, "and then subjected to second class treatment."[13] Marginalization in the paid labor market left women in lower-waged segments of the labor force, with few options for advancing. Citing evidence reported by President Nixon's Task Force on Women's Rights and Responsibilities in 1970, feminist legal advocates invoked the French philosopher Simone de Beauvoir to characterize the result: "Men and women, economically speaking, constitute two castes." And there was no doubt that women were the interlopers. "Women," Trudy Hayden of the ACLU Women's Rights Project concluded, "are thus viewed as a fraud upon the labor market."[14]

Such treatment did not matter in the eyes of most postwar Americans. As Trudy Hayden elaborated, convention held that women worked "for personal convenience" and "to suit their whims." In work that paralleled their attacks on prevailing theories of female selfhood, feminists collected data point after data point and embarked upon a determined publicity campaign to overturn the belief that women did not *really* need to work. The "breadwinner myth" must be refuted, Barbara Leon argued in *Woman's World* in April 1971. A member of the radical feminist group Redstockings, Leon contended that men used the excuse "that women . . . do not really need to work, and can always find a man to support them" to deny women jobs. "This myth can be disproved," Leon avowed, and she marshaled an impressive array of statistics to show that women earners were often heads of households and that the percentage of working wives was highest for low- and middle-income male earners. "In fact," Leon concluded,

married women "must 'moonlight' on two jobs—at home, and in the labor
market—in order to survive economically." Others made the same point.
The Women's Bureau issued a stream of bulletins and brochures that featured the economic roots of wage earning by married women and mothers.
"Underutilization of Women Workers" offered graphic evidence of the
nearly 50 percent of the female work force in 1968 who were either heads
of households (17 percent) or married to a husband earning less than $7,000
per year "at a time when the annual income necessary even for a low standard of living for an urban family of four was estimated at $6,567." "Most
women work to support themselves or others," was the Bureau's conclusion, a death knell to the breadwinner myth.[15]

Speaking on behalf of NOW, Dorothy Haener, leader of the United Auto
Workers women's department and a NOW founder, told a House Education and Labor subcommittee in March 1973 that "the misconceived notion that most women work for 'pin-money' must be buried once and for
all." Minority women in particular suffered from low wages, testified
Haener, as black families more frequently had mothers as single heads of
household and, when a husband was present, more often had employed
mothers. Black feminists called attention to the same issue, emphasizing the
breadwinning needs of black single mothers. Similarly, lesbian feminists
observed that they were permanent members of the workforce and, often,
working mothers as well. Lesbians, noted the well-known San Francisco–
based lesbian rights activist Del Martin, were "cast in the role of breadwinner" and needed high-waged work, professional opportunities, and
childcare centers, just as other working women did.[16]

Simmering discontent at the dismissive attitudes finally burst open in the
second half of the 1960s. As soon as the Equal Employment Opportunity
Commission (EEOC)—the federal agency formed to enforce Title VII of the
Civil Rights Act—began accepting complaints in 1965, working mothers
inundated the commission with testimonials of arbitrary firings, unjust leave
policies, and unequal benefits for pregnant women and mothers. Ruth
Weyand, a lawyer for the International Union of Electrical, Radio and Machine Workers (IUE), described a rush of "as many as 350 charges with
EEOC in one weekend after one local learned of the EEOC ruling in sick-
ness and accident benefits for disabilities arising from pregnancy."[17] Assisted
by their unions, other working women brought similar complaints and initiated lawsuits. Stewardesses launched a well-publicized effort to retain

their jobs upon marriage and pregnancy. "We don't want to cling to the old image of being fly girls. We're professional career women and mothers," a flight attendant named Polly Musch told the *Los Angeles Times*. Local women's groups backed such challenges. In Seattle, a NOW attorney aided pregnant workers at United Airlines in fighting their maternity leave policy.[18]

Ida Phillips received support from a number of organizations, including the NOW Legal Defense and Education Fund, the feminist legal group Human Rights for Women, Inc., and feminists within the American Civil Liberties Union. Her case finally reached the Supreme Court as the feminist legal network challenging maternity and pregnancy employment discrimination came together. Susan Deller Ross was one member of that network. Ross had been transfixed by both Simone de Beauvoir's *The Second Sex* and Betty Friedan's *The Feminine Mystique* as an undergraduate. In the spring of 1970, during her final term of law school at New York University, Ross worked with the pioneering feminist lawyers Pauli Murray and Dorothy Kenyon on the ACLU's friend-of-the-court brief for *Phillips v. Martin Marietta*. Writing the brief changed Ross's career plans. Hoping to keep working on sex discrimination, Ross abandoned a job at a law firm to take up a position at the Equal Employment Opportunity Commission, where she went on to shape the EEOC's guidelines on pregnancy discrimination as a staff lawyer for the Commission and, in 1977, to lead the coalition demanding passage of the Pregnancy Discrimination Act.[19] Labor supporters joined Phillips's feminist advocates in submitting sympathetic briefs, while the NAACP provided her lead legal team. Phillips herself recognized early on the broad civil rights implications of her case early on, seeking out a local black attorney to represent her because, she remembered, "we knew [that] they knew more about civil rights."[20]

As the ridicule peppering the record of oral arguments in Phillips's case attests, the meaning of sex discrimination in employment was highly unsettled in the late 1960s. Feminists faced an uphill battle to overturn the belief that motherhood defined women's work lives as much as it did their family roles. In its ruling on Ida Phillips's job rights, for example, the Court of Appeals found the idea that Congress intended the Civil Rights Act "to require that an employer treat [mothers and fathers] exactly alike in the administration of its general hiring policies" preposterous. "The common experience of Congressmen is surely not so far removed from that of mankind in general," the three justices opined, "as to warrant our attributing to them such an irrational purpose in the formulation of this statute." Indeed, the Appeals Court judges concluded that Ida Phillips had been denied a job not because of her sex, but because of her sex *plus* her motherhood. For Phillips's supporters, such a "sex plus" doctrine would effectively make Title VII toothless, enabling discrimination to continue under the guise of a potentially unlimited number of "sex plus" grounds. "If 'sex plus' stands," wrote one dissenting appeals court judge, "the [Civil Rights] Act is dead."[21]

As the Supreme Court took up the case, then, justices, plaintiff, and defendant debated who raised children: was childrearing the exclusive responsibility of mothers, thus justifying their exclusion—but not fathers'—from the workplace? Who should make that decision—society, or individual women? Feminists argued that women, as individuals, should. Congress had a specific intent to prevent employment based on "stereotyped groups of people," one lawyer supporting Phillips told the justices. "People can't be just put into classes and denied a chance to show their individual ability to perform a job." If they were, that was discrimination. Plaintiff's briefs pointed out that most working mothers needed their jobs to support their families, as did Phillips. The economic cost of forcing women to choose between maternity and employment—costs that men did not have to bear—further deepened the discriminatory element of Martin Marietta's regulation. Those costs effectively curtailed women's right to bear children. Denying mothers employment had an additional impact on minority women, who were heads of households at twice the rate of white women, and intensified the discriminatory effect of the company's rule.[22]

Phillips's supporters returned repeatedly to the theme of the illegitimacy of using sex-role stereotypes to regulate employment. The supposition that all mothers took care of their children in such a way that they couldn't be workers was, they argued, neither fact nor nature, but merely a stereotype. "Title VII seeks to prohibit employment policies based on stereotypic assumptions, prejudgments," insisted Phillips's lawyers, "and requires that applicants for employment be considered on their individual merit." The same was true for men. They could not be excluded from positions just because men had never filled them, nor should the state presume that fathers have different responsibilities toward their children than mothers do.[23]

The emphasis on arbitrary sex-typing about parents' roles presaged the arguments Ruth Bader Ginsburg and other feminists would develop in subsequent cases on pregnancy discrimination. Again and again, Ginsburg led challenges to laws and regulations that categorically assigned breadwinning to men and caregiving to women, as we saw in Chapter 3 with the cases she argued on men's and women's duties in marriage. The Appeals Court's majority decision against Phillips earned a cutting rebuke from Supreme Court Justice Thurgood Marshall for its failure to repudiate such gender stereotypes. "The Court has fallen into the trap of assuming that the [Civil Rights] Act permits ancient canards about the proper role of women to be a basis for discrimination," he remarked scathingly.[24]

In his concurring opinion to the unanimous Supreme Court decision in Phillips's favor, Marshall contended that an employer might require "parents, both mothers and fathers, to provide for the care of their children so that job performance is not interfered with," but it could not establish a separate set of rules for fathers and mothers. The rest of the court, while dismissing the sex plus doctrine, was not so sure. In fact, the joint *per curiam* opinion in Phillips's case left open the possibility that an occupational qualification in which family obligations were "demonstrably more relevant to job performance for a woman than for a man" could exist, thus justifying mothers' exclusion from the workplace.[25] The January 1971 decision in *Phillips v. Martin Marietta* was thus a qualified if significant victory. The court ruled that an employer could not have two separate hiring policies for men and women. Barring some hypothetical qualification making it impossible for a mother but not a father to hold a job, the opinion would hold. But the majority of the justices couldn't quite let go of the idea that such a qualification would inevitably exist.

The "Right to Be Pregnant without Penalty"

If securing mothers the right to a job was the first big hurdle, the next one was securing them the right to keep a job when pregnant—and return to it after delivery. "The greatest single case of sex discrimination in employment," Brenda Feigen Fasteau of the ACLU's Women's Rights Project testified to a suburban New York panel in 1973, is pregnancy. The Women's Rights Project (WRP) made pregnancy one focus of its early cases.[26] Pregnant women's routine dismissal from jobs, mandatory wait periods before returning to work, and loss of seniority and pension credits in the process stimulated a wave of defiance as the implications of Title VII took root. Between 1970 and 1974, feminists debated how to define pregnancy discrimination as sex discrimination and won a first set of skirmishes around pregnancy dismissal and rehiring policies.

Teachers were the visible faces of this battleground. In Toledo, Ohio, they won an agreement to remain in their classrooms until they chose to leave, be reinstated with full benefits, and provide male teachers with paternity leave. Teachers' union locals in Yonkers, New York; Philadelphia, Pennsylvania; Taylor Township, Michigan; Waukegan, Illinois; St. Paul, Minnesota; and San Francisco, California, among others, negotiated new terms on pregnancy or took their districts to court. The American Federation of Teachers, at its 1970 national convention, passed resolutions opposing maternity restrictions, which Marjorie Stern, the chair of the organization's newly formed Women's Rights Committee, introduced to the membership and locals across the country. The lower federal courts decided twenty-eight cases related to pregnancy discrimination between 1971 and 1974; teachers initiated 60 percent of them.[27]

Schoolteachers found allies among local feminists. In San Joaquin County, California, the NOW local worked with the American Federation of Teachers in suing the district school board. At the national level, NOW backed teacher protests in its earliest days: at their second national convention in 1967, for instance, NOW objected to the treatment of Cindy Hill, a public-school music teacher from Chartiers Valley, Pennsylvania, outside Pittsburgh. Hill had lost both leave pay and her job when she gave birth while on a paid sabbatical from teaching in order to earn a master's degree. The school district, NOW proclaimed, had "violated the rights of motherhood, the rights of a married couple to manage its own family, and the basic individual rights of a teacher." The Communications Workers of America and the IUE fought to negotiate pregnancy coverage as well.[28] Yet it was teachers who brought the cases that moved earliest through the federal district courts and eventually to the Supreme Court, where the constitutionality of pregnancy dismissal was finally adjudicated. The feminist lawyers who supported them worked furiously in these years to define those constitutional grounds.

Feminist strategy on maternity benefits and pregnancy discrimination evolved significantly. Long-standing debates among women's activists about providing women workers with special safeguards or treating them similarly to other workers surfaced immediately.[29] NOW began grappling with the issue within months of its founding. In its February 1967 statement of goals, NOW's Task Force on Equal Opportunity in Employment demanded an end to "discrimination on the basis of maternity" and called for "providing paid maternity leave as a form of social security for all working mothers, and the right to return to her job." Hesitancy about the demand for maternity benefits soon arose. Although the organization's Task Force on the Family also called for maternity protections, it argued that NOW should undertake "more detailed discussion of [the] maternity benefit issue before taking any action on this issue." These early NOW activists worried that requiring special workplace benefits for mothers would escalate discrimination. Uncertainty did not, however, prevent the organization from including paid maternity leave and job security for working mothers returning to employment among the eight planks in its Bill of Rights for women passed at its November 1967 convention.[30]

Conflict among leaders in the movement about demanding maternity benefits became heated. Betty Friedan and Catherine East disagreed forcefully. Friedan kept pressing for special maternity benefits. Sonia Pressman Fuentes remembered attending weekly NOW meetings held in Washington, DC apartments to debate the issue as attention to the topic increased, and the lawyer Mary Eastwood recalled, "they were just yelling at each other! Catherine was afraid that [mandated] pregnancy leave would cause employers to discriminate against women more."[31]

The critical breakthrough to the impasse came through East. As the executive secretary at the Citizens' Advisory Council on the Status of Women, East researched and wrote position papers. A consummate insider for the movement, East's analytical brilliance and encyclopedic knowledge of the facts was so often buried behind official reports and statements that friends nicknamed her Deep Throat, after the informant who brought down President Nixon. East drafted a highly influential 1971 law review article, "Childbirth and Child Rearing Leave: Job-Related Benefits," published under the name of Elizabeth Duncan Koontz, the director of the Women's Bureau. According to Koontz, "Discussions of maternity leave in the United States have been characterized by semantic confusion, much emotion, and few facts." Lack of consistency in policies and evolving social norms meant that little consensus existed about what maternity leave even was. "Perhaps it would help to alleviate the semantic confusion," Koontz offered, "if a new term were adopted to refer to leave for childbirth and complications of pregnancy—a term such as *childbirth leave*."[32]

In coining that new terminology, Koontz inaugurated a paradigm shift. "The subject of *child rearing* is a separate topic," she continued. "Only women can bear children, but both men and women are capable of rearing children. The conceptual framework of childbearing and child rearing fits both present and future reality better than . . . [one] that assumes that childbearing and child rearing are both solely the responsibility of women."[33] That simple statement broke the Gordian knot. An approach to pregnancy discrimination that separated childbearing from childrearing disentangled parenting—to be done by both women and men—from pregnancy and delivery. Pregnant women could then be viewed as similar to other workers who needed leave or medical care and retain the same job rights and benefits of any employee.

East was also instrumental in changing government policy on pregnancy and maternity. Her arguments informed the position taken the previous October by the Citizens' Advisory Council on the Status of Women. CACSW's statement of principles on job-related maternity benefits announced: "Childbirth and complications of pregnancy are, for all job-related purposes, temporary disabilities and should be treated as such under any health insurance, temporary disability insurance, or sick leave plan of an employer, union, or fraternal society."[34] The CACSW recommendations on pregnancy encapsulated what the legal historian Deborah Dinner has called the temporary disability paradigm. Equating pregnancy to the array of medical conditions that all workers potentially face, this standard rebutted pernicious stereotypes about pregnancy and its effects on women while carving out the possibility for benefits to cover the costs of childbirth. Moreover, by relying on the distinction between childbirth and childrearing, CACSW resisted the idea that women had sole responsibility for children. In the future, benefits for childrearing could be pursued on behalf of both men and women.[35]

The CACSW recommendations were pivotal. Susan Deller Ross had spent nearly two years working as a staff attorney at the Equal Employment Opportunity Commission, which had only tepidly and reluctantly restrained employer discrimination against pregnant workers in its first few years. In April 1972, the commission issued new guidelines broadly banning pregnancy discrimination along the lines that the CACSW had proposed.[36]

Ross had instigated the change. "That came about," she explained, "because I was talking with Catherine East." The Council had "come up with a policy paper saying 'treat pregnant women the same as other workers who are medically disabled, not worse, not better.' So that was the EEOC approach I pushed for." Other feminist lawyers within the EEOC had argued that a fairer approach would be to highlight the uniqueness of pregnancy and set standards for maternity leave and benefits that all employers must meet. "I struggled with myself on which approach was better," Ross recalled, but she was ultimately persuaded by the logic of the principles East enunciated.[37]

Under these guidelines, federal district courts increasingly reviewed the cases piling up before them, with broadening sympathy to the argument that pregnancy discrimination was sex discrimination.[38] Jo Carol LaFleur taught girls at risk of dropping out of school in Cleveland's Patrick Henry Junior High School. The civil rights movement had provided LaFleur, a young white woman growing up in segregated Richmond, Virginia, with a searing transformation in consciousness. Appalled by her own community's resistance to change, she committed to working with African American communities and students. She was stunned and furious when she became pregnant and the Cleveland school district enforced its policy of mandatory leave without pay. She had to stop teaching when she was four months pregnant, and she was not allowed to return to work until the first semester beginning three months after her child was born. (Unmarried women faced permanent dismissal.) There was something insulting about a policy that kicked her out of classrooms that themselves contained pregnant students.[39]

Disgusted by the blatant sex discrimination in the policy, LaFleur raged at the "Neanderthal thinking of small-minded men." Her teachers' union and the ACLU both refused to help her, and she eventually contacted the local newspaper asking for names of area feminist organizations. She got a number for the Women's Equity Action League (WEAL), formed in 1968, and WEAL member Jane Picker became LaFleur's attorney. Picker took LaFleur's case all the way to the Supreme Court.[40]

The Cleveland school board's attorneys argued that working posed risks to pregnant women and that the potential disruption of a pregnant teacher in the classroom warranted her removal. "Pointing, giggling, laughing and making snide remarks," was a likely outcome, they claimed, "causing in-

terruption and interference with the classroom program of study." Defense
attorneys also raised the specter of white women's vulnerability to black
youth's violence. School violence had risen among Patrick Henry Junior
High's urban, minority students, and defense attorneys suggested LaFleur
risked being jostled by boys in the hallway.[41] LaFleur was particularly flab-
bergasted by the claims that her pregnancy would interfere with everyday
classroom business, pointing out that several students had been pregnant
in her classes and that they had planned a baby shower for her. Not far
from the surface of this courtroom back-and-forth were racially coded fears
about the "place" of white "ladies," dangerous black youth, and lives for
women outside the protective embrace of men.

The Sixth Court of Appeals ruled in LaFleur's favor on July 27, 1972,
just months after the EEOC issued the new guidelines that Susan Deller
Ross had helped shape. The appeals court called the school district's policy
"clearly arbitrary and unreasonable in its overbreadth" and ruled that it
unfairly singled out women for "unconstitutionally unequal restrictions
upon their employment." That students might make snide remarks or point
fingers, one judge noted, was beside the point. "Basic rights such as those
involved in the employment relationship and other citizenship responsibilities," he maintained, "cannot be made to yield to embarrassment."[42] The
Cleveland School Board appealed to the Supreme Court, and LaFleur's
case was joined with that of Susan Cohen, a high-school social-studies
teacher challenging a similar policy in Chesterfield County, Virginia. The
Fourth Court of Appeals had ruled against Cohen, and the higher court
now had conflicting opinions before it.

The two teachers' lawyers continued to push for an interpretation of the
schools' pregnancy dismissal policies as sex discrimination. Treating pregnancy differently from any other medical condition was capricious and biased, while applying stereotypes about pregnant women and women's
roles as mothers to the workplace was simply discriminatory. Leave for
pregnancy should be based instead on individual circumstances, just as employers managed other workers' situations. On January 21, 1974, the
Court ruled in the teachers' favor, agreeing that pregnancy dismissal policies were unconstitutional—but only on procedural grounds. The Justices
were not yet completely sure that pregnancy discrimination warranted full
protection as sex discrimination. As the astute *New York Times* reporter
Linda Greenhouse observed years later, the same Court that, just the year

before, had authoritatively declared the right to abortion "appeared almost tongue-tied in the presence of pregnant school-teachers."[43]

The Right to Benefits like Any Other Worker

LaFleur's narrowly framed decision left the extent of pregnant workers' rights unresolved. Cases in the pipeline, including one scheduled for the Court's docket later that year, posed pressing and difficult questions about the exclusion of pregnant women from temporary disability benefits. It was an opening that feminists seized. Was pregnancy a category *sui generis* or, as feminist lawyers and their allies believed, did treatment of pregnant workers reflect discredited sex-role stereotypes that violated all women's rights to equal employment? While *LaFleur* ruled out pregnancy dismissal and mandatory leave policies, excluding pregnant women from other workplace benefits remained standard practice. Employers routinely forbade the use of sick leave and vacation time for childbirth. They frequently excluded prenatal care and delivery from employer-provided health insurance plans, and, if these were offered, pregnant women typically paid higher rates than fellow workers. It was common for the wives of male workers to have better health coverage when they were pregnant than the female workers themselves did. Pregnant women were systematically denied payments from temporary disability plans when they gave birth.

As the feminist legal network culled information to build their briefs, the ACLU Women's Rights Project compiled an extraordinary listing of such policies. "Punishing Pregnancy: Discrimination in Education, Employment, and Credit," completed by the WRP in October 1973, filled seventy-five pages with unfair treatment directed at pregnant women. In Albuquerque, New Mexico, banks refused to allow employees to use accrued vacation time for maternity leave. Kimberly Clark, one of the largest employers in Wisconsin, prevented women from using their sick days for giving birth. These employers reasoned that pregnancy was a normal condition, so sick benefits did not apply. Time off for maternity typically meant loss of seniority. The City of Houston even subtracted months out for maternity from a woman's accumulated years of service.[44]

The policies piled up in a dizzying array of inconsistency. Employers' arguments about the difficulties of accommodating pregnancy, which they

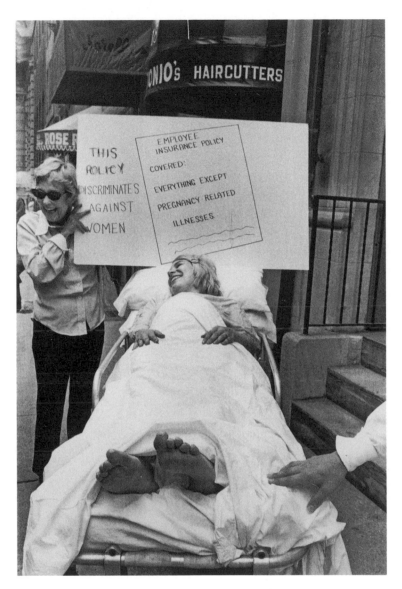

"Benefits for Pregnant Women Demonstration," by Bettye Lane. August 20, 1973. Wheeling a "pregnant woman" down the streets of New York City, feminists drew attention to the gaping holes in employers' coverage of pregnant workers as well as society's failure to see it as discrimination.

typically insisted was a voluntary condition, made little sense to feminists who pointed out that many pregnancies were not voluntary, and that other "voluntary" conditions received accommodations without such problems. Hypocrisies abounded. "When an employee breaks a leg skiing on vacation, no one asks if it was his own fault. A showing of hospitalization or medical treatment and of a temporary inability to work are all that is needed," the Women's Rights Project commented with barely disguised fury, "and so it should be also with childbirth."[45]

At the forefront of feminist legal activists' attention was the exclusion of pregnant workers from temporary disability programs offered both by private employers and some states. Temporary disability provided replacement income for workers incapacitated for a short period. While promoting the idea that pregnancy was a "disability" angered some feminists, feminist lawyers conceived of pregnancy within the broad array of conditions that could prevent *any* worker from being on the job. Prostatectomies, cosmetic surgery, broken limbs, and many other conditions were covered. Why not pregnancy and childbirth? Pregnant workers were like *all* other workers facing conditions that kept them temporarily away from work.

Feminists insisted that providing temporary disability coverage for pregnancy was not simply an equity issue, however. Such coverage provided benefits critically needed by women to support themselves and their families. Without them, mothers faced impoverishment, an inability to provide for their children, or economic dependence. Their constitutionally protected right to abortion was similarly threatened. Ruth Bader Ginsburg told *Ms.* magazine about her dismay that women might be forced to choose between an abortion and raising a child in poverty. "Lawyers must follow up the abortion decision," she insisted, "by pressing for job protection and disability insurance for pregnant women, and child-care centers."[46] Feminists argued that no woman should have her right to bear children constrained by going without a wage or losing her job. Responsibility for preventing those outcomes lay not in presuming men would take care of women, but in supporting mothers through state and workplace benefits.

Workers in the International Union of Electrical, Radio and Machine Workers pressed the issue first with their employers and then before the courts, backed by their legal department's fierce labor rights advocate, Ruth Weyand. IUE members had been bargaining to include pregnancy benefits in their contracts since the 1950s, and they had had some success. But with Title VII and the 1972 EEOC guidelines on pregnancy-related discrimination to back them up, IUE locals took on four hundred employers in a two-year period, and they secured agreements to grant pregnancy disability benefits from many of them. General Electric, with eighty-five thousand unionized and nonunionized employees, fought back, however. The EEOC's new guidelines had led Weyand to advise GE workers to go ahead and file claims for disability benefits; three hundred women demanded the official forms immediately. Women at General Electric soon flooded the company with claims for disability benefits and then inundated the EEOC with charges of discrimination—so much so that IUE members filed charges on denial of sick leave for pregnancy-related causes at a rate well exceeding those for equal pay or promotion complaints.[47] Given that their male bargaining-unit colleagues were entitled to temporary disability benefits for anything from hair transplants to vasectomies, sex discrimination seemed patently clear.

When that still didn't produce change in General Electric's policies, Weyand gathered a set of plaintiffs and filed charges in federal court in March 1972. One plaintiff was Barbara Hall, a woman at GE's plant in Salem, Virginia, who had been required by the company nurse to quit work at her sixth month of pregnancy and made to wait eight weeks after birth to return to work, despite Hall's desires to keep working and return much sooner. Once Hall learned that the EEOC had declared that pregnant workers had a right to disability benefits, she filed a claim, which was denied. Other plaintiffs emerged. A blood clot in her lung disabled Emma Furch, working at a plant in Texas, but GE denied her temporary disability benefits because she was also pregnant. One plaintiff, Sherrie O'Steen, would become famous, her story retold repeatedly. Sherrie O'Steen was working for General Electric in coastal Virginia when she became pregnant in 1972; soon after, her husband abandoned her. O'Steen's foreman let her work to the end of her seventh month of pregnancy, even though the rules required otherwise, but then she was forced to take unpaid leave. She couldn't pay her electricity bills, and she spent over a month in an unheated house with her newborn and toddler, with no working refrigerator or stove, before state welfare payments began. She was back at work as soon as GE would let her inside the plant. Martha Gilbert, the woman who gave her name to the case, worked at the Salem plant with Hall.[48]

Weyand received a favorable ruling in district court in early 1974. Justice Robert R. Merhige, Jr. agreed that pregnancy discrimination constituted sex discrimination. He chastised the company, insisting that Congress never intended to force female employees to "forego a fundamental right, such as a woman's right to bear children," just to keep a job. Judge Merhige rejected GE's argument that women left the labor force upon birth as mere stereotype about sex roles. "While pregnancy is unique to women, parenthood is common to both sexes," but only women, under General Electric policy, lost income "from their participation in the procreative experience."[49] Weyand's *General Electric v. Gilbert* was then joined with another similar suit, *Liberty Mutual Insurance Company v. Wetzel*, in appeal before the Supreme Court.

Weyand arrived for oral arguments in *Gilbert* on January 26, 1976 with a bulging brief—266 pages and expanding. Fellow attorneys referred to it as the "fat yellow one" and cited detail after detail from its comprehensive history of discrimination at GE. Weyand bolstered her case with a brief from the Women's Rights Project of the ACLU, co-written by Ruth Bader Ginsburg and Susan Deller Ross, additional briefs from Wendy Williams with Equal Rights Advocates and from feminist, labor, and public law groups, and a concise, incisive declaration from the government produced by the feminist network inside the EEOC. Rulings by lower courts were going in Weyand's favor, with all six Courts of Appeal hearing pregnancy discrimination cases under Title VII ruling them sex discrimination.[50]

General Electric's attorney preceded Weyand in oral arguments. He rebutted the claim of discrimination. Pregnancy was a voluntary condition, rather than a medical one. He cited the ease of access to contraception and the recent *Roe v. Wade* ruling that, in his words, made abortion "an in-and-out noon-hour treatment" to suggest that pregnancy could be fully planned. He and GE's supporters from the National Association of Manufacturers and the Chamber of Commerce argued that coverage of pregnancy in temporary-disability plans would place onerous costs on business, ones not warranted by women's tendency to use the benefits and then quit. Pregnancy benefits, they claimed, would constitute "a unique form of severance pay." Business arguments in the case reiterated belief in male breadwinning and mothers' inevitable departure from the workplace once they gave birth. At one point, General Electric's attorney raised the unsettling specter that if women were awarded pregnancy benefits, men could ask for paid leave for childcare.[51]

Weyand and her team framed their arguments carefully. A discouraging ruling on a state of California temporary disability program in *Geduldig v. Aiello* in 1974 had made a constitutionally based claim of pure sex discrimination a nonstarter. Instead, they made the case that excluding pregnant women from GE's temporary disability policy violated Title VII's guarantee against employment discrimination. Anchoring employment policy in sex-role stereotypes about women's rightful place produced unequal effects for male and female workers, and it had been made unlawful by the legislation. To suggest, as the company's advocates did, that mothers would simply exploit the benefit as severance pay "embodie[d] an unjustifiable presumption . . . that women have cavalier attitudes toward their jobs, are not the 'breadwinners' in their families and so can be left without income during a period of disability."[52]

Gilbert culminated nearly a decade of evolving arguments by second-wave feminists about how maternity must be protected in the workplace to produce equality. The briefs in the case built on both the feminist deconstruction of sex roles and the knowledge they had painstakingly accumulated about women's economic circumstances. Their fundamental premise was that motherhood and worker must not be mutually exclusive categories—in law or in society. Ruth Bader Ginsburg described the deep-seated beliefs about the natural order of things that she and other feminist lawyers had to overcome. Reflecting on the Court's decision in 1974's *Geduldig v. Aiello*, she thought it was rooted in "a reason not fully acknowledged" by the justices: "Assessment of childbirth not as a short-term episode but as an integral part of a long-term process. . . . Childbirth marks a new period in the woman's life cycle. She will (or ideally should) relinquish her secondary role as gainfully employed worker in favor of her primary role as mother-wife. And in that role, she should be supported by the family's man, not the state or an employer she is destined to leave." Of course, Ginsburg added, with dry sarcasm, the justices in *Geduldig* had ruled against a plaintiff who did not fit that mold.[53]

As it had in *Geduldig*, the Court in *General Electric v. Gilbert* refused to concede Ginsburg's point. On December 7, 1976, the court ruled 6–3 that excluding pregnant women from the company's disability policy merely drew distinctions between pregnant and "non-pregnant persons" and did not constitute sex discrimination. ACLU colleagues in Washington read out the opinion to Ruth Bader Ginsburg over the phone. A "disaster," Ginsburg would write later that day to her longtime feminist law collaborator at the

University of California at Berkeley, Herma Hill Kay. "The most disastrous court decision on women in the last 50 years," was Ruth Weyand's dismayed response. Susan Deller Ross roundly condemned the Court in the *Los Angeles Times*. The Justices had just "legalized sex discrimination." Employers had been given permission to "treat pregnant women as harshly as they like—firing them, refusing to hire them and forcing them to take long, unpaid leaves of absence." Appallingly, Ross went on, "it is even conceivable that employers will refuse to hire any women because they might become pregnant."[54]

The Right to Bear Children

When Susan Deller Ross painted her grim picture of *Gilbert*'s consequences to the readers of the *Los Angeles Times*, she chose her words deliberately, shaping them for a new audience. It was just one day after the decision, but behind the scenes Ross was mobilizing the feminist network to take the issue to Congress. On December 14, the ACLU Women's Rights Project, working with the Pennsylvania Commission for Women, brought together dozens of feminist lawyers and activists, labor leaders, and legislative aides for a meeting at the University of Pennsylvania, a location strategically chosen to bridge the New York–Washington divide. Discussion spilled over into a second day of meetings in Washington. The attendees represented over fifty organizations, and they walked away from the meeting announcing the intent to seek legislation against pregnancy discrimination and the formation of the Campaign to End Discrimination Against Pregnant Workers (CEDAPW). The coalition elected Susan Deller Ross and Ruth Weyand as its co-chairs. Eventually, over two hundred organizations signed coalition mailings in the campaign for passage of the Pregnancy Discrimination Act (PDA).[55]

Feminist legal and advocacy organizations made the work of CEDAPW a number-one priority. NOW, the National Women's Political Caucus, the Women's Equity Action League, the Women's Legal Defense Fund, and the ACLU Women's Rights Project all threw their weight behind the campaign. Unions constituted a second critical arm of the coalition. With Ruth Weyand at the helm, the IUE threw its weight behind the legislation, but the Communications Workers of America, the United Auto Workers, and the AFL–CIO more broadly became active coalition partners. Conscious that amending Title VII raised an unsettling prospect of changing the Civil Rights Act, the coalition also recruited civil rights organizations, with the Leadership Conference on Civil Rights playing a significant role. And then, perhaps in the most unexpected dimension to the coalition, both pro-choice and anti-abortion groups joined. One congressional staffer characterized the PDA as "a decent motherhood bill," and supporters and opponents of abortion found common ground in the bill's promotion of fair working conditions for mothers. Nina Hegsted, lobbying for NOW, commented ruefully, "It has been such a diverse coalition from the beginning. Even Citizens for Life are active on this. NOW will probably not ally itself with the Citizens for Life again *ever*!"[56]

The legislation itself was simple—a few short paragraphs amending Title VII of the Civil Rights Act introduced on March 15, 1977. The paragraphs spelled out the meaning of "because of sex" or "on the basis of sex" to include "because of or on the basis of pregnancy, childbirth, or related medical conditions." The amended language expanded the logic of the temporary disability paradigm to include all employment benefits. Sick leave, vacation leave, and any other employer-provided benefit could not, under the PDA, be denied pregnant workers. The underlying premise was comparability of treatment: workers "similar in their ability or inability to work," whether male or female, should be treated equivalently.[57]

A number of elements were important to campaign leaders in drafting the legislation. First, the fact that pregnancy discrimination was sex discrimination must be unequivocal. Without that, where would the line be drawn? Hard-fought gains such as the right not to take mandatory lengthy unpaid leaves or retention of seniority rights might be stripped away. Coalition leaders argued that women's potential pregnancy and childbirth colored all discrimination against working women.[58] Wendy Williams testified to the Senate Subcommittee on Labor that "the common thread of justification through most policies and practices that have discriminated against all women in the labor force rested ultimately on the capacity of women to become pregnant." Beliefs, she went on, that women "would and, in fact, should get married and have children and leave the work force have led to the view that women are marginal workers not deserving of the emoluments of the 'real' workers in the work force."[59]

Feminists challenged such assumptions about women workers during PDA hearings in April and June 1977 and in public statements. Turning to employment statistics, to testimony from the head of the Women's Bureau, and to evidence that denying pregnant women their jobs harmed them and their families, the Coalition argued that there was no reason to presume that maternity trumped all else in women's lives.[60] Mothers worked because they needed the income. On the eve of the legislation's introduction, Ruth Bader Ginsburg and Susan Deller Ross explained to the readers of the *New York Times* that "millions of gainfully employed women have husbands earning less than $7,000 per year. Families dependent on the income of these women will suffer the harshest impact when no wage replacement attends childbirth." Women's workforce attachment was also a central theme. Toni Sterling, a member of Local 65, United Steelworkers of America, took exception to the assumption of many on the all-male Senate panel that she did not need her job. "There has been a lot of talk about women not returning back to work after having their babies." They were simply misinformed. "Most of us who are working . . . return to work, because we are middle-class. We have to be able to pay to keep that child living. We cannot stay home."[61]

Clarence Mitchell, of the NAACP, alerted Senators to the subtext: "It looks like everything suddenly comes into focus as saying you can't trust these mothers, they're going to chisel and not come back to work. They're going to hang around the house." All too aware of how opponents of welfare routinely defamed poor women on public assistance as "chiselers," Mitchell well understood how requiring that benefits—whether provided by the state or an employer—be given to mothers still violated the expectation that all women should have a male breadwinner looking out for them.[62] The demand to grant pregnant women full economic citizenship—to make them "real" workers in the workforce, with secure jobs, fringe benefits, and income replacement for disability—struck at the heart of a male-breadwinning family order and unsettled deeply held beliefs about who should provide for, and who should take care of, children.

Opponents got that message loud and clear. The National Association of Manufacturers (NAM) maintained that the issue at stake in the Pregnancy Discrimination Act was not one of sex discrimination, but rather "how far society chooses to go in subsidizing parenthood." The Association questioned "how much of the economic responsibility for parenthood will be assumed by those men and women who choose to have children and how much of the responsibility will be assumed by society—either directly through taxation or indirectly through requirements placed on employers." Business critics of the bill connected the dots between the PDA's requirements and feminists' larger goal to make society and business bear greater responsibility for children and families. With rising fury, NAM's statement for congressional committees listed costs Congress *could* impose on employers to subsidize parenthood—"all of a family's medical expenses," "disability benefits for pregnancy," "paid leave to both mothers and fathers for child rearing," "day-care centers." With "its sweeping language and broad implications," the PDA went "too far," in their view.[63]

PDA supporters disagreed with NAM's conclusion, but not its analysis. They located awarding benefits to pregnant workers within a broad array of society's duties to aid women's (and men's) joint breadwinning and parenting. The question of pregnancy disability supports "raises even broader social questions about who is responsible for the propagation of the race," wrote two feminist supporters in the *Los Angeles Times*. Americans could follow the model set by states in Western Europe, where "liberal maternity and paternity leave," "free or inexpensive day-care centers for children of working parents," and "the rights of women to retain seniority and other benefits when returning to work after childbirth" were commonplace. "Why is it," they queried, "that in the United States working women have to deal with pregnancy as a problem and society's stake in childrearing is unacknowledged?"[64]

Feminists emphasized the costs—and the injustice—of that avoidance. In the midst of debate over the PDA, Ruth Bader Ginsburg published a short assessment of sex-discrimination law that noted the problems with the US's failure to protect pregnant workers. She accused the Supreme Court of "ostrich-like responses" to the realities facing pregnant women. Congress, too, had to stop sticking their heads in the sand. "If Congress is genuinely committed to the eradication of sex-based discrimination and promotion of equal opportunity for women," she contended, it will pass the PDA right away and deliver "job security, health insurance coverage, and income maintenance for childbearing women." Bella Abzug reminded her former colleagues pointedly that "Congress never intended that employers could force women to trade off their cherished and constitutionally protected right to bear children as a condition for enjoying the statutory protections embodied in Title VII."[65]

CEDAPW argued further that the Pregnancy Discrimination Act was a "pro-family bill." The alliance that feminist coalition members forged with pro-life groups came from recognition that the right to bear children was tightly linked to the right *not* to bear children, a right guaranteed by the 1973 *Roe v. Wade* decision making abortion an individual woman's constitutionally protected decision. Jacqueline Nolan-Haley, representing American Citizens Concerned for Life, observed that if a woman faced losing income and perhaps a job, "her decision to abort cannot be said to be the product of free choice but of economic coercion." Feminists echoed this point. Wendy Williams bluntly informed Congress that absence of pregnancy disability coverage forced some women to choose "between employment and . . . termination of a pregnancy which they otherwise would not terminate."[66]

The pro-PDA alliance's unity nearly foundered, however, when congressional conservatives, prodded by the Catholic Bishops' Committee for Pro-Life Activities, sought to insert requirements that elective abortions would be excluded from covered medical conditions. Internal tensions within the coalition over how to respond temporarily divided the bill's feminist supporters. In the end, CEDAPW leaders succeeded in getting compromise language inserted that narrowed the constraints on abortion coverage, and still permitted employers to cover the procedure should they wish. The conflict signaled clearly, though, that with the increasingly contentious politics surrounding abortion rights, feminists confronted serious obstacles in defending the right to bear and the right *not* to bear children as two sides of the same coin.[67]

In elaborating how pregnancy discrimination impinged on women's right to bear children, coalition activists underscored one final cost to women: the potential "severe economic consequences"—losses that men did not incur for their parenthood. CEDAPW drew attention to the effects on poor women of going without pay. Sherrie O'Steen, the plaintiff in *Gilbert* who had been forced by General Electric to stop working before and after childbirth, testified that she had ended up on public assistance. The decade's anxieties about soaring welfare rolls inflected the debate as the specter of women pushed out of employment during pregnancy and childbirth and landing on AFDC, the program that supported poor mothers, surfaced repeatedly.[68]

Arguments like these complemented arguments feminists made in other contexts in the same years about the importance of good jobs for women. For both full employment legislation, which President Carter signed into

law just days before the PDA reached his desk, and in hearings for the welfare reform initiative—the Program for Better Jobs and Income (discussed
in Chapter 5), which was introduced within months of the Pregnancy Discrimination Act—antipoverty feminists had joined welfare rights activists
in emphasizing the necessity for jobs that did not leave poor women on a
rollercoaster of public assistance and inadequate employment.[69] PDA advocates thus reinforced the larger shift in feminist activism in the latter part
of the 1970s toward emphasizing jobs over income to support motherhood.
By targeting pregnancy discrimination rather than maternity leave for this
critical legislative campaign, feminists pushed employment ahead of
government-provided income for new mothers. Union women's focus on
pregnancy discrimination and the devastating impact of the *Gilbert* decision lent urgency to feminists' prioritization of the issue. Fears by many
feminist leaders that agitating for paid maternity leave would only deepen
discrimination against women in the workplace also added weight to the
decision. And feminists did not abandon claims for income for childrearing:
within half a dozen years of the PDA's enactment, many coalition leaders
would launch a campaign for paid maternity leave.

Coalition organizers struggled to hold onto the most expansive feminist
rationale for pregnancy rights as the legislation moved through committee.
Congressional proponents, however, shifted the ground and foregrounded
families' needs over women's equality. In introducing the legislation into
Congress, Senator Harrison Williams of New Jersey explained that "the loss
of a mother's salary will have a serious effect on the family unit—making
it difficult for parents to provide their children with proper nutrition and
health care." Feminists conceded the point. Bella Abzug cited the growth
of the "husband and wife breadwinner family" as well as "the growing percentage of families headed by women" and acknowledged that the need to
shield pregnant workers from discrimination was "underscored by today's
economic realities." Yet Abzug batted down the suggestion from Utah's Senator Orrin Hatch that society could not afford disability benefits for pregnant mothers. "I realize there is always a cost—sometimes not only a
financial cost but even a social cost—whenever you have change and provide equality to people and make it possible for people to fulfill their constitutional rights, Senator."[70]

Congress ultimately agreed with Abzug that equality outweighed the
costs. California Representative Augustus Hawkins declared that the

Pregnancy Discrimination Act had to be enacted to overrule the Court's misreading of Congress's intent in *Gilbert*. "I know that when I cast my vote for Title VII [in 1964], I understood that protection to include pregnancy." The bill had the bipartisan support of six Senate and eighty-six House cosponsors, with more signing on. Public support was strong. Mail coming in to Congress ran between eight-to-one and ten-to-one in favor after the bill was introduced. Senator Jim Jeffords of Vermont would conclude, "We seldom see legislation which enjoys such broad-based support throughout the country. It is a pro-life, pro-family bill designed to take discriminatory pressure off the millions of families in this country who want to have children, but need two incomes to survive."[71] Overwhelming majorities voted in favor of the legislation. On October 31, 1978, President Carter signed it into law.

SECURING WOMEN LEGAL protection against pregnancy discrimination and employment rights as mothers was a signal feminist achievement. The fight for those rights drew on a coalescing network of feminist union activists and lawyers as well as major national women's organizations. It was a preeminent concern of the movement for nearly a decade, and the activism penetrated deeply, with cases surfacing not simply from New York or Washington but from Cleveland, rural Virginia, and small towns in central California as well. This was an issue which animated women at the grassroots level.

Through this activism, feminists opened the doors of workplaces to mothers and legally secured the right for mothers and pregnant women to their jobs. They overcame the weight of history to do so. But they didn't just open the door to women in the workplace and abandon them there. First of all, the vast majority of those they represented were already in the workplace and facing discrimination. Feminists argued persuasively that women should not incur either undue penalties for childbirth and childcare nor be denied employment opportunities and face permanent second-class status in the workplace. They battled to guarantee to female employees the full array of entitlements men received as a matter of course. Loss of wages should never be a fear, and no woman should face a no-win situation of impoverishment or dependency if she wanted to bear children. In the process, these second-wave activists rejected the belief that women alone bore responsibility for children. They conceived of a shared social and private obligation in which the state and employers provided income and benefits so that women could fulfill their roles as both mothers and workers. In short, feminists fought long and hard for a fundamental right, which they named the right to bear children.

They changed a nation's opinion, securing by overwhelming majorities legislative endorsement of their position in the Pregnancy Discrimination Act. It was a breathtaking cultural transformation. As symbols, Phillips's case and the anti-pregnancy discrimination campaigns signaled revised conceptions of mothers as workers. Wage earning and motherhood now were, at least in law and increasingly in social belief, compatible. The distinction legal feminists developed that separated childbirth from childrearing laid the foundation for the campaign for the Family and Medical Leave Act (FMLA) that began a few years later. Feminist leaders behind the FMLA had all been active in CEDAPW; Judith Lichtman and Donna Lenhoff, of the Women's Legal Defense Fund, architects of the FMLA, both worked on the PDA.

Like so many victories of this era, it is one half undone. We know that the right to bear children is still partial. Feminists lost the struggle to secure full social benefits for pregnancy and maternity. That this achievement remains incomplete should neither detract from recognition of the hardfought ground these feminist leaders gained nor keep us from understanding the broader vision they articulated.

8

FLEXTIME

Federally Employed Women and the
Drive to Restructure Work

The concept of full-time has remained constant only in that
it is the standard amount of time men work.

—Carol Greenwald, *Ms.*, 1976

S OMETIME IN 1966, Betty Friedan took a research trip to Washington for a
book she had begun to prepare. Through her connections with Catherine East, at the Commission on the Status of Women, and civil and women's
rights lawyer Pauli Murray, she plugged into the city's underground network of women's advocates inside the federal government and set up an
interview with Sonia Pressman, the first female staff attorney with the General Counsel's office at the Equal Employment Opportunity Commission
(EEOC). Despite the hundreds of complaints pouring in from women across
the country, commissioners were refusing to take the problem of sex discrimination seriously. The General Counsel, Pressman's boss, called her
a "sex maniac" for persisting with women's cases. Her frustrations spilled
out into Friedan's waiting notebook. What the country needed, she suggested, was a civil rights organization for women, an NAACP for the
women's movement.

Pressman was among the twenty-one women and men at the organizing conference of the National Organization for Women at the end of October 1966. When the group got off the ground, Pressman kept feeding Friedan and other members of NOW inside information from the EEOC. Just as importantly, she strengthened the widening Washington women's network by joining with other women working for the government to found Federally Employed Women (FEW) two years later.[1]

Federally Employed Women had its origins in a group of senior women in the federal government who participated in a training session for "Women Executives" in April 1968. Pressman attended. Helen Dudley, an instructor with the Department of Agriculture Graduate School, led the seminar and put the question of sex discrimination front and center. Participants found themselves in an impromptu consciousness-raising group, reporting, one after the other, on the jobs they had been denied, the promotions that went to men below them, the slights and indignities of daily work-life, and the hypocrisies of the newly inaugurated "Federal Women's Program." Dorothy Nelms, an African American woman raising two children on her own after a recent divorce, who worked for the Social Security Administration, recalled that Dudley made them "relive all the things we had experienced but had buried. Within four hours we were raging maniacs, we had become so livid." At that point, 34 percent of federal employees were female: 78.7 percent of them were in the lowest civil service grades (GS-1 through GS-6). A meager 1 percent occupied grades 13 or above. At lunch on Saturday, April 20, the group agreed to form a committee to plan a new organization, the symbolically named "TOO FEW—the Organization of Federally Employed Women," and later just F.E.W., Federally Employed Women.[2]

Dedicated to advancing women within the federal workforce, FEW worked to open doors to jobs for women in the civil service, support those bringing discrimination cases, and advance legislation that eradicated employment discrimination against women, particularly those in federal government positions. From the beginning, they forged strong alliances with feminist legislators in Congress, testifying in hearings organized by Oregon Congresswoman Edith Green in 1970 on the slow progress—and, indeed, active resistance—to countering discrimination in government workplaces.[3] One of their signal achievements was to collaborate with Representatives Bella Abzug, Yvonne Brathwaite Burke, and Patricia Schroeder from 1973 to 1978 to secure passage of legislation advancing career-ladder part-time employment and flexible scheduling within the civil service.

Federally Employed Women's efforts on behalf of these bills are emblematic of the feminist goal to restructure workplaces to be more compatible with family responsibilities for both men and women. Second-wave activists wished to remake the workweek itself. They called into question the forty-hours-a-week norm, demonstrating its male-breadwinner bias and the barriers it put up to workplace equality. As an alternative, second-wavers fought for well-paying part-time jobs, complete with benefits and advancement opportunities. They also pursued flexible employment with variable work schedules in order to enable women to accommodate household responsibilities, care for their children, and even have time for themselves. These demands stood alongside feminists' crusades for universal childcare and maternity benefits to create a comprehensive vision of change in American society and workplaces, so that having a job never meant that women also sacrificed their families or stretched themselves so thin they fought exhaustion daily.

Feminists walked a fine line in pursuing part-time and flexible employment. On the one hand, they acknowledged the specific needs of women who, in practice, bore responsibility for running their homes; on the other hand, they attempted to structure solutions in gender-neutral terms. They wanted to uphold the anti-sex-stereotyping principle that *both* women and men needed such changed workplaces. Advocating in these terms extended aspirations feminists had held since early in the twentieth century to transform protective labor laws into universal standards. Those rules had helped reconcile women's wage-earning and family responsibilities by regulating their hours, location, and conditions of work. Protective labor laws had been discarded at the end of the 1960s as discriminatory to women, but second-wave feminists hoped that new flexible and part-time hours regulations could become the kind of egalitarian family-supportive labor standards only dreamed of by earlier feminists.

The arguments that FEW leaders and other feminists made to back part-time employment and flexible work schedules evolved over a period of thirteen years, from the earliest experiments with alternative work schedules in the federal government in 1965 to the 1978 legislation that was finally enacted. The first calls for part-time and flexible alternatives were shaped by the position feminists in the post-World War II labor movement had taken on protective labor laws—women needed accommodations in their work conditions to enable them to fulfill their duties to families and home—but that stance evolved fairly rapidly. The focus remained on accommodating *women*, but the arguments shifted ground. Starting in the early 1970s, feminists contended that change in standard work-hours was urgently needed given the reality that so many women, particularly mothers of young children, now had jobs and still carried most of the family responsibilities. They demanded part-time and flexible hours of work more openly and directly as essential to true workplace equality, but still without substantially questioning the belief that it was women who bore responsibility for household work.

In the mid-1970s, however, feminist proponents argued increasingly forcefully that altered work schedules represented a requirement for true equality—necessary for shifting the balance in the home as well as the workplace and for changing men's roles in the family too. As the legislation neared passage in 1977 and 1978, a final set of claims about the benefits of more part-time and flexible work surfaced. These played to the rising public angst about the "crisis of the family" and insisted that altered work schedules would benefit the family. Feminists embraced the gender-neutral dimension to this focus on the family, but struggled to keep the issue of women's equality part of the debate.

The Standard Workweek and Protective Labor Legislation for Women

Although the eight-hour day had been a rallying cry of the American labor movement since the late nineteenth century, the standard workweek—maximum eight hours of work a day, forty hours a week—was a legacy of the New Deal era. Enacted in 1938, the Fair Labor Standards Act (FLSA) regulated hours of work, established a minimum wage, and required premium overtime pay beyond either eight hours of daily or forty hours of weekly time on the job. In its initial incarnation, the law entrenched long-established labor hierarchies, excluding agricultural and domestic workers, as we have seen in Chapter 4, but also those in retail and service industries, food processing and packing, and all government employees, among others. Overall, only 20 percent of workers received coverage, and they were disproportionately male—39 percent of working men but only 14 percent of female wage earners gained FLSA protections at passage. African American women saw little gain from the legislation: domestic and personal service employed 60 percent of black women in 1930; scarcely one in ten African American women worked in jobs benefitting from the act. Coverage in the decades after World War II expanded to include retail and service workers and state and local government employees, and the FLSA became a jealously guarded labor right, with union leaders determined to protect the standard of an eight-hour day with overtime pay.[4]

Just as importantly, the FLSA propped up male-breadwinning prerogatives. In part, it did so by its effective exclusion of large majorities of working women; moreover, not until the Equal Pay Act of 1963 were equal wages for women mandated. State-level protective labor legislation also remained legal under FLSA. With the forty-hour workweek in place, male union leaders turned their attention in the postwar years to battles for shorter working years (such as through paid vacation and sick leave) and shorter working lives (with stronger retirement provisions) that bolstered their effective earning power. Women in the labor movement saw things differently, but labor leaders largely ignored their calls for fewer hours of work to ease their double day. A gendered vision tailored to white male breadwinners' needs decidedly shaped what historian Dorothy Sue Cobble has called the "politics of time" in the two decades after World War II.[5]

The protective labor legislation that continued to shape many female workers' employment in these years was an achievement of early-twentieth-century women's groups. Aware that no brakes existed on the hours of work employers might demand beyond labor agreements, these maternalist champions sought limits on women's labor in the name of protecting family and motherhood. In the wake of the 1908 *Muller v. Oregon* decision discussed in Chapter 7, they helped secure laws that set maximum hours of work for women, prohibited work at late hours or on weekends, and barred female employees in some settings. For many of their advocates, the laws represented a first step toward universal protections for all workers, male as well as female.

Protective labor laws enjoyed widespread support into the 1960s, including among labor feminists who were advancing women's rights from inside the labor movement. They saw them as the best source of curbs on women's work, which they deemed essential to fulfilling their family roles. Forty-three states and the District of Columbia had woman-only maximum hours laws in 1963. However, passage of the Civil Rights Act, with its last-minute inclusion of the category of sex in Title VII forbidding employment discrimination, tapped into simmering doubts by some women's advocates over whether protective labor laws still benefitted them. Women working behind the scenes on the President's Commission on the Status of Women had already sought to create greater flexibility in protective laws, and they proposed once again expanding the maximum hours controls to men as well as women. In the United Auto Workers, labor feminists urged dissolution of protective laws early on. Employed in a male-dominated industry, where FLSA coverage made a difference, UAW women primarily saw hours limits as disadvantaging them relative to their male peers. After passage of Title VII, extended debate unfolded among women in the labor movement about whether to fight to uphold or dismantle protective labor laws.[6]

In August 1969, the Equal Employment Opportunity Commission made the debate moot. The Commission ruled that single-sex protective laws violated Title VII; when challenged, the courts sided with the commission's interpretation, and state legislatures began either repealing the laws or extending some beneficial ones, such as rest periods and minimum wages, to both women and men.[7] The broad cultural acceptance of protective labor legislation soon evaporated. With protective rules invalidated, labor and other feminist proponents needed to forge new arguments for regulating hours of work and accommodating workplaces to family responsibilities.

TOO FEW: Building a Feminist Organization to Advance Women in the Civil Service

"We feel it is this type of combined effort that will remove the artificial barriers to full equal opportunity for all of our wasted human assets." With these words, Allie Latimer Weeden launched Federally Employed Women's drive to "end sex discrimination in employment in the government service . . . and to further the use of the potential of women in the government." Latimer served as the first president of FEW. She was a lifelong organizer for civil rights and social justice, and she had taken a group of women from the local Presbyterian Interracial Council, which she led, to join the

Selma to Montgomery freedom march. In 1977, she became General Counsel of the General Services Administration—the first woman and the first African American to serve as general counsel of a major federal agency.[8]

FEW built a national membership, establishing chapters in Cincinnati; Huntsville, Alabama; Baltimore; Boston; the San Francisco Bay area; the "Space Coast" in Florida; and Fort Monmouth, New Jersey, among others, by mid-1970. Two thousand attended its annual conference in 1976, representing 125 chapters. Membership numbers equaled those of the Women's Equity Action League.[9] The organization was interracial, with visible black leadership and half of its membership African American in 1970. The Baltimore chapter president, Bernice S. White, for example, worked for the Social Security Administration and wrote a column, "It's NOT a Man's World," for the *Baltimore Afro-American*. Early newsletters featured stories on racial as well as gender equality, and FEW explored "a joint rap session[/]party with black employee caucuses." Those caucuses, observed one member, "have a more sophisticated and hard hitting political approach than we have, and perhaps we could learn from them, and they may need to be educated on women's issues." In the mid-1970s, President Janice Mendenhall identified recruiting Black and Chicana women as an ongoing priority. Still, in FEW's early years, white women predominated in the top posts: as president of the organization, as heads of chapters, and as regional coordinators.[10]

Aware that women remained trapped on the bottom rungs of the civil service, FEW recruited members among the lower general service grades. The first president of the Nashville, Tennessee chapter was Eunice Fisher, a secretary for the US Department of Labor, and her chapter prioritized pro-

"F.E.W. Holds First Annual Conference." *F.E.W.'s News and Views*, July 4, 1970.
Gathering for FEW's first annual national conference, chapter representatives
reported on their activities. The interracial mix of these chapter leaders echoes
the organization's membership.

moting women in lower grades. In 1974, the FEW board endorsed a secre-
taries' "Bill of Rights." More generally, FEW focused on advancement lad-
ders for women within the federal government.[11] At the same time, FEW
cultivated a network of highly placed women leaders both in government
and in the Washington feminist community. Sonia Pressman Fuentes was
not the only original NOW member and leader affiliated with FEW; NOW
founder and legal feminist Mary Eastwood served on the executive committee and in several other leadership roles in FEW, and both Catherine East
and Kathryn Clarenbach, another NOW originator, were honorary members of the organization. When Janice Mendenhall took over FEW's presidency in 1974, she belonged to NOW, the Women's Equity Action League
(WEAL), Women's Lobby, Inc., and the National Women's Political Caucus
(NWPC).[12]

Federally Employed Women belonged within two different traditions of
feminist organizing in this period. The organization shared a mission with
the many women's caucuses that sprouted up inside businesses, professional
associations, and labor unions and occupied common ground with the academic women's associations discussed in Chapter 1.[13] Drawing on the
moral and formal leverage that equal-opportunity programs within the federal government offered, FEW sought to make the federal service an exemplar of women's advancement. Moreover, the federal government was the
single largest employer in the country; action there had the potential to impact 700,000 working women's lives. Concerned, particularly in its early

years, to present a respectable public face, FEW distanced itself from more radical women's liberationist actions. As Daisy Fields, the organization's second president, explained, "We fight with wits—not bricks—but we aim to win."[14]

FEW embraced that strategy, placing it within a second strand of feminist advocacy—the organizing and activism carried out by large national feminist groups. FEW co-sponsored the August 1970 Strike for Equality, worked with other leading feminist organizations like NOW and the National Women's Political Caucus in petitioning the Federal Communications Commission to deny a license to a sexist District of Columbia television station, and were active members of the National Women's Agenda Coalition that advanced a feminist agenda for the National Women's Conference in Houston in 1977. In a 1974 study of women's groups, FEW shared with the NWPC, NOW, and the Women's Equity Action League, among others, interests in social security reform, childcare, domestic worker rights, and flexible work hours. DC FEW recruited members in the mid-1970s by distributing a list of past achievements that included co-sponsoring workshops with the Women's Legal Defense Fund, attending the feminist theater production "Floury Tales," offering "An Introduction to Consciousness Raising," organizing a free film festival on women's issues, and selling T-shirts and dish towels emblazoned with "Uppity Women Unite." DC FEW also joined the short-lived DC Metropolitan Abortion Alliance.[15]

FEW adopted several tactics to move women into and up the ranks of federal employment. They supported training to advance female federal employees while monitoring federal equal employment programs. Grievances and suits alleging discrimination received FEW backing. Enforcing the 1967 Executive Order 11375, which banned sex discrimination in federal employment, shaped many of FEW's initiatives in its first years, and they pressed the Civil Service Commission and the Nixon administration for robust action while demanding real support for the Federal Women's Program. When they met recalcitrance and limited progress, they coupled fighting from within the federal equal employment system with Congressional lobbying. From the beginning, FEW had a Legislative Committee and worked closely with women in Congress. Representative Martha Griffiths received a "Women Are People" award in December 1969 from FEW for her advancement of women's rights. (At the same event, FEW awarded Daniel Patrick Moynihan, who was serving as advisor to President Nixon, the "Undistinguished Service Award," citing him as "the person who contributed the most this year to discrimination against women.") The group wrote dozens of representatives in 1969 in support of bills removing sex discrimination in female federal employees' pension rights; Daisy Fields testified before sex-discrimination hearings convened by Congresswoman Edith Green the next year.[16]

Rallying for the national Women's Strike for Equality on August 26, 1970, FEW members received encouragement and support from across the federal government. It was a hopeful beginning to the coming decade of struggle. Undersecretary of State Alexis Johnson and Secretary of Labor James Hodgson declared "Federal Women's Day," and congresswomen sent upbeat messages full of hopes for sex equality, wider roles for women, and passage of the Equal Rights Amendment. Esther Peterson, the former director of the Women's Bureau and now a representative for the Amalgamated Clothing Workers, vowed, "We are on the way to a society where no one is forced into a predetermined role on account of sex." Above the crowd floated hundreds of red and blue balloons, emblazoned, "Women are on the Way Up!"[17]

Making Part-Time Work Pay: Fair Employment for Working Mothers

A broad official and popular interest in "womanpower" in the 1950s emphasized utilizing female talent in a tight labor market without interfering with women's roles in the home. Part-time work was a popular solution. 1957's *Womanpower*, a report of the National Manpower Council, a group set up in 1951 to study the country's labor market needs, recommended part-time and flexible employment as a way to draw on an untapped potential supply of women workers tied down by family responsibilities. In 1967, about a quarter of American women workers held less-than-full-time positions, the vast majority of them by preference. Women's employment in part-time work accelerated faster than their rise in full-time work in the 1950s and 1960s. High proportions of those seeking such nonstandard employment were middle-aged women, many now following the mid-twentieth-century pattern of returning to work after childrearing burdens eased. Male part-time job-seeking, by contrast, was much lower: in 1967, only one in ten men desired part-time work. Part-time employment for the vast majority of women was dead-end and unremunerative, with most of the jobs in clerical, household, and general service work. Nonwhite women working part-time remained trapped in the household, agricultural, or service work that employed nearly 85 percent of them. "Thus it is evident," the Women's Bureau summed up, "that women who work part time hold, for the most part, the less skilled, less rewarding jobs in our economy."[18]

FEW members were among the earliest feminists to engage the campaign to upgrade part-time work. Experiments with career part-time and alternative work schedules began in several government agencies in the years leading up to FEW's founding. The President's Commission on the Status of Women had recommended leadership by the federal government in creating skilled part-time employment for women in its 1963 report, and a similar recommendation came out of the Federal Women's Award Study Group in 1967. Those recommendations spurred some small-scale experiments, and Federally Employed Women became an active supporter of them. At the Atomic Energy Commission, Dr. Mary Bunting—serving as a commissioner while on a year's leave from Radcliffe—initiated a job-sharing program in 1965 that enabled two professionals to share a position.[19] The program with which FEW had the most direct involvement was the part-time Professional and Executive Corps, begun in late 1967, at the Department of Health, Education, and Welfare (HEW).

Recruiting forty women, all married with children—40 percent with at least one child under six—the HEW project showcased the promise of part-time employment of married mothers. A study of the group by Marjorie Silverberg and FEW member Dr. Lorraine Eyde, both of whom belonged to the Professional and Executive Corps themselves, showed that neither stereotypes about working mothers nor about part-time work held: the HEW Corps members were career committed, demonstrated high productivity, and advanced successfully from their part-time Corps positions. A few cautionary notes were sounded. The earnings of HEW Corps members simply wouldn't support households; for those at entry-level or clerical positions, this option was out of reach. Slowed access to promotions and uncertainty about the extent of fringe benefits also sowed both confusion and frustration. Silverberg and Eyde argued that part-time workers shouldn't have to wait twice as long as others to advance, and that a norm other than

Health, Education, and Welfare Secretary Gardner greets Mrs. Marjorie Silverberg and Mrs. Annabel Hecht at a press conference announcing the formation of HEW Professional and Executive Corps. Photograph by Jerry Hecht, December 19, 1967. Silverberg and Dr. Lorraine D. Eyde featured the corps and its successes as part of their advocacy for better part-time jobs for federal employees.

"man-years worked" needed to be developed. Such issues of sufficient pay and meaningful advancement continued to plague feminist efforts to create equitable part-time work over the next decade.[20]

Pressure to expand part-time employment and flexible work schedules came from a number of directions in the early 1970s. The International Labor Organization, the United Nations agency dedicated to promoting fair labor policies worldwide, endorsed both part-time and flexible work in the private and public sectors, noting their increasing use in developed countries. Several European countries enacted public-sector part-time and flexible employment laws. Flexible scheduling itself had its origins in a proposal by Christel Kammerer, a German management consultant, to address absenteeism and punctuality. Employers were interested for a variety of reasons. Some found that such work schedules also helped with peak demand hours. Bank of America, for example, used part-time workers to ease long lines for midday banking. Those concerned with humanizing workplaces argued that part-time and flexible employment options provided workers with greater control, and they posited that more satisfied workers would also be more productive and less prone to tardiness and absenteeism. After the oil crisis in 1973, many insisted that flexible work schedules would ease traffic congestion, reduce commute times (and create more worker leisure), and contribute to reduced air pollution and energy conservation.[21]

With mounting momentum for part-time and flexible work, the federal government became a prime candidate for pioneering experiments, and in 1973, Representatives Yvonne Brathwaite Burke of California and Bella Abzug of New York proposed the Flexible Hours Employment Act, which set a target of opening 10 percent of executive-branch positions to part-time schedules within five years. In the Senate, Senator John Tunney of California submitted a parallel bill.[22] As debate over the legislation got under way, FEW and feminist legislators began to distance themselves from older arguments about increasing part-time employment so women could work while fulfilling their duties to their families, instead using more recent ideas feminists had developed about women's "dual roles." Hearings held before the Senate Post Office and Civil Service Committee in September 1973 featured Felice Schwartz of Catalyst, a nonprofit agency focused on part-time employment opportunities for professional women. Her testimony provided a telling counterpoint to the ideas feminists were beginning to express.

Felice Schwartz is best known for the feminist outrage her 1989 *Harvard Business Review* article advocating for a "mommy track" stirred up, but Schwartz had been in the business of opening doors to employment for mothers for over twenty-five years.[23] Catalyst, the organization she founded in 1962, channeled its energies into aiding suburban, largely white, college-educated homemakers. Schwartz's goal was to make it possible for women to take paid jobs that could be combined with their family obligations. She justified broadening women's responsibilities by touting the call for getting talented "womanpower" into the workforce. When she founded Catalyst, Schwartz reached out to the Washington feminist network, but although Esther Peterson served on the Board starting in 1965, Schwartz's ties to feminists remained few.[24]

Catalyst was the vanguard of a host of similar organizations: Newtime, Inc., in New York; Options for Women, in Philadelphia; Wider Opportunities for Women and Distaffers, Inc., both in Washington, DC; New Ways to Work, in San Francisco; and Flexible Careers, in Chicago. Schwartz was thus an obvious choice for the Senate to call for the first hearings to be held on the Flexible Hours Employment Act. In her testimony, Schwartz described a pressing need for part-time work for mothers. "Now that women live for 75 years and are urged by population planners to have no more than two children," Schwartz commented emphatically, "it is essential that they be able to pursue careers, if they are to avoid virtual unemployment and frustration during the major portion of their lives." Without such opportunities, women experienced "demeaning" unemployment, while society wasted its "enormous investments" in their education.[25]

Her statement hinted at a growing role for men in family life but never made men and women equally responsible for taking care of the children and the home. Catalyst's position paper, "Flexible Work Schedules," admitted men could benefit from such legislation, but for them, new work schedules promised "more time for active involvement with their families, in society, with leisure pursuits." Catalyst's case for the nonstandard workweek still rested largely on the assumptions of a reliable male breadwinner and underutilized homemaker that had shaped the calls for women's part-time employment since the 1950s. Ultimately, Schwartz assured the assembled Senators, "there are a multitude of women who currently will be very appreciative of such legislation and their husbands are about to find out how much their lives are enhanced when their wives are given this opportunity."[26]

Bella Abzug preceded Schwartz before the committee and presented a joint statement from herself and Yvonne Brathwaite Burke. While striking a note similar to Schwartz's about women's particular desire for part-time employment, Abzug and Burke's statement more openly denounced existing structures as discriminatory and came closer to questioning the assumption that women had primary responsibility for the family. Part-time and flexible work, they said, was essential to enable women to fulfill their dual roles as workers and parents. Indeed, in pushing for *flexible* work schedules, they acknowledged that some needed or wished to work full-time and that an altered work pattern for full-time work might best suit their desires. "The problem of talented women who would like to return to work is great," the two legislators declared, yet mothers' unemployment rate was astronomical, childcare facilities were ridiculously insufficient, and the system was unaccommodating. "With a little help from the Federal

Government . . . we can upgrade the efficiency of current Federal employees who might opt for flexi-hours positions, attract talented women, who because they can't find child care or have some commitments at home, can't work 40 hours a week from 9 to 5." More directly than Schwartz, they included expanding men's role in childrearing in their justification for the bill. Less focused on opportunity for individual women than Schwartz was, the feminists Burke and Abzug highlighted the social structures impeding women's advancement. From their perspective, redesigned workplaces were a precondition for equality.[27]

Daisy Fields, FEW's legislative committee chair and former president, echoed Burke and Abzug in her statement to the committee, drawing attention in particular to the foot-dragging of federal officials. Outright bias in the Civil Service Commission and elsewhere in the government got in the way of making part-time or flexible work real options. The Commission, FEW wrote, has opted for a "passive role in encouraging innovation or creativity in personnel policies and practices." "Leadership must come from the Congress," FEW avowed. The commission's insistence that many jobs could not be performed with an altered work structure had "no basis in fact." FEW took Commissioner Hampton to task specifically for stereotypically claiming "Air Traffic Controller, Border Patrol Officer, Park Ranger, and Forester" would not attract candidates willing to work part-time. Women had gained the right to hold federal jobs where they would carry a firearm just two years before. How would there be a large supply of candidates without training? Park Ranger and Forester, moreover, could well be jobs "ideally suited to husband-wife teams and could be filled on a part-time basis."[28]

Fields stressed that any final legislation must include real benefits and promotion opportunities. Making part-time work "real" jobs was a priority for FEW, and it largely reflected their desire to bring women up through the ranks into professional-grade positions. But the professional and middle-class bias of the organization's leaders meant that there was no acknowledgment in FEW's statements of the needs of single mothers, and the sense that professional opportunity more than earning power was at stake pervaded their presentations. Nowhere in their remarks did either Fields or Abzug connect part-time work to feminist antipoverty activism or the needs of poor mothers on public assistance.

In addition to the Civil Service Commission, which desired to preserve its control over the regulation of government employment, the bill's opponents included the labor unions representing federal employees. Labor feared changes that might undo the protections of the eight-hours-a-day, forty-hours-a-week workweek. Flexible or compressed schedules, after all, might have workers at their jobs for longer hours of work on a given day in exchange for more days off. Loss of premium pay, now mandated by FLSA after eight hours in a day, could occur, as well as compulsory compliance with a schedule that violated FLSA principles. Creating part-time positions could serve as an excuse to downgrade existing full-time jobs into part-time positions that were not as good. For the next five years, responding to this concern became a major challenge for the bill's advocates, and they never fully overcame the resistance of the public-sector unions representing federal employees.[29]

Employment Equity *and* Family Responsibilities: Reshaping the Standard Workweek

Burke and Abzug's Flexible Hours Employment bill stalled in the 93rd Congress, and it took until late September 1975, two years later, before the next round of hearings were held on legislation now titled the "Part-Time Career Opportunities Act." By then, the terrain had shifted substantially. In 1975, and again in hearings in April 1976, legislators heard from a growing chorus of voices—professional human resource specialists and corporate leaders—who had experimented with alternative work schedules that reconfigured rather than reduced the standard workweek. This national movement for alternative work schedules had only tangential ties to the women's movement; rather, it emerged from business interests and social scientists seeking to improve work life and productivity. In the mid-1970s, the movement took off. The US Comptroller General reported that in 1976, a million workers in three thousand firms had positions requiring four-day, forty-hour weeks. Alternative work schedules typically meant full-time employment on nonstandard workweeks—flexible start and end times, compressed schedules with longer hours traded for days off, and various methods of "banking" hours.[30] When Congress reconvened to consider the issue this time around, it had two sets of legislation in front of it, which reflected the rising influence of this movement: in addition to the older one promoting part-time employment in the federal government, another one directly authorized experiments with the kinds of flexible work schedules the new movement called for.[31]

A second issue was on legislators' minds as well. A recession from November 1973 to March 1975, along with rising unemployment, triggered persistent questions about how more part-time employment might affect the economy. Would it create worthwhile opportunities? Or would it lead to permanent substitution of part-time jobs for much needed full-time ones? Would a flood of women entrants in pursuit of new part-time positions crowd out breadwinning men?[32]

Consideration of the part-time and flexible hours bills occurred in the same years as debate over both full employment legislation and President Carter's welfare reform proposal, the Program for Better Jobs and Income (PBJI) discussed in Chapter 5. PBJI and the Full Employment and Balanced Growth Act, which was finally signed in 1978, raised many of the same issues about employment policy, equity, and male breadwinning that part-time and flexible hours legislation did. In each context, feminists—sometimes, in fact, the same activists and lobbyists—resisted equations between women's wage earning and men's unemployment. They challenged prioritizing male breadwinners in programs, demanding recognition of women's distinctive situation and the history of discrimination against them. They pointed out the need to restructure workplaces and labor markets to accommodate the family responsibilities that women bore more heavily than men. Part-time and flexible hours laws, in other words, were embedded in the broad feminist agenda of breaking down the family-wage model of male breadwinning and standard work patterns, while stripping away the legal and policy superstructure supporting them.[33]

With debate over full employment and welfare reform raging, and interest in alternative work schedules expanding rapidly, this second stage of consideration of the part-time and flexible hours bills in 1975 and 1976 elicited broader feminist participation. Joining FEW in supporting the bill were NOW, the Women's Equity Action League, Women's Lobby, Inc., the National Women's Political Caucus, and the Alliance for Displaced Homemakers, along with an expanding roster of feminist national and state legislators. These liberal feminist organizations would take the lead in making the case both that women needed alternative work schedules because they needed the money to support themselves and their families and that they needed the flexibility in a world where affordable, full-time childcare was sorely lacking.

As they did with the fight for universal childcare, radicals stayed out of these national legislative battles. Skeptical about a capitalist system that locked both women and men into a soulless labor system, radicals had limited interest in reforming national policy. Even so, they, too, considered part-time and flexible work a feminist issue. The radical feminists among the five hundred women attending the Congress to Unite Women in November 1969 joined the assembly in demanding "that working hours be made flexible for both men and women" and that "part-time employment . . . be made available for women who want it."[34] Greater elaboration of that demand appeared two years later in *Women: A Journal of Liberation.* "Do we really want to be equal to men in that we spend all day, five days a week for forty years of our lives, working—even at a fascinating, meaningful job?" Marie Carosello Bristol asked. Bristol enumerated a set of benefits to a shorter workweek: easing the burden of "the sisters who have spent their adult lives working forty hours a week away from home *and* forty hours a week doing housework" and giving mothers who wanted to work, but did not want their children in childcare centers, some options.

Writing at a moment of high economic optimism and influenced by the New Left critique of bureaucratic work, Bristol envisioned a twenty-hour workweek freeing people from "a production-centered personality." "Free time to pursue other interests," such as "political action, a vegetable garden, writing, care of small children (their own or others'), painting, further formal or informal education, etc." would be the outgrowth.[35] Surrounded by social movements that dreamed of dramatic shake-ups in workplaces and families—and, for some, even the imminent end of capitalism—radical feminists had little interest in ensconcing relentless shuttling between paid and household labor for women. Instead, they assumed an affluent and technologically advancing United States could afford to transform work itself. Both men and women would be free to parent some of the time and work some of the time, without submitting to a daily grind.

As debate over alternative workweeks expanded after 1973, radicals increasingly feared that rather than the liberation of time and self-development that Bristol imagined, expanded flextime and part-time work would become just another means to extract labor from women. WUSH—Women United for Shorter Hours—an arm of the Workers Action Movement and an offshoot of the socialist Progressive Labor Party, was fighting for forty hours' pay for thirty hours' work in the early 1970s. "Part-time work is what women get all the time," said WUSH's Mary Gelles in 1973 in condemning the bills in Congress. "Women who work part time get less pay and less benefits. We want a shorter week with full benefits."[36] Five years later Ellen Frye, writing in the radical feminist magazine *Off Our Backs*, denounced liberal feminists for embracing "the job-sharing concept."

Rather than seeing opportunity for women in the hype around part-time work and flextime, Frye saw exploitation. Employers gained workers who were cheaper because they often did two-thirds of a job for half-time wages. Plus, benefits were typically nonexistent. Frye warned of employers phasing out full-time work, leaving workers to fend for themselves on unreliable shifts and inadequate hours of work. She held out little hope that part-time work would break down gender stereotypes. "The concept of job-sharing, or to label it more bluntly, high-status part-time employment, is directly linked to the myth of the woman being fully responsible for child rearing and homemaking with hubby providing the economic security blanket." The real result of "job-sharing," according to Frye, was that "thousands of women are forced into juggling two or more part-time jobs with full responsibility for the children and the dishes." More cynical than others, Frye closed with this stinging assessment: "The objective of our government is to incorporate women into the labor market without jeopardizing either the jobs of men or the traditional American family."[37]

As radicals shifted between celebrating part-time work for its promise of a life defined *not* by capitalist imperatives and excoriating it for its perpetuation of class hierarchies and gender norms, they revealed the fault lines and troubling risks in feminist advocacy of nonstandard employment. Feminists within the labor movement, however, were increasingly supportive. At the end of the decade, Working Women, the national organization representing office workers, called for good benefits and protections for part-time workers as well as more flextime and job sharing, and they made the demand "for policies to ease the burden of the working family" part of their "Agenda for the 1980s." Two leading women's labor groups, Union WAGE and the Coalition of Labor Union Women (CLUW), also joined the broader labor movement's appeal for thirty hours' work for forty hours' pay in the 1970s. In 1980, CLUW allied with the Displaced Homemakers Network, Wider Opportunities for Women, and the National Commission on Working Women to issue a "Working Women's Platform." Among many requests, they challenged the presidential candidates and their fellow labor-movement members to "promote alternative work schedules (including flex-time, part-time, compressed workweek, and job sharing) with appropriate benefits."[38]

Despite such declarations, women's labor coalitions never testified for the proposed flex and part-time legislation. They faced united opposition from within the labor movement. Federal employees associations and the AFL–CIO units representing public employees both continued to oppose the bills, not just in 1975 and 1976, but also in the final stage of debate, from 1977 to 1978. Protection of the Fair Labor Standards forty-hour week remained paramount for them. Federal employees had just come under the forty-hour provisions of the FLSA with the same amendments to the act in 1974 that had granted the domestic workers discussed in Chapter 4 their coverage, and labor remained jittery. We "stand," they said, "for labor standard legislation." The "pending bills," the AFL–CIO public employees unit warned ominously in 1975, "provide a dangerous loop-hole in this basic labor standards legislation." Two years later, the message was much the same, "We oppose these [flextime proposals] even on a temporary, experimental basis."[39]

It was, then, liberal feminists in organizations like FEW, NOW, and the Women's Equity Action League who set out the second-wave case for the legislation. They built their arguments from the ground up, citing historic bars to women's employment opportunity because of their family responsibilities. They noted the specific needs of women on the job as a consequence of family labor and, as they were doing in the same years for pregnant workers, refuted the notion that women were merely secondary earners in male-breadwinner households. Writing to members of the House subcommittee reviewing the bill in November 1975, Lynne Darcy, the coordinator of NOW's National Task Force on Compliance and Enforcement, which addressed employment discrimination, and Elaine LaTourelle, the Seattle childcare activist and current NOW Legislative Vice President, pointed out that "an unemployed woman seeking a part-time job is just as 'unemployed' as a person seeking a full-time job; it is not humanly possible to distinguish between their *needs* to be gainfully employed. . . . NOW simply asks that the employment needs and desires of *all* people in the job market be considered equally, and that the growing number of part-time workers no longer be 'sacrificed' for the benefit of the more traditional needs of full-time employees."[40]

Gladys Henrikson, testifying for WEAL and Women's Lobby, Inc., described "a growing rejection of the traditional labor pattern for working mothers" for the assembled committee members and—in the absence of decent childcare options—the acute need for work that did not force women to withdraw from the labor force for a decade or more to meet their family responsibilities.[41] The fact that many single mothers, including those on public assistance, had substantial childcare obligations made part-time work an important option for them as well.

That flexibility in work schedules would also benefit men remained an undercurrent of this round of hearings. Patricia Schroeder cited flexible hours as giving "working fathers" the opportunity "to participate more fully in the raising of their children." NOW was most direct. They took old-fashioned gender-role stereotypes to task, voicing the idea that "in view of a less narrow and gender-based approach to parenthood, increasing numbers of men are expressing the desire for a more central role in the raising of their children." Like women, men would "find in part time work a solution to their two fold ambitions as breadwinners and family men."[42]

Male feminists reiterated this point in their writings. Warren Farrell cited compressed workweeks, flexible schedules, and job sharing in 1974's *The Liberated Man* as means for fathers to free up time to care for children. James Levine made the same case two years later. In a chapter entitled "Making the Time to Care: Part-Time Jobs for Full-Time Fathers," he explored the stigma men faced if they worked part time. Citing the part-time and flexible hours bills before Congress, Levine observed that "the most immediate impact of more part-time job options will be on young mothers"; still, he hoped, "new status for part-time jobs" would lead employers to be "less likely to suspect a man's commitment to the job if he chose to work part time so that he could share in the care of his young children."[43]

As Levine acknowledged, bars to women's advancement and strong societal expectation of their responsibility for children remained the primary focus of the debate around the legislation. Supporters insisted that the massive social changes unfolding before their eyes and the unfair consequences of discrimination made it imperative for society, not just individual women, to adapt. To those who complained that changing the system was too difficult or imposed burdens on some, Linda Teixeira of the Alliance for Displaced Homemakers countered, "Whose system, I ask?" Was it the system that forced "the makers of breakfast and dinner" to "get along somehow" even if they also worked a full day's paid labor? Not at all. "It is, I suggest, the system itself that tampers with the lives of many individuals and ruins them solely because it is inflexible," Teixeira concluded heatedly. Feminists demanded changes in the system that ensured not just scheduling flexibility but also that the part-time and flexible positions opened to women did not exploit them. They offered a unified chorus of voices reiterating FEW's call for promotion opportunities, seniority possibilities, and secure retirement benefits.[44]

The bills once again went nowhere in the 94th Congress, and a renewed push for passage began in 1977. Still ringing in the air was FEW President Janice Mendenhall's forceful avowal that "we cannot condone any practice . . . that denies equal rights and benefits to any group of employees . . . solely because their hours of duty in a scheduled workweek are less than 40."[45]

THE DISCUSSION OF PART-TIME and flexible work developed a new twist in this final round of debate as Americans began more directly facing up to the end of the family wage system. "I speak to you today in behalf of America's families and their children," Urie Bronfenbrenner announced to members of the House Committee on Post Office and Civil Service in late May 1977. An eminent child psychologist and professor of family studies at Cornell University, Bronfenbrenner predicted disaster ahead. "As I am sure you are aware, the American family is currently being subjected to powerfully destructive forces." For the first time, the endangered American family made its way into debates about part-time and flexible work. Belief that the American family was "in crisis" gripped popular and policy debates in the late 1970s, as we saw in the forces shaping President Carter's Program for Better Jobs and Income. Both liberals and conservatives increasingly viewed women's employment through this lens. As early as 1973, Walter Mondale had proposed requiring "Family Impact Statements" for any social policy related to the family—correlates to the environmental impact statements required after 1970. Introducing "the family" into the discussion over nonstandard work schedules altered the tenor of the debate, offering some new points of leverage for feminists while sidestepping the needs of women and the goal of women's equity.[46]

In his testimony, Bronfenbrenner characterized maternal employment and the rising rates of single parenthood as the root cause of danger to American families. Alarmingly, "the middle-class family of today increasingly resembles the low income family of the early 1960s." Evoking the demonized black family of the 1965 Moynihan Report, Bronfenbrenner painted a dire picture: "Who cares for America's children? Who cares?" Bronfenbrenner went on to support more part-time work opportunities for both women and men, and even to note that this alone would not address the needs of single parents for whom the low wages of part-time work simply created added stress. He identified *time* as the critical scarce resource in family lives. This focus on time drew attention to the strains of the mounting hours of paid and household labor carried by women, but in the process, questions of advancement, wage equity, and women's historically disadvantaged position faded. The problem boiled down to "a new American dilemma: the agonizing choice between doing right by one's job versus doing right by one's child."[47]

Feminists—from the representatives sponsoring the legislation, like Pat Schroeder, to FEW and the other women's groups testifying for the bills—resisted reducing the problem of balancing employment and family responsibilities to merely a question of time. For them, first of all, the issue of time remained inextricable from unequal allocation of family and household work to women. Second, rising pressures on women's time came from economic need and from women's just claims for equality, not from the maternal abandonment implicit in so much of the family crisis commentary. Part-time employment, observed Representative Pat Schroeder with some irritation, had nothing to do with "people who get tired of eating bon-bons and watching soap operas" and everything to do with falling incomes and families' need for more than one breadwinner. "Employment policies," said Mae Walterhouse, president of FEW, "can no longer be based on the concept of a single family breadwinner."[48]

From this perspective, the absence of meaningful part-time and flexible work opportunities was "a form of de facto discrimination against women by denying them access to better paying nontraditional and career opportunities." *Time* was not the issue, added Leslie Gladstone, speaking on behalf of WEAL, NOW, NWPC, and Women's Lobby, Inc., but rather, "the rigidity of the traditional 9 to 5 workday" that burdened "the already delicate fabric of American family life." She and other feminists were the first to make the case that the standard workweek itself was discriminatory, and a barrier to women's equality which society had an obligation to redress. "The only thing full time about a 37 ½ hour week is that it is the amount of time usually worked by men, and men are taken as the norm," noted Carol S. Greenwald, Massachusetts's commissioner of banks. Men's lives, she added tartly, should not be held up as the norm "when almost half the labor force is women." It is as if, Pat Schroeder observed, "Somebody thought that the 8-hour day and the 40-hour week was hammered in a stone tablet somewhere."[49]

Carol Greenwald expressed the feminist expectation that society take a role in altering working conditions most fully. After the birth of her children, Greenwald had pioneered part-time employment in the Federal Reserve and then as commissioner of banks. In her testimony, she posed the same question as Bronfenbrenner: "Who is going to care for our children?" Greenwald's answer was strikingly different from his. She insisted that what was at stake was *"society's* needs to insure that our children are well cared for. That is a government concern." Citing laws enacted in France and Sweden, Greenwald demanded a legal right to part-time work, prodding Congress to "mandat[e] that it is a legal right for men and women to hold one's current position on a part-time basis for a certain number of years." Greenwald envisioned a broad package of labor rights, including parental leave and federally funded childcare, as a necessary comprehensive change in the structure of work. Without that kind of reorganization, equality remained elusive. "Only," she concluded, "when the federal government funds day care centers for all and mandates part-time career opportunities as a legal right, only then will women be able to believe that there is a commitment to equal employment opportunity for them. Only then can we feel assured that our children are being well cared for."[50]

Feminists continually returned the debate to this question of genuine conditions for equality. Problems of wage equity, occupational segregation, and women trapped in low-grade positions all hinged on reorganization of society's norms for a "typical" worker. Real part-time work, employment unaffected by having children, and access to more flexible hours: these were what Congress should guarantee.[51]

Both the flexible hours and part-time hours legislation finally made it through Congress in September 1978, and facilitating stable part-time positions has remained a part of federal government employment policy since then. But the flexible hours act contained compromises. Most significant was the replacement of mandatory by voluntary targets for the percentage of federal employees involved in the flexible hours pilots. After some wrangling with the Reagan administration, the act was renewed in 1982; in 1985, Congress permanently authorized alternative work schedules for federal employees.[52] Flexibility has become a labor force watchword—a standard demand not just of feminists, but of liberals and labor as well.

Passage of the two bills happened within months of enactment of both the Pregnancy Discrimination Act and the federal jobs programs for displaced homemakers. Displaced homemaker legislation was also a product of feminist advocacy, as we saw in Chapter 4. It provided training and guidance to women who had dedicated years to homemaking, but now needed to work because of divorce or widowhood.[53] Together, the flexible and part-time employment acts, the displaced homemaker legislation, and the Pregnancy Discrimination Act represent a notable set of feminist legislative successes in the late 1970s. These victories show a movement carrying considerable political clout despite the rising anti-ERA momentum that is more commonly understood to have consumed feminists' energies in these same late 1970s years.

FROM THE FIRST EXPERIMENTS with part-time work, led by women in FEW in the late 1960s, to the final hearings in 1978, feminists struggled to ensure that part-time and flexible employment advanced women's opportunities and equality without reinforcing their marginal status in the workforce. They demanded *good*, permanent part-time positions with benefits, advancement, and flexible schedules to keep women at work when family obligations might have knocked them out of the labor force. They linked employment equity both to workweeks liberated from a forty-hour male norm and to changed roles for men as well as women. Married middle-class professional women remained more in feminists' sightlines than female heads of households on the bottom rungs of the general service ladder. They never quite grappled with the reality that a single parent would be hard pressed to survive on even a good part-time wage. Still, FEW and their feminist allies took on the widely entrenched "standard workweek." They were the ones who pushed the point that change needed to be made to accommodate family labor. They provide more evidence that second-wave feminists did not simply pursue the male full-employment model for women's equity. They did not expect individual women and families to go it alone. Rather, they put forward plans for both business and government to accommodate the family. The sweeping reorganization of the working day that they envisioned completed the feminist campaign for work and family lives where women could live fully in both public and private worlds, unfettered by discrimination.

Of course, this campaign had its limits. It worked much better for middle-class households in which a second, part-time earner could adequately meet family needs. And "flexibility," as labor feared, often became a watchword for greater employer control and for gutting labor's rights and protections in the coming decades, as conservatives gained ground in American politics. The support from government and business was relatively limited—individual women still bore the brunt of the costs of family, in both time and money. And while the federal government was the largest national employer, and a model that many private and public sector employers emulated, the legislation covered only a fraction of the national workforce. The law has yet to extend to business. Even with these limitations, FEW and their allies were, in so many ways, prescient. Flexibility on feminist terms—with gender equity and eradication of sex-role stereotypes as a central goal—is now a widely recognized means to create workplace equality and meet family needs.

CONCLUSION

The Myth of "Having It All"

> The media image of the ideal woman shifted from the fully
> domesticated suburban housewife . . . to the upwardly
> mobile career woman. . . . What is tragic is that the new
> imagery gradually came to *represent* feminism, not only to
> an apolitical public but to many feminists too. . . . The
> face-to-face self-presentation of feminism did not stand a
> chance compared to the media's representation of feminism,
> and what the media presented was not a movement at all,
> but a self–improvement program.
>
> —Barbara Ehrenreich, "The Women's Movements:
> Feminist and Antifeminist," 1981

BY THE END OF THE 1970S, the claim that feminists promised women they could "have it all" but failed them could be found everywhere: on the pages of any women's magazine, in the endless drumbeat of news stories on working women's burdens, or on gloomily intoned television "special reports" on women and the family. Feminism became the target of choice. It was convenient to fault the movement for the strains on families as the new postindustrial economy swept male-breadwinning households away in its ongoing, gradual restructuring of employment. In the years when the Reagan era began to unfold, a highly reductive version of second-wave feminism took over popular conceptions of the movement. As the media peddled the "cult" of having it all—as Letty Cottin Pogrebin had so aptly labeled it—the setbacks of the new conservative era and the new economic realities conspired to obscure a decade and a half of feminist activism on behalf of work and family.

The strangest amnesiac was Betty Friedan herself. Nearly twenty years after *The Feminine Mystique*'s breakthrough, her 1981 book *The Second Stage* added a troubling coda that gave a disconcerting boost to those finding fault with feminism. The book was filled with eyebrow-raising declarations, stinging accusations backed with mere scatterings of evidence, bitterness over the movement's internal struggles, and a disavowal of much of the feminist labor in the realms of work and family. Friedan even perpetuated the having-it-all myth: in the book and in a series of articles that she began publishing in 1979, she argued that the feminist movement had succumbed to a *feminist* mystique that led it to commit two dangerous mistakes.[1]

First, by her account, liberal feminists exclusively "fought for equality in terms of male power." Chafing at women's confinement to home and motherhood, she and other NOW activists had demanded "full participation, power and voice in the mainstream, inside the party, the political process, the professions, the business world."[2] Friedan painted second-wave feminism's proponents—all implicitly white and middle class—as solely concerned with opening doors for women, whom they left to move within the public world on the same terms as men. Efforts to transform marriage, men, and household labor disappeared in Friedan's story of the movement, as did struggles for workplaces accommodating to mothers. As Friedan recounted it, "We told our daughters that they could—and should—have it all. Why not? After all, men do. But the 'superwomen' who are trying to 'have it all,' combining full-time careers and 'stretch-time' motherhood, are enduring such relentless pressure that their younger sisters may not even dare to think about having children."[3] Somehow, it became feminism's legacy to produce stressed-out superwomen. While this was troubling enough, the movement's more damning mistake in Friedan's judgment was the antifamily sexual politics of radical feminists. Friedan served up a caricatured version of the radical feminist critique of the family alongside the diverse antirape, antipornography, pro-abortion, and lesbian rights campaigns of the movement. As Friedan told one lesbian who challenged her, "That's sex . . . not politics."[4]

Friedan blamed feminism's vulnerability at the end of the 1970s on these missteps. "The women's movement has to assume some responsibility" for the opposition it now faced, she claimed. Radicals bore the lion's share. Their sexual politics, she wrote, "made it easy for the so-called Moral Majority to lump E.R.A. with homosexual rights and abortion into one explosive package of licentious, family-threatening sex."[5] In other words, by engaging in struggles over sexual and reproductive freedom, women's rights proponents handed their detractors a potent weapon to use against them. Yet even her own brand of liberal feminism received its share of censure. Focused on overturning the feminine mystique that had defined women by motherhood and homemaking, "we insidiously fell into a feminist mystique, which denied that core of women's personhood that is fulfilled through love, nurture, home." Then sidetracked by "sexual battles," the movement failed to restructure homes and workplaces to give women and men meaningful choices. "Our failure was our blind spot about the family."[6]

It was time to move on to a "second stage." Friedan urged the movement "to transcend that polarization between feminism and the family." Repeating the claim that all supporters of women's advancement had simply accepted the antinomy between work and home as a given, Friedan called for reconciling the two through government-funded childcare, family leaves, "child allowances" for full-time parenting, flexible workplaces, and greater participation of men—as if feminists had not demanded these all along.[7] It was a stunning and perplexing rewriting of the movement's own history that erased the broad swath of feminist work on behalf of childcare, maternity rights in the workplace, and egalitarian marriage.

Not surprisingly, fellow feminists roundly panned *The Second Stage*. Radicals objected to the mischaracterization of their position on the family and to the claim that sexual politics was somehow a mere incendiary diversion that stopped the main thrust of the movement in its tracks. Susan Faludi, writing in her bestseller *Backlash*, accused Friedan of indulging in "the tantrums of a fallen leader" who offered up only "a murkily defined new order that is heavy on old Victorian rhetorical flourishes." The radical activist and writer Ellen Willis pointed out the absurdity of Friedan's narrative of feminism: "The family is and always has been a central concern of feminism," she wrote. "Friedan is really saying that feminists should embrace the current trend toward mindless sentimentality about the family and abandon our abrasive habit of analyzing and criticizing it." The New

Right cheered the book. Phyllis Schlafly was jubilant, hailing Friedan for having just hammered "another nail in the coffin of feminism."[8]

When Betty Friedan could earn Phyllis Schlafly's praise for attacking feminism, something was up. How could "the mother of the movement" write such a travesty of feminist history? The years from 1979 to 1982 were a low point for the women's movement; on this, her critics agreed with Friedan. "Feminism is at a critical point in its history," commented Ellen Willis in her 1981 review of Friedan's book. "The momentum of the movement has drastically slowed, and if it is to survive, let alone progress, it must regroup and begin a new offensive."[9] The highs of passing the Pregnancy Discrimination Act, displaced homemaker legislation, and FEW-supported flex- and part-time hours laws in 1978 were followed by a dry spell. Feminist policy proposals stalled out: the Program for Better Jobs and Income faded, leaving poor women vulnerable while new childcare initiatives gained little traction. In January 1979, President Carter fired Bella Abzug as the head of his National Advisory Committee for Women after she protested upcoming cuts in public programs benefitting women.[10] In March 1979, the first deadline for ratifying the Equal Rights Amendment expired, three states short of approval. A Herculean effort to extend the ratification deadline by three years drained energies already depleted by the long fight for ratification. Feminism was increasingly vulnerable. Weariness, disillusionment, and battle fatigue set in among leaders and grassroots feminists alike. A painful reckoning over movement strategy unfolded as the ERA dream crashed to an end on June 30, 1982, when the amendment's three-year ratification extension expired without any progress.

A book hoping to move on to a "second stage" was not so surprising, then, but its needless reiteration of the having-it-all myth about feminism was. Other factors help explain Friedan's use of the shorthand. She was a journalist writing for the very magazines that invented and perpetuated the having-it-all ideal. As her biographer Daniel Horowitz has observed, her 1970s articles alternated between hard-hitting analysis and cliché-filled formula.[11] Having it all had come to dominate media characterization of the women's movement. In 1978, Enjoli famously sold perfume with a jingle that made feminists' blood boil: "I can bring home the bacon, fry it up in a pan and never, never, never let you forget you're a man." The advertisement's print tagline read "the eight hour perfume for the twenty-four hour woman." Journalists spread doubts about feminist goals as they reported on women under pressure from the "superwoman squeeze," who suffered the exhaustion of the "go-it-alone grind." By 1985, feminism's legacy was a given in popular accounts. The bestselling *Smart Women/Foolish Choices* informed its readers that their struggles were "an unfortunate consequence of feminism," which had "created a myth among women that the apex of self-realization could be achieved only through autonomy, independence, and career."[12]

The rising conservative movement pounced on this characterization. The Reverend Jerry Falwell's Moral Majority, founded in 1979, added fuel to the growing pro-family movement led by anti-E.R.A. activists like Schlafly. In his first two years in office, an actively hostile President Reagan advanced legislation that undid years of feminist work. Both pro-family and main-stream conservatives equated feminism with careerism and sexual liber-tinism. Relentless, withering attacks charged feminism with putting the family in crisis. For conservatives, the movement threw women into the workforce, left children vulnerable, contributed to men's unemployment, and weakened society's foundations. Paul Weyrich, called the "Father of the New Right" by some, celebrated the unmasking of "the lie of femi-nism": "Women are discovering they can't have it all," he crowed. "They are discovering that if they have careers, their children will suffer, their family life will be destroyed. It used to be we were the only ones who were saying it. Now I read about it everywhere."[13]

Friedan's fixation on the family also reflected ongoing misgivings about its fate. The country faced a deeply unsettled period as the underpinnings of the family wage system came apart and the social, cultural, and legal formations predicated on it stretched to the breaking point. The economics of the family became particularly urgent at the end of the decade. Inflation had topped 11 percent in December 1979, with unemployment at a worri-some 6 percent. They would keep rising for three years running. As Friedan observed, "Sheer economic need, exposed and escalated with undeniable urgency by inflation, gives most women in the 1980s, married or single, no choice but to work."[14] The combination of economic dislocation and the ongoing influx of women into the workplace fed a pervasive belief that the American family was in crisis.

Scholars, journalists, and politicians alike portrayed the family as an en-dangered species. The child advocate Urie Bronfenbrenner published his 1977 analysis of the family for the *Washington Post* under the headline,

"The Calamitous Decline of the American Family," while the *New York Times* titled its coverage equally forebodingly, predicting that "The Family Could Become a Relic by the Year 2000." Many saw white middle-class families facing the same dangerous disintegration they had diagnosed in inner-city black families the decade before. It was not only conservatives who blamed feminism for the crisis. The prominent child psychologist Dr. Lee Salk told *US News and World Report* readers that the "sexual revolution and the women's movement" were at fault.[15] Scholars rushed to diagnose the problems of the American family, spawning new journals, organizing conferences, and raising plenty of funding. In 1977, Congress responded to the "national drift toward the disintegration of the family unit" with a helpful "National Family Week."[16]

President Carter eventually convened a White House Conference on Families in the summer of 1980—or rather, he was forced to run three conferences across the country when liberals and conservatives could not agree on the meeting's agenda. The two sides could not even find consensus on the name of the conference itself: was it a conference on "the family," in its singular traditional form, or on "families," in their varied single-parent, cohabiting, gay, or dual-career forms? Increasingly, conservatives lined up to argue that the country should dedicate itself to restoration of the male-breadwinner ideal, whereas liberals, feminists, and other allies embraced the revolution in family forms and sex roles of the previous twenty years.[17] The decade's rhetoric of family crisis boiled down to a deeply entrenched cultural conflict over the family's future after the demise of the family wage.

The conservative response was to shore up the male-breadwinning family. Leaders of the pro-family movement, such as Schlafly and Weyrich, argued that families with men earning money and women taking care of the home were the foundation of any properly ordered society. Schlafly supported preferential hiring for male family breadwinners and maintained that preventing employers from preferring fathers in hiring caused "reverse discrimination" against men as the principal family earner. Schlafly postulated "a man's right and ability to fulfill his role as provider" as a parallel to "the right of his wife to be a full-time homemaker." "It is only right and just that [a man] earn more" than a woman, she told a Senate hearing on sex discrimination in the workplace, in April 1981. In fact, women's secondary position in the labor market was "not sex discrimination. It [was] career choice." She opposed any policy that would require workplaces to accommodate women's family responsibilities.[18]

Self-appointed "pro-family" advocates designed a program to restore male-breadwinning households that embraced conservative arguments about government and the market. Schlafly contended that "the biggest single assault on the role of motherhood today, as well as on the family unit, is government-caused inflation."[19] This became a standard argument of the New Right. According to Richard Viguerie, the leader of the conservative Free Congress Foundation, New Right supporters rejected guaranteed annual incomes and welfare because "federal spending eats into the family's income, forcing mothers to go to work to pay for food, clothing, shelter and other family basics." Conservative diagnostics of the country's economic woes often blamed a dip in productivity on a male workforce threatened by competition from women and a younger generation of men lacking proper male vigor.[20] In tandem with market conservatives, pro-family activists demanded smaller government to lower the tax burdens on families, reduce inflation, and reestablish households with male providers. Essentially, they wished for policies to shore up the family wage system.

While most mainstream liberals rejected the conservative call to turn back the clock, many continued to express deep ambivalence about the loss of the domestic ideal. In a 1977 *Psychology Today* special report on "The American Family in Trouble," Senator Walter Mondale worried about juvenile crime, rising rates of out-of-wedlock pregnancy, teen suicide, and physical abuse, among other social issues, all of which required a range of "family-strengthening initiatives."[21] Liberals' investment in the male-breadwinner family shaped their policy agenda late into the Carter years, as the Program for Better Jobs and Income revealed. A kind of push-pull between acknowledging the new realities and anxiety about their implications loomed over the 1980 White House Conference on Families. On the one hand, the Conference's official report agreed that families in America were no longer the idealized 1950s family of the television show *The Waltons* (if they ever had been), but neither were they "some version of a counter-culture commune." The Agenda for Action adopted by the Conference verged on schizophrenia. Action item number one—urging "business and labor to consider new policies and practices in the workplace to reduce the conflict between responsibilities as parents and employees"—was followed immediately by action item number two—seeking "an end to the unintended but still destructive tax, welfare, health and other governmental policies which discriminate against marriage and help break up families." Policy prescriptions vacillated between making employers and society take up the costs of family and children and shoring up marriage and the private home. The report settled on a doctrine of "choice" that let them have it both ways: accepting a woman's choice to work should she wish (and it was definitely framed as a woman's dilemma), but reaffirming the home as the bedrock in the fight against social dangers like drugs, alcohol, and teen pregnancy.[22]

What some liberals seemed to fear most deeply with the erosion of the family wage system/male-breadwinner ideal was the loss of an idealized paternal authority and a nurturing mother. The historian and cultural critic Christopher Lasch became the most vocal of those who bemoaned waning patriarchs. His surprise 1978 bestseller, *The Culture of Narcissism: American Life in an Age of Diminishing Expectations* expressed his disillusionment with the Left and his dislike of changes wrought by the women's movement. The year before, he had already argued in *Haven in a Heartless World: The Family Besieged* that over the twentieth century, the mounting clout of experts in the "helping professions" had dangerously undermined parental authority, particularly the father's. Without strong authoritative fathers and affectionate mothers, the nation produced children who grew up as narcissists, lacking spine and moral direction, in a culture in thrall to consumption and celebrity.[23]

Lasch had a counterpart in what sociologist Judith Stacey called the "new conservative feminism." Its leading voice, the ethicist and political philosopher Jean Bethke Elshtain, warned that feminist proposals to restructure the family dangerously collapsed the boundaries between public and private, and eroded boundaries essential to maintain traditional feminine values critical to society's well-being. Her prescriptions to protect those values, which she termed "social feminism," involved retaining the private family sphere with women at the center, particularly for nurturing children—a position not so different from welfare mothers' demand for a right to care for their children, but without the income to sustain their economic autonomy in the process. All told, Elshtain favored preserving the family wage system.[24]

Liberals looked out at the changes wrought by the economic forces dissolving the family wage system while still entangled in the gendered imagination of the male-breadwinner model. The domestic ideal's hold was tenacious, and many liberals at the end of the 1970s wondered how far it was possible to step away from it without causing social disintegration. None really wanted to roll back women's equality, but they were unsure what it would bring in terms of women's life pathways, the rearing of children, and the reconstruction of public and private domains.

Feminists saw promise, not crisis, in the changes in the family. To them, dismantling the male-breadwinner ideal was positive and, indeed, a precursor to women's equality. In November 1979, at a daylong conference on the Future of the Family organized by the NOW Legal Defense and Education Fund, Betty Friedan delivered a keynote speech that previewed ideas from *The Second Stage*. But Muriel Fox, president of the fund, sounded a different note. She told conference planners, "We do not share the frequently voiced opinion that American families are in a state of hopeless collapse." "We will accept the inevitability of continuing future change in the relationships and roles of men, women and children within families. And we will seek new responses to the conditions that are the cause and effect of such change."[25] From the second wave's inception, feminists had envisioned transformations in the family that destroyed the male-breadwinner norm.

The movement's drive for family change was multipronged. Radical feminists offered the most eviscerating critiques, with many voicing doubt that the patriarchal family could ever be disentangled from capitalism or that social equality was possible within it. Others upended the breadwinner norm by advocating acceptance of family pluralism—lesbian and gay families, cohabiting couples, single parents, even those never wed, and other voluntary alliances. This was family defined as "who you come home to," observed Betty Friedan. Feminists embraced such pluralism. They focused their energies on transforming intimate relationships, fatherhood, care, and workplaces to secure women's autonomy and equality within reimagined public and private worlds. As Gloria Steinem described it in *Ms.*, in December 1979, feminists still had in front of them difficult struggles to secure "a redistribution of power in families, a revolution in the way children are raised and by whom, flexible work schedules outside the home, [and] recognition of work done by women (and men) in the home."[26]

The social organization of family and workplace envisioned by secondwavers was ultimately the most responsive, of any conceived at the time, to the changed shape of the economy. In the decade and a half after the publication of *The Feminine Mystique*, feminists working from many directions forged a new model to replace the domestic ideal. In this conception, all adults were potential wage earners, with roles defined not by gender stereotype but by household needs and the individuals within it. Both women and men received adequate wages to provide for their households, whether or not those households had more than one earner. Adults shared and negotiated who did what work at home and outside, with meaningful choices possible because of a system of public and employer-sponsored supports like universal childcare, paid leaves, and family allowances. Conversely, both government and companies provided support for families to care for children, the elderly, the ill, and the disabled, even full-time if needed. In the work and family ideal, second-wave feminists offered a wholesale reworking of the gender and family order installed with the rise of the separate spheres ideology in the nineteenth century.[27]

Not surprisingly, this vision is not fully achieved. At its origins, it seemed radical and extreme to most Americans. As conservatives dug in their heels to retain the male-breadwinner norm, their opposition undercut feminist ambitions and brought many of their proposals to a standstill. The women's movement did not succeed in getting broad public or employer-provided supports for workers' families: universal free childcare remains a dream, paid family leave is only just now moving seriously onto politicians' agendas, and workfare has replaced welfare rights activists' demands for income supports for caregiving. The stretched supermom that Betty Friedan described in *The Second Stage* is still squeezing too much into too few hours, and women keep bearing the brunt of family labor, now on top of increasing hours of paid work outside the home. The greatest beneficiaries of changed roles for women are also those who have benefitted the most in the American economy over the last forty years: professional women, overwhelmingly white. Poor women and women of color have remained the most vulnerable. For feminists, these remain deeply discouraging outcomes.

Yet dismay at how much remains to be done must not obscure what has been accomplished. Feminists had some signal successes. They reconstructed the female self. Consciousness-raising groups, spirited academic rebuttals of dominant paradigms in sociology and psychology, along with women of color's resistance to male nationalists' aspirations for male-breadwinner households helped relegate to oblivion the voices of experts who defined a woman's natural destiny in motherhood and the home. In parallel work, male feminists reimagined healthy fatherhood. The value of household labor has been recognized in social security, pension, and divorce law, as well as in the inclusion of domestic workers in the protections of the Fair Labor Standards Act. A mother's right to work was created as a network of child-care centers developed from local grassroots initiatives. Flexible work schedules gained traction in the federal government. Granted, feminists' greatest successes came when costs to society and to business were the least, but it is still critical to understand that they aimed to achieve a set of ambitious goals that embodied a more comprehensive vision for the work and family ideal. The feminism-as-having-it-all myth has become so ingrained that it continues to render much of this important work invisible.

And despite the backlash and a public image that reduced their aspirations to the impoverished slogan of "having it all," feminists forged ahead in the 1980s. Policies to benefit work and family remained central to multiple feminist campaigns. Donna Lenhoff, a veteran of the Pregnancy Discrimination Act campaign who worked at the Women's Legal Defense Fund, reunited what she called "the PDA alumnae association" in 1984, just after she received the first call from legislators looking to write new family leave legislation. Lenhoff and another PDA alumna, Judith Lichtman, went on to lead the coalition fighting for passage of the Family and Medical Leave Act (FMLA).[28] Colorado congresswoman Pat Schroeder, co-chair of the Congressional Caucus for Women's Issues, informed her fellow representatives that this legislation "would allow the United States to shake itself of a static model of the American family in which the father works and the mother stays at home." Updating the feminist call for a right to bear children, Schroeder then proclaimed, "No longer will job or economic security be traded against the needs of the family."[29]

Union women were strong allies in the FMLA campaign. The Coalition of Labor Union Women (CLUW) organized the American Family Celebration in Washington, DC in May 1988 a mass demonstration in support of the FMLA, to demand "responsible government action *now* for a national family policy," including "family and medical leave, quality childcare, services for the elderly . . . and economic justice."[30] Women's advocates within the labor movement turned labor's attention to work and family issues. CLUW, 9to5, National Association of Working Women, and the Service Employees International Union (SEIU) were among the unions describing demands for childcare as urgent, undertaking feasibility studies, providing locals with model contract clauses on women's issues, distributing the 1983 handbook *Bargaining for Child Care*, and leading a Future of Work Project.[31]

Other feminists joined efforts to preserve childcare funding in the face of cutbacks slated by the Reagan administration. Catherine East, now the legislative director for the National Women's Political Caucus, worked to expand before- and after-school care programs, develop information and referral clearinghouses, and support childcare programs in public housing and for low-income college students. With potentially devastating cuts looming, East noted that feminist strategy had been "to spend our limited resources seeking incremental gains for low income families in the Congress" while working for larger gains at the state and local level.[32] Feminists also sought to expand dependent care tax credits across the decade.

A number of women's organizations, including Federally Employed Women, were also part of the seventy-eight member Coalition on Women and the Budget, which issued annual reports documenting the "inequality of sacrifice" that Reagan budget proposals imposed on women. They joined other groups in objecting to cuts, in particular to Aid to Families with Dependent Children (AFDC). Feminist advocates continued to produce research exposing the consequences of the feminization of poverty and to call for policy adjustments.[33] Antipoverty feminists in a new National Coalition on Women, Work, and Welfare Reform were steadfast in emphasizing the importance of both good jobs and an adequate minimum standard of support. Avril Madison, the director of Wider Opportunities for Women—a Washington, DC organization working with displaced homemakers, poor women, female offenders, and others seeking employment that was not dead-end—pointed out how sex, race, and age discrimination curtailed poor women's opportunities for employment. AFDC still failed them by offering contradictory incentives for job training and employment and by slotting women into programs designed for male breadwinners. Welfare mothers and their activist allies focused on enabling self-sufficiency. They supported programs to foster economic autonomy that rested upon vigorous antidiscrimination enforcement and improved wages, coupled with increased assistance. Joyce Miller of CLUW told thousands assembled for a 1981 Solidarity Day march that "we need programs that will nurture our children while we are at work and elder care that will help our sick and aged parents."[34]

In 1983 and 1984, Maine Congresswoman Olympia Snowe, co-chair of the Congressional Caucus for Women's Issues, convened hearings of the Joint Economic Committee focused on "the dual role women play as wage earners and as mothers." At the April 1984 hearings, she stressed that "the availability of reliable child care [was] an important component of [women's] ability to enter and remain in the work force." She brought a parade of feminist activists before the committee to talk about pay equity, low wages in occupations traditionally dominated by women, and expanding women's access to nontraditional employment, as well as needs for childcare, programs for poor women, and retirement security for older women. "A lifetime of job segregation, wage discrimination and the difficulties of balancing work and family responsibilities" all contributed directly to women's vulnerability as they aged, Snowe testified at the hearings. The Caucus introduced packages of legislation throughout the 1980s, and Congress slowly endorsed some of their elements. In addition to job-related benefits, legislation advanced under the 1981 Economic Equity Act's umbrella responded to ongoing feminist concerns, such as inequitable treatment of homemakers—through pensions for military spouses—and the feminization of poverty—via an expanded Earned Income Tax Credit for low-income workers. The 1984 Retirement Equity Act, for example, required treating breaks in employment service for pregnancy, birth, and adoption as hours of service toward retirement credits.[35]

A new, self-identified work and family field brought together academics, activists, human relations specialists, labor department officials, business leaders, and some union leaders. Feminists led the new movement's efforts to alter corporate policies to facilitate wage earning and parenting. The Conference Board, a business think tank in New York, began the Work and Family Information Center and the Work/Life Leadership Council in 1983 under the stewardship of Dana Friedman, a feminist with roots in daycare activism. The information center was a clearinghouse on work and family issues, while the leadership council sponsored sessions that brought together people from across the entire spectrum. In March 1987, the US Department of Labor and the Bureau of National Affairs, a publisher of business and policy information and analysis, brought together nearly a thousand participants from forty-three states for a two-day conference, "Work and

Family: Seeking a New Balance." At the end of the decade, Friedman joined forces with Ellen Galinsky to found the Families and Work Institute in order to conduct research into the changing workforce and family.[36]

In the 1980s, the work and family movement concentrated much of its attention on business to shape the "responsive workplace," as the researchers Sheila Kamerman and Alfred Kahn aptly called it. The work and family field helped generate corporate accountability where there had been none, and, with self-conscious media savvy, it built public expectations for a new responsibility to be taken up by the American "corporate welfare state." The first steps tended to involve childcare, but by mid-decade, cutting-edge firms were promoting what came to be called "cafeteria plans" allowing employees to choose from among a range of benefits and services that best met their personal needs.[37]

James Levine joined the Families and Work Institute when it opened in 1989. His Fatherhood Project continued to fight to involve men in fathering and childcare. Male feminists advocated for family leave and workplace flexibility, arguing that men needed the changes as much as women.[38] Participation in household labor shifted considerably in the 1980s. Arlie Hochschild's 1989 book *The Second Shift* famously argued that the feminist revolution had stalled in the home, where women put in a second shift for household work. More recent studies show a pattern in which women did less household work as their hours of paid labor rose—while men faced mounting pressure to "pick up some of the slack." The burden on women continued to be heavier than on men, and many more women were in single-parent households by the end of the 1980s. Nevertheless, things improved: in 1975, married mothers used to spend four times as many hours as married fathers on household work, but by 1985, the proportion was halved: they now did just twice as many hours.[39]

All of these efforts happened in the changed context of the 1980s. Feminists' scope for action was much narrower, and a more constrained public discourse closed many options. The Reagan administration's commitment to slash social programs and its hostility to welfare in particular left women's activists on the defensive, fighting simply to maintain social supports for poor women and childcare. The kinds of legislative gains made in the decade tended to come in less controversial areas, such as retirement security for older women, and they emphasized private over public solutions for meeting caregiving and dependents needs. Republican officials pushed private employer solutions. Feminists in the new work and family field leapt on the possibilities such business initiatives promised, but these were a pale shadow of what feminists dreamed. Such policies also favored the needs of middle-class and professional women, largely white, over poor women and minorities.

The prevailing anxiety about the end of the family wage system and its shake-up of the domestic ideal put working mothers under intense scrutiny. Feminists found it much more difficult to advance claims based on women's continued disadvantage and inequity. In the hands of many liberals (and occasionally conservatives) "work and family" became a more anodyne call for piecemeal adjustments rather than the revolutionary restructuring feminists pursued. Feminists by no means relinquished their broader ideals, but throughout the 1980s, they struggled to reconcile commitment to women with the politically necessary terms of family policies.[40]

In the long run, the terms of the debate centered on work and family rather than the conservative-favored male breadwinning. Work and family, or increasingly, "working families," took center stage in the 1988 presidential election, and they have never yet left the heart of political discourse.[41] In a strange twist of fate, by 1996, even conservatives claimed to support working families by establishing the Campaign for Working Families political action committee, albeit with a policy agenda far from that of feminists. Liberals and progressives have turned to the Working Families Party, organized in New York in 1998. The Labor Project for Working Families, founded in 1992, advises unions on how to bargain and advocate for family-friendly workplaces and social policies. Started by women's and labor activist Netsy Firestein, the project recently led the successful campaign for paid family leave in the state of California.[42] Organizations with "working family" in their names now join women's groups like the National Partnership for Women and Families (formerly the Women's Legal Defense Fund) in carrying on advocacy for work and family policies.

The specter of having it all continues to haunt American cultural and political life in paradoxical ways. On the one hand, it does encapsulate a dream. Feminists did (and do) aspire to reconstruct personal, family, social, and economic life to create full *but* sustainable lives for women and men—the "all" of the slogan. Yet in the first decades of the twenty-first century, "having it all" rightly distills women's frustration and resentment at having been left holding the bag for social changes that never materialized. It has been easy to blame feminism for this paradox and to discard the aspiration with the bitterness. They just got it wrong in the first place, many say. But the history of feminism shows this judgment misses the mark. Second-wave feminists of the 1960s and 1970s had a bold vision that started with the inner worlds of women and men, embraced both homes and workplaces, and came up with redistributive social policies for sustainable family and work lives. The social change they imagined hit roadblocks as the economic stresses of the late twentieth century recalibrated family economics and as social and economic conservatives successfully countered feminist claims. Historians know that the domestic ideology of the nineteenth century was built piecemeal, advancing unevenly over decades. Dismantling it has been a similarly uneven process. We must credit feminists with taking on the battle to replace the family wage with a new, more egalitarian and just ordering of family and work life.

As second-wave feminists carried out those campaigns, they provided a road map. Their vision to organize intimate lives as partnerships remains essential, along with recognition that such partnerships are sometimes marital, sometimes not, and that many adults live without mates. The host of state benefits that accrue to married couples, from social security to custody rights, still need today the same kind of rigorous feminist analysis to reveal their inequities.[43] Involving fathers in their children's lives and men in the home remains a hurdle. Women in this country still spend on average an hour more than men in caring for children each day, and they pay the price in a variety of ways, from the "motherhood penalty" in wages to greater stress.[44] Yet projects reminiscent of the one founded by James Levine steadfastly advocate for feminist-inspired fathering. And like the 1970s buzz over marital agreements, contemporary campaigns for "equally shared parenting" strive to model egalitarian childrearing, housecleaning, and breadwinning.[45]

The struggle to give economic value to household labor is ongoing. Wages for housework groups with roots in the 1970s continue to organize.[46] Paid domestic labor has shifted form in recent decades: fewer work as in-home domestic and childcare workers, while jobs as home health aides and personal attendants have soared.[47] The workforce draws heavily on nonwhite and immigrant women; wages remain low, while immigrant status, including lacking papers, leaves many vulnerable to exploitation. Despite some expansion of their rights in recent years, many private domestic workers still lack basic labor protections like those offered by the Family and Medical Leave Act. A surge in organizing of paid care workers began again in the late twentieth century. Domestic workers associations and unionized home-healthcare workers have won some important victories.[48]

The second-wave insight that equality requires "a right to bear children" with laws and policies to back it up should stay front and center. Discrimination against mothers persists. Scholars have documented the "maternal wall" in employment that leaves mothers lagging behind both men and childless women in wages and advancement. Because paid benefits for pregnant workers come through private employers (except in five pioneering states and the District of Columbia), many mothers still go without pay when they give birth. Feminist organizations have persevered in pressing for paid maternity leave, as well as for paid sick leave that can be used for oneself or family members. Sweden and other Scandinavian countries remain the lodestar—models to emulate—as they were in the 1970s.[49]

Federally Employed Women continues to join other feminist organizations in advocating for flexible work without stigma or penalty. Resurrecting the feminist demand for childcare as a universal right could rally a broad coalition by connecting children's wellbeing with the greater public good, as it did in 1971. The United States lags far behind other industrialized countries where comprehensive national systems are the norm. Childcare remains very costly. Those in the lower-middle income spectrum bear the largest burdens, since the government still restricts subsidized childcare to low-income families. Interest in a guaranteed annual income has spiked recently. As welfare rights and antipoverty feminists showed us, a clear-eyed focus on meeting the needs of poor mothers must be part of the conversation.[50]

It can seem impossible to bring such a vision to fruition. But then, there was no blueprint whatsoever for a new world when feminists got started fifty years ago.

Second-wave feminism changed how Americans think and act so dramatically that we can almost no longer conceive how profoundly the movement transformed our society. The women's movement was instrumental in fighting for a vision of fairness that many Americans take for granted in their daily lives today. It changed basic expectations about what counts as women's nature, what constitutes just treatment in the workplace, who is responsible for cleaning bathrooms and putting children to sleep, and what life pathways women and men can follow, along with many more of the cultural, legal, and social frameworks that constrained women's lives in 1960. And it was not that feminists overpromised: their comprehensive conception of reorganized family and work lives carried wide appeal and elicited broad support. Rather, feminism's opponents clawed back. They successfully resisted the legislative, legal, and workplace changes the movement's champions sought. Their rhetorical triumph in distorting the movement's goals has buried the breathtaking scope of the feminist dream.

It is time to recover that vision, and to tell the world what having it all truly means.

ABBREVIATIONS

―――――

Archival Collections

Baxandall-Gordon, TAM.210 — Rosalyn Baxandall and Linda Gordon Research Files on Women's Liberation, TAM.210, Tamiment Library/Robert F. Wagner Labor Archives, New York University.

Collections at the Schlesinger Library, Radcliffe Institute, Harvard University

Alexander Papers, Schlesinger — Dolores Alexander. Papers of NOW officer Dolores Alexander, 1960–1973.

Carabillo-Meuli Papers, Schlesinger — Toni Carabillo and Judith Meuli Papers, c. 1890–2008.

East Papers, Schlesinger — Catherine Shipe East Papers, 1941–1995.

Eastwood Papers, Schlesinger — Mary O. Eastwood Papers, 1915–1983.

NOW Legal/Educ., Schlesinger — National Organization for Women Legal Defense and Education Fund Records, 1968–2008.

NOW Newsletters, Schlesinger — National Organization for Women Chapter Newsletter Collection, 1967–2008.

NOW Records, Schlesinger — National Organization for Women Records, 1959–2002.

Tully-Crenshaw Records, Schlesinger — Tully-Crenshaw Feminist Oral History Project Records, 1961–2001.

WOW Records, Schlesinger   Wider Opportunities for Women Records, 1965–1987.

Collections in the Sophia Smith Collection, Smith College

Empl. Coll., SSC, MS 456   Employment Collection, 1817–1991, MS 456.

WLC, SSC, MS 408   Women's Liberation Collection, 1959–2006, MS 408.

WRC, SSC, MS 397   Women's Rights Collection, 1789–2000, MS 397.

ERACAP, SSC, MS 310   Equal Rights Amendment Campaign Archives Project (ERACAP) Records, 1970–1985, MS 310.

Congressional Hearings

Hearings 1973   *Flexible Hours Empl't. Hearing Before the Comm. on Post Office and Civil Service, S., 93d Cong. (1973).*

Hearings 1975   *Alt. Work Schedules and Part-Time Career Opportunities in the Fed. Gov't. Hearings Before the Subcomm. on Manpower and Civil Service. of the Comm. on Post Office and Civil Service, H., 94th Cong. (1975).*

Hearings 1976   *Changing Patterns of Work in America, 1976. Hearings Before the Subcomm. on Empl't, Poverty, and Migratory Labor of the Comm. on Labor and Pub. Welfare, S., 94th Cong. (1976).*

Hearings 1977   *Part-Time Empl't and Flexible Work Hours. Hearings Before the Subcomm. on Employee Ethics and Utilization of the Comm. on Post Office and Civil Service, H., 95th Cong. (1977).*

Hearings 1978   *Flexitime and Part-Time Legislation. Hearing Before the Comm. on Gov'tal Affairs, S., 95th Cong. (1978).*

Hearings 1979   *National Policy Proposals Affecting Midlife Women. Hearings Before the Subcomm. on Ret. Income and Empl't of the Select Comm. on Aging, H., 96th Cong. (1979).*

Joint Hearings 1977

Administration's Welfare Reform Proposal. Joint Hearings Before the Welfare Reform Subcomm. of the Comm. on Agric., Comm. on Educ. and Labor, Comm. on Ways and Means, part 2, H., 95th Cong. (1977).

PDA—Senate Hearings

Discrimination on the Basis of Pregnancy, 1977. Hearings Before the Subcomm. on Labor of the Comm. on Human Res., S., 95th Cong. (1977).

PDA—House Hearings

Legislation to Prohibit Sex Discrimination on the Basis of Pregnancy, Part 2. Hearing Before the Subcomm. on Empl't Opportunities of the Comm. on Educ. and Labor, H., 95th Cong. (1977).

NOTES

Introduction

1. Letty Cottin Pogrebin, "Can Women Really Have It All?: Should We?," *Ms.*, March 1978, 47. See also Elizabeth Cagan, "The Selling of the Women's Movement," *Social Policy* 9 (May/June 1978): 4–12; and Ruth Rosen, *The World Split Open: How the Modern Women's Movement Changed America* (New York: Viking, 2000), 295–314.

2. "Pogrebin, "Can Women Really Have It All?," 48.

3. Ibid.

4. The metaphor of first, second, and third waves to describe US women's movements has come under both criticism and defense by historians. I retain the terminology of second wave for two specific reasons. The first is merely chronological: it supplies a useful shorthand for the surge of women's activism in the 1960s and 1970s and a way to vary the book's terminology. The second reason is more substantive: while I agree that the wave metaphor can incorrectly suggest an absence of activism in other periods, there was a vibrant, grassroots movement in these years; it deserves to be recognized as such. My hope is to broaden the tent of what "counts" as second-wave activism by bringing together strands of organizing most typically kept separate in the scholarship. Debate over the *waves* metaphor is synthesized in Kathleen A. Laughlin, et al., "Is It Time to Jump Ship? Historians Rethink the Waves Metaphor," *Feminist Formations* 22 (Spring 2010): 76–135.

5. Nancy MacLean, "Postwar Women's History: The 'Second Wave' or the End of the Family Wage?," in *A Companion to Post-1945 America*, ed. Jean-Christophe Agnew and Roy Rosenzweig (Malden, MA: Blackwell, 2006), 237–238. See also Alice Kessler-Harris, *In Pursuit of Equity: Women, Men, and the Quest for Economic Citizenship in 20th-Century America* (New York: Oxford University Press, 2001); Nancy F. Cott, *Public Vows: A History of Marriage and the Nation* (Cambridge: Harvard University Press, 2000), 157–158; and Sonya Michel, *Children's Interests/Mothers' Rights: The*

Shaping of America's Child Care Policy (New Haven: Yale University Press, 1999), 1–3.

6. Although the phrase did not come into common usage until the 1980s, the terminology of *work and family* usefully captures both the range of issues and the contemporary terminology with which we describe them. See Kirsten Swinth, "Post-Family Wage, Postindustrial Society: Reframing the Gender and Family Order through Working Mothers in Reagan's America," *Journal of American History* 105 (September 2018). At the same time, there is one caveat: the language of *family* can obscure the plurality of family forms that have always existed and which were the subject of debate in the period of this study. I use it here without a normative presumption but with the awareness that, in the 1960s and 1970s, it pointed to the debate over the normative family form: a heterosexual, nuclear family, with a male head of household.

7. Robert O. Self, *All in the Family: The Realignment of American Democracy since the 1960s* (New York: Hill and Wang, 2012), 5.

8. Kessler-Harris, *In Pursuit of Equity*, 5–6.

9. Barry Bluestone and Bennett Harrison, *The Deindustrialization of America: Plant Closings, Community Abandonment, and the Dismantling of Basic Industry* (New York: Basic Books, 1982); Judith Stein, *Pivotal Decade: How the United States Traded Factories for Finance in the Seventies* (New Haven: Yale University Press, 2010); and Sarah Kuhn and Barry Bluestone, "Economic Restructuring and the Female Labor Market: The Impact of Industrial Change on Women," in *Women, Households, and the Economy*, ed. Lourdes Benería and Catharine R. Stimpson (New Brunswick: Rutgers University Press, 1987), 9.

10. Drew Desilver, "For Most Workers, Real Wages Have Barely Budged for Decades," *Fact Tank*, October 9, 2014, Pew Research Center, www.pewresearch .org/fact-tank/2014/10/09/for-most-workers-real-wages-have-barely-budged-for -decades/; Claudia Goldin, *Understanding the Gender Gap: An Economic History of American Women* (New York: Oxford University Press, 1990), 17; Wendy Wang, Kim Parker, and Paul Taylor, *Breadwinner Moms: Mothers Are the Sole or Primary Provider in Four-in-Ten Households with Children; Public Conflicted about the Growing Trend* (Washington, DC: Pew Research Center, 2013), assets .pewresearch.org/wp-content/uploads/sites/3/2013/05/Breadwinner_moms_final .pdf, 20; Leah Platt Boustan and William J. Collins, "The Origins and Persistence of Black-White Differences in Women's Labor Force Participation," NBER Working Paper Series, Working Paper 19040 (Cambridge, MA: National Bureau of Economic Research, May 2013), 43; and Eliot Janeway, "Reviving the Economy: If Women Can't Do It, No One Can," *Working Woman*, October 1977, 67.

11. Marjorie J. Spruill, *Divided we Stand: The Battle over Women's Rights and Family Values that Polarized American Politics* (New York: Bloomsbury, 2017); Self, *All in the Family*; Bruce J. Schulman and Julian E. Zelizer, eds., *Rightward Bound: Making America Conservative in the 1970s* (Cambridge: Harvard University Press, 2008); and Rebecca E. Klatch, *Women of the New Right* (Philadelphia: Temple University Press, 1987).

12. Although I draw attention to Chicana and other Latina activists throughout the book, their experiences warrant much fuller development than I am able to offer. Asian American feminists similarly deserve further investigation along these

lines. In this book, I have concentrated on the largest groups in order to make it possible to sketch out the overarching story of feminist work and family activism. For starting points, see Alma M. García, ed., *Chicana Feminist Thought: The Basic Historical Writings* (New York: Routledge, 1997); Maylei Blackwell, *¡Chicana Power!: Contested Histories of Feminism in the Chicano Movement* (Austin: University of Texas Press, 2011); Mitsuye Yamada, "Asian Pacific American Women and Feminism," in *This Bridge Called My Back: Writings by Radical Women of Color*, ed. Cherríe Moraga and Gloria Anzaldúa, 2nd ed. (New York: Kitchen Table, Women of Color Press, 1983), 71–75; Susie Ling, "The Mountain Movers: Asian American Women's Movement in Los Angeles," *Amerasia* 15 (1989): 51–67; and Esther Ngan-Ling Chow, "The Development of Feminist Consciousness among Asian American Women," *Gender and Society* 1 (September 1987): 284–299. On Native Americans' very different engagement with feminism, see Andrea Smith, "Native American Feminism, Sovereignty, and Social Change," *Feminist Studies* 31 (Spring 2005): 116–132; and Annelise Orleck, *Rethinking American Women's Activism* (New York: Routledge, 2015), 138–144.

13. Stephanie Gilmore, *Feminist Coalitions: Historical Perspectives on Second-Wave Feminism in the United States* (Urbana: University of Illinois Press, 2008). This study joins other recent work in drawing attention to shared purposes that crossed political and racial lines. While I fully acknowledge that crucial differences existed and that coalition building was messy, often temporary work, I nonetheless argue that feminist attention to work and family issues only comes into focus when we study the movement through those topics. This book thus highlights overlapping concerns and connects streams of activism that are more typically separated.

14. For the most recent example, see Anne-Marie Slaughter, "Why Women Still Can't Have It All," *The Atlantic*, July/August 2012, 85–102. See also Joan Kron, "The Dual-Career Dilemma," *New York Magazine*, October 25, 1976, 49–50; Judy Mann, "The Superwoman Image Is Beginning to Crack," *The Washington Post*, January 18, 1980, C1; Lynn Langway, et al., "The Superwoman Squeeze," *Newsweek*, May 19, 1980, 72–79; Barbara J. Berg, "Mothers Against Mothers," *Washington Post*, January 3, 1986, B5; Felice N. Schwartz, "Management Women and the New Facts of Life," *Harvard Business Review* 67 (January–February 1989): 65–76; Nina Darnton, "Mommy vs. Mommy," *Newsweek*, June 4, 1990, 64–67; and Lisa Belkin, "The Opt-Out Revolution," *New York Times Sunday Magazine*, October 26, 2003, 42–47, 58, 85–86. Self-help books have also perpetuated the having-it-all myth. See Joyce Gabriel and Bettye Baldwin, *Having it All: A Practical Guide to Overcoming the Career Woman's Blues* (New York: M. Evans and Company, 1980); Helen Gurley Brown, *Having It All: Love, Success, Sex, Money, Even If You're Starting with Nothing* (New York: Simon and Schuster, 1982); and Carol Osborn, *Enough Is Enough: Exploding the Myth of Having It All* (New York: Putnam, 1986). For a good summary, see Joan C. Williams, Jessica Manvell, and Stephanie Bornstein, "'Opt Out' or Pushed Out?: How the Press Covers Work/Family Conflict" (San Francisco: The Center for WorkLife Law, University of California, Hastings College of the Law, 2006), worklifelaw .org/pubs/OptOutPushedOut.pdf.

Feminist critiques are plentiful: Ellen Goodman, "Superworkingmom or Superdrudge?," December 1976 and "Your Better Basic Supermother," May 1976, in Ellen Goodman, *Close to Home* (New York: Simon and Schuster, 1979), 88–89 and 180–181; Barbara Ehrenreich and Deirdre English, "Blowing the Whistle on the 'Mommy Track,'" *Ms.*, July/August 1989, 56–58; Rebecca Traister, "Can Modern Women 'Have It All?,'" *Salon*, June 21, 2012, www.salon.com/2012/06 /21/can_modern_women_have_it_all/; and Ruth Rosen, "Who Said 'We Could Have It All?,'" *Opendemocracy.net*, August 2, 2012, www.opendemocracy.net /5050/ruth-rosen/who-said-"we-could-have-it-all".

15. Histories of the movement abound. I have found particularly insightful Flora Davis, *Moving the Mountain: The Women's Movement in America Since 1960* (New York: Simon and Schuster, 1991); Rosen, *The World Split Open*; Sara Evans, *Personal Politics: The Roots of Women's Liberation in the Civil Rights Movement and the New Left* (New York: Vintage Books, 1980); Sara M. Evans, *Tidal Wave: How Women Changed America at Century's End* (New York: Free Press, 2003); Estelle Freedman, *No Turning Back: The History of Feminism and the Future of Women* (New York: Ballantine, 2002); Dorothy Sue Cobble, Linda Gordon, and Astrid Henry, *Feminism Unfinished: A Short, Surprising History of American Women's Movements* (New York: Liveright, 2014); Orleck, *Rethinking American Women's Activism*; and Alice Echols, *Daring to Be Bad: Radical Feminism in America, 1967–1975* (Minneapolis: University of Minnesota Press, 1989). Feminists did, of course, take crucial steps to redress workplace inequality. For a starting point, see Katherine Turk, *Equality on Trial: Gender and Rights in the Modern American Workplace* (Philadelphia: University of Pennsylvania Press, 2016).

Helpful and important discussions of feminist commitments to transform work and family include Catherine East, "Critical Comments on *A Lesser Life: The Myth of Women's Liberation in America*" (Washington, DC: National Women's Political Caucus, July 15, 1986); and Cynthia Harrison, "'A Revolution But Half Accomplished': The Twentieth Century's Engagement with Child-Raising, Women's Work, and Feminism," in *The Achievement of American Liberalism: The New Deal and Its Legacies*, ed. William H. Chafe (New York: Columbia University Press, 2002), 243–274. The most extended pre-history of work and family feminism is Dorothy Sue Cobble's study of postwar labor activists, *The Other Women's Movement: Workplace Justice and Social Rights in Modern America* (Princeton: Princeton University Press, 2004). Alice Kessler-Harris's pathbreaking work on women's economic citizenship has influenced my thinking in important ways as well; see especially *In Pursuit of Equity*.

Sociologists, political scientists, and policy analysts have paid extensive attention to the problem of work-family conflict, often proposing policy prescriptions filtered through feminist lenses. Yet neither history nor the second-wave feminist movement is a primary concern of this research. See Faye J. Crosby, ed., *Spouse, Parent, Worker: On Gender and Multiple Roles* (New Haven: Yale University Press, 1987); Arlie Hochschild, *The Second Shift: Working Parents and the Revolution at Home* (New York: Viking, 1989); Joan Williams, *Unbending Gender: Why Work and Family Conflict and What to Do About It* (New York: Oxford University Press, 2000); Jerry A. Jacobs and Kathleen Gerson, *The Time Divide: Work, Family and Gender Inequality* (Cambridge: Harvard University

Press, 2004); and Kathleen Gerson, *The Unfinished Revolution: How a Generation is Reshaping Family, Work, and Gender in America* (New York: Oxford University Press, 2010). This literature is vast; for a state of the field, see Marcie Pitt-Catsouphes, Ellen Ernst Kossek, and Stephen Sweet, eds., *The Work and Family Handbook: Multi-Disciplinary Perspectives and Approaches* (Mahwah, NJ: Lawrence Erlbaum Associates, 2006); and Teri Ann Lilly, Marcie Pitt-Catsouphes, and Bradley K. Googins, *Work-Family Research: An Annotated Bibliography* (Westport, CT: Greenwood Press, 1997). An early important text is Rosabeth Moss Kanter, *Work and Family in the United States: A Critical Review and Agenda for Research and Policy* (New York: Russell Sage Foundation, 1977).

16. Betty Friedan, *It Changed My Life: Writings on the Women's Movement* (New York: Dell, 1977), 188. See also Davis, *Moving the Mountain*, 281; Christine Stansell, *The Feminist Promise: 1792 to the Present* (New York: Modern Library, 2010), 263; and Evans, *Tidal Wave*, 55.

17. On welfare rights, see Premilla Nadasen, "Expanding the Boundaries of the Women's Movement: Black Feminism and the Struggle for Welfare Rights," *Feminist Studies* 28 (Summer 2002): 270–301; Premilla Nadasen, *Welfare Warriors: The Welfare Rights Movement in the United States* (New York: Routledge, 2005); Marisa Chappell, *The War on Welfare: Family, Poverty, and Politics in Modern America* (Philadelphia: University of Pennsylvania Press, 2010); Felicia Kornbluh, *The Battle for Welfare Rights: Politics and Poverty in Modern America* (Philadelphia: University of Pennsylvania Press, 2007); and Annelise Orleck, *Storming Caesar's Palace: How Black Mothers Fought Their Own War on Poverty* (Boston: Beacon Press, 2005). An excellent new study on domestic worker organizing is Premilla Nadasen, *Household Workers Unite: The Untold Story of African American Women Who Built a Movement* (Boston: Beacon Press, 2015).

On feminist legal activism, see Serena Mayeri, *Reasoning from Race: Feminism, Law, and the Civil Rights Revolution* (Cambridge: Harvard University Press, 2011); Cary Franklin, "The Anti-Stereotyping Principle in Constitutional Sex Discrimination Law," *New York University Law Review* 85 (April 2010): 83–173; and Lise Vogel, *Mothers on the Job: Maternity Policy in the US Workplace* (New Brunswick: Rutgers University Press, 1993). Particularly significant for sharing my broad approach to feminism is the work of legal historian Deborah Dinner, including "The Universal Childcare Debate: Rights Mobilization, Social Policy, and the Dynamics of Feminist Activism, 1966–1974," *Law and History Review* 28 (August 2010): 577–628; "Recovering the *LaFleur* Doctrine," *Yale Journal of Law and Feminism* 22 (2010): 343–406; "The Costs of Reproduction: History and the Legal Construction of Sex Equality," *Harvard Civil Rights—Civil Liberties Law Review* 46 (August 2011): 415–495; "Strange Bedfellows at Work: Neomaternalism in the Making of Sex Discrimination Law," *Washington University Law Review* 91 (2014): 453–530; and "The Divorce Bargain: The Fathers' Rights Movement and Family Inequalities," *Virginia Law Review* 102 (2016): 79–152. On pregnancy discrimination and feminists in the labor movement, see Susan M. Hartmann, *The Other Feminists: Activists in the Liberal Establishment* (New Haven: Yale University Press, 1998).

Additional important work on feminist engagements with motherhood, marriage, and family includes Lauri Umansky, *Motherhood Reconceived: Feminism and the Legacies of the Sixties* (New York: New York University Press, 1996); Self, *All in the Family*; Rebecca Jo Plant, *Mom: The Transformation of Motherhood in Modern America* (Chicago: University of Chicago Press, 2010); and Alison Lefkovitz, *Strange Bedfellows: Marriage in the Age of Women's Liberation* (Philadelphia: University of Pennsylvania Press, 2018).

A new generation of scholarship on the movement has revised familiar narratives of the foci and interests of both liberal and radical feminists. This work emphasizes coalition building across race and class, greater complexity in women of color's involvement in the movement, and local and grassroots feminism outside the hothouse of New York, particularly in Midwestern and Western locations. See Gilmore, ed., *Feminist Coalitions*; Nancy A. Hewitt, ed., *No Permanent Waves: Recasting Histories of US Feminism* (New Brunswick: Rutgers University Press, 2010); Kathleen A. Laughlin and Jacqueline L. Castledine, eds., *Breaking the Wave: Women, Their Organizations, and Feminism, 1945–1985* (New York: Routledge, 2011); Stephanie Gilmore, *Groundswell: Grassroots Feminist Activism in Postwar America* (New York: Routledge, 2013); Anne M. Valk, *Radical Sisters: Second-Wave Feminism and Black Liberation in Washington, DC* (Urbana: University of Illinois Press, 2008); Judith Ezekiel, *Feminism in the Heartland* (Columbus: Ohio State University Press, 2002); Anne Enke, *Finding the Movement: Sexuality, Contested Space, and Feminist Activism* (Durham: Duke University Press, 2007); Daniel Winunwe Rivers, *Radical Relations: Lesbian Mothers, Gay Fathers, and Their Children in the United States since World War II* (Chapel Hill: University of North Carolina Press, 2013); Kimberly Springer, *Living for the Revolution: Black Feminist Organizations, 1968–1980* (Durham: Duke University Press, 2005); Benita Roth, *Separate Roads to Feminism: Black, Chicana, and White Feminist Movements in America's Second Wave* (New York: Cambridge University Press, 2004); and Blackwell, *¡Chicana Power!*.

1. Self

1. Betty Friedan, "I Say: Women Are People, Too!," *Good Housekeeping*, September 1960, 60–61, 162; Saylor's letter can be found at "'Women are People, Too!': The Groundbreaking Article by Betty Friedan," *Good Housekeeping*, August 9, 1910, www.goodhousekeeping.com/life/career/advice/a18890/1960 -betty-friedan-article/. See also Stephanie Coontz, *A Strange Stirring: The Feminine Mystique and American Women at the Dawn of the 1960s* (New York: Basic Books, 2011), 25–26; and Daniel Horowitz, *Betty Friedan and the Making of The Feminine Mystique: The American Left, the Cold War, and Modern Feminism* (Amherst: University of Massachusetts Press, 1998), 194–195.

2. Benjamin Nelson, ed., *Freud and the Twentieth Century* (Cleveland: World Publishing, 1957), qtd. in Louis Menand, "The Stone Guest," *The New Yorker*, August 28, 2017, 77.

3. Ellen Herman, *The Romance of American Psychology: Political Culture in the Age of Experts, 1940–1970* (Berkeley: University of California Press, 1995),

277–279; and Elizabeth Singer More, "Best Interests: Feminists, Social Science, and the Revaluing of Working Mothers in Modern America" (PhD diss., Harvard University, 2012), 11.

4. Ruth Feldstein, *Motherhood in Black and White: Race and Sex in American Liberalism, 1930–1965* (Ithaca: Cornell University Press, 2000), 57–58, 142–144; and Alice O'Connor, *Poverty Knowledge: Social Science, Social Policy, and the Poor in Twentieth-Century US History* (Princeton: Princeton University Press, 2001), 112–113.

5. Joanne Meyerowitz, "Beyond the Feminine Mystique: A Reassessment of Postwar Mass Culture, 1946–1958," *Journal of American History* 79 (March 1993): 1455–1482; National Manpower Council, *Womanpower: A Statement, with Chapters by the Council Staff* (New York: Columbia University Press, 1957); More, "Best Interests," 157, 149–159; and Lois Meek Stolz, "Effects of Maternal Employment on Children: Evidence from Research," *Child Development* 31 (December 1960): 752.

6. Alice Kessler-Harris, *In Pursuit of Equity: Women, Men, and the Quest for Economic Citizenship in 20th-Century America* (New York: Oxford University Press, 2001), 216–221.

7. Betty Friedan, *The Feminine Mystique*, 20th anniv. ed. (New York: Dell, 1983), 123–124; Mari Jo Buhle, *Feminism and Its Discontents: A Century of Struggle with Psychoanalysis* (Cambridge: Harvard University Press, 1998), 208–210; and More, "Best Interests," 164–177.

8. Friedan, *Feminine Mystique*, 70; and Vivian Gornick and Barbara K. Moran, eds., *Woman in Sexist Society: Studies in Power and Powerlessness* (New York: Basic Books, 1971), xii–xiii.

9. Sara Davidson, "An 'Oppressed Majority' Demands Its Rights," *Life*, December 1969, 69; and Diane Narek, "A Woman Scientist Speaks," November 20, 1969, 1–2, in *Redstockings First Literature List (Fall 1969) and a Sampling of its Materials*, Redstockings.org, www.redstockings.org/index.php/adp-catalog/test.

10. "Click! Moments of Truth," anonymous letter, *Ms.*, July 1972, 45.

11. Vivian Gornick, "The Next Great Moment in History Is Ours," in *Liberation Now! Writings from the Women's Liberation Movement*, ed. Deborah Babcox and Madeline Belkin (New York: Dell, 1971), 38.

12. Frances M. Beal, "Double Jeopardy: To Be Black and Female," 1969, in *Sisterhood Is Powerful: An Anthology of Writings from the Women's Liberation Movement*, ed. Robin Morgan (New York: Vintage, 1970), 384. See also Beverly Jones, "The Dynamics of Marriage and Motherhood," 1968, in *Sisterhood Is Powerful*, ed. Morgan, 63.

13. Lauri Umansky, *Motherhood Reconceived: Feminism and the Legacies of the Sixties* (New York: New York University Press, 1996), 50; and More, "Best Interests," 169–174.

14. Martha Shelley, "Gay Is Good," 1970, in *Out of the Closets: Voices of Gay Liberation*, 20th anniv. ed., ed. Karla Jay and Allen Young (New York: New York University Press, 1992), 33; and "Letty Cottin Pogrebin," *Makers*, www.makers.com/letty-cottin-pogrebin.

15. Agatha Beins, *Liberation in Print: Feminist Periodicals and Social Movement Identity* (Athens: University of Georgia Press, 2017), 7–10, 21, 49, 150; and

Anne M. Valk, "Living a Feminist Lifestyle: The Intersection of Theory and Action in a Lesbian Feminist Collective," *Feminist Studies* 28 (Summer 2002): 316, 326.

16. Beins, *Liberation in Print*, 4, 30, 35, 63; Kristen Hogan, "Women's Studies in Feminist Bookstores: 'All the Women's Studies Women Would Come In,'" *Signs* 33 (Spring 2008): 600; Judith Sealander and Dorothy Smith, "The Rise and Fall of Feminist Organizations in the 1970s: Dayton as a Case Study," *Feminist Studies* 12 (Summer 1986): 325; Morgan, ed., *Sisterhood Is Powerful*, xv–xvi; and "Letty Cottin Pogrebin," *Makers*.

17. National Organization for Women, "Statement of Purpose," October 29, 1966, as reprinted in Toni Carabillo, Judith Meuli, and June Bundy Csida, eds., *Feminist Chronicles, 1953–1993* (Los Angeles: Women's Graphics, 1993), 159; Betty Friedan, "Our Revolution Is Unique," in *Voices of the New Feminism*, ed. Mary Lou Thompson, 1970 (Boston: Beacon Press, 1975), 37; Wilma Scott Heide, Know, Inc., "Human Rights Are Indivisible," n.d., p. 2 (box 2, folder 6) WLC, SSC, MS 408; and Betty Friedan and Jacquelyn Reinach, "Liberation, Now!," music by Jacquelyn Reinach and J. Rene (Claro Music Corporation, 1970).

18. "Statement by Chicago Women's Liberation," February 1969, in *Sisterhood Is Powerful*, ed. Morgan, 595–596; Janet Hews, "On Becoming a Radical Woman," *Lilith* (Fall 1968): 4; and Radicalesbians, "The Woman-Identified-Woman," 1970, in *Radical Feminism: A Documentary Reader*, ed. Barbara A. Crow (New York: New York University Press, 2000), 235–237. For how, after 1975, a new cultural feminism reshaped feminist ideas of motherhood again, see Umansky, *Motherhood Reconceived*, 118–131.

19. Boston Women's Health Book Collective, *Our Bodies, Ourselves: A Book by and for Women* (Boston: Simon and Schuster, 1971), 10, 154; and Marlene Dixon, "A Position Paper on Radical Women in the Professions: Or, Up from Ridicule," *Lilith* (Fall 1968): 20.

20. Beal, "Double Jeopardy," 386; Mary Reinholz, "Storming the All Electric Doll House," *Los Angeles Times West Magazine*, June 7, 1970, 57; and Eleanor Holmes Norton, "For Sadie and Maude," in *Sisterhood Is Powerful*, ed. Morgan, 399–402.

21. Beal, "Double Jeopardy," 384, 383; and Doris Wright, "Angry Notes from a Black Feminist," 1970, in *Dear Sisters: Dispatches from the Women's Liberation Movement*, ed. Rosalyn Baxandall and Linda Gordon (New York: Basic Books, 2000), 37.

22. Beal, "Double Jeopardy," 384; and Wright, "Angry Notes from a Black Feminist," 37.

23. Norton, "For Sadie and Maude," 402–403; Serena Mayeri, *Reasoning from Race: Feminism, Law, and the Civil Rights Revolution* (Cambridge: Harvard University Press, 2011), 48; and Toni Morrison, "What the Black Woman Thinks about Women's Lib," *New York Times Sunday Magazine*, August 22, 1971, 63. See also Lacey Fosburgh, "Dealing with Feminism in Black and White," *Los Angeles Times*, March 20, 1974, E1.

24. Third World Women's Alliance, "Women in the Struggle," 1971, in *Radical Feminism*, ed. Crow, 464.

25. Maylei Blackwell, *¡Chicana Power! Contested Histories of Feminism in the Chicano Movement* (Austin: University of Texas Press, 2011), 2, 6–7, 96–104;

Benita Roth, *Separate Roads to Feminism: Black, Chicana, and White Feminist Movements in America's Second Wave* (New York: Cambridge University Press, 2004), 139. See also Elena H. García, "Chicana Consciousness: A New Perspective, A New Hope," 1973, in *Chicana Feminist Thought: The Basic Historical Writings*, ed. Alma M. García (New York: Routledge, 1997), 39–40.

26. García, ed., *Chicana Feminist Thought*, 8; and Enriqueta Longauex y Vasquez, "The Mexican American Woman," 1969, in *Sisterhood Is Powerful*, ed. Morgan, 432, 428. Appearing originally as "The Women of La Raza," *El Grito del Norte* 2 (July 6, 1969), it was widely reprinted. Blackwell, *¡Chicana Power!*, 139–140.

27. Vasquez, "Mexican American Woman," 432.

28. "Roles," *Chicana Week*, University of Texas, May 1975, in *The Chicana Feminist*, ed. Martha P. Cotera (Austin: Information Systems Development, 1977), 22–23.

29. See Morrison, "What the Black Woman Thinks"; Mayeri, *Reasoning from Race*, 43–48; and Roth, *Separate Roads to Feminism*, 166–171.

30. Letty Cottin Pogrebin, "Twelve Outspoken Women," video, *Makers*, www.makers.com/videos/5546696fe4b08df3b6dcbd54; and Gainesville Women's Liberation, "What We Do at Meetings," in *Dear Sisters*, ed. Baxandall and Gordon, 70–71. See also Pamela Allen, "The Small Group Process," 1970, and June Arnold, "Consciousness Raising," 1970, in *Radical Feminism*, ed. Crow, 277–286.

31. Estelle Carol, "Chapter Report," Chicago, *Voices of the Women's Liberation Movement* 1 (March 1968): 5; and Monica Mercado and Katherine Turk, "'Second-Wave' Feminism on Campus," in *On Equal Terms: Educating Women at the University of Chicago*, web exhibit (Chicago: University of Chicago Library, Special Collections Research Center, 2009), www.lib.uchicago.edu/collex/exhibits/exoet/second-wave-feminism/.

32. Sandie North, "Women's Liberation Hits the Suburbs," *Family Circle*, November 1970, 22.

33. Jean Pascoe, "Suburban Women's Lib: Turning Mrs. into Ms.," *McCall's*, September 1973, 36.

34. Combahee River Collective, "A Black Feminist Statement," in *This Bridge Called My Back*, ed. Moraga and Anzaldúa, 213; Kimberly Springer, *Living for the Revolution: Black Feminist Organizations, 1968–1980* (Durham: Duke University Press, 2005), 45; and Blackwell, *¡Chicana Power!*, 83–84.

35. Morton A. Lieberman and Gary R. Bond, "The Problem of Being a Woman: A Survey of 1,700 Women in Consciousness-Raising Groups," *Journal of Applied Behavioral Science* 12 (1976): 369; Anita Shreve, *Women Together, Women Alone: The Legacy of the Consciousness-Raising Movement* (New York: Viking, 1989), 194, 198–199; and Pascoe, "Suburban Women's Lib."

36. Vivian Gornick, "Consciousness," 1971, in *Radical Feminism*, ed. Crow, 297–299, 291; and Morrison, "What the Black Woman Thinks," 66.

37. Naomi Weisstein, "Psychology Constructs the Female," in *Woman in Sexist Society*, ed. Gornick and Moran, 133–135, 137. See Herman, *Romance of American Psychology*, 280–282.

38. Kate Millett, *Sexual Politics* (New York: Doubleday, 1970), excerpted in *Radical Feminism*, ed. Crow, 127; and Weisstein, "Psychology Constructs the Female," 140.

39. See Mary Brown Parlee, "Psychology," *Signs* 1 (Autumn 1975): 119–38; Mary Crawford and Jeanne Marecek, "Psychology Reconstructs the Female 1968–1988," *Psychology of Women Quarterly* 13 (June 1989): 147–165; and Abigail J. Stewart and Andrea L. Dottolo, "Feminist Psychology," *Signs* 31 (Winter 2006): 493–509. See also Sue Cox, *Female Psychology: The Emerging Self* (Palo Alto, CA: Science Research Associates, Inc., 1976); and Marcia Millman and Rosabeth Moss Kanter, *Another Voice: Feminist Perspectives on Social Life and Social Science* (Garden City, NY: Doubleday, 1975).

40. Pauline Bart, "Depression in Middle-Aged Women," in *Woman in Sexist Society*, ed. Gornick and Moran, 116, 115.

41. Ravenna Helson, "The Changing Image of the Career Woman," *Journal of Social Issues* 28 (June 1972): 33–46; Carol Ehrlich, "The Male Sociologist's Burden: The Place of Women in Marriage and Family Texts," *Journal of Marriage and Family* 33 (August 1971), 425; and Matina Horner, "Fail: Bright Women," *Psychology Today*, November 1969, in *Up Against the Wall, Mother . . . On Women's Liberation*, ed. Elsie Adams and Mary Louise Briscoe (Beverly Hills, CA: Glencoe Press, 1971), 304.

42. Alice S. Rossi, "Women in the Seventies: Problems and Possibilities," keynote speech, Barnard Conference on Women, April 17, 1970, reprint by *Know, Inc.* (Pittsburgh, PA), p. 1066, (box 2, folder 7) WLC, SSC, MS 408; and Alice S. Rossi, "Equality between the Sexes: An Immodest Proposal," *Daedalus* 93 (Spring 1964): 608, 615.

43. Rossi, "Equality between the Sexes," 611; and Rossi, "Women in the Seventies," 1065. See More, "Best Interests," 182–188.

44. Rossi, "Equality between the Sexes," 608, 625, 649.

45. Arlie Russell Hochschild, "A Review of Sex Role Research," *American Journal of Sociology* 78 (January 1973): 1011–1029; Lenore J. Weitzman, "Sex Role Socialization," 1970–1971, in *Women: A Feminist Perspective*, ed. Jo Freeman (Palo Alto, CA: Mayfield Publishing Company, 1975), 105–144; and Helena Z. Lopata and Barrie Thorne, "On the Term 'Sex Roles,'" *Signs* 3 (Spring 1978): 718–721. See also Myra Marx Ferree, Shamus Rahman Khan, and Shauna A. Morimoto, "Assessing the Feminist Revolution: The Presence and Absence of Gender in Theory and Practice," in *Sociology in America: A History*, ed. Craig Calhoun (Chicago: University of Chicago Press, 2007), 438–479; Barbara Laslett, "Feminist Sociology in the Twentieth-Century United States: Life Stories in Historical Context," in *Sociology in America*, ed. Calhoun, 480–502; and More, "Best Interests," 188–217.

46. Jessie Bernard, *The Future of Motherhood* (New York: Penguin Books, 1975). On Bernard, see Laslett, "Feminist Sociology," 488–492.

47. Bernard, *Future of Motherhood*, 105, 158.

48. Ibid., 185–186, 140; and Herman, *Romance of American Psychology*, 290–292.

49. Bernard, *Future of Motherhood*, 341, 364.

50. Women's Caucus, "Women's Caucus Statement and Resolutions to the General Business Meeting of the American Sociological Association," September 3, 1969, *The American Sociologist* 5 (February 1970): 63; and Pamela Ann Roby, "The Women's 1969 Sociology Caucus, Sociologists for Women in Society and the ASA: A Forty Year Retrospective of Women on the Move," 2009, Sociologists for Women in Society, https://socwomen.org/about/history-of-sws/the -women/; Leonore Tiefer, "A Brief History of the Association for Women in Psychology, 1969–1991," *Psychology of Women Quarterly* 15 (December 1991): 635–649; Mary Roth Walsh, "Academic Professional Women Organizing for Change: The Struggle in Psychology," *Journal of Social Issues* 41 (Winter 1985): 17–27; and Cary Franklin, "The Anti-Stereotyping Principle in Constitutional Sex Discrimination Law," *New York University Law Review* 85 (April 2010): 83–173. NOW members led these first women's caucuses. See "NOW's FIRST DE-CADE . . . A Few Highlights," program of 10th anniversary national conference, 1977, pp. 16–20 (box 21, folder 4) NOW Records, Schlesinger.

51. Gornick and Moran, eds., *Woman in Sexist Society*; Thompson, ed., *Voices of the New Feminism*; Freeman, ed., *Women: A Feminist Perspective*; Adams and Briscoe, eds., *Up Against the Wall*; Morgan, ed. *Sisterhood Is Powerful*; Babcox and Belkin, eds., *Liberation Now!*; Anne Koedt, Ellen Levine, and Anita Rapone, eds., *Radical Feminism* (New York: Quadrangle, 1973); and Jessie Bernard, *The Future of Marriage* (New York: World Publishing, 1972).

52. Helen Dudar, "Women's Lib: The War on 'Sexism,'" *Newsweek*, March 23, 1970, 71; and Sophy Burnham, "Women's Lib: The Idea You Can't Ignore" *Redbook*, September 1970, 190.

53. Karen Oppenheim Mason, John L. Czajka, and Sara Arber, "Change in US Women's Sex-Role Attitudes 1964–1974," *American Sociological Review* 41 (August 1976): 587–588.

2. Fatherhood

1. Pranay Gupte, "Women Here Hail Date of Suffrage," *New York Times*, August 26, 1973, 1. See also "Men's Liberation Protests 'Success Objects,'" press release, [August 1973] (box 48, folder 3) NOW Records, Schlesinger.

2. Betty Friedan, "Woman: The Fourth Dimension," 1964, in *It Changed My Life: Writings on the Women's Movement* (New York: Dell, 1977), 69–70; Betty Friedan, *The Feminine Mystique*, 20th anniv. ed. (New York: Dell, 1983), 386, 391–392; and Jo Ann Levine, "Betty Friedan," *Christian Science Monitor*, April 1, 1974, F1. See also Betty Friedan, "Beyond Women's Liberation," *McCall's*, August 1972, 136.

3. On the NOW Task Force on the Masculine Mystique, see Warren Farrell, *The Liberated Man: Beyond Masculinity—Freeing Men and their Relationships with Women* (New York: Bantam Books, 1974), 140–141; and "NOW Task Force on the Masculine Mystique," November 1973 (box 48, folder 3) NOW Records, Schlesinger.

4. Farrell, *Liberated Man*, xxi–xxvi.

5. Warren Farrell, curriculum vitae, [1973] (box 48, folder 3) NOW Records, Schlesinger; Myra MacPherson, "Husbands, Lovers and the 'Free' Male: Going Beyond Masculinity," *Washington Post,* February 21, 1973, B1, B3; and "In His Own Words: Getting Men to Hold Hands—On the Road to Liberation," *People,* January 20, 1975, 48–51.

6. "The Masculine Mystique Task Force. An Open Letter to NOW Members," TS, 2 pp. c. 1972 (box 210, folder 22) NOW Records, Schlesinger; and "NOW Task Force on the Masculine Mystique."

7. Susan Faludi, *Backlash: The Undeclared War against American Women* (New York: Anchor Books, 1991), 302–303; Don Andersen, "Warren the Success Object," in *For Men against Sexism: A Book of Readings,* ed. Jon Snodgrass (Albion, CA: Times Change Press, 1977), 146; and Farrell, curriculum vitae.

8. "Men's Liberation Protests 'Success Objects.'"

9. Barbara Ehrenreich, *The Hearts of Men: American Dreams and the Flight from Commitment* (New York: Anchor Books, 1983), 14–26; Hendrik M. Ruitenbeck, *Psychoanalysis and Male Sexuality* (New Haven, CT: College and University Press, 1966), 12, qtd. in Ehrenreich, *Hearts of Men,* 14; and Joseph H. Pleck, *The Myth of Masculinity* (Cambridge: MIT Press, 1981), 4–9, 126–128.

10. Bruno Bettelheim, "Fathers Shouldn't Try to Be Mothers," 1956, and Haim Ginott, *Between Parent and Child,* 1975, qtd. in James A. Levine, *Who Will Raise the Children? New Options for Fathers (and Mothers)* (Philadelphia: Lippincott, 1976), 22.

11. Agatha Beins, *Liberation in Print: Feminist Periodicals and Social Movement Identity* (Athens: University of Georgia Press, 2017), 37; and Denys Howard, "Men Doing Childcare for Feminists," in *For Men against Sexism,* ed. Snodgrass, 137, 135–137.

12. Judith Newton, *From Panthers to Promise Keepers: Rethinking the Men's Movement* (Lanham, MD: Rowman & Littlefield Publishers, 2005), 116–117.

13. Newton, *From Panthers to Promise Keepers,* 63, 57–70; and Michael S. Kimmel, *Manhood in America: A Cultural History,* 2nd ed. (New York: Oxford University Press, 2006), 179–180.

14. Michael A. Messner, "The Limits of 'The Male Sex Role': An Analysis of the Men's Liberation and Men's Rights Movements' Discourse," *Gender and Society* 12 (June 1998): 256; Joseph H. Pleck and Jack Sawyer, eds., *Men and Masculinity* (Englewood Cliffs, NJ: Prentice-Hall, 1974), 1–2; Barbara J. Katz, "A Quiet March for Liberation Begins," 1973, and "Berkeley Men's Center Manifesto," 1973, in *Men and Masculinity,* ed. Pleck and Sawyer, 152–156, 173–174; and "The Men's Group Directory," *M: Gentle Men for Gender Justice* 3 (Summer/Fall 1980): 18–20. See also Rob A. Okun, ed., *Voice Male: The Untold Story of the Pro-Feminist Men's Movement* (Northampton, MA: Interlink Books, 2014); Michael A. Messner, *Politics of Masculinities: Men in Movements* (Thousand Oaks, CA: SAGE Publications, 1997); and Kenneth Clatterbaugh, "Literature of the US Men's Movements," *Signs* 25 (Spring 2000): 883–894.

15. Joe Interrante, "Dancing along the Precipice: The Men's Movement in the '80s," *Radical America* 15 (September/October 1981): 54–56; Alan E. Gross, Ronald Smith, and Barbara Strudler Wallston, "The Men's Movement: Personal

Versus Political," in *Social Movements of the Sixties and Seventies*, ed. Jo Freeman (New York: Longman, 1983), 72–73, 78; and Newton, *From Panthers to Promise Keepers*, 123.

16. Farrell, *Liberated Man*; Jack Nichols, *Men's Liberation: A New Definition of Masculinity* (New York: Penguin Books, 1975); Marc Feigen Fasteau, *The Male Machine* (New York: McGraw Hill, 1974); Mike Bradley, et al., *Unbecoming Men: A Men's Consciousness-Raising Group Writes on Oppression and Themselves* (Washington, NJ: Times Change Press, 1971); Snodgrass, ed., *For Men against Sexism*, 6–8; and Pleck and Sawyer, eds., *Men and Masculinity*.

17. Messner, "Limits of 'The Male Sex Role,'" 273; Leonard Schein, "Dangers with Men's Consciousness-Raising Groups," in *For Men against Sexism*, ed. Snodgrass, 131–132; Paul Carlo Hornacek, "Anti-Sexist Consciousness-Raising Groups for Men," in *For Men against Sexism*, ed. Snodgrass, 129; and "Berkeley Men's Center Manifesto," 173–174. See also Lisa Hammel, "Men's Lib—Almost Underground, but a Growing Movement," *New York Times*, August 9, 1972, 42.

18. Hammel, "Men's Lib—Almost Underground"; Robert Brannon, "The Male Sex Role: Our Culture's Blueprint of Manhood, and What It's Done for Us Lately," first published in *The Forty-Nine Percent Majority: The Male Sex Role*, ed. Deborah S. David and Robert Brannon (Menlo Park, CA: Addison-Wesley, 1976), 7–10; Jack Sawyer, "On Male Liberation," 1970, in *Men and Masculinity*, ed. Pleck and Sawyer, 170, 172–173; and Messner, "Limits of 'The Male Sex Role,'" 256.

19. Messner, "Limits of 'The Male Sex Role,'" 260; Brannon, "The Male Sex Role," 12; and Katz, "A Quiet March for Liberation," 155.

20. Newton, *From Panthers to Promise Keepers*, 118, 122; Robert A. Fein, "Men and Young Children," in *Men and Masculinity*, ed. Pleck and Sawyer, 61.

21. Fasteau, *Male Machine*, 92; and Fein, "Men and Young Children," 61.

22. Okun, ed., *Voice Male*, 1–48.

23. Lisa Hammel, "Men's Lib: An Unorganized but Significant Movement," *New York Times*, June 11, 1974, 46; "In His Own Words," 49; Farrell, *Liberated Man*, 129–131, 135–138, 339–340; Bryan E. Robinson, "Men Caring for the Young: A Profile," in *Men's Changing Roles in the Family*, ed. Robert A. Lewis and Marvin B. Sussman (New York: Haworth Press, 1986), 152; Debra G. Klinman and Rhiana Kohl, *Fatherhood USA: The First National Guide to Programs, Services, and Resources for and about Fathers* (New York: Garland, 1984), 52; and Fein, "Men and Young Children," 61–62.

24. Robert Staples, "The Myth of the Impotent Black Male," in *The Black Male in America: Perspectives on His Status in Contemporary Society*, ed. Doris Y. Wilkinson and Ronald L. Taylor (Chicago: Nelson-Hall, 1977), 137, 139; and Robert Staples, "The Myth of the Black Matriarchy," in *The Black Male in America*, ed. Wilkinson and Taylor, 174–187. See also Leonor Boulin Johnson, "Perspectives on Black Family Empirical Research, 1965–1978," in *Black Families*, 2nd ed., ed. Harriette Pipes McAdoo (Newbury Park, CA: Sage, 1988), 91–106.

25. Review of Robert B. Hill, "The Strengths of Black Families," in *Equal Opportunity Review* (May 1973), 2; Marie F. Peters, "Notes from the Guest

Editor," *Journal of Marriage and Family* 40 (November 1978): 655; John Lewis McAdoo, "A Black Perspective on the Father's Role in Child Development," in *Men's Changing Roles in the Family*, ed. Lewis and Sussman, 124–125, 129; and Pleck, *Myth of Masculinity*, 126–128.

26. Joseph H. Pleck, "Psychological Frontiers for Men," *Rough Times* 3, no. 6 (1973): 14–15; and Joseph H. Pleck, "My Male Sex Role—and Ours," *WIN Magazine*, April 1974, 8–12, repr. in *The Forty-Nine Percent Majority*, ed. David and Brannon, 253–264 and in *Our Sociological Eye: Personal Essays on Society and Culture*, ed. Arthur B. Shostak (Port Washington, NY: Alfred, 1977), 93–102. See also Messner, "Limits of 'The Male Sex Role,'" 260.

27. "The Workshop Begins," in Libby A. Cater and Anne Firor Scott, *Women and Men: Changing Roles, Relationships and Perceptions* (New York: Praeger, 1977), 11; and Joseph H. Pleck, curriculum vitae, June 2008, in author's possession.

28. Joseph H. Pleck, "The Psychology of Sex Roles: Traditional and New Views," in *Women and Men*, ed. Cater and Scott, 181, 186, 193. See also Joseph H. Pleck, "The Male Sex Role: Definitions, Problems, and Sources of Change," *Journal of Social Issues* 32 (Summer 1976): 155–164; and Joseph H. Pleck, "Masculinity—Femininity," *Sex Roles* 1 (June 1975): 161–178.

29. Pleck, "My Sex Role—and Ours," in *The Forty-Nine Percent Majority*, ed. David and Brannon, 263; and Pleck, "The Male Sex Role: Definitions, Problems, and Sources of Change," 161. See also Joseph H. Pleck, "Men's Power with Women, Other Men, and Society: A Men's Movement Analysis," in *The Women Say, the Men Say: Women's Liberation and Men's Consciousness—Issues in Politics, Work, Family, Sexuality, and Power*, ed. Evelyn Shapiro and Barry Shapiro (New York: Delta, 1979), 260.

30. Pleck, "Men's Power with Women, Other Men, and Society," 261; and Pleck, "The Psychology of Sex Roles," in *Women and Men*, ed. Cater and Scott, 198.

31. Kimmel, *Manhood in America*, 188; and Pleck, *Myth of Masculinity*, 159–160.

32. Joseph H. Pleck, "The Work-Family Role System," *Social Problems* 24 (April 1977): 417–427; Pleck, curriculum vitae; and Joseph H. Pleck, "Men's Family Work: Three Perspectives and Some New Data," *The Family Coordinator* 28 (October 1979): 485. Pleck co-edited this special issue of *The Family Coordinator* on "Men's Roles in the Family."

33. Lisa Hammel, "A Scholarly 'Homemaker-Father' Studies Others like Himself," *New York Times*, December 14, 1974, 18; Levine, *Who Will Raise the Children?*, 13–14; and Farrell, *Liberated Man*, 340. See also "James A. Levine (1946–)" in *Work and Family in America: A Reference Handbook*, ed. Leslie F. Stebbins (Santa Barbara: ABC-CLIO, 2001), 115–116; and "Jim Levine," Levine, Greenberg, and Rostan Literary Agency, lgrliterary.com/who-we-are/team/jim-levine/.

34. Levine, *Who Will Raise the Children?*, 16, 13.

35. Hammel, "Scholarly 'Homemaker-Father'"; Levine, *Who Will Raise the Children?*, 176, 160; and James A. Levine, "Redefining the Child Care 'Problem'—Men as Child Nurturers," *Childhood Education* 54 (December 1977): 61.

36. Levine, *Who Will Raise the Children?*, 90–91.

37. Ibid., 91–93, 158–159; and Levine, "Redefining the Child Care 'Problem,'" 58–59.

38. Levine, *Who Will Raise the Children?*, 161–175; Hammel, "Scholarly 'Homemaker-Father;'" Joyce Maynard, "Do Fathers Make Good Mothers?," *Ladies' Home Journal*, March 1979, 152–154; and Lynn Langway, et al., "A New Kind of Life with Father," *Newsweek*, November 30, 1981, 93–97.

39. Fein, "Men and Young Children"; Robert A. Fein, "Research on Fathering: Social Policy and an Emergent Perspective," *Journal of Social Issues* 34 (1978): 127; and Ross D. Parke, *Fathers* (Cambridge: Harvard University Press, 1981).

40. Klinman and Kohl, *Fatherhood USA*, 277; Pleck, curriculum vitae; Levine, "Redefining the Child Care 'Problem,'" 57; Joseph H. Pleck, "Paternal Involvement: Revised Conceptualization and Theoretical Linkages with Child Outcomes," in *The Role of the Father in Child Development*, 5th ed., ed. Michael E. Lamb (Hoboken, NJ: Wiley, 2010): 59; James A. Levine, Joseph H. Pleck, and Michael E. Lamb, "The Fatherhood Project," in *Fatherhood and Family Policy*, ed. Michael E. Lamb and Abraham Sagi (Hillsdale, NJ: Lawrence Erlbaum, 1983), 105–106; and *Child Care and Equal Opportunity for Women* (Washington, DC: United States Commission on Civil Rights, 1981).

41. Klinman and Kohl, *Fatherhood USA*, 277. I offer here the first analysis of which I am aware that identifies such a profeminist fatherhood movement, and much research needs to be done to locate and map its grassroots elements. Work on advocates for fatherhood that note some of these actions but don't yet consider it a systematic movement includes Newton, *From Panthers to Promise Keepers*, 160–164; and Levine, Pleck, and Lamb, "Fatherhood Project." For a more skeptical assessment, see Robert L. Griswold, *Fatherhood in America: A History* (New York: Basic Books, 1993).

This movement should not be confused with the fathers' rights movement, which has been more widely studied. See Deborah Dinner, "The Divorce Bargain: The Fathers' Rights Movement and Family Inequalities," *Virginia Law Review* 102 (2016): 79–152; Michael Kimmel, *Angry White Men: Masculinity at the End of an Era* (New York: Nation Books, 2013), 135–168; and Jocelyn Elise Crowley, *Defiant Dads: Fathers' Rights Activists in America* (Ithaca: Cornell University Press, 2008), 14–38.

42. Klinman and Kohl, *Fatherhood USA*, 149–153.

43. Michael E. Lamb, Graeme Russell, and Abraham Sagi, "Summary and Recommendations for Public Policy," in *Fatherhood and Family Policy*, ed. Lamb and Sagi, 250–251. For the antifeminist implications of custody reform, see Dinner, "Divorce Bargain."

44. Lamb, et al., "Summary and Recommendations," 248–249; and Klinman and Kohl, *Fatherhood USA*, 183, 191.

45. *Kramer vs. Kramer*, dir. Robert Benton (Culver City, CA: Columbia Pictures, 1979).

46. Molly Haskell, "Hers," *New York Times*, February 11, 1982, C2.

47. Nita Gilson Kurmins, "Walk a Mile in their Moccasins: Steps to Solving 'Gender Game,'" *Christian Science Monitor*, February 29, 1988, 24; and Warren Farrell, *The Myth of Male Power: Why Men Are the Disposable Sex* (New York: Simon and Schuster, 1993). See also Faludi, *Backlash*, 303–304.

48. Farrell, *Myth of Male Power*, 364–365; Dinner, "Divorce Bargain," 113; and Klinman and Kohl, *Fatherhood USA*, 154. See also Alison Lefkovitz, *Strange Bedfellows: Marriage in the Age of Women's Liberation* (Philadelphia: University of Pennsylvania Press, 2018), 48–53.

49. Klinman and Kohl, *Fatherhood USA*, xv–xvi; *Mr. Mom*, dir. Stan Dragoti (Santa Monica: Twentieth-Century Fox, 1983; MGM, 2000); *Tootsie*, dir. Sydney Pollack (Culver City, CA: Columbia Pictures, 1982); Bill Cosby, *Fatherhood* (Garden City, NY: Doubleday, 1986); and S. Adams Sullivan, *The Father's Almanac* (New York: Doubleday, 1980). See also Desson Howe, "Families: Sometimes Father Knows Best," *Washington Post*, September 25, 1984, C5; and Frank F. Furstenberg, Jr., "Good Dads—Bad Dads: Two Faces of Fatherhood," in Andrew J. Cherlin, *The Changing American Family and Public Policy* (Washington, DC: The Urban Institute, 1988), 193.

50. Maxine P. Atkinson and Stephen P. Blackwelder, "Fathering in the 20th Century," *Journal of Marriage and Family* 55 (November 1993): 981.

51. Levine, *Who Will Raise the Children?*, 177; Patti Hagan, "Dr. Spock Tells Why He No Longer Sings in Praise of Hims," *New York Times*, October 13, 1973, 30; and Sharon Hays, *The Cultural Contradictions of Motherhood* (New Haven: Yale University Press, 1996), 205n54.

52. Benjamin Spock, "Mothers Who Try to Be All Things," *Redbook*, March 1969, 60; Eric Page, "World's Pediatrician Dies at 94," *New York Times*, March 17, 1998, B10; and Benjamin M. Spock, "Male Chauvinist Spock Recants—Well, Almost," *New York Times Sunday Magazine*, September 12, 1971, 98, 100–101.

53. Spock, "Male Chauvinist Recants," 100; Hagan, "Dr. Spock Tells Why"; and "Ms. Heroes: Men Who've Taken Chances and Made a Difference," compiled by Ellen Sweet, *Ms.*, July/August 1982, 104.

54. Luix Overbea, "Family and Jobs Are Top Priorities for Urban League in '85," *Christian Science Monitor*, July 19, 1985, www.csmonitor.com/1985/0719/aurban.html; Klinman and Kohl, *Fatherhood USA*, 107–108; and Newton, *From Panthers to Promise Keepers*, 169–171.

55. Klinman and Kohl, *Fatherhood USA*, back cover, 271–273, 277; Glenn Collins, "Redefining the Role of Fathers," *New York Times*, June 13, 1983, B9; Levine, Pleck, and Lamb, "The Fatherhood Project," 102; Lamb and Sagi, eds., *Fatherhood and Family Policy*, 5; and Pleck, curriculum vitae.

56. Phyllis Schlafly, *The Power of the Positive Woman* (New Rochelle, NY: Arlington House, 1977), 93, 96.

57. *Babies and Briefcases: Creating a Family-Friendly Workplace for Fathers. Hearing Before the Select Comm. on Children, Youth, and Families*, H., 102nd Cong. 34 (1991) (statement of James Levine).

58. Amanda Goldrick-Jones, *Men who Believe in Feminism* (Westport, CT: Praeger, 2002), 40; Newton, *From Panthers to Promise Keepers*, 124; Messner, "Limits of 'The Male Sex Role,'" 265; Messner, *Politics of Masculinities*, 52–54; and Okun, ed., *Voice Male*.

3. Partners

1. Joan Didion, "The Women's Movement," *New York Times Book Review*, July 30, 1972, 2; Norman Mailer, "The Prisoner of Sex," *Harper's Magazine*, March 1971, 91; and Alix Shulman, "A Marriage Agreement," *Up from Under* 1 (August/September 1970): 5–8. For the agreement's history, see Alix Kates Shulman, "A Marriage Disagreement, or Marriage by Other Means," in *The Feminist Memoir Project: Voices from Women's Liberation*, ed. Rachel Blau DuPlessis and Ann Snitow (New York: Three Rivers Press, 1998), 294–295.

2. "Alix Kates Shulman," *Jewish Women's Archive*, jwa.org/feminism/shulman-alix-kates.

3. Leora Tanenbaum, "The Liberation of an Ex-Prom Queen," *Ms.*, November/December 1997, 84; Alice Echols, *Daring to Be Bad: Radical Feminism in America, 1967–1975* (Minneapolis: University of Minnesota Press, 1989), 94; and Charlotte Templin, "An Interview with Alix Kates Shulman," *The Missouri Review* 24 (Winter 2001), 114.

4. Shulman, "Marriage Disagreement," 284–88.

5. Ibid., 284, 288.

6. Ibid., 291; and Shulman, "A Marriage Agreement," 6.

7. Scholars of both marriage and feminism have explored the feminist critique of marriage but not situated it within a larger campaign to reconstruct work and family broadly. See Alison Lefkovitz, *Strange Bedfellows: Marriage in the Age of Women's Liberation* (Philadelphia: University of Pennsylvania Press, 2018); Nancy F. Cott, *Public Vows: A History of Marriage and the Nation* (Cambridge: Harvard University Press, 2000); Stephanie Coontz, *Marriage, a History: From Obedience to Intimacy or How Love Conquered Marriage* (New York: Viking, 2005); and Kristin Celello, *Making Marriage Work: A History of Marriage and Divorce in the Twentieth-Century United States* (Chapel Hill: University of North Carolina Press, 2009).

8. Dorothy Sue Cobble, *The Other Women's Movement: Workplace Justice and Social Rights in Modern America* (Princeton: Princeton University Press, 2004), 122–123. For early-twentieth-century feminists' proposal for "companionate" marriage, see Christina Simmons, *Making Marriage Modern: Women's Sexuality from the Progressive Era to World War II* (New York: Oxford University Press, 2009); and Nancy F. Cott, *The Grounding of Modern Feminism* (New Haven: Yale University Press, 1987), 156–158.

9. Howard Hayghe, "Families and the Rise of Working Wives—An Overview," *Monthly Labor Review* 99 (May 1976): 13; Wendy Wang, Kim Parker, and Paul Taylor, "Breadwinner Moms," report, Pew Research Center, May 29, 2013, assets.pewresearch.org/wp-content/uploads/sites/3/2013/05/Breadwinner_moms_final.pdf, 20; Leah Platt Boustan and William J. Collins, "The Origins and Persistence of Black-White Differences in Women's Labor Force Participation," NBER Working Paper Series, Working Paper 19040 (Cambridge, MA: National Bureau of Economic Research, May 2013), 43; and Nancy MacLean, *Freedom Is Not Enough: The Opening of the American Workplace* (Cambridge: Harvard University Press, 2006), 16–20. See also Claudia Goldin, *Understanding the*

Gender Gap: An Economic History of American Women (New York: Oxford University Press, 1990).

10. Celello, *Making Marriage Work*, 107; Betty Friedan, "Woman: The Fourth Dimension," 1964, and "The Crises of Divorce," 1974, in *It Changed My Life: Writings on the Women's Movement* (New York: Dell, 1977), 68–70, 417; and "And Changing Occupations," *Women's Lobby Quarterly* 2 (October 1975), 11–13.

11. Heather Booth, Evi Goldfield, and Sue Munaker, "Toward a Radical Movement," 1968, and Kate Millett, "Theory of Sexual Politics," 1970, in *Radical Feminism: A Documentary Reader*, ed. Barbara A. Crow (New York: New York University Press, 2000), 58–60, 124; and Flora Ellen Hardy, letter, *Voice of the Women's Liberation Movement* 6 (February 1969): 15. For other radical feminists in a similar vein, see Betsy Warrior, "Housework: Slavery or Labor of Love," 1971, and Sheila Cronan, "Marriage," 1971, in *Radical Feminism*, ed. Anne Koedt, Ellen Levine, and Anita Rapone (New York: Quadrangle, 1973), 208–221. See also Celello, *Making Marriage Work*, 105, 109; Lefkovitz, *Strange Bedfellows*, 26–29; and Echols, *Daring to be Bad*, 145–148, 170, 178. Echols rightly points out important differences among radical feminist groups' interpretations of how marriage oppressed women.

12. Evelyn Reed, "Women: Caste, Class or Oppressed Sex?," *International Socialist Review* 31 (September 1970), 17; Shulamith Firestone, "The Women's Rights Movement in the US: A New View," in *Notes from the First Year*, ed. Shulamith Firestone (New York: New York Radical Women, 1968), 6–7; and Millett, "Theory of Sexual Politics," 134.

13. Eleanor Holmes Norton, "For Sadie and Maude," in *Sisterhood Is Powerful: An Anthology of Writings from the Women's Liberation Movement*, ed. Robin Morgan (New York: Vintage, 1970), 400; and Serena Mayeri, *Reasoning from Race: Feminism, Law, and the Civil Rights Revolution* (Cambridge: Harvard University Press, 2011), 48.

14. Booth, Goldfield, and Munaker, "Toward a Radical Movement," 60; and National Organization for Women, "Statement of Purpose," October 29, 1966, in Toni Carabillo, Judith Meuli, and June Bundy Csida, eds., *Feminist Chronicles, 1953–1993* (Los Angeles: Women's Graphics, 1993), 159–160.

15. Cronan, "Marriage," 219; Ellen Willis, "Whatever Happened to Women? Nothing—That's the Trouble," *Mademoiselle*, September 1969, 208; Martha Shelley, "On Marriage," *The Ladder* 13 (October–November 1968): 46–47; and Anne M. Valk, "Living a Feminist Lifestyle: The Intersection of Theory and Action in a Lesbian Feminist Collective," *Feminist Studies* 28 (Summer 2002): 310–311.

16. Naomi Weisstein, "An Anlaysis of the Oppression of Women as Related to a Consideration of the Nature of Social Systems (Society)," October 1969, Chicago Women's Liberation Union Papers, Chicago History Museum, qtd. in Alison Lefkovitz, "The Problem of Marriage in the Era of Women's Liberation" (PhD Diss., University of Chicago, 2010), 46; and Cronan, "Marriage," 214. See also The Feminists, "Women: Do You Know the Facts about Marriage?," 1969, in *Sisterhood Is Powerful*, ed. Morgan, 601–603.

17. Linda Gordon, "Families," [1971], TS, p. 1 (box 7, folder 5) Baxandall-Gordon, TAM.210, reprinted in a slightly different form in *Women: A Journal of Liberation* (Fall 1969) and as Linda Gordon, "Functions of the Family," in *Voices*

from Women's Liberation, ed. Leslie B. Tanner (New York: Signet, 1970), 181–188; and Lefkovitz, *Strange Bedfellows*, 27–28.

18. National Organization for Women, "Statement of Purpose," 162.

19. Gordon, "Functions of the Family," in *Voices from Women's Liberation*, ed. Tanner, 188; and Heidi Hartmann, "Capitalism, Patriarchy, and Job Segregation by Sex," *Signs* 1 (Spring 1976): 137.

20. Karol Hope, "The Single Mother Experience," *Momma: The Newspaper/Magazine for Single Mothers*, December 1, 1972, 1; and Barbara Omolade, "Sisterhood in Black and White," in *Feminist Memoir Project*, ed. DuPlessis and Snitow, 394.

21. Gloria Steinem, "Women's Lives Will Change in Every Way" in "What Kind of Future for America," *US News and World Report*, July 7, 1975.

22. Mailer, "The Prisoner of Sex," 41–92; and Shulman, "Marriage Disagreement," 295–296.

23. On deconstructing coverture, see Lefkovitz, *Strange Bedfellows*, 39–40, 74; and Cott, *Public Vows*, 209.

24. Susan Edmiston, "How to Write Your Own Marriage Contract," *New York Magazine*, December 20, 1971, 71; Rae André, *Homemakers: The Forgotten Workers* (Chicago: University of Chicago Press, 1981), 221–223; Lenore J. Weitzman, "Legal Regulation of Marriage: Tradition and Change. A Proposal for Individual Contracts and Contracts in Lieu of Marriage," *California Law Review* 62 (July–September 1974): 1169–1288; "New Marriage Styles," *Time*, March 20, 1972, 56–57; and Sherry Blackman, letter, *Ms.*, May 1973, 8.

25. Sussman study cited in "Ties That Bind," *Time*, September 1, 1975, 62.

26. "New Marriage Styles," 66; and Madelon Bedell, "Supermom! We Are Never Tired; We Are Never Afraid; But, Oh, the Guilt!," *Ms.*, May 1973, 100.

27. Rosabeth Moss Kanter, *Commitment and Community: Communes and Utopias in Sociological Perspective* (Cambridge: Harvard University Press, 1972); Rosabeth Moss Kanter, ed., *Communes: Creating and Managing the Collective Life* (New York: Harper and Row, 1973); Timothy Miller, *The 60s Communes: Hippies and Beyond* (Syracuse: Syracuse University Press, 1999); and Cheri Register, interview by Anne Enke, August 29, 1996, qtd. in Anne Enke, *Finding the Movement: Sexuality, Contested Space, and Feminist Activism* (Durham: Duke University Press, 2007), 64.

28. Marlene Dixon, "Why Women's Liberation?," *Ramparts*, December 1969, 61; Margaret Benston, "The Political Economy of Women's Liberation," *Monthly Review* 21 (September 1969): 13–27; Echols, *Daring to Be Bad*, 222–237; and Keith Melville, *Communes in the Counter Culture: Origins, Theories, Styles of Life* (New York: Morrow, 1972).

29. Betty Rollin, "What's Women's Lib Doing to the Family? Plenty!," *Look*, January 26, 1971, 40; Lillian Faderman, *Odd Girls and Twilight Lovers: A History of Lesbian Life in Twentieth-Century America* (New York: Penguin Books, 1992), 238–239; and Sarah Kershaw, "My Sister's Keeper," *New York Times*, February 1, 2009, ST1. See also Vicki Cohn Pollard, "The Five of Us (With a Little Help from Our Friends)," 1971, in *Dear Sisters: Dispatches from the Women's Liberation Movement*, ed. Rosalyn Baxandall and Linda Gordon (New York: Basic Books, 2000), 222–224.

30. Miller, *60s Communes*, 59, 155–56; and Barbara Balogun Jackson, "Marriage as an Oppressive Institution/Collectives as Solutions," in *Voices from Women's Liberation*, ed. Tanner, 295.

31. Vivian Estellachild, "Hippie Communes," *Women: A Journal of Liberation* (Winter 1971): 40–43; and Gretchen Lemke-Santangelo, *Daughters of Aquarius: Women of the Sixties Counterculture* (Lawrence: University Press of Kansas, 2009), 163–64.

32. "Help Wanted: Female," *Ladies' Home Journal*, August 1970, 67–68; Joan Jordan, *The Place of American Women: Economic Exploitation of Women* (Boston: New England Free Press, 1968), 20; "Editorial," *Up from Under* 1 (January/February 1971): 4; and Dolores Hayden, *The Grand Domestic Revolution: A History of Feminist Designs for American Homes, Neighborhoods and Cities*, rev. ed. (Cambridge: MIT Press, 1982), 188–195, 204, 207–210.

33. Shulman, "A Marriage Agreement," 8; Sara Davidson, "An 'Oppressed Majority' Demands Its Rights," *Life*, December 1969, 78; and Sheli Wortis, "The Home," TS, 1970, p. 6 (box 7, folder 9) Baxandall-Gordon TAM.210.

34. Sidney Abbott and Barbara Love, "Is Women's Liberation a Lesbian Plot?," in *Woman in Sexist Society: Studies in Power and Powerlessness*, ed. Vivian Gornick and Barbara K. Moran (New York: Basic Books, 1971), 437, 449–450; Jill Johnston, "Selections from *Lesbian Nation*," 1973, in *Radical Feminism*, ed. Crow, 342; "Loving Another Woman" in *Radical Feminism*, ed. Koedt, Levine, and Rapone, 89; and Martha Shelley, "Lesbianism and the Women's Liberation Movement," in *Women's Liberation: Blueprint for the Future*, ed. Sookie Stambler (New York: Ace Books, 1970), 129.

35. "The Marriage Experiments," *Life*, April 28, 1972, 41–76.

36. "Ties That Bind"; "New Marriage Styles"; Rollin, "What's Women's Lib Doing to the Family?"; John P. Hayes, "Marriage Contracts: Why Couples Want them and How to Write Your Own," *Glamour*, January 1978, 20–22; "Special Home Furnishings Section: The New American Marriage," *New York*, October 25, 1976, 40–48. See other articles in this special issue of *New York*, especially Elin Schoen, "Seven Two-Career Couples" and Anne Roiphe, "Keeping and Carrying the House Together," *New York*, October 26, 1976, 40–48, 54–55. See also Susan J. Douglas and Meredith W. Michaels, *The Mommy Myth: The Idealization of Motherhood and How It Has Undermined Women* (New York: Free Press, 2004), 43–45.

37. Judy Klemesrud, "'Obsolete' Divorce Laws Assailed at NOW Conference Here," *New York Times*, January 21, 1974, 32; Carl R. Rogers, *Becoming Partners: Marriage and its Alternatives* (New York: Delacorte, 1972); Robert E. Burger, *The Love Contract: Handbook for a Liberated Marriage* (New York: Van Nostrand Reinhold, 1973); and Cott, *Public Vows*, 208.

38. Irene Backalenick, "Suburban Housewives Striving to Become 'The New Woman,'" *New York Times*, March 31, 1972, 34.

39. "American Women," Report of the President's Commission on the Status of Women (Washington, DC: 1963), 47–48. See also Alice Kessler-Harris, *In Pursuit of Equity: Women, Men, and the Quest for Economic Citizenship in 20th-Century America* (New York: Oxford University Press, 2001), 213–225. Successor commissions to the PCSW developed the partnership ideal in tandem with

feminists. See Catherine East, "New Commissions Move the Issues Forward," TS, pp. 4–5 (box 7, folder 65) East Papers, Schlesinger.

40. Norton, "For Sadie and Maude," 403–404; Cellestine Ware, "The Black Family and Feminism: A Conversation with Eleanor Holmes Norton," *Ms.* preview issue, Spring 1972, 95–96; Mayeri, *Reasoning from Race*, 26, 42–49, 230; and Premilla Nadasen, "Expanding the Boundaries of the Women's Movement: Black Feminism and the Struggle for Welfare Rights," *Feminist Studies* 28 (Summer 2002): 282.

41. National Organization for Women, "Task Force on the Family," TS (box 42, folder 5) NOW Records, Schlesinger; "Equality in Family Relations. A Report of the Task Force on Marriage, Divorce, and Family Relations," October 1972 (box 30, folder 68) NOW Records, Schlesinger; and Judith Hole and Ellen Levine, *Rebirth of Feminism* (New York: Quadrangle Books, 1971), 213.

42. Olof Palme, "The Emancipation of Man," reprinted in *Journal of Social Issues* 28 (June 1972): 237–246; "Report to the United Nations, 1968: The Status of Women in Sweden," in *Voices of the New Feminism*, ed. Mary Lou Thompson (Boston: Beacon Press, 1970), 155–177; and Kenneth M. Davidson, Ruth Bader Ginsburg, and Herma Hill Kay, *Text, Cases, and Materials on Sex-Based Discrimination* (St. Paul, MN: West Publishing Company, 1974), 936–948.

43. Ruth Bader Ginsburg, "Gender and the Constitution," *University of Cincinnati Law Review* 44 (1975): 13; and Elizabeth Duncan Koontz, "Childbirth and Child Rearing Leave: Job-Related Benefits," *New York Law Forum* 17 (1971): 501, 481.

44. Sandie North, "The 50/50 Marriage: Is This What Women Want?," *Look*, October 5, 1971, 57; *F.E.W.'s News and Views* 2, no. 4 (July 1970): 4; and Richard J. Meislin, "Poll Finds More Liberal Beliefs on Marriage and Sex Roles, Especially among the Young," *New York Times*, November 27, 1977, 75. On the Bems, see also Jean Murphy, "An Equalitarian Marriage and How it Works," *Los Angeles Times*, February 20, 1972, F1.

45. Ginsburg, "Gender and the Constitution," 27; Neil S. Siegel and Reva B. Siegel, "*Struck* by Stereotype: Ruth Bader Ginsburg on Pregnancy Discrimination as Sex Discrimination," *Duke Law Journal* 59 (2010): 783; Amy Leigh Campbell, "Raising the Bar: Ruth Bader Ginsburg and the ACLU Women's Rights Project," *Texas Journal of Women and the Law* 157 (Spring 2002): 157–243; and "The History of the ACLU Women's Rights Project," American Civil Liberties Union, www.aclu.org/sites/default/files/field_document/wrp_history.pdf.

46. Ginsburg, "Gender and the Constitution," 42; and Cary Franklin, "The Anti-Stereotyping Principle in Constitutional Sex Discrimination Law," *New York University Law Review* 85 (April 2010): 88. See also Siegel and Siegel, "*Struck* by Stereotype"; and Joan C. Williams, "Jumpstarting the Stalled Gender Revolution: Justice Ginsburg and Reconstructive Feminism," *Hastings Law Journal* 63 (2012): 1267–1296.

47. Franklin, "Anti-Stereotyping Principle," 97–98, 111.

48. Joan Williams has calculated that twelve of fourteen cases in these years took this orientation. Williams, "Jumpstarting the Stalled Gender Revolution," 1273.

49. Ginsburg, "Gender and the Constitution," 14; and Franklin, "Anti-Stereotyping Principle," 136. See also Lefkovitz, *Strange Bedfellows*, 23–26.

50. Martha W. Griffiths, "Sex Discrimination in Income Security Programs," *Notre Dame Law Review* 49 (February 1974): 534.

51. Katharine T. Bartlett, "Feminist Legal Scholarship: A History through the Lens of the *California Law Review*," *California Law Review* 100 (April 2012): 389–391; and Cott, *Public Vows*, 206. See the work of Herma Hill Kay, notably "Making Marriage and Divorce Safe for Women," *California Law Review* 60 (November 1972): 1683–1700; "Making Marriage and Divorce Safe for Women Revisited," *Hofstra Law Review* 32 (Fall 2003): 71–92; and "From the Second Sex to the Joint Venture: An Overview of Women's Rights and Family Law in the United States During the Twentieth Century," *California Law Review* 88 (December 2000): 2017–2094. On the Uniform Marriage and Divorce Act, see Ginsburg, "Gender and the Constitution," 24; and "Marriage and Divorce Act, Model Summary," www.uniformlaws.org/ActSummary.aspx?title=Marriage%20 and%20Divorce%20Act,%20Model. See also Lefkovitz, *Strange Bedfellows*, 56–70.

52. Ginsburg, "Gender and the Constitution," 27; and Joan M. Krauskopf and Rhonda C. Thomas, "Partnership Marriage: The Solution to an Ineffective and Inequitable Law of Support," *Ohio State Law Journal* 35 (1974): 558–600.

53. "HERA: Homemakers' Equal Rights Association," September 1980 (box 46, folder 40) NOW Records, Schlesinger; and National Organization for Women, "ERA and Homemakers, Partnership in Marriage," ERA Countdown Shoot 1981 (box 5) ERACAP, SSC, MS 310.

54. IWY Project, Recognition of the Economic Contribution of the Home-maker, "Fact Sheet #5: Legal Rights of the Homemaker and the Impact of ERA," October 1975 (box 19, folder 19) East Papers, Schlesinger; and Catherine East, "Effects of the ERA on the Homemaker," speech at the National Press Club, April 10, 1976 (box 7, folder 2) East Papers, Schlesinger. See also Evelyn Nakano Glenn, *Forced to Care: Coercion and Caregiving in America* (Cambridge: Harvard University Press, 2010), 100–101.

55. Catherine East, Address to "Homemaker: Career in Transition" Seminar, MS, October 19, 1977, pp. 8–9 (box 7, folder 21) East Papers, Schlesinger.

56. Ginsburg, "Gender and the Constitution," 34.

57. Koontz, "Childbirth and Child Rearing Leave," 488–502; Gary L. Ackerman, "Child-Care Leave for Fathers," *Ms.*, September 1973, 118–119; and Maurice Carroll, "US Backs Child-Care Leaves For Men in a School Case Here," *New York Times*, January 6, 1973, 1.

58. "Task Force on the Family," [1967]; Maren Lockwood Carden, *The New Feminist Movement* (New York: Russell Sage Foundation, 1974), 106; and "Statement of Ms. Aileen C. Hernandez to the Joint Economic Committee, US Congress," July 11, 1973, p. 14 (box 46, folder 18) NOW Records, Schlesinger.

59. Coontz, *Marriage, A History*, 247–262; and Cott, *Public Vows*, 200–227.

60. Phyllis Schlafly, "What's Wrong with 'Equal Rights' for Women?," *Phyllis Schlafly Report*, February 1972.

4. Housework

1. "Women Arise: The Revolution That Will Affect Everybody," *Life*, September 4, 1970, 16; "Women on the March," *Time*, September 7, 1970, 20; Lee Dye, "L.A. 'Women's Lib' Marchers Greeted by Cheers and Jeers," *Los Angeles Times*, August 27, 1970, 1; and Linda Charlton, "Women March down Fifth in Equality Drive," *New York Times*, August 27, 1970, 30. See also Betty Friedan, *It Changed My Life: Writings on the Women's Movement* (New York: Dell, 1977), 185–206; Bonnie J. Dow, *Watching Women's Liberation, 1970: Feminism's Pivotal Year on the Network News* (Urbana: University of Illinois Press, 2014), 144–167; and Susan J. Douglas, *Where the Girls Are: Growing up Female with the Mass Media* (New York: Three Rivers Press, 1994), 177–186.

2. Friedan, *It Changed My Life*, 205.

3. Douglas, *Where the Girls Are*, 179; CBS News, "Women's Liberation circa 1970, 2009," August 26, 1970, https://youtu.be/E9TlSiMSdPk; Dow, *Watching Women's Liberation*, 160; Patricia Bradley, *Mass Media and the Shaping of American Feminism, 1963–1975* (Jackson: University Press of Mississippi, 2003), 118; and Judy Klemesrud, "It Was a Great Day for Women on the March," *New York Times*, August 30, 1970, section 4, p. 4.

4. Dow, *Watching Women's Liberation*, 156–158; and Douglas, *Where the Girls Are*, 185–186.

5. Lisa Levenstein, "'Don't Agonize, Organize!': The Displaced Homemakers Campaign and the Contested Goals of Postwar Feminism," *Journal of American History* 100 (March 2014): 1114–1138; Mary Ziegler, "An Incomplete Revolution: Feminists and the Legacy of Marital-Property Reform," *Michigan Journal of Gender and Law* 19 (2013): 259–292; and Premilla Nadasen, *Household Workers Unite: The Untold Story of African American Women Who Built a Movement* (Boston: Beacon Press, 2015), 124–147.

6. Alix Kates Shulman, "A Marriage Disagreement, or Marriage by Other Means," in *The Feminist Memoir Project: Voices from Women's Liberation*, ed. Rachel Blau DuPlessis and Ann Snitow (New York: Three Rivers Press, 1998), 296; "June 1969: A Blast of Redstockings Feminism," www.redstockings.org /index.php/june-1969-a-blast-of-redstockings-feminism; and Pat Mainardi, "The Politics of Housework," in *Sisterhood Is Powerful: An Anthology of Writings from the Women's Liberation Movement*, ed. Robin Morgan (New York: Vintage, 1970), 501–510.

7. Mainardi, "Politics of Housework," 505, 507.

8. Ibid., 507, 503.

9. Judy Syfers, "Why I Want a Wife," 1971, in *Radical Feminism*, ed. Anne Koedt, Ellen Levine, and Anita Rapone (New York: Quadrangle Books, 1973), 60–62. On Sudsofloppen, see Elizabeth Sullivan, "Sudsofloppen: Consciousness-Raising and the Small Group as Free Space" *FoundSF*, www.foundsf.org/index .php?title=Sudsofloppen:_Consciousness-Raising_and_the_Small_Group_as_Free _Space.

10. Maren Lockwood Carden, *The New Feminist Movement* (New York: Russell Sage Foundation, 1974), 106; and Letty Cottin Pogrebin, "The Working Woman," *Ladies' Home Journal*, April 1972, 56.

11. Susan Brownmiller, "'Sisterhood Is Powerful': A Member of the Women's Liberation Movement Explains What It's All About" *New York Times Sunday Magazine*, March 15, 1970, 136; Sara Evans, *Tidal Wave: How Women Changed America at Century's End* (New York: Free Press, 2003), 54; Rae André, *Homemakers: The Forgotten Workers* (Chicago: University of Chicago Press, 1981), 98; and Stephanie Roberts, "I Hereby Resign as Keeper of This House," *Ms.*, May 1977, qtd. in André, *Homemakers*, 103–104. For more examples, see André, *Homemakers*, 104–110.

12. Pat Mainardi, "The Politics of Housework," 506, 502–503; Carol Hanisch and Elizabeth Sutherland, "Women of the World Unite—We Have Nothing to Lose but Our Men," in *Notes From the First Year*, ed. Shulamith Firestone (New York: New York Radical Women, 1968), 14; and Ellen Willis, "Whatever Happened to Women? Nothing—That's the Trouble. A Report on the New Feminism," *Mademoiselle*, September 1969, 208.

13. Meredith Tax, "Woman and Her Mind," 1970, in *Radical Feminism: A Documentary Reader*, ed. Barbara A. Crow (New York: New York University Press, 2000), 496; and Vivien Leone, "Domestics," 1970, in *Radical Feminism*, ed. Crow, 516, 519–520.

14. US Department of Commerce, "Consumer Income," Current Population Reports, series P-60, no. 78 (May 20, 1971); and Gloria Steinem, *ABC Nightly News*, January 25, 1972, qtd. in Susan J. Douglas and Meredith W. Michaels, *The Mommy Myth: The Idealization of Motherhood and How It Has Undermined Women* (New York: Free Press, 2004), 45.

15. Kirsten Lise Fermaglich, "'The Comfortable Concentration Camp': The Significance of Nazi Imagery in Betty Friedan's *The Feminine Mystique* (1963)," *American Jewish History* 91, no. 2 (2003): 205–232; and bell hooks, *Feminist Theory: From Margin to Center*, 2nd ed. (Cambridge, MA: South End Press, 2000), 1–3.

16. "Help Wanted: Female," *Ladies' Home Journal*, August 1970, 67.

17. Margaret Benston, "The Political Economy of Women's Liberation," *Monthly Review*, September 1969: 13–27; Marlene Dixon, "The Rise of Women's Liberation," *Ramparts Magazine*, December 1969, 57–63; and Ellen Malos, ed., *The Politics of Housework* (New York: Schocken Books, 1980), 31. See also Nona Glazer-Malbin, "Housework," *Signs* 1 (Summer 1976): 916–919.

18. Michigan Women's Commission, "Fact Sheet #1: Inclusion of Homemakers in National Measures of Production and Income," in annual report 1975–1976, appendix 1 (Lansing: Michigan Women's Commission, 1976), 40; Keith Love, "How Do You Put a Price Tag on a Housewife's Work?," *New York Times*, January 13, 1976, 40; Joann Vanek, "Housewives as Workers," in *Women Working: Theories and Facts in Perspective*, ed. Ann H. Stromberg and Shirley Harkness (Palo Alto, CA: Mayfield, 1978), 404; and Janice Peskin, "Measuring Household Production for the GNP," *Family Economics Review* 20 (June 1982): 17.

19. Evelyn Shapiro and Barry Shapiro, eds., *The Women Say, the Men Say: Women's Liberation and Men's Consciousness* (New York: Delta, 1979), 19; "The Worth of Wives," *News for and from Housewives for ERA*, March 29, 1975 (box 25, folder 12) WRC, SSC, MS 397; Love, "Price Tag"; Wendyce Brody, "Economic Value of a Housewife," *Research and Statistics Note*, US Dep't of Health Educ.

and Welfare, Soc. Sec. Admin. Office of Research and Statistics, note 9, August 28, 1975 (box 19, folder 19) East Papers, Schlesinger; and André, *Homemakers*, 114–115.

20. Nancy Folbre, "The Unproductive Housewife: Her Evolution in Nineteenth-Century Economic Thought," *Signs* 16 (Spring 1991): 463–484; and Ann Crittenden Scott, "The Value of Housework—For Love or Money," *Ms.*, July 1972, 56–57.

21. Maud Anne Bracke, "Between the Transnational and the Local: Mapping the Trajectories and Contexts of the Wages for Housework Campaign in 1970s Italian Feminism," *Women's History Review* 22 (2013): 626–630; Malos, ed., *The Politics of Housework*, 21–24; Mariarosa Dalla Costa and Selma James, "The Power of Women and the Subversion of the Community," in *The Politics of Housework*, ed. Malos, 160–195; and Silvia Federici, "Wages Against Housework" (Bristol, UK: Power of Women Collective and Falling Wall Press, April 1975). For earlier incarnations, see Nancy F. Cott, *The Grounding of Modern Feminism* (New Haven: Yale University Press, 1987), 77–78.

22. Leone, "Domestics," 519; "Leone, Vivien," in *Feminists Who Changed America, 1963–1975*, ed. Barbara J. Love (Urbana: University of Illinois Press, 2006), 276; and Linda Gordon, "Functions of the Family," in *Voices from Women's Liberation*, ed. Leslie B. Tanner (New York: Signet, 1971), 184.

23. "Federici, Sylvia," in *Feminists Who Changed America*, ed. Love, 142; Alison Lefkovitz, *Strange Bedfellows: Marriage in the Age of Women's Liberation* (Philadelphia: University of Pennsylvania Press), 27–29; and Silvia Federici and Arlen Austin, eds., *Wages for Housework: The New York Committee, 1972–1977—History, Theory, and Documents* (Brooklyn, NY: Autonomedia, 2017).

24. Federici, "Wages against Housework," 1, 5.

25. New York Wages for Housework Committee, "Housework—Unpaid Work. The Crime against Women Internationally," 1976, in *Wages for Housework*, ed. Federici and Austin, 49; and New York Wages for Housework Committee, "Wages for Housework: From the Government. For ALL Women," 1975, in *Wages for Housework*, ed. Federici and Austin, 54.

26. "International Wages for Housework Campaign," n.d., freedomarchives.org /Documents/Finder/DOC500_scans/500.020.Wages.for.Housework.pdf; Kathleen Hendrix, "L.A. Pair Seeks Wages for Women's Unpaid Work," *Los Angeles Times*, July 28, 1985, D1; Greg Childs, "Black Intellectual History and STEM: A Conversation with Dr. Chanda Prescod-Weinstein," *Black Perspectives*, August 29, 2016, www.aaihs.org/black-intellectual-history-and-stem-a-conversation-with-chanda -prescod-weinstein/; and "Wages for Housework: From the Government. For ALL Women."

27. Federici, "Wages against Housework," 5, emphasis in original; Carol Lopate, "Pay for Housework?," *Social Policy* 5 (September/October 1974): 27–31; Heidi I. Hartmann, "The Unhappy Marriage of Marxism and Feminism: Toward a More Progressive Union," *Capital and Class* 3 (Summer 1979): 5–7; Malos, *The Politics of Housework*, 35–38; Lefkovitz, *Strange Bedfellows*, 29; and Nicole Cox and Silvia Federici, *Counter-Planning from the Kitchen: Wages for Housework—A Perspective on Capital and the Left* (New York: New York Wages

for Housework Committee and Falling Wall Press, 1975), 9. See also Betsy Warrior and Lisa Leghorn, *Houseworker's Handbook*, 3rd ed. (Cambridge, MA: Woman's Center, 1975).

28. Crittenden Scott, "Value of Housework," 57; Hartline, qtd. in André, *Homemakers*, 171; and André, *Homemakers*, 171–176.

29. National Organization for Women, "On-Site Program of Tenth Anniversary Conference," April 1977, p. 8 (box 21, folder 4) NOW Records, Schlesinger.

30. American Council of Life Insurance survey, cited in André, *Homemakers*, 112; Crittenden Scott, "Value of Housework," 58; and Louise Kapp Howe, *Pink Collar Workers* (New York: Putnam, 1977), 211.

31. Charlton, "Women March down Fifth," 30; and Betty Berry, "Report of NOW–NY Marriage and Divorce Committee," [1970], pp. 4–5 (box 25, folder 3) East Papers, Schlesinger.

32. Howe, *Pink Collar Workers*, 229.

33. Ibid., 200.

34. Berry, "Report of NOW–NY Marriage and Divorce Committee," 1, 3–4; and "Housewives' Bill of Rights," *Ladies' Home Journal*, August 1970, 67. On Berry, see "Berry, Betty Blaisdell," in *Feminists Who Changed America*, ed. Love, 41.

35. Jane Roberts Chapman, "Conclusions," in *Women into Wives: The Legal and Economic Impact of Marriage*, ed. Jane Roberts Chapman and Margaret Gates (Beverly Hills, CA: Sage Publications, 1977), 295; and Martha W. Griffiths, "How Much Is a Woman Worth? The American Public Policy," in *Economic Independence for Women: The Foundation for Equal Rights*, ed. Jane Roberts Chapman (Beverly Hills, CA: Sage Publications, 1976), 31–35. See also Alice Kessler-Harris, *In Pursuit of Equity: Women, Men, and the Quest for Economic Citizenship in 20th-Century America* (New York: Oxford University Press, 2001), 292–293; and Patricia A. Seith, "Congressional Power to Effect Sex Equality," *Harvard Journal of Law and Gender* 36 (2013): 15–16.

36. Anna Quindlen, "NOW's President: 'I Definitely See the Movement Coming of Age,'" *New York Times*, September 2, 1977, 36; Ben A. Franklin, "A New President for NOW: Eleanor Marie Cutri Smeal," *New York Times*, April 28, 1977, 18; and Patricia Schroeder to Eleanor Smeal, 2 May 1977 (box 46, folder 38) NOW Records, Schlesinger.

37. Prepared statement of Eleanor Cutri Smeal, *Hearings 1979*, 107–108, 110, and *passim*, 107–111.

38. "Housewives NOW," c. 1976 (box 47, folder 2) NOW Records, Schlesinger; "Changing Role of Homemaker Examined. . . . Experts Vary Widely in Viewpoints," press release, Homemaker in Transition Conference, October 1977 (box 7, folder 21) East Papers, Schlesinger; and Eleanor Smeal to Susan Brown, 5 January 1978 (box 46, folder 38) NOW Records, Schlesinger.

39. Prepared statement of Eleanor Cutri Smeal, *Hearings 1979*, 34; and "Changing Role of Homemaker Examined." On income sharing, see Berry, "Report of NOW–NY Marriage and Divorce Committee," 3; Kathleen Gallagher, "Report Says Homemakers' Rights Bleak; Financial Footing Fragile," *The Tennessean*, clipping, April 25, 1977 (box 46, folder 38) NOW Records, Schlesinger; and "The 'Bonnie Plan,'" *News for and from Housewives for ERA* 3, no. 3, March 29, 1975 (box 25, folder 12) WRC, SSC, MS 397.

40. Susan Kinsley, "Women's Dependency and Federal Programs," in *Women into Wives*, ed. Chapman and Gates, 89.

41. Suzanne Kahn, "Valuing Women's Work in the 1970s Home and the Boundaries of the Gendered Imagination," *Harvard Journal of Law and Gender* (2013): 3–5; and Kinsley, "Women's Dependency," 89.

42. *Hearings Before the Joint Econ. Comm., Congr. of the United States, on the Econ. Problems of Women, pt. 2*, 93rd Cong., 305 (1973) (Statement of Carolyn Shaw Bell, Katharine Coman Professor of Econ., Wellesley Coll., Wellesley, Mass.); Kahn, "Valuing Women's Work," 6; and André, *Homemakers*, 215.

43. Kahn, "Valuing Women's Work," 7; Nancy M. Gordon, "Institutional Responses: The Social Security System," in *The Subtle Revolution: Women at Work*, ed. Ralph E. Smith (Washington, DC: Urban Institute Press, 1979), 231–243; and prepared statement of Eleanor Cutri Smeal, *Hearings 1979*, 108–110.

44. Spencer Rich, "Hill Widens Old-Age Aid for Women," *Washington Post*, January 10, 1978, A8; André, *Homemakers*, 213–214, 216–217; Gordon, "Institutional Responses," 239–243, 255; Kahn, "Valuing Women's Work," 8–9; and Seith, "Congressional Power to Effect Sex Equality," 22, 27–28, 57.

45. Enid Nemy, "Almost All Agree—Women Marrying Should Know Their Rights," *New York Times*, August 10, 1973, 33; "Report of NOW–NY Marriage and Divorce Committee"; and "Now, Homemaker's Insurance," *News for and from Housewives for ERA*, 4, no. 3, October–November 1976 (box 46, folder 40) NOW Records, Schlesinger. On NOW's divorce reform activism, see also "NOW Task Force on Marriage, Divorce and Family Relations," November 1973 (box 30, folder 54) NOW Records, Schlesinger; Judy Klemesrud, "'Obsolete' Divorce Laws Assailed at NOW Conference Here," *New York Times*, January 21, 1974, 32; and Ziegler, "An Incomplete Revolution."

46. "Report of the Task Force on Marriage, Divorce and Family Relations," October 1972 (box 30, folder 68) NOW Records, Schlesinger; Ziegler, "An Incomplete Revolution," 277; and Elizabeth Coxe Spalding, national coordinator, NOW Task Force on Marriage and Divorce, "Statement," c. 1975 (box 30, folder 68) NOW Records, Schlesinger.

47. DiFlorido v. DiFlorido, 459 Pa. 650, 331 A.2d 179 (1975), qtd. in Lefkovitz, *Strange Bedfellows*, 61; Lefkovitz, *Strange Bedfellows*, 59–61; and Ziegler, "An Incomplete Revolution."

48. Lefkovitz, *Strange Bedfellows*, 33, 68–69; Fern Schumer, "Fairness New Byword," *Chicago Tribune*, March 24, 1981, C1, cited in Lefkovitz, *Strange Bedfellows*, 65; and Ziegler, "An Incomplete Revolution," 278, 282–283. Lefkovitz offers a more equivocal assessment of the long-term outcome of feminist legal and legislative efforts to reform marriage and divorce; see 65–74.

49. Beverly Cederberg, "Displaced as Homemaker, She Builds New Life," *Valley News*, August 22, 1976, 4, qtd. in Levenstein, "Don't Agonize, Organize!," 81–119; and Levenstein, "Don't Agonize, Organize!," 1117–1119. See also Laurie Shields, *Displaced Homemakers: Organizing for a New Life* (New York: McGraw-Hill, 1981).

50. Shields, *Displaced Homemakers*, ix, xii. On Shields and Sommers' biographies, see Shields, *Displaced Homemakers*, 25–27; and Levenstein, "Don't Agonize, Organize!," 1119–1120, 1122.

51. Levenstein, "Don't Agonize, Organize!," 1122–1124; and Susan M. Hartmann, *The Other Feminists: Activists in the Liberal Establishment* (New Haven: Yale University Press, 1998).

52. Shields, *Displaced Homemakers*, 62–64; and Levenstein, "Don't Agonize, Organize!," 1122–1124, 1130.

53. Shields, *Displaced Homemakers*, 112; Jill Nelson, "Displaced Homemakers: Who's Displacing Whom?," *Encore American and Worldwide News*, April 16, 1979, 18–19, qtd. in Levenstein, "Don't Agonize, Organize!," 1131–1132; and Levenstein, "Don't Agonize, Organize!," 1131–1134.

54. National Organization for Women, "ERA and Homemakers: Partnership in Marriage," ERA Countdown Shoot, 1981 (box 5) ERACAP, SSC, MS 310. See also National Organization for Women, "Dollars and Cents Feminism," pamphlet, [mid 1970s] (box 209, folder 18) NOW Records, Schlesinger; "No Retreat from Equality," pamphlet, c. 1979 (box 209, folder 18) NOW Records, Schlesinger; and NOW/ERA Referendum Committee, Television Advertisements, "Homemaker," 1980, repr. in Dan Itzkowitz, "How Did Iowa Coalitions Campaign for the Equal Rights Amendment in 1980 and 1992?," in *Women and Social Movements* (Alexander Street Press, 2002), doc. 9A. On pro-ERA housewives' organizations, see "Homemakers' Equal Rights Association," September 1980 (box 46, folder 40) NOW Records, Schlesinger; "Housewives for ERA," pamphlet, [mid-1970s] (box 25, folder 12) WRC, SSC, MS 397; and "Homemakers for ERA Organize," *Tuscaloosa News*, November 2, 1979, 6.

55. National Commission on the Observance of International Women's Year, *". . . to Form a More Perfect Union . . .": Justice for American Women* (Washington, DC: US Government Printing Office, 1976), 232; and *The Spirit of Houston: The First National Women's Conference—An Official Report to the President, the Congress and the People of the United States* (Washington, DC: US Government Printing Office, 1978), 93, 167. See also Marjorie J. Spruill, *Divided We Stand: The Battle Over Women's Rights and Family Values That Polarized American Politics* (New York: Bloomsbury, 2017), 205–261.

56. Bella Abzug, "Speech by Bella Abzug, Presiding Officer," *Spirit of Houston*, 219.

57. Premilla Nadasen, "Power, Intimacy, and Contestation: Dorothy Bolden and Domestic Worker Organizing in Atlanta in the 1960s," in *Intimate Labors: Cultures, Technologies, and the Politics of Care*, ed. Eileen Boris and Rhacel Salazar Parreñas (Stanford: Stanford University Press, 2010), 208–210.

58. Phillip Shabecoff, "To Domestics: A Minimum Wage Is a Raise," *New York Times*, June 6, 1973, 30, qtd. in Premilla Nadasen, "Citizenship Rights, Domestic Workers, and the Fair Labor Standards Act," *Journal of Policy History* 24, no. 1 (2012): 90; Nadasen, *Household Workers Unite*, 61–71. See also Phyllis Palmer, "Outside the Law: Agricultural and Domestic Workers under the Fair Labor Standards Act," *Journal of Policy History* 7, no. 4 (1995): 416–440; Eileen Boris and Premilla Nadasen, "Domestic Workers Organize!," *Working USA: The Journal of Labor and Society* 11 (December 2008): 413–437; Eileen Boris and Jennifer Klein, *Caring for America: Home Health Workers in the Shadow of the Welfare State* (New York: Oxford University Press, 2012); Dorothy Sue Cobble, "'A Spontaneous Loss of Enthusiasm': Workplace Feminism and the Transformation

of Women's Service Jobs in the 1970s," *International Labor and Working-Class History* 56 (Fall 1999): 23–44; and Evelyn Nakano Glenn, *Forced to Care: Coercion and Caregiving in America* (Cambridge: Harvard University Press, 2010).

59. Boris and Nadasen, "Domestic Workers Organize!," 423; and Nadasen, *Household Workers Unite*, 104–105.

60. Edith Barksdale Sloan, keynote address, July 17, 1971, National Committee on Household Employment (NCHE) Records, Landover, MD, qtd. in Nadasen, *Household Workers Unite*, 78. On Sloan and the HTA, see Nadasen, *Household Workers Unite*, 58–61, 71–73, 77–79; Boris and Klein, *Caring for America*, 127–128; and "Of Note—Edith Barksdale Sloan," *Washington Post*, February 15, 2012, B7.

61. "Domestics at Session Ask Gains," *New York Times*, October 10, 1972, 47; keynote address by Congresswoman Shirley Chisholm, 1972, NCHE Records, qtd. in Boris and Nadasen, "Domestic Workers Organize!," 423; and "Domestics Fight for New Way of Life," *Chicago Defender*, August 21, 1971, 14. On HTA membership, see Nadasen, *Household Workers Unite*, 79; and Boris and Klein, *Caring for America*, 127.

62. Josephine Hulett, interview by Janet Dewart, "Household Help Wanted: Female," *Ms.*, February 1973, 46. See also Nadasen, *Household Workers Unite*, 73–77, 139.

63. Nadasen, *Household Workers Unite*, 128, 136, 138–139; Nadasen, "Citizenship Rights," 83–85; Palmer, "Outside the Law," 427–428; and Anastasia Hardin, "Making the Dignity of Our Labor a Reality," Master's thesis (Rutgers University: 2013), 58–59.

64. Hardin, "Making the Dignity of Our Labor a Reality," 60, 62–65; Nadasen, *Household Workers Unite*, 136; and Boris and Nadasen, "Domestic Workers Organize!," 423.

65. Nadasen, *Household Workers Unite*, 134; and Nadasen, "Citizenship Rights," 84.

66. Edith Lynton, "Toward Better Jobs and Better Service in Household Work," New York Commission on Human Rights, 1972, qtd. in Hardin, "Making the Dignity of Our Labor a Reality," 59–60; Boris and Klein, *Caring for America*, 137; and Nadine Brozan, "Bargaining Legislation for Domestics May Have Wide Impact," *New York Times*, April 28, 1975, 48.

67. Edith Sloan, keynote address, *NCHE News* 2 (July 1971), qtd. in Hardin, "Making the Dignity of Our Labor a Reality," 23; Hardin, "Making the Dignity of Our Labor a Reality," 27, 42; and Geraldine Miller, interview by Loretta J. Ross, October 14, 2004, transcript, p. 30, Voices of Feminism Oral History Project, Sophia Smith Collection, Smith College. See also Nadasen, *Household Workers Unite*, 82–103; and Cobble, "Spontaneous Lack of Enthusiasm," 34–35.

68. Palmer, "Outside the Law," 419; and Nadasen, *Household Workers Unite*, 125–129.

69. Gen. Subcomm. on Labor of the Comm. on Educ. and Labor, *Fair Labor Standards Amendments of 1973, H.R. 4757 and H.R. 2831*, 93d Cong. 208, 206, 242 (1973) (statements of Edith B. Sloan and Dorothy Haener and Kee Hall, National Organization for Women). For the hearings, see Palmer, "Outside the Law," 428–432; and Glenn, *Forced to Care*, 139–142.

70. Palmer, "Outside the Law," 430–431; and Brennan, qtd. in Nadasen, *Household Workers Unite*, 132.

71. The Subcomm. on Labor of the Comm. on Labor and Public Welfare, S., *Legislative History of the Fair Labor Standards Amendments of 1974 (Public law 93–259)* (Washington, DC: US Government Printing Office, 1976), vol. 2., 1818; and NCHE, "Minimum Wage Coverage for Domestics: At Last!!!," press release, April 8, 1974, qtd. in Nadasen, *Household Workers Unite*, 142.

72. Nadasen, *Household Workers Unite*, 139–140.

73. Boris and Klein, *Caring for America*; and Glenn, *Forced to Care*, 174–182.

5. Care Work

1. Betty Friedan, *It Changed My Life: Writings on the Women's Movement* (New York: Dell, 1977): 178, 185, 222; Kathy Russell, *Divided Sisters: Bridging the Gap between Black Women and White Women* (New York: Anchor Books, 1996), 200; Joan Steinau Lester, *Fire in My Soul* (New York: Atria Books, 2003), 177; and Dick Schaap, "The Ten Most Powerful Men in New York," *New York Magazine*, January 4, 1971, 26.

2. Felicia Kornbluh, *The Battle for Welfare Rights: Politics and Poverty in Modern America* (Philadelphia: University of Pennsylvania Press, 2007), 1, 14, 25, 160.

3. This chapter draws on Premilla Nadasen, "Expanding the Boundaries of the Women's Movement: Black Feminism and the Struggle for Welfare Rights," *Feminist Studies* 28 (Summer 2002): 270–301; Premilla Nadasen, *Welfare Warriors: The Welfare Rights Movement in the United States* (New York: Routledge, 2005); Marisa Chappell, *The War on Welfare: Family, Poverty, and Politics in Modern America* (Philadelphia: University of Pennsylvania Press, 2010); Kornbluh, *Battle for Welfare Rights*; and Annelise Orleck, *Storming Caesars Palace: How Black Mothers Fought Their Own War on Poverty* (Boston: Beacon Press, 2005). Other important studies include Guida West, *The National Welfare Rights Movement: The Social Protest of Poor Women* (New York: Praeger, 1981); Premilla Nadasen, Jennifer Mittelstadt, and Marisa Chappell, *Welfare in the United States: A History with Documents* (New York: Routledge, 2009); Jill S. Quadagno, *The Color of Welfare: How Racism Undermined the War on Poverty* (New York: Oxford University Press, 1994); and Martha F. Davis, "Welfare Rights and Women's Rights in the 1960s," in *Integrating the Sixties: The Origins, Structures, and Legitimacy of Public Policy in a Turbulent Decade*, ed. Brian Balogh (University Park: Pennsylvania State University Press, 1996), 144–165.

4. Molly Ladd-Taylor, *Mother-Work: Women, Child Welfare, and the State, 1890–1930* (Urbana: University of Illinois Press, 1994); and Nadasen, *Welfare Warriors*, 140.

5. Diana Pearce, "The Feminization of Poverty: Women, Work, and Welfare," *Urban and Social Change Review* 11 (1978): 28–36; and Sara S. McLanahan and Erin L. Kelly, "The Feminization of Poverty: Past and Future," in *Handbook of the Sociology of Gender*, ed. Janet Saltzman Chafetz (New York: Kluwer Academic/Plenum, 1999), 127–145.

6. DWAC Press Advisory, n.d., Downtown Welfare Advocacy Records, Social Welfare History Archives, University of Minnesota, qtd. in Chappell, *War on Welfare*, 194.

7. Johnnie Lea Tillmon, interview by Nick Kotz and Mary Lynn Kotz, November 26, 1974, Nick Kotz Papers, Wisconsin Historical Society, qtd. in Kornbluh, *Battle for Welfare Rights*, 48. See also Robert McG. Thomas, Jr., "Johnnie Tillmon Blackston, Welfare Reformer, Dies at 69," *New York Times*, November 27, 1995, B10. For the movement's beginnings and NWRO's origins, see Nadasen, *Welfare Warriors*, 2–3, 13–43; Nadasen, "Expanding the Boundaries," 275–276; and Kornbluh, *Battle for Welfare Rights*, 14–38, 60–61.

8. Premilla Nadasen, "Welfare's a Green Problem: Cross-Race Coalitions in Welfare Rights Organizing," in *Feminist Coalitions: Historical Perspectives on Second-Wave Feminism in the United States*, ed. Stephanie Gilmore (Urbana: University of Illinois Press, 2008), 178–195; Nadasen, "Expanding the Boundaries," 276–277, 286–289; West, *National Welfare Rights Movement*, 44–45, 50; Felicia Kornbluh, "To Fulfill Their 'Rightly Needs': Consumerism and the National Welfare Rights Movement," *Radical History Review* 69 (1997): 77–78; Maylei Blackwell, *¡Chicana Power!: Contested Histories of Feminism in the Chicano Movement* (Austin: University of Texas Press, 2011), 146–149; and Johnnie Tillmon, "Welfare Is a Women's Issue," *Ms.*, Spring 1972, 111.

9. Nadasen, "Expanding the Boundaries," 274, 291–292; Chappell, *War on Welfare*, 30–35, 102–103, 170; Chappell, "Rethinking Women's Politics in the 1970s: The League of Women Voters and the National Organization for Women Confront Poverty," *Journal of Women's History* 13 (Winter 2002): 155–179; Aileen C. Hernandez and Letitia P. Sommers, "The First Five Years, 1966–1971," Chicago, National Organization for Women, 1971, pp. 14, 22 (box 1, folder 1) NOW Records, Schlesinger; and Orleck, *Storming Caesars Palace*, 194. See also Davis, "Welfare Rights and Women's Rights in the 1960s."

10. Nadasen, "Expanding the Boundaries, 276; and Chappell, *War on Welfare*, 28–29.

11. Nadasen, *Welfare Warriors*, 4–5; and Chappell, *War on Welfare*, 50–51. On ADC's origins, see also Mary Poole, *The Segregated Origins of Social Security: African Americans and the Welfare State* (Chapel Hill: University of North Carolina Press, 2006).

12. Nadasen, *Welfare Warriors*, 7, 135–136.

13. For the FAP debate, see Chappell, *War on Welfare*, 65–105; Nadasen, *Welfare Warriors*, 157–191; Kornbluh, *Battle for Welfare Rights*, 142–160; and Quadagno, *Color of Welfare*, 117–134.

14. Nadasen, *Welfare Warriors*, 161–162, 168–170; and Chappell, *War on Welfare*, 58–63.

15. Nadasen, *Welfare Warriors*, 159–161.

16. Ohio Steering Committee for Adequate Welfare, "Ohio's Continuing Welfare Disgrace," flyer, 1969, William Howard Whitaker Papers, Ohio Historical Society, qtd. in Nadasen, *Welfare Warriors*, 164; Nadasen, *Welfare Warriors*, 157, 164, 219–220; Chappell, *War on Welfare*, 100; and Hernandez and Sommers, "The First Five Years," 14.

17. Chappell, *War on Welfare*, 57–61; and Nadasen, *Welfare Warriors*, 158.

18. Cassie B. Downer, in Milwaukee County Welfare Rights Organization, *Welfare Mothers Speak Out: We Ain't Gonna Shuffle Anymore* (New York: Norton, 1972), qtd. in Nadasen, *Welfare Warriors*, 166; Nadasen, *Welfare Warriors*, 165–167; and Tillmon, "Welfare Is a Women's Issue," 112.

19. Beulah Sanders, "Multiple Jeopardies of the Welfare Mother," in *Women's Role in Contemporary Society: The Report of The New York City Commission on Human Rights, September 21–25, 1970* (New York: Avon Books, 1972), 476–477; Nadasen, *Welfare Warriors*, 178–181; Ben A. Franklin, "Welfare Parley Cautious on Nixon," *New York Times*, August 24, 1969, 34; Tillmon, qtd. in Orleck, *Storming Caesars Palace*, 125; and Kornbluh, *Battle for Welfare Rights*, 1, 154–156.

20. Nadasen, *Welfare Warriors*, 167–168, 179–180; and Kornbluh, *Battle for Welfare Rights*, 156.

21. Beulah Sanders, George Wiley, and Carl Rachlin, "Statement to the House Ways and Means Committee," 27 October 1969, George Wiley Papers, State Historical Society of Wisconsin, qtd. in Nadasen, *Welfare Warriors*, 179; Chappell, *War on Welfare*, 73–76, 82–83; and Richard Armstrong, "The Looming Money Revolution Down South," *Fortune*, June 1970, 68.

22. Nadasen, *Welfare Warriors*, 181; Chappell, *War on Welfare*, 91; and Kornbluh, *Battle for Welfare Rights*, 150.

23. Nadasen, *Welfare Warriors*, 182, 186–188; Chappell, *War on Welfare*, 92–93, 97; Kornbluh, *Battle for Welfare Rights*, 157–160; and Quadagno, *Color of Welfare*, 134.

24. Nadasen, Mittelstadt, and Chappell, *Welfare in the United States*, 74; and Chappell, *War on Welfare*, 194.

25. Chappell, *War on Welfare*, 158, 170–171, 191; Marisa Chappell, "Demanding a New Family Wage: Feminist Consensus in the 1970s Full Employment Campaign," in *Feminist Coalitions*, ed. Gilmore, 255, 271. A telling survey of NOW members in 1975 gave priority to "employment/economic security" but strongly preferred compliance with anti-discrimination laws as a strategy over full employment or a guaranteed income (*War on Welfare*, 169–170). For a more critical assessment of the network, see Nadasen, *Welfare Warriors*, 219–221.

26. Chappell, *War on Welfare*, 171–172.

27. *Joint Hearings 1977*, 664; US Bureau of the Census, *Characteristics of the Population Below the Poverty Level, 1978*, Current Population Reports, series P-60, no. 124 (Washington, DC: US Government Printing Office, 1980), 5; and Pearce, "Feminization of Poverty," 35.

28. "Downtown Welfare Advocacy Center to All Welfare Coalition Folks Who Attended the April 5th Working Meeting for May 11th Action," n.d., Downtown Welfare Advocacy Center Records, Social Welfare History Archives, University of Minnesota, qtd. in Chappell, *War on Welfare*, 177.

29. Ruby Duncan, qtd. in Orleck, *Storming Caesars Palace*, 232; and Chappell, *War on Welfare*, 194, and more generally on the shift to jobs, 176–182. See also "Strategy for NOW's Action on Full Employment Legislation," [1976] (box 54, folder 72) NOW Records, Schlesinger.

30. Chappell, *War on Welfare*, 182; testimony of Eve Dembaugh, records of the President's Commission for National Agenda for the Eighties, Carter Library,

Atlanta, qtd. in Chappell, *War on Welfare*, 177–178; and Ruby Duncan, qtd. in Orleck, *Storming Caesars Palace*, 233.

31. "Carter Says Plans of Government Should Keep Families Together," *New York Times*, June 19, 1977, 16; President Carter to the Congress of the United States, 6 August 1977, Carter Library, Atlanta, qtd. in Chappell, *War on Welfare*, 184; Chappell, *War on Welfare*, 187; and Orleck, *Storming Caesars Palace*, 242.

32. Chappell, *War on Welfare*, 188, 194–195; "National Council on Women, Work and Welfare Statement," 16 September 1977, League of Women Voters Papers, Library of Congress, Washington, DC, qtd. in Chappell, *War on Welfare*, 195; and Orleck, *Storming Caesars Palace*, 242.

33. Chappell, *War on Welfare*, 189–195; National Women's Agenda, 1978, Women's Action Alliance Records, Sophia Smith Collection, Smith College, qtd. in Chappell, *War on Welfare*, 195; and Carol Payne to Executive Officers, 11 May 1977, League of Women Voters Papers, Library of Congress, Washington, DC, qtd. in Chappell, *War on Welfare*, 195.

34. Nancy S. Barrett, "Women in the Job Market: Unemployment and Work Schedules," in Ralph E. Smith, *The Subtle Revolution: Women at Work* (Washington, DC: Urban Institute, 1979), 93.

35. *Joint Hearings Before the Welfare Reform Subcomm. of the Comm. on Agric., Comm. on Educ. and Labor Comm. on Ways and Means, H., on H.R. 9030*, 95th Cong. (1977) (Ruth Clusen, testimony), qtd. in Chappell, "Rethinking Women's Politics," 169; Chappell, *War on Welfare*, 195–197; and Jo Freeman, untitled document, n.d., Downtown Welfare Advocacy Center Records, Social Welfare History Archives, University of Minnesota, qtd. in Chappell, *War on Welfare*, 196.

36. Heather L. Ross, "Poverty: Women and Children Last," in *Economic Independence for Women: The Foundation for Equal Rights*, ed. Jane Roberts Chapman (Beverly Hills, CA: Sage Publications, 1976), 137–154.

37. *Joint Hearings 1977*, 671.

38. Ruby Duncan, qtd. in Orleck, *Storming Caesars Palace*, 232; and Beulah Sanders, *Hearings on Family Assistance Plan, H.R. 16311*, November 18–19, 1970, Nick Kotz Papers, Wisconsin Historical Society, qtd. in Kornbluh, *Battle for Welfare Rights*, 156.

39. Tillmon, "Welfare Is a Women's Issue," 116.

6. Childcare

1. Rosalyn Baxandall, "City Money for Nursery Schools Now Available," *Woman's World*, April 15, 1971, 6; Susan Edmiston, "The Psychology of Day Care," *New York Magazine*, April 5, 1971, 39; "Rosalyn Baxandall on Women's Liberation and the History and Politics of Day Care in New York City," *Talking History*, radio program, Albany: State University of New York at Albany, December 29, 2005, www.albany.edu/talkinghistory/arch2005july-december .html; and Rosalyn Baxandall, "Cooperative Nurseries," 1970, in *Radical Feminism: A Documentary Reader*, ed. Barbara A. Crow (New York: New York University Press, 2000), 404.

2. "Rosalyn Baxandall Interview," final copy, 1991, transcript, pp. 29–30 (box 12, folder 3) Tully-Crenshaw Records, Schlesinger; and Rosalyn Baxandall, interview with author, January 19, 2009. See also Edmiston, "Psychology of Day Care," 41–42.

3. Florence Falk-Dickler to NOW chapter presidents, convenors, and chairladies and chapters' child care committees, July 31, 1970 (box 42, folder 35) NOW Records, Schlesinger Library.

4. Emilie Stoltzfus, *Citizen, Mother, Worker: Debating Public Responsibility for Child Care after the Second World War* (Chapel Hill: University of North Carolina Press, 2003); and Deborah Dinner, "The Universal Childcare Debate: Rights Mobilization, Social Policy, and the Dynamics of Feminist Activism, 1966–1974," *Law and History Review* 28 (August 2010): 585.

5. Elizabeth Rose, *A Mother's Job: The History of Day Care, 1890–1960* (New York: Oxford University Press, 1999), 211.

6. National Conference on the Day Care of Children, "Excerpts Related to the Day Care of Children," [summer 1960?], Women's Bureau Records, National Archives, Silver Springs, MD, qtd. in Sonya Michel, *Children's Interests / Mothers' Rights: The Shaping of America's Child Care Policy* (New Haven: Yale University Press, 1999), 228.

7. Patrick Moynihan, undated memo to Mrs. Peterson, Esther Peterson Collection, Schlesinger Library, qtd. in Alice Kessler-Harris, *In Pursuit of Equity: Women, Men, and the Quest for Economic Citizenship in 20th-Century America* (New York: Oxford University Press, 2001), 223; Kessler-Harris, *In Pursuit of Equity*, 222–223; and Stoltzfus, *Citizen, Mother, Worker*, 225–231.

8. Rose, *A Mother's Job*, 213–214.

9. "NOW Statement of Purpose," October 29, 1966, in *Feminist Chronicles, 1953–1993*, ed. Toni Carabillo, Judith Meuli, and June Bundy Csida (Los Angeles: Women's Graphics, 1993), 161–162.

10. "Task Force on the Family report," November 1967, p. 1 (box 42, folder 5) NOW Records, Schlesinger. See also "Report of the Task Force on Employment," November 1967 (box 42, folder 5) NOW Records, Schlesinger.

11. "NOW Bill of Rights in 1968, Adopted at the 1967 National Convention," in *Feminist Chronicles*, ed. Carabillo, et al., 214.

12. *L.A. Women's Liberation Newsletter*, March 1972, 9; "Third World Women and the Workforce," *Triple Jeopardy* 3, September / October 1973 (box 3, folder 19) Baxandall-Gordon, TAM.210; and Benita Roth, *Separate Roads to Feminism: Black, Chicana, and White Feminist Movements in America's Second Wave* (New York: Cambridge University Press, 2004), 146.

13. "Congress to Unite Women," press release, November 24, 1969 (box 10, folder 16) Alexander Papers, Schlesinger.

14. Natalie M. Fousekis, *Demanding Child Care: Women's Activism and the Politics of Welfare, 1940–1971* (Urbana: University of Illinois Press, 2011), 151–152, 155–157; and Premilla Nadasen, "Expanding the Boundaries of the Women's Movement: Black Feminism and the Struggle for Welfare Rights," *Feminist Studies* 28 (Summer 2002): 285.

15. "Free 24-Hour Childcare Centers—Community Controlled," August 26 Women's Strike, 1970 (box 84, folder 1) NOW Records, Schlesinger; Dinner,

"Universal Childcare Debate," 589; Judith Hole and Ellen Levine, *Rebirth of Feminism* (New York: Quadrangle Books, 1971), photo section between 242–243; and Karen DeCrow, "NOW," *The Beacon*, November 1970 (box 1, folder 39) NOW Records, Schlesinger.

16. George Lardner, Jr., "Child Care Program Urged," *Washington Post*, December 20, 1970, A3; Barbara A. Chandler, "The White House Conference on Children: A 1970 Happening," *The Family Coordinator* 20 (1971): 195–198; and "Report to the President," White House Conference on Children (Washington, DC: US Government Printing Office, 1970).

17. "Falk-Dickler, Florence," in *Feminists Who Changed America, 1963–1975*, ed. Barbara J. Love (Urbana: University of Illinois Press, 2006), 139; and Betty Friedan, *It Changed My Life: Writings on the Women's Movement* (New York: Dell, 1977), 188. NOW's active role in fighting for childcare in these pivotal years has not been widely recognized. See Florence Falk-Dickler to NOW board of directors, 15–17 January 1971 (box 33, folder 38) NOW Records, Schlesinger; and Dinner, "Universal Childcare Debate," 613–614.

18. Florence F. Dickler, national coordinator of child day care to all chapters of the National Organization for Women, c. early 1970 (box 42, folder 35) NOW Records, Schlesinger; NOW Task Force on Child Care to all local NOW chapter presidents and Child Care Committee chairmen, [mid-1970] (box 42, folder 35) NOW Records, Schlesinger; Florence Falk-Dickler, coordinator, National Task Force on Child Care to chapter presidents, conveners, and chairladies, chapters' Child Care Committees, 31 July 1970 (box 33, folder 37) NOW Records, Schlesinger. For one response, see Albuquerque NOW, "Newsletter," October and December 1970 (box 16, folder 2) NOW Newsletters, Schlesinger.

19. Aileen Hernandez to Florence Falk-Dickler, 24 July 1970 (box 33, folder 37) NOW Records, Schlesinger; Florence Falk-Dickler to Wilma Scott Heide, 9 August 1970 (box 33, folder 37) NOW Records, Schlesinger; Florence Falk-Dickler to Gene Boyer, 9 October 1970 (box 33, folder 37) NOW Records, Schlesinger; Florence Falk-Dickler to NOW board members, 25 October 1970 (box 33, folder 37) NOW Records, Schlesinger; and Florence Falk-Dickler to NOW board members, 6 December 1970 (box 33, folder 36), NOW Records, Schlesinger. On the internal debate, see Falk-Dickler to NOW board members, 25 October 1970; Gene Boyer to Florence Falk-Dickler and NOW board members, 3 November 1970 (box 33, folder 36) NOW Records, Schlesinger; Maggie Quinn to Florence Falk-Dickler and NOW board members, 5 November 1970 (box 33, folder 37) NOW Records, Schlesinger; and Florence Falk-Dickler to NOW executive board, 29 November 1970 (box 33, folder 36) NOW Records, Schlesinger.

20. Falk-Dickler to Boyer, 9 October 1970; Falk-Dickler to NOW board, 25 October 1970; and Falk-Dickler to NOW board, 6 December 1970.

21. The Women's Caucus of the White House Conference on Children, press release, [December 1970] (box 33, folder 38) NOW Records, Schlesinger.

22. Florence Falk-Dickler to NOW board of directors, 15–17 January 1971 (box 33, folder 38) NOW Records, Schlesinger; and "Chronological Summary of National Organization for Women Conference Resolutions, Policies, and Board Decisions, 1966–1971," pp. 17–19 (box 1, folder 7) NOW Records, Schlesinger.

23. Patricia Lynden, "What Day Care Means to the Children, the Parents, the Teachers, the Community, the President," *New York Times Sunday Magazine*, February 15, 1970, 30–31, 72–88; Nan Ickeringill, "Story of a Day Care Center: Venture of Faith Born of Desperation," *New York Times*, February 5, 1969, 50; Gloria Steinem, *Outrageous Acts and Everyday Rebellions* (New York: Holt, Rinehart and Winston, 1983), 5–7; Judy Klemesrud, "It Was Ladies Day at Party Meeting," *New York Times*, December 14, 1970, 62; Enid Nemy, "They're Black, So Feminism Has Even More Obstacles than Usual," *New York Times*, November 7, 1973, 42; Baxandall, interview with author; and Michael T. Kaufman, "50 City Day Centers Fight Income Limit," *New York Times*, January 6, 1972, 39. See also Dinner, "Universal Childcare Debate," 595.

24. Baxandall, "City Money for Nursery Schools," 6; Alfonso A. Narvaez, "Parents Hold Day-Care Offices Three Hours to Demand Changes," *New York Times*, January 27, 1970, 39; and Juan M. Vasquez, "Day-Care Centers to Get City Help," *New York Times*, November 6, 1970, 39.

25. Andrea Estepa, "When a 'Sister' Is a Mother: Maternal Thinking and Feminist Action, 1967–1980," in *US Women's History: Untangling the Threads of Sisterhood*, ed. Leslie Brown, Jacqueline Castledine, and Anne Valk (New Brunswick: Rutgers University Press, 2017), 157–158; and Day Creamer and Heather Booth, "Action Committee for Decent Childcare: Organizing for Power," 1970, in *Radical Feminism*, ed. Crow, 408, 410.

26. Kimberly J. Morgan, "A Child of the Sixties: The Great Society, the New Right, and the Politics of Federal Child Care," *Journal of Policy History* 13, no. 2 (2001): 223; Michel, *Children's Interests/Mothers' Rights*, 248; Theodore Taylor, executive director, Day Care and Child Development Council of America to "Friends," 29 July 1971 (box 42, folder 35) NOW Records, Schlesinger; and Joyce D. Miller, "The Urgency of Child Care," *American Federationist* 82 (1975): 7.

27. Rochelle Beck and John Butler, "An Interview with Marian Wright Edelman," *Harvard Educational Review* 44 (February 1974): 69; Morgan, "Child of the Sixties," 225–226; Carol Joffe, "Why the United States Has No Child-Care Policy," in *Families, Politics, and Public Policy*, ed. Irene Diamond (New York: Longman, 1983), 177–178; and Jill Norgren, "In Search of a National Child Care Policy: Background and Prospects," *Western Political Quarterly* 34 (March 1981): 133. Other national liberal feminist groups were not in a position to participate in the campaign: the Women's Equity Action League had a focus on education; the Women's Action Alliance and National Women's Political Caucus were founded too late.

28. Mamie Moore, Day Care and Child Development Council of America to Ann Scott, NOW vice-president for legislation, 27 February 1973 (box 42, folder 34) NOW Records, Schlesinger.

29. Wilma Scott Heide to Congress member, House Committee on Education and Labor, [1971] (box 42, folder 36) NOW Records, Schlesinger; "Statement by Vicki Lathom, Member, National Board of Directors, Child Care Task Force, National Organization for Women," May 18, 1971, US Senate, *Joint Hearings Before the Subcomm. on Empl't, Manpower and Poverty and the Subcomm. on Children and Youth of the Comm. on Labor and Public Welfare*, 92nd Cong., pt. 3 751–754 (1971); and "Urgent," National Task Force on Child Care and national

legislative vice president to chapters, board of directors, task force coordinators, 22 April 1971 (box 42, folder 34) NOW Records, Schlesinger; and "Why Feminists Want Child Care," included with "Urgent" mailing, 22 April 1971 (box 42, folder 34) NOW Records, Schlesinger.

30. "Newsletter," Denver NOW, June 14, 1971 (box 4) NOW Newsletters, Schlesinger.

31. Vicki Lathom, "Latest on Brademas Child Care Bill," July 2, 1971 (box 42, folder 35) NOW Records, Schlesinger; Vicki Lathom, "Day Care Legislative Wrap Up," October 29, 1971 (box 42, folder 35) NOW Records, Schlesinger; Ann Scott to NOW members and chapter presidents, 1 November 1971 (box 42, folder 35) NOW Records, Schlesinger; and "Urgent! Urgent! Urgent!" Child Care Task Force to all NOW members, 1 November 1971 (box 30, folder 57) NOW Records, Schlesinger. For responses, see NOW chapter newsletters April–December 1971 in Denver (box 4), Albuquerque, New Mexico (box 16, folder 2), Central New York (box 17, folder 2), and Kansas City (box 14) NOW Newsletters, Schlesinger.

32. Morgan, "Child of the Sixties," 221–238; Robert O. Self, *All in the Family: The Realignment of American Democracy since the 1960s* (New York: Hill and Wang, 2012), 128–131; Michel, *Children's Interests/Mothers' Rights*, 250–51; and Dinner, "Universal Childcare Debate," 615–616.

33. Edward F. Zigler and Jody Goodman, "The Battle for Day Care in America: A View from the Trenches," in *Day Care: Scientific and Social Policy Issues*, ed. Edward F. Zigler and Edmund W. Gordon (Boston: Auburn House, 1982), 344; Richard Nixon, "Veto of the Economic Opportunity Amendments of 1971," December 9, 1971, *The American Presidency Project*, ed. Gerhard Peters and John T. Woolley, University of California, Santa Barbara, www.presidency.ucsb.edu/ws/?pid=3251; and NOW, "Why Feminists Want Child Care."

34. Hon. John Brademas, telephone interview by Kimberly Morgan, August 4, 1997, qtd. in Morgan, "Child of the Sixties," 238; Rochelle Beck, "Beyond the Stalemate in Child Care Public Policy," in *Day Care*, ed. Zigler and Gordon, 308–309; Dinner, "Universal Childcare Debate," 617–618; and Carole Faye Simkin, "Child Care and Household Expenses under the New Section 214: Is This Really the Reform We Were Waiting For?," *Women's Rights Law Reporter* 1 (1973): 15–28.

35. Other examples include Boston, Massachusetts ("Coming in June—Day Care Teach-In," *The New Broom*, May 1971: 3); Kansas City, Missouri (Carol Hannah, "Day Care," *Newsletter*, Kansas City Women's Liberation Union, April–May 1973, 3–6); Iowa City, Iowa (Mary Frances Berry, *The Politics of Parenthood: Child Care, Women's Rights, and the Myth of the Good Mother* [New York: Penguin Books, 1993], 128); Detroit, Michigan (Women's Caucus, People Against Racism [box 3, folder 17] Baxandall-Gordon, TAM.210); Dayton, Ohio (Judith Ezekiel, *Feminism in the Heartland* [Columbus: Ohio State University Press, 2002], 46); and Los Angeles, California ("Child-Care Co-ops," *Los Angeles Women's Liberation Newsletter* December 1971, 1). See also Lauri Umansky, *Motherhood Reconceived: Feminism and the Legacy of the Sixties* (New York: New York University Press), 46–50.

36. Rosalyn Fraad Baxandall, "Catching the Fire," in *The Feminist Memoir Project: Voices from Women's Liberation*, ed. Rachel Blau DuPlessis and Ann

Snitow (New York: Three Rivers Press, 1998), 217; and Baxandall, "City Money for Nursery Schools," 6. On Liberation Nursery, see also Baxandall, "Cooperative Nurseries"; Baxandall, interview with author; and "Rosalyn Baxandall on Women's Liberation."

37. Edmiston, "Psychology of Day Care," 42.

38. Baxandall, "Cooperative Nurseries," 404–405; Furies Action, "Day Care," 1971, in *Radical Feminism*, ed. Crow, 419; and Daniel Winunwe Rivers, *Radical Relations: Lesbian Mothers, Gay Fathers, and Their Children in the United States since World War II* (Chapel Hill: University of North Carolina Press, 2013), 159–160. See also Phyllis Taube Greenleaf, "Liberating Children from Sex Roles," in *The Day Care Book: The Why, What, and How of Community Day Care*, ed. Vicki Breitbart (New York: Alfred A. Knopf, 1974), 147–173.

39. Baxandall, "City Money for Nursery Schools," 6; Baxandall, interview with author; and Deborah Babcox, "The Liberation of Children," 1971, in *Radical Feminism*, ed. Crow, 416.

40. Baxandall, "Catching the Fire," 219; and Baxandall, interview with author. See also Amy Kesselman, Heather Booth, Vivian Rothstein, and Naomi Weisstein, "Our Gang of Four: Friendship and Women's Liberation," in *Feminist Memoir Project*, ed. DuPlessis and Snitow, 48.

41. Baxandall, "Catching the Fire," 219; Baxandall, interview with author; and Louise Gross and Phyllis MacEwan, "On Day Care," in *Voices from Women's Liberation*, ed. Leslie B. Tanner (New York: Signet, 1971), 199–207.

42. "City Money for Nursery Schools" appeared in the Redstockings newspaper, *Woman's World*; "Cooperative Nurseries" was printed in *Women: A Journal of Liberation* in 1970 and in Sookie Stambler, ed., *Women's Liberation: Blueprint for the Future* (New York: Ace Books, 1970), 217–223; and "Who Shall Care for Our Children? The History and Development of Day Care in the United States" appeared in Jo Freeman, ed., *Women: A Feminist Perspective* (Palo Alto, CA: Mayfield Publishing, 1975): 88–102.

43. Alice Echols, *Daring to Be Bad: Radical Feminism in America, 1967–1975* (Minneapolis: University of Minnesota Press, 1989), 98; "Rosalyn Baxandall Interview," final copy, 1991, transcript, p. 27 (box 12, folder 3) Tully-Crenshaw Records, Schlesinger; and "Lowen, Marilyn Norma," in *Feminists Who Changed America*, ed. Love, 286–287. I have not been able to locate a reliable listing of all such centers nor find an accurate count. Many were under the radar; some lasted a brief time. The evidence suggests that centers with radical feminist participation numbered in the hundreds. Judith Hole and Ellen Levine cite forty to sixty centers in New York City as of 1971 (*Rebirth of Feminism*, 309). On specific centers, see "Female Liberation of Chapel Hill Newsletter," September 27, 1971, 2; Ezekiel, *Feminism in the Heartland*, 46; and Edmiston, "Psychology of Day Care," 46. See also *The Working Mother*, Summer 1971, p. 2, Fall 1971, pp. 6–7, 11–12, Fall 1972, pp. 11, 16–17, and Winter 1972–1973, p. 3.

44. Baxandall, interview with author; and Baxandall, "Catching the Fire," 218.

45. Rivers, *Radical Relations*, 141; "NOW's Child Care Accomplishments," December 1973 (box 42, folder 37) NOW Records, Schlesinger; Aileen C. Hernandez and Letitia P. Sommers, "The First Five Years, 1966–1971," National Organization for Women, Chicago, 1971, pp. 22, 24, 26, 28 (box 1, folder 1) NOW Records, Schlesinger; Wichita NOW newsletter, September 20, 1971 (box 9)

NOW Newsletters, Schlesinger; and Washington, DC NOW newsletter, January 1972 (box 5, folder 2) NOW Newsletters, Schlesinger.

46. Fousekis, *Demanding Childcare*, 157, 212n67; and Kaufman, "50 City Day Centers Fight Income Limit." For earlier centers organized by black women, see Nancy MacLean, *Freedom Is Not Enough: The Opening of the American Workplace* (Cambridge: Harvard University Press, 2006), 136; and Robyn Ceanne Spencer, "Engendering the Black Freedom Struggle: Revolutionary Black Womanhood and the Black Panther Party in the Bay Area, California," *Journal of Women's History* 20 (March 2008): 105–106.

47. Dinner, "Universal Childcare Debate," 608–609; Albuquerque NOW newsletter, August 1970 (box 16, folder 2) NOW Newsletters, Schlesinger; and Rivers, *Radical Relations*, 118.

48. Eileen Boris and Sonya Michel, "Social Citizenship and Women's Right to Work in Postwar America," in *Women's Rights and Human Rights: International Historical Perspectives*, ed. Patricia Grimshaw, Katie Holmes, and Marilyn Lake (New York: Palgrave, 2001), 208–209; Dinner, "Universal Childcare Debate," 608; and Miller, "Urgency of Child Care," 7–8.

49. Joyce F. Goldman, "Vacuum-Packed Day Care," *Ms.*, March 1975, 80–82; and Dinner, "Universal Childcare Debate," 602–603.

50. Barbara Winslow, "Primary and Secondary Contradictions in Seattle: 1967–1969," in *Feminist Memoir Project*, ed. DuPlessis and Snitow, 239; and Wanda Adams, "Seattle's Campus Day Care War," in Day Care and Child Development Council, *Action for Children*, October 1970, p. 4 (box 33, folder 37) NOW Records, Schlesinger. On Wanda Adams, see Michael Mauney, "Dropout Wife," *Life*, March 17, 1972, 36–37.

51. NOW Child Care Workshop, December 4, 1971 (box 1, folder 325) National Organization for Women, Seattle-King County Chapter Records, 1970–1976, accession no. 2287-002, University of Washington Special Collections, Seattle; "Child Care Syllabus, A NOW Publication" c. October 1971 (box 209, folder 51) NOW Records, Schlesinger; and Seattle NOW, "Herstory," nowseattle.org/about-us/.

52. Seattle NOW, "Herstory"; and Emily Lieb, "City Council Committee Names First Seattle Women's Commission Members on April 6, 1971," August 14, 2007, HistoryLink.org, historylink.org/file/8205.

53. Constantine Angelos, "Jackie Griswold, 61, Helped Push through Reform of State Rape Laws," *Seattle Times*, June 29, 1992, community.seattletimes.nwsource.com/archive/?date=19920629&slug=1499760; and Finding aid for Jacqueline (Jackie) Griswold Papers, MS 119, Washington State Historical Society, Tacoma, WA, www.washingtonhistory.org/imu/api/file/10456.

54. Richard Ruopp, et al., *Technical Appendices to the National Day Care Study: Background Materials. Final Report of the National Day Care Study. Vol. IV-A* (Cambridge, MA: Abt Associates, 1980), 245; on the number of centers, see 258–259.

55. Ibid., 259.

56. Linda Francke and Dorothy Pitman Hughes, "Child Care Centers: Who, How, and Where," *Ms.*, December 1971, 102; Breitbart, *The Day Care Book*; and Warren Farrell, *The Liberated Man* (New York: Bantam Books, 1974), 340.

57. Joan M. Bergstrom and Jane R. Gold, "How to Choose the Right Child-Care Program," *Ms.*, March 1975, 84, 95–96.

58. Morgan, "Child of the Sixties," 236; and Marjorie J. Spruill, *Divided We Stand: The Battle over Women's Rights and Family Values that Polarized American Politics* (New York: Bloomsbury, 2017).

59. James A. Levine, "The Prospects and Dilemmas of Child Care Information and Referral," in *Day Care*, ed. Zigler and Gordon, 379; Sharon L. Kagan and Theresa Glennon, "Considering Proprietary Child Care," in *Day Care*, ed. Zigler and Gordon, 403; and Michel, *Children's Interests / Mothers' Rights*, 251–253.

60. Levine, "Prospects and Dilemmas," 381.

61. Susan Paynter, "'Dropout Wife': A New Chapter in Herstory," *Seattle Post Intelligencer*, May 12, 2002, www.seattlepi.com/news/article/Dropout-Wife-A-new-chapter-in-herstory-1087102.php; Angelos, "Jackie Griswold"; and "Eleanor Marie Cutri Smeal," in Donna Hightower-Langston, *A to Z of American Women Leaders and Activists* (New York: Facts on File, 2002), 213–214.

62. Barbara Sprung, *The Women's Action Alliance Guide to Non-Sexist Early Childhood Education* (New York: Women's Action Alliance, Inc., 1974), 1; and Lori Rotskoff and Laura L. Lovett, eds., *When We Were Free to Be: Looking Back at a Children's Classic and the Difference It Made* (Chapel Hill: University of North Carolina Press, 2012).

63. Levine, "Prospects and Dilemmas," 380; and Ruopp, et al., *Technical Appendices to the National Day Care Study*, 253.

64. Belle Canon, "Child Care Where You Work," *Ms.*, April 1978, 83–86; "Where Day Care Is Everybody's Business," *Ms.*, August 1979, 25; and Kirsten Swinth, "Post-Family Wage, Postindustrial Society: Reframing the Gender and Family Order through Working Mothers in Reagan's America," *Journal of American History* 105 (September 2018).

65. Molly Lovelock, "Bringing Up Baby: The Day Care Question," 1981, in *Frontline Feminism, 1975–1995: Essays from Sojourner's First 20 Years*, ed. Karen Kahn (San Francisco: Aunt Lute Books, 1995), 145.

7. Maternity

1. "Women and Work," *Ladies' Home Journal*, August 1970, 64–65; and Judith Michaelson, "The Justices Saw it Her Way," *New York Post Weekend Magazine*, January 30, 1971, 1. On Phillips's case, see also Ann Marie Boylan, "*Ida Phillips vs. Martin Marietta Corporation*," *Women's Rights Law Reporter* 1 (1971): 11–21; and Serena Mayeri, *Reasoning from Race: Feminism, Law, and the Civil Rights Revolution* (Cambridge: Harvard University Press, 2011), 51–54.

2. Michaelson, "Justices Saw it Her Way."

3. Betty Friedan, *It Changed My Life: Writings on the Women's Movement* (New York: Dell, 1977), 177, 183; Coletta Reid, "Women Oppose Carswell," *Off Our Backs*, February 27, 1970, 5; Mayeri, *Reasoning from Race*, 54; and Michaelson, "Justices Saw it Her Way."

4. Martha Chamallas, "Mothers and Disparate Treatment: The Ghost of *Martin Marietta*," *Villanova Law Review* 44 (January 1999): 343–347; and Boylan, "*Phillips vs. Martin Marietta*," 12–20.

5. "Women and Work," 65; and Trudy Hayden, "Punishing Pregnancy: Discrimination in Education, Employment, and Credit," Women's Rights Project, American Civil Liberties Union (New York: ACLU Reports, October 1973): 33. On the legal status of mothers and pregnant workers in the second half of the 1960s, see Hayden, "Punishing Pregnancy"; and Lise Vogel, *Mothers on the Job: Maternity Policy in the US Workplace* (New Brunswick: Rutgers University Press, 1993), 38–39.

6. Margaret Ann Sipser, "Maternity Leave: Judicial and Arbital Interpretation, 1970–1972," *Labor Law Journal* 24 (March 1973): 182. They also called it "the right to be pregnant without penalty." See Hayden, "Punishing Pregnancy," 3.

7. Ruth Bader Ginsburg, "Gender and the Constitution," *University of Cincinnati Law Review* 44 (1975): 38.

8. "Labor Force Participation Rates of Women, by Presence and Age of Youngest Child, Selected Years, 1947–1996," US H., Comm. on Ways and Means, *1998 Green Book*, 105th Cong. 661 (1998). See also Claudia Goldin, *Understanding the Gender Gap: An Economic History of American Women* (New York: Oxford University Press, 1990), 174–177.

9. Muller v. Oregon, 208 US 412 (1908); and Alice Kessler-Harris, "The Paradox of Motherhood: Night-Work Restrictions in the United States," in *Gendering Labor History* (Urbana: University of Illinois Press, 2007), 223.

10. Kessler-Harris, "Paradox of Motherhood," 225.

11. Dorothy Sue Cobble, *The Other Women's Movement: Workplace Justice and Social Rights in Modern America* (Princeton: Princeton University Press, 2004), 127–129; and Eileen Boris and Sonya Michel, "Social Citizenship and Women's Right to Work in Postwar America," in *Women's Rights and Human Rights: International Historical Perspectives*, ed. Patricia Grimshaw, Katie Holmes, and Marilyn Lake (New York: Palgrave, 2001), 201–204.

12. Elizabeth Duncan Koontz, "Childbirth and Child Rearing Leave: Job-Related Benefits," *New York Law Forum* 17 (1971): 490; Cobble, *Other Women's Movement*, 123; and Susan M. Hartmann, *The Other Feminists: Activists in the Liberal Establishment* (New Haven: Yale University Press, 1998), 44.

13. Joan Jordan, *The Place of American Women: Economic Exploitation of Women* (Boston: New England Free Press, 1968), 14; and Kathleen Peratis and Elizabeth Rindskopf, "Pregnancy Discrimination as a Sex Discrimination Issue," *Women's Rights Law Reporter* 2 (1975): 26.

14. Diane L. Zimmerman, "*Geduldig v. Aiello*: 'Pregnancy' Classifications and the Definition of Sex Discrimination," *Columbia Law Review* 75 (March 1975): 478; and Hayden, "Punishing Pregnancy," 55. See also Alice Kessler-Harris, *A Woman's Wage: Historical Meanings and Social Consequences*, updated ed. (Lexington: University Press of Kentucky, 2014), 122–123.

15. Hayden, "Punishing Pregnancy," 54–55; Barbara Leon, "Fewer Jobs for Women," *Women's World*, April 15, 1971, 2; and Department of Labor, *Underutilization of Women Workers* (Washington, DC: US Government Printing Office, 1971), 1.

16. Statement of Dorothy Haener and Kee Hall before the Gen. Labor Subcomm. of the H. Educ. and Labor Comm., March 15, 1973 (box 46, folder 17, 4) NOW Records, Schlesinger; Cellestine Ware, "The Relationship of Black Women

to the Women's Liberation Movement," 1970, in *Radical Feminism: A Documentary Reader*, ed. Barbara A. Crow (New York: New York University Press, 2000), 111; "Third World Women and The Workforce," *Triple Jeopardy* 3 (September–October 1973): 6; and Martin, qtd. in Sidney Abbott and Barbara Love, "Is Women's Liberation a Lesbian Plot?," 1971, in *Radical Feminism*, ed. Crow, 323.

17. Alice Kessler-Harris, *In Pursuit of Equity: Women, Men, and the Quest for Economic Citizenship in 20th-Century America* (New York: Oxford University Press, 2001), 246–247; Cobble, *Other Women's Movement*, 215; and Ruth Weyand to Edith Ann Ardissone, 20 March 1973, Murray Papers, Schlesinger, qtd. in Hartmann, *Other Feminists*, 228 n54.

18. Betty Liddick, "Tail Slogan Hits Bottom, Say Stewardesses," *Los Angeles Times*, January 25, 1974, E1; Dorothy Sue Cobble, "'A Spontaneous Loss of Enthusiasm': Workplace Feminism and the Transformation of Women's Service Jobs in the 1970s," *International Labor and Working-Class History* 56 (Fall 1999): 28; and Aileen C. Hernandez and Letitia P. Sommers, "The First Five Years, 1966–1971," Chicago, National Organization for Women, 1971, p. 24 (box 1, folder 1) NOW Records, Schlesinger. See also Kathleen M. Barry, *Femininity in Flight: A History of Flight Attendants* (Durham: Duke University Press, 2007).

19. "Transcription of the Oral History Interview with Susan Deller-Ross," July 8, 2003, National Archive of Clinical Legal Education, 13–14, lib.law.cua .edu/nacle/Transcripts/Deller-Ross.pdf. On Ross, see also "Tribute: The Legacy of Ruth Bader Ginsburg and WRP Staff," Women's Rights Project, American Civil Liberties Union, www.aclu.org/other/tribute-legacy-ruth-bader-ginsburg; and Eve Cary, "Life Faces Portia: How Feminists Are Changing the Law," *Ms.*, April 1974, 94.

20. Michaelson, "The Justices Saw it Her Way." For Phillips's supporters, see Chamallas, "Mothers and Disparate Treatment," 341.

21. Phillips v. Martin Marietta Corp., 411 F.2d 1 (US App., 5th Cir. 1969), in Kenneth M. Davidson, Ruth Bader Ginsburg, and Herma Hill Kay, *Text, Cases, and Materials on Constitutional Aspects of Sex-Based Discrimination* (St. Paul, MN: West Publishing Company, 1974), 464; and Phillips v. Martin Marietta Corp., 416 F.2d 1257 (on petition for rehearing), in *Sex-Based Discrimination*, ed. Ginsburg, et al., 466.

22. Qtd. in Boylan, "*Phillips vs. Martin Marietta*," 16. On oral arguments, see also Mayeri, *Reasoning from Race*, 52–54; Eileen Boris, "Where's the Care?," *Labor: Studies in Working-Class History of the Americas* 11 (2014): 44–45; and Chamallas, "Mothers and Disparate Treatment," 344–348.

23. Qtd. in Boylan, "*Phillips vs. Martin Marietta*," 14–15.

24. Neil S. Siegel and Reva B. Siegel, "*Struck* By Stereotype: Ruth Bader Ginsburg on Pregnancy Discrimination as Sex Discrimination," *Duke Law Journal* 59 (2010): 771–798; and Phillips v. Martin Marietta Corp., 400 US 542, 545 (1971).

25. *Phillips v. Martin Marietta Corp.*, 400 US 542, 544 (1971); and Chamallas, "Mothers and Disparate Treatment," 342.

26. Linda Greenhouse, "Westchester Women Testify on Employment Bias," *New York Times*, April 1, 1973, 72; "Tribute: The Legacy of Ruth Bader Gins-

burg and WRP Staff"; and Amy Leigh Campbell, "Raising the Bar: Ruth Bader Ginsburg and the ACLU Women's Rights Project," *Texas Journal of Women and the Law* 11 (Spring 2002): 209–216.

27. Marjorie Stern, "An Insider's View of the Teachers' Union and Women's Rights," *The Urban Review: Issues and Ideas in Public Education* 6 (September 1973): 47–49; and Deborah Dinner, "Recovering the *LaFleur* Doctrine," *Yale Journal of Law and Feminism* 22 (2010): 350–354. See also Mayeri, *Reasoning from Race*, 63–69.

28. Dinner, "Recovering the *LaFleur* Doctrine," 354; and National Organization for Women, press release, November 20, 1967, in *Feminist Chronicles: 1953–1993*, ed. Toni Carabillo, et al. (Los Angeles: Women's Graphics, 1993), 219. See also "The First Five Years, 1966–1971," 18. On other union negotiations, see Koontz, "Childbirth and Child Rearing Leave," 493–495; and Carolyn York, "Bargaining for Work and Family Benefits," in *Women and Unions: Forging a Partnership*, ed. Dorothy Sue Cobble (Ithaca, NY: ILR Press, 1993), 138.

29. See Wendy W. Williams, "Equality's Riddle: Pregnancy and the Equal Treatment / Special Treatment Debate," *New York University Review of Law and Social Change* 13 (1984–1985): 325–380. See also Kessler-Harris, *In Pursuit of Equity*, 261–267; and Cobble, *The Other Women's Movement*, 182–190.

30. "Task Force on Equal Opportunity in Employment," [1967] (box 46, folder 20) NOW Records, Schlesinger; "National Organization for Women Task Force on the Family," [November] 1967 (box 42, folder 5) NOW Records, Schlesinger; and "NOW Bill of Rights in 1968," [1967] (box 1, folder 2) NOW Records, Schlesinger.

31. Mary Eastwood interview, March 14, 2005, qtd. in Kevin S. Schwartz, "Equalizing Pregnancy: The Birth of a Super-Statute," *Yale Law School Student Prize Paper Series*, paper 41 (May 7, 2005): 26–27.

32. Anthony Ramirez, "Catherine East, 80, Inspiration for National Women's Group," *New York Times*, August 20, 1996, B6; Catherine East testimony transcript, *Gilbert v. General Electric*, [1976], pp. 137–138 (box 10, folder 13) East Papers, Schlesinger; and Koontz, "Childbirth and Child Rearing Leave," 480–481.

33. Koontz, "Childbirth and Child Rearing Leave," 481. This framework was widely adopted. See Hayden, "Punishing Pregnancy," 24–25.

34. Citizens' Advisory Council on the Status of Women, "Job-Related Maternity Benefits," October 29, 1970, p. 1 (box 9, folder 7) Empl. Coll., SSC, MS 456.

35. Deborah Dinner, "The Costs of Reproduction: History and the Legal Construction of Sex Equality," *Harvard Civil Rights-Civil Liberties Law Review* 26 (August 2011): 450–456; and Deborah Dinner, "Strange Bedfellows at Work: Neomaternalism in the Making of Sex Discrimination Law," *Washington University Law Review* 91 (2014): 472. See also discussion of these developments in Davidson, et al., *Sex-Based Discrimination*, 496–497.

36. Association of American Colleges, "Employment Policies Regarding Pregnancy, Maternity and Childbirth. A Digest of Guidelines Issued by the Equal Employment Opportunity Commission on April 5, 1972," February 1973 (box 3b, folder 3) Empl. Coll., SSC, MS 456. See also Dinner, "Costs of Reproduction," 456–457.

37. "Transcription of the Oral History Interview with Susan Deller-Ross," 15–16; Susan Deller Ross interview, October 20, 2004, as cited in Schwartz, "Equalizing Pregnancy," 24; and Schwartz, "Equalizing Pregnancy," 23–24.

38. Mayeri, *Reasoning from Race*, 67–68; Dinner, "Recovering the *LaFleur* Doctrine," 376–377; and Sipser, "Maternity Leave," 182.

39. Jo Carol Nesset-Sale, "From Sideline to Frontline: The Making of a Civil Rights Plaintiff—A Retrospective by the Plaintiff in *Cleveland Board of Education v. LaFleur*, a Landmark Pregnancy Discrimination Case," *The Georgetown Journal of Gender and the Law* 7 (2006): 9–12; and Dinner, "Recovering the *LaFleur* Doctrine," 363–364.

40. Nesset-Sale, "From Sideline to Frontline," 14, 16–17; and Dinner, "Recovering the *LaFleur* Doctrine," 365.

41. Arguments cited in Sipser, "Maternity Leave," 177. See "Maternity Leave," 177–178; and Dinner, "Recovering the *LaFleur* Doctrine," 367–368.

42. Ruling cited in Sipser, "Maternity Leave," 178. See also Mayeri, *Reasoning from Race*, 67.

43. Dinner, "Recovering the *LaFleur* Doctrine," 395–400; Nancy Woloch, *A Class by Herself: Protective Laws for Women Workers, 1890s–1990s* (Princeton: Princeton University Press, 2015), 239; and Linda Greenhouse, *Becoming Justice Blackmun: Harry Blackmun's Supreme Court Journey* (New York: Henry Holt, 2005), 215.

44. Hayden, "Punishing Pregnancy," 37–39.

45. Ibid., 40–41.

46. Cary, "Life Faces Portia," 94.

47. Hartmann, *Other Feminists*, 35, 43–44; Bart Barnes, "EEOC Counsel Ruth Weyand Identified as Crash Victim," *Washington Post*, November 20, 1986, B10; Dinner, "Costs of Reproduction," 423–424; and Schwartz, "Equalizing Pregnancy," 41–42.

48. Fred Strebeigh, *Equal: Women Reshape American Law* (New York: Norton, 2009), 107–109; and Hartmann, *Other Feminists*, 44. On *General Electric v. Gilbert*, see Dinner, "Costs of Reproduction," 423–431; Schwartz, "Equalizing Pregnancy," 41–57; and Strebeigh, *Equal*, 104–135.

49. Gilbert v. General Electric Company, 375 F. Supp. 367, 382, 381 (E.D. Va.), https://law.justia.com/cases/federal/district-courts/FSupp/375/367/1669167/.

50. Strebeigh, *Equal*, 125–128; Schwartz, "Equalizing Pregnancy," 64; and Nicholas Pedriana, "Discrimination by Definition: The Historical and Legal Paths to the Pregnancy Discrimination Act of 1978," *Yale Journal of Law and Feminism* 21 (2009): 10. Feminist groups included the Women's Legal Defense Fund, NOW, and WEAL.

51. Strebeigh, *Equal*, 126; Dinner, "Costs of Reproduction," 425; and Melissa Ann McDonald, "Labor Pains: Sex Discrimination and the Implementation of Title VII, 1964–1980," PhD diss. (University of California Santa Barbara, 1993), 428.

52. Brief of American Civil Liberties Union and National Education Association as Amici Curiae at 43, Liberty Mut. Ins. Co. v. Wetzel, 424 US 737, no. 74–1245 (1976), qtd. in Dinner, "Costs of Reproduction," 428.

53. Ginsburg, "Gender and the Constitution," 42.

54. Schwartz, "Equalizing Pregnancy," 59; Ginsburg and Weyand's responses cited in Mayeri, *Reasoning from Race*, 114; and Philip Hager, "Court

Upholds Bars on Benefits for Pregnancy," *Los Angeles Times*, December 8, 1976, A6.

55. Schwartz, "Equalizing Pregnancy," 58, 62–63; Dinner, "Costs of Reproduction," 470; and Mayeri, *Reasoning from Race*, 119.

56. Maria Landolpho, associate counsel to Senate Labor Subcommittee, interview with Dr. Anne Costain, May 20, 1977, qtd. in Schwartz, "Equalizing Pregnancy," 65–66; Nina Hegsted, acting head of the NOW Legislative Office, interview with Dr. Anne Costain, May 6, 1977, qtd. in Schwartz, "Equalizing Pregnancy," 67. On CEDAPW, see Schwartz, "Equalizing Pregnancy," 63–66; and Susan Gluck Mezey, *Elusive Equality: Women's Rights, Public Policy, and the Law* (Boulder, CO: Lynne Rienner, 2003), 192.

57. "The Pregnancy Discrimination Act of 1978," www.eeoc.gov/laws/statutes /pregnancy.cfm.

58. Ruth Bader Ginsburg and Susan Deller Ross, "Pregnancy and Discrimination," *New York Times*, January 25, 1977, 33; and Lesley Oelsner, "Recent Supreme Court Rulings Have Set Back Women's Rights," *New York Times*, July 8, 1977, 32. See also Campaign to End Discrimination Against Pregnant Workers (CEDAPW), "The Williams/Hawkins Bill: Fact Sheet," c. 1977 (box 54, folder 72) NOW Records, Schlesinger; and statement of Susan Deller Ross, co-chair CEDAPW and staff attorney, ACLU, *PDA—Senate Hearings*, 117–118. On congressional debate, see Dinner, "Costs of Reproduction," 470–473; "Strange Bedfellows," 494–516; Schwartz, "Equalizing Pregnancy," 77–110; and Strebeigh, *Equal*, 138–139.

59. Statement of Wendy W. Williams, Georgetown University Law Center, *PDA—Senate Hearings*, 113. Schwartz, "Equalizing Pregnancy" also quotes Williams on this point; see p. 85.

60. Schwartz, "Equalizing Pregnancy," 91–92; and statement of David J. Fitzmaurice, president, IUE, *PDA—House Hearings*, 108.

61. Ginsburg and Deller Ross, "Pregnancy and Discrimination"; and statement of Toni Sterling, Local 65, United Steelworkers of America, *PDA—Senate Hearings*, 294.

62. Clarence Mitchell, National Association for the Advancement of Colored People and Leadership Conference on Civil Rights, *PDA—Senate Hearings*, 108. On Mitchell, see also Schwartz, "Equalizing Pregnancy," 91.

63. Statement of the National Association of Manufacturers on H.R. 6075, *PDA—House Hearings*, 79–80.

64. Erica Black Grubb and Andrea Hricko, "Pregnancy Ruling: Who's Responsible for Propagation," *Los Angeles Times*, January 30, 1977, D2. See also Letty Cottin Pogrebin, "Anatomy Isn't Destiny," *New York Times*, May 6, 1977, 21.

65. Ruth Bader Ginsburg, "Some Thoughts on Benign Classification in the Context of Sex," *Connecticut Law Review* 10 (1978): 826–827; and statement of Bella S. Abzug, presiding officer, National Commission on the Observance of International Women's Years, *PDA—Senate Hearings*, 309. See also Statement of Wendy Williams, *PDA—Senate Hearings*, 115.

66. CEDAPW, "Fact Sheet"; statement of Jacqueline M. Nolan-Haley, special counsel, American Citizens Concerned for Life, Inc., *PDA—Senate Hearings*, 432; and statement of Wendy W. Williams, *PDA—Senate Hearings*, 115.

67. Joyce Gelb and Marian Lief Palley, *Women and Public Policies: Reassessing Gender Politics*, rev. ed. (Charlottesville: University Press of Virginia, 1996), 169–171, 173.

68. CEDAPW, "Fact Sheet."

69. Marisa Chappell, *The War on Welfare: Family, Poverty, and Politics in Modern America* (Philadelphia: University of Pennsylvania Press, 2010), 136–138.

70. Remarks of Senator Harrison A. Williams, Jr., joint press conference regarding introduction of a bill to amend Title VII of the Civil Rights Act of 1964 to prohibit sex discrimination on the basis of pregnancy, childbirth, and related medical conditions, March 15, 1977, qtd. in Schwartz, "Equalizing Pregnancy," 79; and statement of Bella S. Abzug, *PDA—Senate Hearings*, 309, 313. See also Dinner, "Costs of Reproduction," 470–471; and Dinner, "Strange Bedfellows," 505.

71. Senate Committee on Labor and Human Resources, *Legislative History of the Pregnancy Discrimination Act of 1978: Public Law 95–555* (Washington, DC: US Government Printing Office, 1980), 12; Schwartz, "Equalizing Pregnancy," 80; and Cong. Rec. 38,574 (Oct. 14, 1978) (statement of Sen. Jeffords).

8. Flextime

1. Betty Friedan, *It Changed My Life: Writings on the Women's Movement* (New York: Dell, 1977), 115–116; Sonia Pressman Fuentes, "Timeline of Some of Sonia Pressman Fuentes' Activities through Nov. 4, 2004," www.erraticimpact.com/~feminism/html/FUENTES_timeline.htm; Sonia Pressman Fuentes, "Representing Women," *Frontiers* 18, no. 3 (1997): 98, 101–103; and Sonia Pressman Fuentes, "The Beginning of the Second Wave of the Women's Movement and Where We Are Today: A Personal Account," *Cornell Law Faculty Working Papers*, paper 54 (April 2009). Friedan's meeting with Pressman may have occurred in 1965, but definitely preceded the formation of NOW.

2. Pressman Fuentes, "Timeline"; Allie Weeden, "The Founding of F.E.W," *F.E.W. Facts* 1, no. 1 (1969); Elizabeth Shelton, "'Federally Employed Women' Is Formed to Push Equal Rights," *Washington Post*, September 24, 1968, C3; Sara M. Evans, *Tidal Wave: How Women Changed America at Century's End* (New York: Free Press, 2003), 82; and Judith Hole and Ellen Levine, *Rebirth of Feminism* (New York: Quadrangle Books, 1971), 99.

3. Weeden, "Founding of F.E.W."; Hole and Levine, *Rebirth of Feminism*, 99–100; and Lee Ann Banaszak, *The Women's Movement Inside and Outside the State* (New York: Cambridge University Press, 2010), 106–107.

4. Alice Kessler-Harris, *In Pursuit of Equity: Women, Men, and the Quest for Economic Citizenship in 20th-Century America* (New York: Oxford University Press, 2001), 105–106; Ruth Milkman, "Women Workers and the Fair Labor Standards Act, Past and Present," in *A Paper Series Commemorating the 75th Anniversary of the Fair Labor Standards Act* (Berkeley: Department of Labor with the Institute for Research on Labor and Employment, University of California, Berkeley, 2013), 282–284; and Jean Collier Brown, "The Negro Woman Worker," The Women's Bureau, Washington, DC, bulletin no. 165 (1938), 2.

5. Dorothy Sue Cobble, *The Other Women's Movement: Workplace Justice and Social Rights in Modern America* (Princeton: Princeton University Press, 2004), 139–141. Cobble borrows the "politics of time" from the sociologist Carmen Sirianni (139).

6. Ibid., 171–172, 186–190; and Kessler-Harris, *In Pursuit of Equity*, 262–263. For earlier debates, see Nancy Woloch, *A Class by Herself: Protective Laws for Women Workers, 1890s–1990s* (Princeton: Princeton University Press, 2015), 171–174.

7. Woloch, *A Class by Herself*, 201–202, 212–214.

8. Weeden, "Founding of F.E.W."; and "Allie B. Latimer," in The 24th Annual Margaret Brent Awards Luncheon program, ABA Annual Meeting, Boston, August 10, 2014, p. 17. See also "Federally Employed Women," in *US Women's Interest Groups: Institutional Profiles*, ed., Sarah Slavin (Westport, CT: Greenwood Press, 1995), 186–190; and Banaszak, *Women's Movement*, 105–108.

9. "A Few Facts about F.E.W.," pamphlet, c. 1970 (box 2, folder 17a) Eastwood Papers, Schlesinger; Anne N. Costain, "The Struggle for a National Women's Lobby: Organizing a Diffuse Interest," *The Western Political Quarterly* 33 (December 1980): 483; and "Janice Mendenhall Video," in *FEW Video Archives*, www.few.org/video-archives/.

10. Judy Nicol, "Federal Women in Job Quest," *Los Angeles Times*, November 15, 1970, G22; "F.E.W. Holds First Annual Conference," *F.E.W.'s News and Views* 2, no. 4 (1970), 3; Dorothy Frank, "Making Equality of Opportunity a Reality," *F.E.W.'s News and Views* 2, no. 4 (1970), 6; "Suggestions for FEW," c. 1974 (box 3, folder 18) Eastwood Papers, Schlesinger; and Janice Mendenhall, "For President Federally Employed Women" c. 1974 (box 3, folder 18) Eastwood Papers, Schlesinger. On leadership positions, see Federally Employed Women, "Our Story," FEW.org, www.few.org/about-us/few-history/our-story/. Two of the first seven presidents of FEW (1968–1980) were African American: Allie Latimer Weeden and Dorothy Nelms. Chapter leadership is harder to determine, but of the eight chapter presidents whose race could be determined from the first eleven chapters chartered, two were African American ("A Few Facts about F.E.W."). All seven (of ten total for the organization) regional coordinators identified by biography and photograph in 1976 were almost certainly white. "Meet Your Regional Coordinators," *F.E.W.'s News and Views* 9, no. 4 (1976), 4–5.

11. "F.E.W. Holds First Annual Conference," 4; "Bill of Rights," March 9, 1974 (box 3, folder 18) Eastwood Papers, Schlesinger; "FEW History," FEW.org, www .few.org/about-us/few-history/; and "FEW Is . . ." c. 1978 (box 52, folder 21) Carabillo-Meuli Papers, Schlesinger.

12. FEW, "Executive Committee Meeting," March 30, 1970 (box 3, folder 17b) Eastwood Papers, Schlesinger; FEW, "The F.E.W. Phone Book," December 1974 (box 3, folder 19) Eastwood Papers, Schlesinger; "How Different Are Women?," program of FEW 1st National Conference, June 19–20, 1970 (box 3, folder 17b) Eastwood Papers, Schlesinger; and Mendenhall, "For President Federally Employed Women."

13. Mary Scott Welch, "How Women Just like You Are Getting Better Jobs," *Redbook*, September 1977, 121, 176–86; and Nancy MacLean, "The Hidden

History of Affirmative Action: Working Women's Struggles in the 1970s and the Gender of Class," *Feminist Studies* 25 (Spring 1999): 42–78.

14. Marlene Cimons, "Uncle Sam as a Fair Employer," *Los Angeles Times*, September 7, 1970, H1; US Bureau of the Census, *Statistical Abstract of the United States: 1981*, 102d ed. (Washington, DC: US Government Printing Office, 1981), table 462, p. 270; and "To Be—Or Not to Be—Belligerent," *F.E. W.'s News and Views* 2, no. 3 (1970), 2.

15. On FEW as a liberal feminist organization, see "F.E.W. Holds Equal Rights for Women Rally in Lafayette Park on August 26," *F.E. W.'s News and Views* 3, no. 1 (1970); Maren Lockwood Carden, *The New Feminist Movement* (New York: Russell Sage Foundation, 1974), 146; Cynthia Harrison, "Creating a National Feminist Agenda: Coalition Building in the 1970s," in *Feminist Coalitions: Historical Perspectives on Second-Wave Feminism in the United States*, ed. Stephanie Gilmore (Urbana: University of Illinois Press, 2008), 39; and Costain, "Struggle for a National Women's Lobby," 488. On DC FEW, see "An Invitation to Join DC FEW" (box 3, folder 18b) Eastwood Papers, Schlesinger; and Anne M. Valk, *Radical Sisters: Second-Wave Feminism and Black Liberation in Washington, DC* (Urbana: University of Illinois Press, 2008), 103.

16. "FEW: A History of Progress," *FEW's News*, August 31, 1997; Federally Employed Women, "Federally Employed Women: Celebrating A Rich 45-Year History of Activism and Accomplishments" (Alexandria, Virginia: Federally Employed Women, 2013): 5–15; Federally Employed Women, "Our Story"; and the following in *F.E. W.'s News and Views*: "The Federal Women's Program" and Tina Lower, "FWP 1969 Review Seminar," in volume 1, no. 2 (June 1969); "F.E.W. Gives Griddle Iron Party," "A Long Way to Go," "Congressmen Reply (!) to F.E.W. Letter," and "F.E.W. Seeks Improvements in F.W.P.," in volume 2, no. 2 (1970); and "Progress (?) on Equal Rights," in volume 2, no. 4 (1970), 2.

17. "F.E.W. Holds Equal Rights for Women Rally"; and Cimons, "Uncle Sam as a Fair Employer."

18. National Manpower Council, *Womanpower: A Statement, with Chapters by the Council Staff* (New York: Columbia University Press, 1957), 37; Kessler-Harris, *In Pursuit of Equity*, 211–212; and Women's Bureau, Dep't of Labor, *Part-Time Empl't of Women*, report #WB 68–151 (Washington, DC: US Government Printing Office, April 1968), 1–3.

19. Daisy Fields, Federally Employed Women to Honorable John V. Tunney, 5 April 1973, in *Hearings 1973*, 27–28; Florence Perman to Senator Gale McGee, 19 October 1973 (box 10, folder "Part-time Documentation") WOW Records, Schlesinger; Women's Bureau, Dep't of Labor, *Part-Time Empl't of Women*, 4; and statement of Allene Joyce Skinner, dir., Women's Program Div., Dep't of HUD, *Hearings 1977*, 68–69.

20. Marjorie M. Silverberg and Lorraine D. Eyde, "Career Part-Time Employment: Personnel Implications of the New Professional and Executive Corps," *Good Government* 88 (Fall 1971), 11–19; Marjorie M. Silverberg, "Part-Time Careers in the Federal Government," *The Bureaucrat* 1, no. 3 (Fall 1972): 247–251; and HEW Federal Women's Program, "Part-Time Employment: A Manager's Alternative in Staffing," *Hearings 1973*, 135–136.

21. Marion Janjic, "Part-Time Work in the Public Service," *International Labour Review* 105 (1972): 335–349; Roger Ricklefs, "Temporary Duty: Em-

ployees, Employers Both Discover the Joys of Part-Time Positions," *Wall Street Journal*, March 7, 1973, 1; Sam Zagoria, "When Work Schedules Are Flexible," *Washington Post*, September 9, 1973, G4; Stanley D. Nollen and Virginia H. Martin, *Alternative Work Schedules, Part 1: Flexitime—An AMA Survey Report* (New York: AMACOM, 1978), 17–29; and statement of Hon. Gladys Noon Spellman, *Hearings 1977*, 2.

22. *Hearings 1973*, 3, 58. On the Congressional debates, see also Halcyone H. Bohen and Anamaria Viveros-Long, *Balancing Jobs and Family Life: Do Flexible Work Schedules Help?* (Philadelphia: Temple University Press, 1981), 36–55.

23. Felice N. Schwartz, "Management Women and the New Facts of Life," *Harvard Business Review* 67 (January–February 1989): 65–76. On Schwartz, see Elizabeth Singer More, "Best Interests: Feminists, Social Science, and the Revaluing of Working Mothers in Modern America," PhD diss. (Harvard University, 2012), 256–309.

24. Catalyst, *Our History*, www.catalyst.org/who-we-are/our-history; and More, "Best Interests," 269.

25. Statement of Felice Schwartz, president of the Catalyst org., *Hearings 1973*, 108.

26. Ibid., 110–111.

27. Statement of Hon. Bella Abzug, *Hearings 1973*, 54, 53–56.

28. Daisy Fields, FEW to Hon. John V. Tunney, April 5, 1973, statement of Daisy B. Fields, chairman of the Legislative Comm. for Federally Employed Women, Inc. (FEW), and Federally Employed Women, Inc., additional statements, *Hearings 1973*, 116, 28, 111–116.

29. Statement of Clyde M. Webber, national president, Am. Federation of Gov't Employees and Francis S. Filbey, general president, Am. Postal Workers Union, AFL–CIO to Hon. Gale W. McGee, *Hearings 1973*, 17–21.

30. *Changing Patterns of Work in Am., 1976. Hearings Before the Subcomm. on Empl't, Poverty, and Migratory Labor, of the Comm. on Labor and Pub. Welfare, S.*, 94th Cong. 472 (1976) (statement of Isabel Sawhill, senior research assoc. and dir. of a program of research on women at The Urban Institute); statement of Gail S. Rosenberg, president, National Council for Alternative Work Patterns," *Hearings 1977*, 173–177; Rosabeth Moss Kanter, "Work in a New America," *Daedalus* 107 (Winter 1978): 59; and US Comptroller General, *The Federal Role in Improving Productivity—Is the National Center for Productivity and Quality of Working Life the Proper Mechanism?* (Washington, DC: US Government Printing Office, 1978).

31. *Hearings 1975*.

32. Nancy S. Barrett, "Women in the Job Market: Unemployment and Work Schedules," in *The Subtle Revolution: Women at Work*, ed. Ralph E. Smith (Washington, DC: Urban Institute Press, 1979), 63–98; and Marisa Chappell, "Demanding a New Family Wage: Feminist Consensus in the 1970s Full Employment Campaign," in *Feminist Coalitions: Historical Perspectives on Second-Wave Feminism in the United States*, ed. Stephanie Gilmore (Urbana: University of Illinois Press, 2008), 259–261.

33. Chappell, "Demanding a New Family Wage"; "Women and Full Employment Workshops, June 12, 1976," (box 54, folder 72) NOW Records, Schlesinger;

and Carol S. Greenwald, "Part-Time Work," in *American Women Workers in a Full Employment Economy: A Compendium of Papers* (Washington, DC: US Government Printing Office, 1977): 182–191.

34. "Congress to Unite Women: Report from the New York City Meeting of November 21, 22, 23, 1969," in *Radical Feminism*, ed. Anne Koedt, Ellen Levine, and Anita Rapone (New York: Quadrangle, 1973), 307.

35. Marie Carosello Bristol, "The 20-Hour Work Week," *Women: A Journal of Liberation* 2 (1971): 30–31.

36. Marlene Cimons, "Family Chores Change Work Week," *Washington Post*, August 16, 1973, G1.

37. Ellen Frye, "Job-Sharing, or the Myth of What Women Want," *Off Our Backs*, October 31, 1978, 4–5.

38. Karen Nussbaum, *Office Work in America* (Cleveland: Working Women, 1982), bcrw.barnard.edu/archive/workforce/Office_Work_in_America.pdf, 8, ii; Diane Balser, *Sisterhood and Solidarity: Feminism and Labor in Modern Times* (Boston: South End Press, 1987): 127, 185; and "Working Women's 1980 Platform," reprinted in Philip S. Foner, *Women and the American Labor Movement: From the First Trade Unions to the Present* (New York: Free Press, 1982), 497–500.

39. Statement of the Public Employee Department, American Federation of Labor and Congress of Industrial Organizations (AFL–CIO), *Hearings 1975*, 148, 167.

40. Lynne Darcy and Elaine Latourell [LaTourelle], National Organization for Women to Members of the Subcommittee on Manpower and Civil Service, 7 November 1975 (box 54, folder 70) NOW Records, Schlesinger.

41. Statement of Gladys E. Henrikson, task force coordinator on flexible hours and part-time employment legislation, Women's Equity Action League and Women's Lobby, Inc., *Hearings 1975*, 71.

42. Statement of Hon. Patricia Schroeder, *Hearings 1975*, 22; and statement of the National Organization for Women, *Hearings 1975*, 144.

43. Warren Farrell, *The Liberated Man* (New York: Bantam Books, 1974), 135–138; and James Levine, *Who Will Raise the Children? New Options for Fathers (and Mothers)* (Philadelphia: Lippincott, 1976), 98, 66–98.

44. Prepared statement of Linda Teixeira, legislative coordinator, Alliance for Displaced Homemakers, *Hearings 1975*, 81. On feminist demands, see also Statement of Gladys E. Henrikson; and statement of Jinx Melia, division manager of TransCentury Corp., *Hearings 1975*, 76. On FEW, see statement of Janice Mendenhall, president of Federally Employed Women, *Hearings 1975*, 133–36; "Minutes of the Meeting of the Executive Committee," FEW, April 25, 1975 (box 3, folder 20) Eastwood Papers, Schlesinger; and HEW Professional and Executive Corps to Honorable Gale W. McGee, 12 December 1974 (box 10, folder "Part-time Abzug/Tunney/Burke Bill") WOW Records, Schlesinger. See also "Flexitime and Part-Time—A Status Report," *F.E.W.'s News and Views*, February/March 1976, 14.

For other women's groups, see Lynne Darcy and Elizabeth Cox to NOW chapter legislative coordinators, "Legislation on Flexible Hours and Part-Time Employment," 13 November 1975 (box 54, folder 70) NOW Records, Schlesinger; Judy Flynn, "The Implications of Flexitime: Particularly For Women," report prepared for the National Organization for Women, January 31, 1977 (box 54, folder 71) NOW Records, Schlesinger; and Virginia H. Martin, *Hours of Work When Workers Can Choose: The Experience of 59 Organizations with Employee-Chosen Staggered Hours and Flexitime* (Washington, DC: Business and Professional Women's Foundation, 1975).

45. Statement of Janice Mendenhall, 134.

46. Statement of Professor Urie Bronfenbrenner, *Hearings 1977*, 25; and *Am. Families: Trends and Pressures, 1973, Hearings before the Subcomm. on Children and Youth, of the Comm. on Labor and Pub. Welfare, S.,* 93rd Cong. 69 (1973).

47. Statement of Urie Bronfenbrenner, 27, 29.

48. Representative Patricia Schroeder, *Hearings 1977*, 128; and prepared statement of Mae Walterhouse, president, Federally Employed Women, Inc., *Hearings 1977*, 77.

49. Statement of Leslie Gladstone, joint testimony on behalf of Women's Equity Action League, Nat'l Org. for Women, Nat'l Women's Political Caucus, and Women's Lobby, *Hearings 1977*, 32; prepared statement of Carol S. Greenwald, commissioner of banks, Commonwealth of Massachusetts, *Hearings 1978*, 44; and Representative Patricia Schroeder, *Hearings 1977*, 29. On Greenwald, see "Several States Experiment: 'Flexible' Public Jobs Gain Acceptance," *Los Angeles Times*, July 27, 1977, D7.

50. Testimony of Carol S. Greenwald, *Hearings 1978*, 38, emphasis added; and prepared statement of Carol S. Greenwald, *Hearings 1978*, 43–45.

51. Statement of Mae Walterhouse, 74–79; and testimony of Lynne Revo Cohen, director, part-time careers, Women's Lobby, *Hearings 1978*, 71–75.

52. Mike Causey, "Part-Time Job Bill Enacted," *Washington Post*, September 28, 1978, C2; Georgetown University Law Center, "Federal Employees Part-Time Career Employment Act of 1978," *Workplace Flexibility 2010* (Washington, DC: Georgetown University Law Center, 2006).

53. Commentators at the time connected the bills; see "100 Bills Affecting Women Are Still before Congress," *New York Times*, July 8, 1977, 32; and "Lobbyists on Women's Rights Press Congress for Action," *New York Times*, August 13, 1977, 28.

Conclusion

1. Daniel Horowitz, *Betty Friedan and the Making of* The Feminine Mystique: *The American Left, the Cold War, and Modern Feminism* (Amherst: University of Massachusetts Press, 1998), 235–236; and Susan Faludi, *Backlash: The Undeclared War against American Women* (New York: Anchor Books, 1991), 318–324.

2. Betty Friedan, "Feminism's Next Step," *New York Times Sunday Magazine*, July 5, 1981, 14; and Betty Friedan, *The Second Stage* (New York: Summit Books, 1981), 27.

3. Betty Friedan, "Feminism Takes a New Turn," *New York Times Sunday Magazine*, November 18, 1979, 92. See also Friedan, *Second Stage*, 58, 79.

4. Friedan, *Second Stage*, 319.

5. Friedan, "Feminism's Next Step," 15.

6. Ibid., 14; and Friedan, *Second Stage*, 203.

7. Friedan, "Feminism's Next Step," 14; Friedan, *Second Stage*, 260–263; and Friedan, "Feminism Takes a New Turn," 92.

8. Faludi, *Backlash*, 322–323; Ellen Willis, "Betty Friedan's 'Second Stage': A Step Backward," *The Nation*, November 14, 1981, 494; and Phyllis Schlafly, "Betty Friedan and the Feminist Mystique," *Phyllis Schlafly Report*, March 1988, 3, qtd. in Faludi, *Backlash*, 319. See also Linda Gordon and Marla Erlien, "The Politics of Puritanism," *The Nation*, November 28, 1981, 578–579; and Herma Hill Kay, "Do We Suffer From a Feminist Mystique?," *New York Times Book Review*, November 22, 1981, 1, 33.

9. Willis, "Friedan's 'Second Stage,'" 494.

10. Edward Walsh, "Abzug Praises President—And Then He Fires Her," *Washington Post*, January 13, 1979, A1.

11. Horowitz, *Betty Friedan*, 234.

12. Bill Abrams, "TV Ads, Shows Struggle to Replace Bygone Images of Today's Mothers," *Wall Street Journal*, October 5, 1984, 35; Lynn Langway, et al., "The Superwoman Squeeze," *Newsweek*, May 19, 1980, 72–79; and Connell Cowan and Melvyn Kinder, *Smart Women/Foolish Choices* (New York: New American Library, 1985), 16, qtd. in Faludi, *Backlash*, xii.

13. Paul Weyrich, interview with Susan Faludi, 1988, qtd. in Faludi, *Backlash*, 229–230. On conservative accusations that feminism destroyed the family, see *Backlash*, 232–237; and Rebecca E. Klatch, *Women of the New Right* (Philadelphia: Temple University Press, 1987), 122–127.

14. Bureau of Labor Statistics, Department of Labor, "Databases, Tables and Calculators by Subject," www.bls.gov/data/; and Friedan, *Second Stage*, 70.

15. Urie Bronfenbrenner, "The Calamitous Decline of The American Family," *Washington Post*, January 2, 1977, 65; Joan Cook, "The Family Could Become a Relic by the Year 2000, Sociologist Says," *New York Times*, June 2, 1977, 47; Natasha Zaretsky, *No Direction Home: The American Family and the Fear of National Decline, 1968–1980* (Chapel Hill: University of North Carolina Press, 2007), 13, 209; and "The 'Traditional Family Will Make a Comeback': Interview with Dr. Lee Salk, Child Psychologist," *US News and World Report*, June 16, 1980, qtd. in Marisa Chappell, *The War on Welfare: Family, Poverty, and Politics in Modern America* (Philadelphia: University of Pennsylvania Press, 2010), 162.

16. Marshall Berman, "Family Affairs," *New York Times Book Review*, January 15, 1978, 6–7, 20; and Chappell, *War on Welfare*.

17. Marjorie J. Spruill, *Divided We Stand: The Battle over Women's Rights and Family Values That Polarized American Politics* (New York: Bloomsbury, 2017), 299–303; Bruce Schulman, *The Seventies: The Great Shift in American Culture, Society, and Politics* (Cambridge, MA: DaCapo Press, 2002), 187–189; and Robert O. Self, *All in the Family: The Realignment of American Democracy Since the 1960s* (New York: Hill and Wang, 2012), 333–335.

18. "How E.R.A. Will Hurt Men," *Phyllis Schlafly Report*, May 1975; Phyllis Schlafly, *The Power of the Positive Woman* (New Rochelle, NY: Arlington House, 1977), 93–95; and *Hearings on Sex Discrimination in the Workplace, Comm. on Labor and Human Res., US S.*, 97th Cong. 412, 414 (1981) (testimony by Phyllis Schlafly).

19. *Hearings on Sex Discrimination in the Workplace, Comm. on Labor and Human Res., US S.*, 97th Cong. 421 (1981) (testimony by Phyllis Schlafly). Conservatives also sought policies to regulate sexuality, reproduction, and education in ways that rolled back feminist gains. See Karen Flax, "Women's Rights and the Proposed Family Protection Act," *University of Miami Law Review* 36 (1981): 141–163.

20. Richard A. Viguerie, *The New Right: We're Ready to Lead*, rev. ed. (Falls Church, VA: Viguerie Co., 1981), 158; Self, *All in the Family*, 382–383; and Zaretsky, *No Direction Home*, 110.

21. Walter Mondale, "Introducing a Special Report: The Family in Trouble," *Psychology Today*, May 1977, 39; and Chappell, *War on Welfare*, 163.

22. White House Conference on Families, *Listening to America's Families: Action for the 80s—A Summary of the Report to the President, Congress and Families of the Nation* (Washington, DC: White House Conference on Families, 1980), 12, 9, and 10; and Matthew D. Lassiter, "Inventing Family Values," in *Rightward Bound: Making America Conservative in the 1970s*, ed. Bruce J. Schulman and Julian E. Zelizer (Cambridge: Harvard University Press, 2008), 24–25.

23. Zaretsky, *No Direction Home*, 202–206; and Wini Breines, Margaret Cerullo, and Judith Stacey, "Social Biology, Family Studies, and Antifeminist Backlash," *Feminist Studies* 4 (February 1978): 43–67.

24. Judith Stacey, "The New Conservative Feminism," *Feminist Studies* 9 (Autumn 1983): 566–567; and Mari Jo Buhle, *Feminism and Its Discontents: A Century of Struggle with Psychoanalysis* (Cambridge: Harvard University Press, 1998), 310–311. Stacey also considers Betty Friedan a new conservative feminist.

25. Enid Nemy, "Women's Movement Sets Its Sights on the Future of the Family," *New York Times*, November 20, 1979, B11; and Friedan, "Feminism Takes a New Turn," 92.

26. Friedan, *Second Stage*, 319; and Gloria Steinem, "The Way We Were—And Will Be," *Ms.*, December 1979, 71, qtd. in Self, *All in the Family*, 336–337.

27. The historians Marisa Chappell and Dorothy Sue Cobble have called this a "degendered family wage." Cobble points out that postwar labor feminists demanded a "provider wage." Both have important overlaps with the work and family ideal I introduce here, although it is more expansive, including transformations within intimate relationships and households as well as the social wage. Chappell, *War on Welfare*, 158, 168, 248; and Dorothy Sue Cobble, *The Other Women's Movement: Workplace Justice and Social Rights in Modern America* (Princeton: Princeton University Press, 2004), 118–119. See also Alice Kessler-Harris and Karen Brodkin Sacks, "The Demise of Domesticity in America," in *Women, Households, and the Economy*, ed. Lourdes Benería and Catharine R. Stimpson (New Brunswick: Rutgers University Press, 1987), 75–77.

28. Ronald D. Elving, *Conflict and Compromise: How Congress Makes the Law* (New York: Touchstone, 1995): 19–20. On the highly contentious debate over paid pregnancy leave, see Deborah Dinner, "Strange Bedfellows at Work: Neomaternalism in the Making of Sex Discrimination Law," *Washington University Law Review* 91 (2014): 519–523. For the "rumbling of feminist ideas through mainstream institutions," see Sara M. Evans, *Tidal Wave: How Women Changed America at Century's End* (New York: Free Press, 2003), 191–202.

29. Pat Schroeder, House Subcommittee on Civil Service, September 1986, in "Statements from Senate and House Sponsors of the Family and Medical Leave Act," Press Kit, Family and Medical Leave Coalition, October 7, 1987 (box 352, folder 18) NOW Legal/Educ., Schlesinger.

30. "Our Nation Needs Strong Families," flyer for American Family Celebration, c. April or May 1988, qtd. in Eileen Boris and Sonya Michel, "Social Citizenship and Women's Right to Work in Postwar America," in *Women's Rights and Human Rights: International Historical Perspectives*, ed. Patricia Grimshaw, Katie Holmes, and Marilyn Lake (New York: Palgrave, 2001), 213.

31. John J. Sweeney and Karen Nussbaum, *Solutions for the New Work Force: Policies for a New Social Contract* (Washington, DC: Seven Locks Press, 1989), xv; and Boris and Michel, "Social Citizenship," 210–211.

32. Catherine East, "Critical Comments on *A Lesser Life: The Myth of Women's Liberation in America*" (Washington, DC: National Women's Political Caucus, July 15, 1986), 9.

33. "Reagan's '85 Budget Unfair to Women, Norton Charges," *Jet*, April 16, 1984, 7; Janice Mall, "About Women: New Report on Effects of Budget Cuts," *Los Angeles Times*, July 13, 1986, J8; and Nancy Folbre, "The Pauperization of Motherhood: Patriarchy and Public Policy in the United States," *Review of Radical Political Economics* 16 (Winter 1984): 72–88.

34. *Hearing Before the Joint Econ. Comm.*, 98th Cong. 144–145 (1984) (statement of Avril Madison, executive dir. of WOW, Inc., "Problems of Working Women"); Joyce Miller, "Speech at Solidarity Day," September 19, 1981, Coalition of Labor Union Women Records, Detroit, qtd. in Chappell, *War on Welfare*, 225; and *War on Welfare*, 214–241.

35. *Hearing Before the Joint Econ. Comm.*, 98th Cong. 1–2 (1984) (statement of Olympia Snowe, "Problems of Working Women"); and Patricia A. Seith, "Congressional Power to Effect Sex Equality," *Harvard Journal of Law and Gender* 36 (2013): 1–87.

36. Kirsten Swinth, "Post-Family Wage, Postindustrial Society: Reframing the Gender and Family Order through Working Mothers in Reagan's America," *Journal of American History* 105 (September 2018).

37. Ibid.

38. James A. Levine, *Getting Men Involved: Strategies for Early Childhood Programs* (New York: Families and Work Institute, 1993); Joseph Pleck, "Fathers and Infant Care Leave," in Edward F. Zigler and Meryl Frank, eds., *The Parental Leave Crisis: Toward a National Policy* (New Haven: Yale University Press, 1988), 177–191; and Graham L. Staines and Joseph H. Pleck, "Work Schedule Flexibility and Family Life," *Journal of Occupational Behaviour* 7 (April 1986): 147–153.

39. Arlie Hochschild, *The Second Shift: Working Parents and the Revolution at Home* (New York: Viking, 1989); and Suzanne M. Bianchi, Liana C. Sayer, Melissa A. Milkie, and John P. Robinson, "Housework: Who Did, Does or Will Do It, and How Much Does it Matter?," *Social Forces* 91 (September 2012): 57–58.

40. For similar conclusions about 1980s feminism's constraints, see Chappell, *War on Welfare*, 214–241; Seith, "Congressional Power," 36; Serena Mayeri, "Filling in the (Gender) Gaps, A Response to Patricia Seith," *Harvard Journal of Law and Gender* 36 (2013): 4–9; and Marisa Chappell, "Reagan's 'Gender Gap' Strategy and the Limitations of Free-Market Feminism," *Journal of Policy*

History 24, no. 1 (2012): 115–134. No scholarly consensus about the impact of 1980s feminist activism exists, and many assessments are more skeptical than the one presented here. See Cynthia Harrison, "'A Revolution But Half Accomplished': The Twentieth Century's Engagement with Child-Raising, Women's Work, and Feminism," in *The Achievement of American Liberalism: The New Deal and Its Legacies*, ed. William H. Chafe (New York: Columbia University Press, 2003), 243–274; and Self, *All in the Family*, 327.

41. *Working family* initially entered the American cultural and political lexicon interchangeably with *working-class family*, but in the late 1980s it became a commonplace term to describe working- and middle-class American households facing the dual pressures of wage earning and care responsibilities.

42. Campaign for Working Families, www.cwfpac.com/home; Working Families Party, workingfamilies.org/; Labor Project for Working Families, familyvaluesatwork.org/laborproject; Netsy Firestein and Nicola Dones, "Unions Fight for Work and Family Policies—Not for Women Only," in *The Sex of Class: Women Transforming American Labor*, ed. Dorothy Sue Cobble (Ithaca: Cornell University Press, 2007), 140–154; and Ruth Milkman and Eileen Appelbaum, *Unfinished Business: Paid Family Leave in California and the Future of US Work-Family Policy* (Ithaca: Cornell University Press, 2013).

43. Serena Mayeri, "Foundling Fathers: (Non-)Marriage and Parental Rights in the Age of Equality," *Yale Law Journal* 125 (June 2016): 2292–2392.

44. Suzanne Bianchi, Nancy Folbre, and Douglas Wolf, "Unpaid Care Work," in *For Love and Money: Care Provision in the United States*, ed. Nancy Folbre (New York: Russell Sage Foundation, 2012), 47, 54, 58; and Suzanne M. Bianchi, John P. Robinson, and Melissa A. Milkie, *Changing Rhythms of American Family Life* (New York: Russell Sage Foundation, 2006), 136–137.

45. "MenCare: A Global Fatherhood Campaign," https://men-care.org; and "The Fatherhood Project: Connecting Fathers and Children," www.thefather hoodproject.org/; Marc Vachon and Amy Vachon, *Equally Shared Parenting: Rewriting the Rules for a New Generation of Parents* (New York: Penguin, 2010); and Francine Deutsch, *Halving It All: How Equally Shared Parenting Works* (Cambridge: Harvard University Press, 1999).

46. Silvia Federici, *Revolution at Point Zero: Housework, Reproduction, and Feminist Struggle* (Oakland, CA: PM Press, 2012); and "Housework as Work: Selma James on Unwaged Labor and Decades-Long Struggle to Pay Housewives," *Democracy Now!* (April 16, 2012). www.democracynow.org/2012/4/16 /housework_as_work_selma_james_on.

47. Mignon Duffy, *Making Care Count: A Century of Gender, Race, and Paid Care Work* (New Brunswick: Rutgers University Press, 2011), figure 2.2, p. 25, figure 2.5, p. 32; US Census Bureau, "Employment by Industry: 2000 to 2010," *Statistical Abstract of the United States: 2012* (Washington, DC: US Government Printing Office, 2012), table 620, p. 339; and Heidi Shierholz, *Low Wages and Scant Benefits Leave Many In-Home Workers Unable to Make Ends Meet* (Washington, DC: Economic Policy Institute, November 25, 2013), table 1, p. 4 and table 11, p. 22.

48. Premilla Nadasen, "Citizenship Rights, Domestic Work, and the Fair Labor Standards Act," *Journal of Policy History* 24, no. 1 (2012): 88; Shierholz, "Low Wages and Scant Benefits," 2, 22; Pierrette Hondagneu-Sotelo, "Domésticas

Demand Dignity," in *Women's America: Refocusing the Past*, 8th ed., ed. Linda K. Kerber, et al. (New York: Oxford University Press, 2016), 759–775; Domestic Workers United, www.domesticworkersunited.org/index.php/en/; National Domestic Workers Alliance, www.domesticworkers.org; and Eileen Boris and Jennifer Klein, *Caring for America: Home Health Workers in the Shadow of the Welfare State* (New York: Oxford University Press, 2012).

49. Faye J. Crosby, Joan C. Williams, and Monica Biernat, "The Maternal Wall," *Journal of Social Issues* 60 (December 2004): 675–682; National Partnership for Women and Families, "State Paid Family and Medical Leave Insurance Laws" (February 2018), www.nationalpartnership.org/research-library/work-family/paid -leave/state-paid-family-leave-laws.pdf; and Chris Weller, "These 10 Countries Have the Best Parental Leave Policies in the World," *Business Insider*, August 22, 2016, www.businessinsider.com/countries-with-best-parental-leave-2016-8.

50. US Equal Employment Opportunity Commission, "EEOC Women's Work Group Report," December 2013, www.eeoc.gov/federal/reports/women _workgroup_report.cfm; and Judith Shulevitz, "It's Payback Time for Women," *New York Times*, January 10, 2016, SR1.

ACKNOWLEDGMENTS

The chapters of this book can be measured by the windows I have looked out of as I sat before my computer—the sweet spring light of New York, the rust-red of baking summer *machambas* in Maputo, the effortless passage of boats on the wintry gray East River. As the seasons passed, my debts mounted.

Grants from the American Council of Learned Societies, the Arthur and Elizabeth Schlesinger Library on the History of Women in America, and the Sophia Smith Collection of Women's History at Smith College, as well as research grants and a faculty fellowship from Fordham University provided critical support. Librarians and archivists have been patient with my countless requests. I particularly thank Diana Carey and Ellen Shea at the Schlesinger, and Christine Campbell and Charlotte Labbé at Fordham. Rosalyn Baxandall graciously granted an interview. For permission to use images, I also thank Ann Crittenden, Silvia Federici, and Gary O'Neil, as well the many others who helped me chase down obscure works.

Colleagues have shared their insight and time with extraordinary generosity. Thanks to Deborah Dinner, Ann Fabian, Alice Kessler-Harris, Melani McAlister, and Premilla Nadasen, as well as to the readers for Harvard University Press, and my terrific editor, Andrew Kinney. The Fordham history department has unstintingly supported me. I thank especially Elaine Crane, Nancy Curtin, Chris Dietrich, Richard Gyug, Maryanne Kowaleski, Héctor Lindo-Fuentes, David Myers, Silvana Patriarca, Nick Paul, Thierry Rigogne, Susan Wabuda, and Rosemary Wakeman, as well as the chairs who saw me through this project—Doron Ben-Atar, David Hamlin, and Daniel Soyer. Glenn Hendler has been a fantastic comrade in arms, as has Anne Fernald. Jonathan Crystal, Stephen Freedman, John Harrington, and Mike Latham generously ushered this project forward. I am deeply saddened that Stephen Freedman will not see the book in print. Carina Ray inspired me to *write*. Nancy Cott remains a steadfast and inspiring mentor. Mindy Werner kept me from writing in circles—and kept me on track—all the way from day one.

Melissa Arredia, Maria Calvello, Sal Cipriano, and Jordyn May provided excellent research assistance. Christine Kelly gave a critical boost to the manuscript's first incarnation. Audra Cooke and April Acosta fielded a steady stream of calls and emails. The team at Harvard University Press oversaw the final stages with grace and persistence: the assistance of Kate Brick, Stephanie Vyce, Olivia Woods, and especially Kerry Higgins Wendt is deeply appreciated. Audiences at Cedar Crest College, Fordham University, and Harvard University let me preview my ideas.

Friends have drunk countless glasses of wine with me and provided respite and hospitality. Thanks to Sarah and Ben Alexander, Stuart Krichevsky, Sheila McCullough, Juliette Mead, Craig Pintoff, Roger and Marina Post, Peter Post, Terry Ratigan, and Jennifer Topping. Debora Worth saw me through the ups and downs. In Mozambique, Gifty Gerritsen, Mirita Rodrigues, Monika Sommer, Marc de Tollenaere, and Stuart Williams kept me going. Esperança Albertina Homuana, Alison Postighone, Maria Romero, Elineide da Silva, and Lindsay Vigoda helped immeasurably.

Jocelyn Mason backed this project from its earliest days. My family has been there all along: Carol Anderson, Max Deibert, Bob Swinth, Mark Swinth, and the Portland clan. I miss Kitty Powell—I think she would have liked this book. After long days in the archive, Polly Chatfield gave me a landing pad and delightful conversation over Scotch. My mother, Heather Jackson, has been a rock. Eva Badowska, Pam Dorman, and Stefanie Pintoff have been my lifeline. This book is much better for Beryl Satter's incisive mind and dedicated friendship. Thierry read, and read again, and then was there with champagne and more.

This book is for Gabriel and Alison Swinth, for the joy they bring me every day.

ILLUSTRATION CREDITS

———

p. 14   "I am woman giving birth to myself," by Marta Thoman. Frontispiece to Sue Cox, *Female Psychology: The Emerging Self* (Palo Alto, CA: Science Research Associates, Inc., 1976).

p. 22   "The Bitch versus the Balless Wonder," by Hanako. Schlesinger Library, Radcliffe Institute, Harvard University.

p. 25   "Liberation, Now!" by Betty Friedan and Jacquelyn Reinach, music by Jacquelyn Reinach and J. Rene. Dolores Alexander. Papers of NOW officer Dolores Alexander, 1960–1973 (box 10, folder 17), Schlesinger Library, Radcliffe Institute, Harvard University.

p. 43   "Let's Share Child Care." © Bettye Lane. David M. Rubenstein Rare Book and Manuscript Library, Duke University.

p. 50   Detail of photograph by Frank White, *People*, January 20, 1975, p. 48.

p. 59   "Father and Child at Demonstration." © Bettye Lane. Bettye Lane Photographs, Schlesinger Library, Radcliffe Institute, Harvard University.

p. 71   "The Shulmans at Home," by Arthur Schatz. The Life Picture Collection/Getty Images/159398358.

p. 88   "NOW=Partnership in Marriage." By permission of National Organization for Women–New York City (NOW–NYC). National Organization for Women: New York City Chapter Records, Tamiment Library/Robert F. Wagner Labor Archives, New York University.

p. 91   "First Women's March down Fifth Avenue." © Bettye Lane. Bettye Lane Photographs, Schlesinger Library, Radcliffe Institute, Harvard University.

p. 98   "Women's Liberation, New York." By permission of Ken Regan/Camera 5.

p. 107   "Help Wanted." By permission of Ann Crittenden.

p. 111   "All Work and No Pay." Courtesy of Silvia Federici.

p. 114   Doonesbury © 1977 G. B. Trudeau. Reprinted with permission of Andrews McMeel Syndication. All rights reserved.

p. 136   "Women's Teach-In at Wayne State University." Association of Faculty Women Records, WSR000559, "Cynthia Colvin, President's Files: 1970–1971" (box 3, folder 4), Walter P. Reuther Library, University Archives, Wayne State University.

p. 149   "Pro Day Care and Welfare Demonstrator Confronts a KKK Member in Front of Convention Center." © Bettye Lane. Bettye Lane Photographs, Schlesinger Library, Radcliffe Institute, Harvard University.

p. 159   "Day Care Demonstration at City Hall." © Bettye Lane. Bettye Lane Photographs, Schlesinger Library, Radcliffe Institute, Harvard University.

p. 173   "The Lollipop People. A Case for Child Care NOW!" By permission of the National Organization for Women (NOW). Schlesinger Library, Radcliffe Institute, Harvard University.

p. 184   "International Women's Year March." © Bettye Lane. Bettye Lane Photographs, Schlesinger Library, Radcliffe Institute, Harvard University.

p. 197   "Benefits for Pregnant Women Demonstration." © Bettye Lane. Bettye Lane Photographs, Schlesinger Library, Radcliffe Institute, Harvard University.

p. 216   "F.E.W. Holds First Annual Conference." By permission of Federally Employed Women (FEW). Schlesinger Library, Radcliffe Institute, Harvard University.

p. 221   Photograph by Jerry Hecht, HEW. Marjorie M. Silverberg and Lorraine D. Eyde, "Career Part-Time Employment: Personnel Implications of the New Professional and Executive Corps," *Good Government* 88 (Fall 1971): 14.

INDEX